STALKER!

STALKER!
CHRIS WALKER
THE AUTOBIOGRAPHY

WITH NEIL BRAMWELL

HarperSport
An Imprint of HarperCollins*Publishers*

HarperCollins*Publishers*
77–85 Fulham Palace Road
Hammersmith, London W6 8JB

www.harpercollins.co.uk

First published in hardback in 2007 by HarperSport
an imprint of HarperCollins London
First published in paperback in 2008

3

A CIP catalogue record for this book
is available from the British Library

ISBN-13   978 0 00 725986 1
ISBN-10   0 00 725986 7

Printed and bound in Great Britain by
Clays Ltd, St Ives plc

Picture credits
All photographs supplied by the author with the exception of the following:
Double Red 4 (bottom) and 5 (bottom); Foggy Petronas Racing 6 (bottom),
7 (top); Fox and Wasp 9 (top); Gold & Goose 10 (top), 11 (top);
Keith Martin 5 (centre); Mick Farman 10 (bottom) 11 (bottom left and right);
Rizla Suzuki 14 (top and bottom), 15 (top left and right), 16 (top), 16 (centre);
Yvonne Lishman Photography 12 (centre left and right), 12 (bottom), 13 (top).

To my dad, John
My best friend

Contents

Introducing Stalker

There was only one place I could spend my last night as a single man – the barn conversion at the home of my best man, Jamie Gamble, where I had lived during some of my more eventful bachelor days, earning it the nickname of the Porn Barn. I had been out for a couple of beers with a few of the boys and was in bed for just after midnight. I rang Rachel to check that she was OK.

'I'm so excited. Are you?' I said. 'I miss you. Wish you were here.' I hadn't seen her for all of three hours! I might as well not have bothered going to bed, though, because I literally didn't sleep a wink. At 6 a.m. I got up to put the final touches to my speech and sent Rachel a text, not expecting an answer for hours. But one came straight back as she could not sleep either. I also received a dawn text from Jamie: 'Wha y'up ta?' This was the universal greeting amongst the Stalker clan. Jamie was actually one of the major pre-wedding headaches. You try finding a style of suit to fit a midget groom and a giant best man. But the rest of the ushers were peaking at their brown pin-striped suits, especially Mad Dog, aka Mark Davies, who had only previously ordered suits from catalogues and sent them back after wearing them once.

The nerves didn't start to kick in until five minutes before the ceremony was due to start at 1 o'clock, at St Augustine's Church, Flintham, which was crammed full of family and friends. Then, at five past, the dude on the organ stopped and there was an awkward silence. Still no sign of Rachel. I imagined everyone thinking: 'She's done one. I knew she would see sense!' After another five minutes Jamie whispered: 'Want me to stand on the pew, Nobby, and see if I can see anything out of the window?' Then the organ started again and I turned round to see her. She was perfect in every way. Just stunning. Of all the things I have done, the places I have been and the sights I have seen, this was the best feeling I had ever had – without doubt the proudest moment of my life.

Rachel wasn't aware that over the previous couple of weeks me and the lads had been doing up her little blue 1967 Fiat 500. We kept it round at my mate Dean Gregory's because he has a valeting business and I spent so much time round there with Steve Cottam, or Wee Man, a motocrossing pal, that I'm sure she thought I had a last-minute bird on the go. Deano gave it a bare-metal respray, and another motocross chum, Ian Cherry, fitted new ivory leather upholstery. It looked better than a showroom Bentley Continental. Deano made a 'Just Married #9' sticker for the back window, and his little boy sprayed up some cans to tie to the bumper. Her face was a picture when we walked out of the church grounds where it was parked, ready for us to drive home, and with just enough space for our dog, Nobby, in his new Paul Smith designer lead in the back.

A string quartet played in the garden and drinks were served on the lawn at 2.30. Jamie Whitham was pissed by 3.00. His wife, Andrea, was pissed by 3.05. And I think everyone was pissed before the speeches. With the help of Rachel's mum I had managed to get hold of footage to play on the big screen of Rachel as one of the few kids who ever appeared on the television programme, *Jim'll Fix It*. On the show she read her letter in her squeaky 8-year-old voice:

Dear Jim
I saw my first ballet with my mum when I was 3.
Please could you fix it for me to dance the White Cat and Puss in Boots pas de deux from the ballet Sleeping Beauty?
Rachel Freer, age 8

P.S. I am not allowed on pointed toes yet as I am only eight.

It then showed her dancing in full costume with Puss in Boots, before pulling off her cat mask to reveal that smiley face that hasn't changed a bit. In my wedding speech I read out my pretend letter to the show:

Dear Jim
I saw my first brolly girl when I was 3. I actually met my first brolly girl when I was about 23 and over the next ten years discovered what a strange breed they can be … very beautiful girls with all the bits in the right places but just not quite right upstairs!
  Please could you fix it for me to finally meet a girl of equal beauty but with an IQ in at least double figures.
  Chris Walker, age 33 and a half

P.S. Big rockets would be a real bonus and whilst I've never shied away from a challenge I'm only a midget so one under 6 feet tall would be good!

I hadn't been too nervous about my speech; it was the first dance that I was worried about. With Rachel being a professional dancer we didn't just want to do a slow smooch. But I have two left feet. So during the week Rachel had set about trying to teach me a routine in the marquee. After the first half hour I sat down on the floor and said: 'I can't do this. Why can't I just sit on a chair in the middle and you dance around me?'

'I'm not doing a dirty lap dance for you on our wedding night,' she laughed. 'Well, not until later, anyway!' So I persevered and we came up with a routine to 'Don't Stop Me Now' by Queen, which started slowly but then kicked into life with a few trick lifts. At the end we received a bigger cheer than when you are on the rostrum at BSB. Only when that was out of the way could I get on with drinking. We wanted to use the money we had saved by not hiring a big flash venue to make sure that the guests didn't have to keep putting their hands in their pockets. So there was a free bar all night and I think that Cal Crutchlow and Rat Boy, Stuart Eastham, got through eleven bottles of champagne. There was a Robbie Williams tribute act and some of Rachel's dancing friends handed out cocktails dressed in showgirl outfits, before their can-can routine. All I could see inside the marquee was teeth – everyone was all smiles.

Then Craig Jones had the bright idea of racing me on a yard of Guinness. The prize for my narrow victory? Two tequila slammers. From then on in I was like an actor in a Bruce Lee film. Words were coming out of my mouth, but not in sync with my lips. I had to shuffle everywhere like a geisha girl because if I tried to take a step it was like one giant step for mankind. My last meaningful act was to sneak Magpie, one of the ushers, into the bridesmaids' bedroom. Rachel then had to drag me out confused, because I thought it was my last night of freedom! I was certainly in no fit state to consummate our marriage.

So I just sat on the edge of the bed in total contentment and couldn't help thinking that I was the luckiest man in the world to have just shared the best day of my life with such a loving family and fantastic set of friends; to have made a living doing something I love; and to have finally found love with Rachel.

Sure, I'd had my share of bad luck along the way, on and off track. I have lost count of the number of times I have suffered badly broken bones, and maybe that adversity has helped people to recognize and appreciate my determination to try and succeed in all circumstances. But, for every low, there had been so many more highs.

It's certainly fair to say there was never a dull moment, and now, as I enter the later chapters of my racing career, seems as good a time as any to share the events and people that have shaped my life. So you will discover the family influences, from my dad in particular, that have sparked my love of motorbikes and my hunger for speed. You will be taken down the occasionally rocky path of my personal life. You will meet the mad bunch of mates that I have collected down the years, and hear about (most of) their escapades! You will be able to sit in judgement on my numerous scrapes with the law. (I've just started yet another driving ban, by the way!) You might wince at my medical history, including the trauma of Bell's Palsy. You will be allowed behind the scenes to assess the difficult decisions which structured my career. You will see that I have, without doubt, made some mistakes. But you will, I'm sure, get to know the real Stalker. (That's me, by the way, not my actual stalker!) You will also hopefully learn that whatever the Stalker does, wherever he is doing it, he gives everything he has – and does it with a smile.

And that smile could not have been bigger as I lay back, still wearing my shoes, suit, tie – and the *Jim'll Fix It* badge Rachel's mum had given me – just gazing at my perfect bride. Somebody, somehow, had sure fixed it for the Stalker…

1

Baby Stalker

'Ahhh! John, come and look at our Christopher,' whispered my mum, Christine.

She was paying her nightly visit to my bedroom, just before she turned in. Mum had to do this because I was a serial bed-wetter. (Do I really want to be revealing stuff like this? Oh well, might as well start as I mean to go on!) Each night she gently woke me up and led me to the toilet, to try and prevent soiled sheets later. This became a bit of a ritual for me, and for a few years I would occasionally sleep-walk to the toilet at around that same time. Unfortunately I dragged my pillow with me and managed to pee all over it before returning to bed to put my head back down on the now sodden pillow, which wasn't ideal!

This time I was fast asleep and Mum and Dad witnessed the first clue that a 3-year-old Stalker would spend his life obsessed with motorbikes: left thumb in my mouth, my right hand revving an imaginary throttle, and under the sheets my leg was kick-starting the bike.

'I think it might be time to give him his first ride on a motorbike,' said my dad with pride.

It was probably no great surprise that I was showing these signs at such an early age as I always remember being around engines of some form or another. My granddad started that trend as he was constantly involved with transport machinery – and often with disastrous consequences. There is no doubt that Herbert Walker is a larger-than-life character and he remains the life and soul of any party. He can hardly walk now but he doesn't let that curb his appetite for life and he still tinkers with his own motorbike, although he can't even sit on the thing, and he still manages to get into scrapes.

A little paddle ferry links Dartmouth to Kingswear and if you miss a crossing it's something like a thirty-minute drive across the nearest bridge. The word 'belligerent' has been used on a few occasions to describe the Walker men, but in my granddad's case it's usually accompanied by 'old sod'. He had approached the ferry slipway in his Vauxhall Cavalier SRi – so it must have been around twenty years ago when they were still cool – but belligerently ignored the 'No More' signs. As the paddles started up and the ferry started to pull out into the river he calculated that there was still enough time for him to make it up the ramp. There wasn't! Even if he had wanted to change his mind, which I very much doubt would have happened, the front valance of his car had become hooked onto the ramp and the ferry was dragging him into the river. The car eventually came to a halt in four feet of water and it wasn't long before he was joined inside by fishes swimming round his neck. An intricate operation to extract my granddad from the car was set in motion, but not before a local TV camera crew had arrived to film the whole saga. The first the rest of the family, and the whole country, were to know about it was when the footage was broadcast on breakfast television news the following morning, read by Anna Ford.

He remains to this day one of my biggest supporters and tries to make it to as many races as possible with his cronies. He keeps up to speed with everything that is happening via the internet and was even the oldest member of the Foggy Petronas Racing fan club when I was racing for them. I wish he lived closer so that I could see more of him because I think the world of him.

Granny Joan was always content to play the supporting role, and probably didn't have much choice. While Granddad might be hiding out in his den – the office he locked himself away in to watch telly when we were creating mayhem around the house and in their garden – Granny would keep us all busy. It's not a particularly laddish thing to admit to but I enjoyed her teaching me how to cook, and there was nothing better than getting my hands stuck into a chocolate cake mix. I will have a go at making most things, especially now I have an Aga and don't have to worry the same about burning meals in an electric oven. I cook a mean chilli, even if I say so myself. But it was probably my granny's cooking that resulted in my granddad being nearer to 20 stone rather than 10!

The only grandparent I have lost was Granddad Johnson. Roy died when I was a teenager, having also retired to Devon after working as an accountant for Plessy in Nottingham. During the war he served in the Royal Navy on the motor torpedo boats, commonly known as MTBs. On one mission his boat was hit and sunk off the coast of Holland but he managed to save himself and the ship's flag before it went down, and it still hangs in his local church to this day. Funnily enough they lived on the opposite side of the River Dart to my other grandparents, in Kingswear. They could probably just about see each other through their curtains, and when Granddad Johnson was alive it was nice that they went on holidays together as couples. He was a real gentleman, well-to-do and well-spoken, but not posh. He was also very well-dressed; his dad had run a gentleman's outfitters and when Granddad Johnson died my Granny Margaret found about fifty unopened shirts, two hundred brand new ties and thirty untouched pairs of shoes. He was a real waste-not-want-not type, and on every birthday he would send, along with a card and a bit of money, a letter detailing ways of how I could save money throughout life, such as using a tea bag three times.

Granny Johnson is a bit of a Wonder Woman. At the age of 86 she still smokes twenty a day and has a glass of wine or two every day, yet she is still brand new. Whereas my granddad was quiet and reserved and could sit and examine his stocks and shares for hours, Granny never stops talking. The Walker women, my mum and my sister, have a bit of a mad streak and I think this is where it comes from. I try to get down there once a year to see everyone and she still treats me as grannies do, fussing over my every move. She never watches my races until she knows that I am OK, otherwise her cigarette tally might reach thirty a day. And we try not to let her know if I have had a bad crash until I am fully recovered, explaining that I haven't been doing a lot of racing for a while. In fact, she probably thinks I have a normal day job as well.

Granddad Walker was the first in the family to race bikes, scramblers and also road racers, although his size prevented him from being an Agostini. My dad is a very different personality, much more reserved, but he definitely shared a daredevil love of speed. Dad was bought his first bike at the age of 15, a James 150 complete with screen and leg shields. Along with the exhaust, these were promptly discarded as he rushed to the top of the biggest hill in the area to see just how fast it would go.

He must have inherited some of the mischievousness off Granddad Walker and, like most adolescents, was often in trouble. He was expelled from Nottingham High School for Boys – and I am pretty impressed by the way he got thrown out. At the front of the school is a life-size bronze statue of one of the founders of the school in his army uniform. My dad somehow stumbled across information that he actually deserted the army. So, with a couple of mates, he crept back into the school grounds at night-time and painted the statue yellow. The place was in uproar the next morning and there was a manhunt to find the perpetrator of such a terrible act. I think it was the yellow paint still on my dad's hands that gave him away, and he wasn't invited back to resume his history lessons!

Despite this slight setback he was determined to gain some qualifications and studied A-levels at People's College, now known as Clarendon. He did not finish the course due to a combination of the distraction of the local vicar's daughter and an accident on his way back to college for an afternoon exam, in which he nearly lost his leg when a truck pulled out on him on Wilford Hill. One of the tarpaulin hooks on the side of the lorry went straight through his helmet and could have fractured his skull. But his leg was a real mess, with fractures to the fibula and tibia. The doctors at the hospital wanted to amputate immediately, but fortunately his mum and dad were on holiday and could not be traced to provide permission. So they had no choice but to try and pin it back together in a five-hour operation in which a plate was inserted in exactly the same spot where I have one now. But his suffering did not end there and gangrene got into the wound while he was in traction for almost two months during a three-month stay in hospital. He later contracted shingles on his honeymoon, which affected his eyesight and resulted in him being placed on the Blind Register. He still walks with a bit of a limp, which is almost undetectable, but his eyesight is now nearly perfect. So all in all he was very lucky not to have suffered even more.

During and after college he had a succession of mechanical or engineering jobs, usually costing his employer much more than his actual value to the company.

One of many was at an ice-cream company called Tonibell, where he maintained their fleet of ice-cream vans. One time when he was assigned to pick up a broken-down ice-cream van, he asked for help from his best pal, John Small, commonly known as Noddy for some unknown reason. It was a bit of a Laurel and Hardy pairing: Dad had the common sense and Noddy was a bit of a daft lad. Dad decided to drive the tow vehicle while Noddy steered the van. Or at least that was the plan! But when Dad checked in the rear-view mirror that everything was OK, Noddy was nowhere to be seen and the van appeared to be steering itself. Dad did a double-take and could just about make out that Noddy's leg was on the wheel while he stretched into the back of the van, helping himself to a 99 from the freezer! The next time a van broke down Dad thought it might be better if he was to do the steering. Noddy convinced him that, because the towing vehicle was a lot smaller than the ice-cream van, they needed a long tow-rope as the brakes did not respond as well when the van's engine was off. All seemed to be going smoothly until they reached a T-junction onto a busy main road. Noddy pulled out comfortably but didn't leave enough time for the slack to be taken up before a Robin Reliant T-boned the tow-rope before Dad's van had even turned a wheel. It did a full roll before coming to rest, the driver bewildered and clutching the steering wheel of a guillotined shell of his former car like something out of *Wacky Races*. Time for Dad move on again! And all of a sudden our cupboards were no longer full of ice-cream cones and Flakes!

It was probably at this point that Dad decided he needed to fend more for himself so he bought a small lock-up garage with Noddy. The pair bought second-hand cars and fixed them up to sell them on for a profit. My dad was the grafter whereas Noddy thought he was the brains and the business. The business took off when they bought a few bikes to do up, but quite how it became so successful, when Noddy was actually out shagging and boozing all the time, was probably more down to Dad's input and his obsession with bikes. Around this time the council slapped a compulsory purchase order on the garage. With a bit of cash in their hands, my dad and Noddy decided to go their separate ways and my dad set up a Suzuki dealership in Langley Mill called John Walker Superbikes.

Dad had always looked the part of a biker in his early 20s, with the typical big Rockers' quiff in those days of Mods and Rockers. He was a member of a gang called The Aces, which was emblazoned across their leather jackets. Dad and The Aces used to try and impress the birds by riding their old café-style tricked-up bikes – his first was a 500 Norton Dominator, which he then upgraded to a Triumph Tiger 110 – up and down the University Boulevard in Nottingham, and it's no surprise that he met my mum in a typical bikers' café. He was about 7 stone wet through and was barely able to fend for himself. So it wasn't difficult for Mum to immediately win him over when she invited him round and made her speciality – cheese boats. Recipe: Cook a jacket potato, scoop out the potato and mix with cheese and butter. Refill the potato with this mixture; add sliced tomato followed by grated cheese on top and melt under the grill. (Mum has also taught Rachel how to make them. She knows the secret to a happy marriage!) Before too long my sister Wendy was on the way, and a couple of years later I was born in the flat above the garage – while Dad was respraying an E-type Jaguar downstairs. Home births were pretty common in those days, and legend has it that Mum was up and hoovering within a couple of hours of giving birth, making sure everything was tidy because my granddad was on his way round to look at the new addition to the family.

Some people are born into wealth and privilege, but my good fortune has been to have had a very stable family background. My mum and dad are still very close. You will never see them sat on opposite sides of the room – they are always next to each other on the sofa. It's a marriage based on old-school values – my dad has always been the breadwinner and my mum's mission now that she is retired is to see to his every need – but it is a marriage to aspire to, that's for sure.

I still have to watch my step with my mum, though. She always greets me with a big squeeze, to which I reply: 'Don't squeeze me too hard or I'll fart.'

'Oh, Christopher' – it's only Christopher when I'm in trouble – 'you are horrible, you really are!' she responds, followed by a dead-arm punch. I don't think she knows her own strength sometimes, and those blows are not ideal just before a race. She struck up an immediate bond with Rachel and will always stick up for her if I am playfully picking on her.

My earliest memories are at my parents' second home, a semi-detached on Lindon Grove in a village called Gedling, on the outskirts of Nottingham.

Mum drove a Mini Cooper S – they were still probably doing the Monte Carlo Rally in those days – and it was a big moment for a little Stalker, when he could stand up on the back seat and touch the roof with his head, even if it was a couple of years later than most kids. There was no room in the garage for Mum's car as it was littered with Dad's bikes, and also contained a clapped-out Austin Ruby, which looked more like our rabbit's hutch because of all the shit in it. The rabbit, cat and dog all combined to ruin one of Dad's finest hours in that house. With Mum ill in bed upstairs – and it took a lot to take Mum out of action in the kitchen – Dad was forced to cook the family dinner. All was going smoothly until he dropped the roast chicken on the kitchen floor and continued to serve it up, ignoring the fact that it looked like it had done a couple of laps of the kitchen, collecting bits of dog, cat and rabbit along the way. We have had a poodle in the family for as long as I can remember, and Bozil had been handed down by my grandparents. So he was a bit decrepit, farted a lot and, having no teeth, had to resort to nibbling you with his gums.

Our house was at the top of a gentle slope, but when your dad plonks you on a push bike for the first time and points you downhill, a gentle slope seems like a 1:2 gradient, especially to a kid my size. Until that moment my only experience on wheels was with my little red toy bus or my sister Wendy's tricycle. (She struggled to balance on her tricycle then, and still struggles with balance on her feet now!) My bus was the business. In those days toys were unbreakable, not made out of the crap they are today. So I could bomb around on it over little jumps and there would never be a dint. And even though I could barely reach the pedals of the trike, I could still build up a fair amount of speed. But to go from four wheels to three and immediately down to just two was a pretty big step forward. Of course stabilizers hadn't even been considered – stabilizers were for poofs!

'Just hang on and start pedalling like mad when you start going up the other side,' Dad advised, before giving me a helping hand off down the hill. When I came wobbling back into view about five minutes later, without a scratch on me or the bike, it was clear from the relief on his face that he half-expected never to see me again.

That early crash had not dented his own enthusiasm for motorbikes, and he was a pretty handy racer at club championship level, despite not starting until he was in his 30s. He won the local Granby Cup and at one stage had a cupboard full of trophies. My mum has since slung them all out, allowing him to keep only one, which looks like an urn. She has promised to keep his ashes in it. At one point he intended to enter the national championships and bought the previous year's championship-winning 125cc Honda from Clive Houghton, who owned Racing Lines at Derby. However, Dad was running a business and I think those family commitments proved more important and he didn't actually compete at national level. From what I have heard, though, he was exceptionally talented and could well have raced professionally if he had not taken it up so late.

Having witnessed those first sleepy signs that his 3-year-old son had inherited the family passion for bikes, there was no time like the present to nurture that enthusiasm. Dad was already planning to take me out on his Kawasaki Z1B the very next day – when Stalker was to reach his first biking milestone …

2

Schoolboy Stalker

'Dad, when do you think I might be able to have a go?' I had been plucking up enough courage to ask for weeks. He was now lovingly polishing his bike, and this seemed like a good time to pounce.

'Funny you should ask that. Only the other night we were thinking that you are old enough to have a ride now. Go and get your helmet and I will take you down to the river,' he said.

Mum and Dad might have decided that the time was right, but the law thought otherwise. As long as a kid's legs were long enough to touch the footrests they could be a passenger. But there was no way I would be safe on the back because my legs didn't even stretch round the seat! So Dad plonked me on the tank in front of him, told me to hang on tight to the chrome bit of the handlebars – I couldn't reach the grips – and off we went. I had experienced nothing like it before. It was a beautiful sunny day, the wind rushed through the long blond curls that were poking out the sides of my open-faced helmet and I was transfixed as Dad changed up though the gears. The speedo pointer crept up and up until – Check Me Out! – the 3-year-old Stalker had reached a ton, 100 miles an hour, for the first time. I was hooked on speed.

Dad took me down to the River Trent, past the Ferry Boat pub, and back home round the side roads. When he lifted me off I hit the ground running straight round to the home of my friend, Anthony

Shepherd, to tell him the news. Needless to say he wanted a go, and Dad reluctantly agreed to take him out for a shorter spin around the estate. It wasn't short enough, though. Dad had literally turned the corner from the house when he heard the dreaded police sirens and was asked to pull over. He was promptly awarded an endorsement on his licence for illegally carrying a child on a public highway – and he wasn't happy!

His mood might also have been influenced by the realization that he was going to have to fork out for my first bike soon. And sure enough, just before my fourth birthday I was taken to a shop just round the corner from my granny's home in Beeston to choose my first rocket. A couple of the possible options had gears, but we went for an Italjet 50 automatic off-road bike, yellow with a blue stripe through the centre. The like of it has never been seen since! It became even more distinct when Dad added Bug1 on the front. My nickname was Bug because I was such an ugly baby that Dad christened me Ugly Bug straight away!

Dad had to put a couple of spacers in the levers because I could not reach the brakes, and then set about teaching me how to ride in our garden at Gedling. We soon moved to a house on a new estate in Ripley, to be nearer to the new bike shop that Dad had set up, John Walker Superbikes. There was a field at the back of this house and I was in my element racing round it and finding anything to jump over, much to the farmer's discontent. Soon Dad simply referred to my bike as 'the Italian piece of shit', due to its chequered starting record. But that wasn't my department and I loved it. I lived for Sunday mornings when Dad would get his own bike out and take me up to Chrich Chase or Ambergate Woods, two popular spots for motorbike riders. My aim was always to keep up with him and we used one of the old alarm clocks with two big bells on the top to signal the start of the race. These trips were a good way of keeping me in line. Dad's ultimate threat, if I hadn't tidied my room or done my chores, was 'Right you little sod, no biking this weekend.' I think that kids who do have a hobby or a sport at an early age are much easier to control.

It says a lot that I have had to look up the name of my junior school, Shirley Road. While my attendance record there was very good, except for maybe taking the odd day off to watch my dad at a track day at Cadwell Park, I was rarely there in spirit. It also took me ages to get out of the habit of the afternoon nap I had been used to at home, and I regularly nodded off in lessons in the middle of the afternoon. When I wasn't actually asleep I whiled away the hours daydreaming about Barry Sheene or counting down the minutes until the final bell, when Mum or Dad would be waiting to take me and my sister to the motorbike shop. I spent hours there, trying to help Dad de-grease the AP50s, but in actual fact making them look even dirtier. Or I would just wander around with a spanner in my hand, attempting to look useful but not having a clue what to do with it. In fact I was probably anything but useful, asking a million annoying questions to any of the mechanics. 'What does that do?' 'What happens when I press this?' I must have been a bit like Andy, the wheelchair character in *Little Britain*: 'I want that one!'

I was fairly well behaved at school and generally knew right from wrong. For instance, I knew it was wrong for me to go up behind a girl who was doing a handstand against the wall and, egged on by a big group of pals from our Amber Heights estate, karate chop her in the 'jack and danny'. So the bollocking I received, as she lay crippled in the schoolyard, was thoroughly deserved. But I didn't think it was fair when I was fingered when 50p went missing from the tuck shop. In the days when Space Invaders crisps were only 5p, this was a serious crime, although the principle of innocent until proven guilty went straight out the window. Everyone was asked to turn out their pockets and, sure enough, I had a 50p piece, so despite the fact that I couldn't reach the tuck shop counter I was marched to the headmaster's office to receive the slipper. 'This isn't right,' I thought. 'I'm being whacked because my mum wanted some potatoes on the way home!'

This taught me a vital lesson: if you are going to be punished for things you haven't done, you might as well have some fun doing the stuff you should be punished for! At secondary school, Ripley Mill Hill, I developed the knack of being cheeky enough to be popular with the other kids, but not enough to be disliked by the teachers. Even so, I used to dread parents' evening when Mum and Dad would continually hear comments like 'Chris could do so much more,' or 'He's a lovely lad and I can't bring myself to tell him off.' I guess I was lucky enough or clever enough, or probably a bit of both, to push the boundaries without over-stepping them.

Some subjects were a complete waste of time, such as History and French, although there have been times when I wished I could have spoken more than a couple of words of French. More of that to come! I was pretty good at Biology – Dad said that was because it was about tits and fannies. More of that to come too! And I enjoyed Chemistry because you could set fire to things. I also loved PE and, being pretty nippy, played a few games on the wing for the rugby team. But my favourite subjects were all with my favourite teacher, Eric Webster. He taught technical drawing, metalwork and a motor vehicle engineering course, and he reminded me of my granddad in that he always had a story to tell and always had time for you. The way into the good books of Mr Webster, and his sidekick Cyril, was to stop by the canteen on the way to their department and take them a mug of tea and some cream cakes. These simple offerings meant you could stay with them all day, missing other lessons and helping to teach the younger kids how to do a bit of brazing. Looking back, it possibly didn't do me a lot of good, but it was better than learning about the Battle of Blinkin' Hastings.

I certainly wasn't the kind of kid who came home, watched *Blue Peter* and then went upstairs to start his homework. In fact I have no recollection of ever doing any homework, although I had a 100 per cent attendance record in the early years of secondary school. Then, when the teachers started to strike, school started to become a real chore. On some days we had to cycle into school in the morning, were home again by lunchtime if a certain teacher was on strike, and were then expected to go back again in the afternoon for one final lesson. That wasn't for me! I rebelled and simply stopped going to school. I missed the whole of the final year and have never sat an exam in my life. I was no dunce, but no genius either, and was of the opinion that a practical education was going to be better for me than mediocre qualifications.

During the previous year I had started helping out a little at the bike shop where my best motocrossing mate, Sean Balls, worked. I popped in on the way home after school and learnt the basics of being a mechanic. I already knew that was where my future lay. So when the strikes started it was easier to spend the day working at Dad's shop than travelling to and from school, as the kids who lived nearer did. Mum and Dad weren't happy with the situation but they knew I was learning a useful trade. At the age of 15 I could already perform the work of a trained mechanic of 25 years old, while good students were leaving school unable to write a cheque. I was being educated in the real world at a time when kids with qualifications were struggling to find any job. Occasionally I would answer the phone at the shop and it would be the headmaster wanting to speak to Dad, not knowing it was me on the other end of the line. When he did ever get through, Dad simply sounded surprised that the school hadn't seen me either. I guess Mum and Dad were satisfied knowing that I was keeping out of mischief, which I was starting to get a bit of form for.

It was a similar story out of school; I had to be doing something practical. At an early age I was mad on Lego, which progressed to Meccano, and then on to Scalextric. Later on a lot of my spare time was spent working on or riding my bike and the option of playing a radio-controlled car with pals on the street seemed a bit naff in comparison. But I managed to remain an integral part of a fairly big gang of lads who all lived in the same area and looked after each others' backs. Having such a strong interest in bikes as well as spending such a lot of time around adults, at the bike shops and while motocrossing, meant that I didn't have much time for the usual petty schoolboy squabbles. I had already learnt at junior school to meet confrontation head-on, when the obligatory tough girl in school, Catherine Thornley, challenged me to a fight in the cloakroom after school. There was no obvious reason why she picked on me, except for the fact that I was a little squirt. Part of me was wary about fighting a girl and part of me was worried about being beaten up, because there was no way of avoiding the cloakroom as I had to pick up my coat. A bloodthirsty crowd had gathered as Catherine started to reel off the rules of engagement.

'Right, no kicking, no biting, no hair-pulling …'

I don't know what triggered it but, mid-sentence, I punched her so hard in the stomach, which was exactly the right height for me, that I could feel her spine. She was bent double for minutes, gasping for breath, during which time she presumably decided that she would never pick on me again.

Being a part of a big group of lads could, however, mean big trouble. Don't get me wrong, me and my pals on the estate weren't tearaways. I guess it could be called innocent mischief. However, getting into my teenage years there was perhaps a bit more mischief than innocence.

We tried to use a bit more imagination than simple door-knocking or fireworks through letter-boxes. The sport of hedge-jumping – running through as many hedges and gardens as possible in one stint by clambering over hedges and fences – had to be renamed hedge-mountaineering for me and I was invariably the one left staring the snarling dog in the face.

One near-neighbour had the look of a sergeant-major and, with the aid of a stick, walked with a limp. We soon convinced ourselves that he was an ex-Green Beret. He was still pretty mobile and could chase after us and would carry on his search in his car when we escaped, as we always did. On Halloween most of the neighbours realized it was a smart move to give us a couple of quid or some sweets. The Green Beret gave us nothing. Big mistake! One of the lads, Kevin Goodwin, who was usually in the thick of the action because he had older brothers and was therefore as hard as nails, had been given a bag of sweets earlier in the night so we emptied the bag and searched for the messiest pile of dog shit we could find. I crept up to Green Beret's front door and set fire to the bag and rang the doorbell. It caught alight spectacularly and I scarpered across the road to where the rest of the lads were hiding behind a hedge. Sure enough, Green Beret flung open the front door and stamped out the fire in his slippers. He was incandescent when he realized that his beloved slippers were now covered in prime dog shit, while we were doing all we could not to wet ourselves.

The estate we lived on was only partly built, so there was always a building site nearby to get up to no good in. We knocked down the big show home signs to make ramps for our bikes, or messed around filling the cement mixers with all kinds of crap. But the big temptations were the dumper trucks, which were so old and clapped out that the labourers did not think about immobilizing them. We found one that had to be started manually with a crank handle and I think it took three of us swinging on the handle to eventually start her up. It slowly chugged into life and we jumped on board, hearts pounding, to crunch it into first gear. Until that point we were in hysterics. Then we realized that the steering wheel was too stiff to turn and we had no idea how to stop the old girl, which was chug, chug, chugging merrily towards the front wall of a new house, which had only been built that day. Our last hope was a mound of cement which lay in its path, but the dumper stubbornly chugged its way over this, at which point we had no option but to jump off in blind panic. After flattening a few spades it smashed straight into the wall and, with the wheels now raised from the ground by the pile of rubble underneath, chugged away until it ran out of diesel. We vanished into the night and were so scared that we didn't even mention it to each other for weeks. Every time the phone went we expected it to be the police.

Then, of course, there were the inevitable experiments with alcohol. The first happened when I cycled over to see a friend in nearby Heage on my BMX. His parents ran a pub and, sure enough, we found ourselves in the cellar sampling a few bottles of beer. When you drink for the first time, though, you do not actually realize you are drunk and I was more than happy to cycle back home. My area of expertise on my BMX was pulling wheelies, and if I concentrated I could wheelie the whole length of Heage Road, a fairly busy main road. On this day I was struggling to focus, never mind concentrate. I managed to get the front wheel in the air but didn't have the coordination to use the finger covering the back brake so I looped over the back and landed on my head. A Good Samaritan in a Volvo stopped when he saw me sprawled on the edge of the road, but it did not occur to him that I had been drinking. He loaded my bike into the back and drove me carefully back home, my head spinning all the way. Mum also fell for the banged head explanation for my grogginess and packed me straight off to bed. When I both looked and felt brand new in the morning I was in the clear again. On a later occasion Dad caught me and a friend sat in front of his drinks cabinet, swigging away at all the disgusting concoctions like Drambuie and Tia Maria. That earned me a month of car-washing duty on the condition that he didn't tell Mum – although I wasn't stupid enough to believe that she didn't ever find out these things.

So life was good for the young Stalker. I had a great family life, a brilliant hobby, a great bunch of mates, no school, a few quid in my pocket, the ability to talk myself out of trouble – what more could a teenage lad ask for? Oh yes, a bird! And, what's more, one with big tits whose dad owned a sweet shop!

Amanda Smith was a 13-year-old girl trapped in the body of a woman. Everything seems bigger when you are tiny but I swear I have never seen a bigger pair of boobs to this day – they were like a pair of Arai helmets. When I told Dad that my new girlfriend was coming round he probably expected a sweet and innocent little girl with pigtails, not the vision asking, 'Is Chris coming out to play?' when he opened the door to her. He probably thought, 'No, but I will!'

'Chris! Amanda is here for you,' he shouted and then, muttering under his breath as he passed me on the stairs, added: 'Bloody hell, you were born with your shirt on, you were!' I don't think he realized by then that I was on free sweets as well.

But we all know, when it comes down to it, that women spell trouble. And I blame Amanda for my first serious scrape with the law …

3

Outlaw Stalker

The fact that Amanda used to give me piggy-backs home from school should have been a sign that it was not a match made in heaven. I was still immature around girls. I was into my motorbike and BMX, not girly things like kissing and holding hands. It was pleasant enough going round to her house for tea, and I could happily stare at her boobs for hours. But, as she approached 15 she needed a man and not a little Munchkin Stalker. Having already coped with the wounder of her dad selling the sweet shop and now facing a lifetime of having to pay for my own chocolate, an even bigger blow was just around the corner.

I remember the date, 29 December, for two reasons. It was Mum's birthday, so she was out for a meal with Dad. I also remember that I was skint, having saved up all my pocket money to buy the latest Spandau Ballet tape, or something equally shit, for Amanda's Christmas present. I arrived at her house, which was only just around the corner, shortly after tea, and Amanda took me up to her bedroom. She nervously closed the door and I thought, 'I could be about to get my end away for the first time here.'

'Listen, Chris. You are a really good friend and I really like you but I don't really want to be your girlfriend any more. I hope you are not angry and we will still see a lot of each other at school. I have tried to explain everything in this letter,' she said. I could tell she was quite upset so I had to keep a lid on my own emotions.

'Right, I think I will read this at home. Guess I should be going then. See you around,' I replied, trying to sound as casual as possible and trying not to think how I would be able to replace those rockets, or what I could have spent her Christmas present money on.

But I was devastated. Nobody enjoys being blown out and I trudged home dejected, tears building up, thinking of ways I could tell my mates without losing face. All of a sudden there was a screech of tyres as a Bedford van, amber lights flashing furiously on the roof, pulled up to the kerb. It had Derbyshire County Council written on the side. I peered in to see five or six mates crammed in, two in the front and the rest in the back, all jumping up and down and shouting their heads off at their new-found toy, which had been 'acquired' from the local compound. This was before the days of CCTV and armed guards, so keys could be left in vehicles without expecting them to go walkabout. The lad in the passenger seat wound his window down and shouted, 'Chris! Look what we've found. Come on, get in.'

'Fuck me, I'm having some of that,' I thought. Amanda went clean out of my mind. I scrambled in through the passenger door on top of the lad who was already there, but the crush didn't last for long. As soon as my passenger door closed, the driver's side door was flung open and we were dragged out by the cops. The van wasn't a gritter, so they didn't need to be Poirot to work out that it had no reason to be out and about, lights flashing, at 8 p.m. It was just bad luck that the police were passing when my mates stopped to pick me up.

We were all bundled into the backs of numerous police vans and taken down to the station, where we were asked to empty our pockets. To add insult to injury they read the note that Amanda had earlier given me. But that was the least of my worries. I was absolutely shitting myself, especially about what would happen when Mum and Dad found out. It was the first time I had been in real trouble with the police and I guess I wouldn't feel too different if the same thing happened today. Dad was particularly hard on me, not necessarily for getting involved but for getting caught, and I was grounded for an eternity.

We were all charged with taking without consent. Nowadays you are not in the loop unless you have an ASBO, but this was before even twoc-ing was fashionable, so I did feel that I had let the family down. After appearing in court I was fined £63.16p and ordered to spend twenty-four hours at an attendance centre. This meant two hours every Saturday for twelve weeks, marching around carrying big wooden benches with all the real criminals and with every chance of learning how to become one of them, so it wasn't in the slightest bit correctional. I was very intimidated and kept my head down, counting down the hours until I could be back on my bike at the weekends.

It was perhaps a good job that I started motocross racing at around that time, or I might have ended up in more bother. After my Italjet, my next bike was a Yamaha TY80 trials bike. It wasn't a Dougie Lampkin-style full-on trials bike but it still had four gears and a clutch and was ideal for a kid my size. I raced against Dad and one of his mechanics, Arthur, on makeshift trials courses that we built in the field or in the woods. Dad rode his Suzuki Beamish, which was the same colour as my old Italjet but with a chrome frame – they are still a good-looking bike if you see them now – while Arthur rode a pre-65 BSA Bantam. I took after Dad in that I was quick between the obstacles but had very little finesse. Sure, I was ten times better than any of my mates that had not grown up with bikes, who ripped the back mudguard off as soon as they let the clutch out. But there were certainly no early indications that I was going to make a living riding motorbikes.

Occasionally Dad, Arthur and a few mates would take part in an organized trial and I would go along with my bike. It was at one of these events that I had my first unsuccessful taste of competition. The schoolboys were allowed to tackle certain sections of the course, the biggest challenge being a steep bank with five separate stages. Dad's fatherly advise amounted to: 'Go on, lad, just go at it flat out.' So I hit the bottom at full speed and literally flew up to stage three before crashing and sliding down to the bottom. I could not wait to complete a lap to have another go. I already had another lad, riding a Whitehawk 80 which was essentially the same as my bike but with bigger wheels, as a benchmark, although it was soon obvious that I was pretty useless. Dad was probably already starting to realize that I needed to move on.

The next big step in my motorbike education came out of the blue. I had just turned 12 and, having been out on my BMX after school, came home for tea to hear that Dad had beaten me to it and was back from work really early. Even more unusual, he was out in the back field on his bike – or at least I thought it was his bike. I rushed over to see what he was up to and caught the look of disappointment that I had spoilt his surprise before I noticed the surprise itself. He was running in a brand-new Yamaha YZ80G that he had bought for me. It was a couple of years out of date but as far as I was concerned it was the business. I had been used to an uncomfortable trials bike without a real seat, but this thing had a padded seat and was air-cooled. I was champing at the bit to get out there.

'Now whatever you do, Chris, don't rev it too much. We still need to run the engine in a bit more,' Dad warned. So off I went and was careful to move slowly up through the gears, just as I had been told.

'This is naff! It's not as quick as my Italjet,' I thought, trying to conceal my disappointment as I plodded round the field a few times.

'Right, that should do it,' Dad said. 'Just be careful the first time you open the throttle.'

'Yeah, right,' I thought, 'like I really need to be careful on this shitter!'

The power band of the Italjet and the TY80 had both been very linear and predictable. I guess in reality they didn't have a power band of any sort! But this Yamaha was a completely different beast. The film *Star Wars* was on at the time and the only thing I could compare it to was the *Millenium Falcon* starship. Now we all know that at sub-light velocities the *Millenium Falcon* left a lot to be desired. But switch her into superluminal mode and there was no equal. (Don't worry, I'm not a *Star Wars* freak – I got that from a website!) The bike made a noise like a swarm of angry bees and the hedge bottoms started to fly past, just like the stars in outer space.

I could not get my breath and this was very possibly the first time I ever swore. 'Fuckin' 'ell,' I muttered as I tried to regain control. When I returned to where Dad was proudly standing it was easy to tell that he knew he had made the right choice.

The rule was that I could only ride it when Dad was around, but I already knew that rules are there to be broken and I would often sneak out before Dad was back from work. The problem with that policy was crashing. Then I had to get the bike back to the garage and cleaned up before he was home. And I must have crashed that bike so many times.

As soon as I had my new motocross bike I started bending Dad's ear about starting to race. It was one thing disappearing off to the local woods on a Sunday morning, but taking racing seriously was a different matter. That was an all day of a job and Dad simply didn't have the time to spare while running a family business with Mum. So he would fob me off with: 'You can go racing when you are 14.' This was probably not a random date, as he probably had a certain size of bike in mind for me to start off on. We always had to take my size into consideration. Even when I bought my first road bike at the age of 16 my feet would not touch the floor.

Dad's plan was to enter me in a couple of races at the end of the season, to see whether I took to it and enjoyed it before forking out for a more up-to-date bike. But I did need the proper equipment for even a couple of races, especially with Mum bending Dad's ear in the background about making sure I was safe. So the first I knew about my impending motocross race début was when Dad came home with a brand-new Nolan N19E full-face helmet, which was nearly as big as I was. I think the bottom of it actually touched my shoulders. Over the next couple of weeks I accumulated the full body armour, new boots and padded jacket and trousers, and I could barely walk with it all on. That didn't dampen the growing anticipation of the first race, though.

I don't think I actually slept in my new gear the night before the race, but I certainly wore it on the way to a freezing place on the side of a windswept hill called Oughtibridge, near Barnsley. There were butterflies in the stomach on the Sunday morning as the flasks were filled, butties wrapped and van loaded with bikes and dog. You can't beat that feeling, and I still get it now when I set off with Rachel and Nobby to a motocross meeting. Amanda Smith was still on the scene for this first race, which possibly added to the nervousness as I would have been keen to impress. But impress I did not. In the three races I was last, last and … last!

I made it round the first lap of the morning practice but it was already clear that I didn't have a clue what I was doing. I was no longer racing against my dad in the field, wearing an old sweatshirt and a pair of wellies. I was up against lads who had been doing this every weekend for six or seven years and I was a raw beginner at full-on motocross. This showed in the first race, when I was comprehensively lapped. And it went downhill from there. One of the 'seasoned professionals' went down in front of me during the second race and I could not avoid running over his legs. Nothing like that had ever happened to me before and I was horrified. I stopped immediately to see if he was OK and apologize, but was on an upslope and lost control of my bike, which rolled back over him. He just looked up at me as if to say, 'Who is this twat on the Yamaha YZ80?'

Dad had been watching intently and came up with a plan for the final race of the day. 'You have got to get off to a better start, lad. You are being left for dead,' he said. This was probably because it was the first time I had started behind an elastic tape, which was released by the starter. So with Dad's words fresh in my ears I pinned it for the final race, but unfortunately before the elastic was out of the way. As my bike wheelied off down the straight after the others I rolled around in the mud on the start-line trying to untangle myself from the elastic. Out of the corner of my eye I could see Dad slowly wandering over, shaking his head as the marshals tried to reunite me with my bike.

There was plenty of time to reflect on my performance on the way home, caked in mud from head to toe because I only had one set of gear and no change of clothes. Amanda was probably already starting to pen her letter dumping me. And I was pretty bewildered. OK, my bike was probably a couple of years older than the ones the other kids were riding, but that had not made a blind bit of difference. This was a reality check that I had a huge gulf to bridge. Just because I was the fastest kid on my estate did not mean I was actually any good. I had two choices: to give it up as a bad job or roll up my sleeves and make sure I improved. I chose the latter. It was time to get my brave head on.

I obviously convinced Dad that my heart was in it because my next combined Christmas and birthday present was a new water-cooled version of the Yamaha YZs, ready for the new season in the YMSA Inter-80s class. What's more I had another new set of gear, so at least I could get changed at lunchtime now. But, new bike or no new bike, I had to start exactly where I had left off – at the back. No matter what I tried I just could not get the hang of jumps. I tried holding the throttle flat out and I tried shutting off at the top of the jump. There was always the same result. And it didn't really help that, as with trials riding, my mentor didn't exactly have all the answers. Dad just based himself next to the biggest jump at the start of the race because he knew I would come off on nearly every lap. There were times when I went missing for the whole twenty minutes, stranded on some banking trying to get the bike upright. I was learning the hard way, but what I lacked in natural talent and experience I made up for in heart.

This probably came from Dad. He used to box as a kid, and by all accounts he was pretty tough. He was also the most fearless and fastest of his mates on a bike. But those qualities were not going to make up for the seven years of experience that the other kids had on me. When I stayed on and finished a race I did not do too badly, and there were several motivating factors to do better.

For one, I did not enjoy losing – and still don't. I was not a bad loser, certainly no Carl Fogarty! But I felt bad for disappointing Dad, who had given up his day off after working hard all week. And, like any kid, I wanted to walk into school on Monday morning with my head held high and with a trophy to show my mates.

I received my first piece of silverware, or plasticware to be more precise, for coming thirteenth overall. I still have it in pride of place at home. I looked after it like the Holy Grail and carried it everywhere in my rucksack. Before long I was ninth and then seventh in the main class, then within a couple of years I was challenging the fast lads for the big trophies that were awarded to the top three places. I had done enough to be invited to the regional Champion of Champions event, spread over two days, where the real class acts like Paul Malin and Jamie Dobb would be competing in other classes. This was a real family affair and one of the few times Mum would come to watch because we could make a full weekend of it, staying in a bed and breakfast or camping. The downside of Mum being there is that she insisted on cleaning my face between races by spitting on her hanky and wiping off the mud. Dad was only ever concerned about cleaning my air filter or making sure there was enough two-stroke oil in the petrol.

My main concern at this event was that I was out of my depth once more. Having worked so hard to be on a par with the lads that I raced against every week, it was crushing to find out that there was now a whole new gulf to bridge. So I spent the weekend crashing my brains out.

Ability was not my only disadvantage if I wanted to stay at school-boy level. I still wasn't big enough to ride a 125cc bike so, when I was too old for the 80cc class, rather than race my 80cc bike against 125cc bikes, Dad thought it might be an idea to start racing in AMCA events for adults. This was also where some of the older lads I had become friendly with, such as Sean Balls, were competing, so it made sense from that aspect too. Now you were graded on ability and not age. By then I had swapped the YZ80 for a Kawasaki KX80. It was not necessarily a lot faster than the Yamaha but it was easier to ride because it had a lot more grunt, whereas the Yamaha had no bottom-end power. Kawasakis were also a lot easier to buy parts for locally, and an engine kit to make it up to 100cc, which we used later, was available.

Once again we decided to test the new class out towards the end of the season rather than throw ourselves into it for a full season. So at Warsop Sandbowl I found myself on the starting grid staring up at some huge bloke revving his Maico 490 thinking, 'What the hell am I doing here?' But it was one of the few times when size didn't matter because most of these guys were beginners. I won all three races in the Junior Open class and was immediately upgraded to the Seniors class. This was more of a challenge but it did not take too long before

I was in the Experts class. That's when we took the opportunity to use the 100cc kit because, although I really needed to be on a 125 at this stage, I was still at least a foot off fitting on one.

The motocross scene now dominated my life. We had moved to Nottingham, where Dad had set up another shop, Fox's, and sponsored one of the top motocross riders in our region, John Reynolds. I had lost contact with a lot of my pals from school and the estate and was spending more and more time with my new motocross pals, particularly Sean Balls, who ironically was now going out with Amanda Smith, and another handy rider, Simon Hayes, who was seeing my sister. (I fancied his sister, too, but didn't get anywhere!) His mum and dad owned a dairy farm way off the beaten track and I loved mucking around up there, where we could get away with anything. This was where I learned to drive, long before getting my licence. We also used to fix lights onto our Honda ATC70s and tear around in the dark and snow.

One day we ventured out of his fields up to the notorious Ambergate Woods, sensibly packing some straps in case we got into any difficulties. We were tearing along a path at the top of a ridge, with a 20-foot drop onto rocks below. The path was barely wide enough for ramblers, let alone these three-wheeled all-terrain machines (they sound glamorous but actually only had Honda C70 engines in them) and it was probably no great surprise when one of my wheels went over the side. I thought that me and the bike were doomed to be smashed on the rocks below but I managed to lunge and grab a branch on the way down. Miraculously I stopped myself from falling but, equally unlikely, the ATC had become caught on my boot so I was left swinging from the branch with a trike dangling from my leg. Simon peered over the edge and averted disaster by managing to lasso me with the straps and drag me to safety. Needless to say I rode a bit steadier for the rest of the day.

Although motocrossing was my main focus, road bikes were never far away from my mind during those teenage years. I barely remember going to watch my dad road racing, as I was only about 5 before he packed in to concentrate on his young family and the business. Those were the days when the likes of Barry Sheene could be winning a GP one week and then racing at Cadwell Park the next, and Dad also took me to a few of these events. I did not go anywhere without my autograph book, and I still have the page saying: To Bugs from Barry Sheene. I also loved watching racing on telly and looked up to the likes of Kenny Roberts, the massive Dutchman Will Hartog in his white leathers, Randy Mamola and Freddie Spencer.

I also rode to school on my BMX and, when I started disappearing from school, used it to get to Jervis Motorcycle shop in Ripley to see Sean, where he worked for the owner, Graham Clifton. As I approached the age of 16 I was itching to ditch the BMX, which I could now wheelie for England, and have my motorbike licence. I applied at the earliest opportunity, only to receive the shock of my life when the provisional licence arrived in the post – complete with an endorsement for nine points from the incident with the Derbyshire County Council van, which my selective memory had forgotten all about. I was already walking a tightrope without having legitimately turned a wheel!

Still, this was not going to put me off, and I inherited the Kawasaki AE50 that had been bought for my sister two years earlier. It soon became clear that Wendy wasn't exceptionally safe on her bike. She wasn't scared, just not particularly adept. For instance, if she ever took a wrong turn she would wait until she reached the next round-about, which might be four or five miles away, rather than do a U-turn. There were always new bits of plastic hanging off the bike, evidence of her latest scrape. It was obvious she wasn't going to last! So when it came to the choice of not having a daughter any more or having to get up bright and early to give her a lift into Nottingham Art College, there was no option for Mum and Dad and the bike sat in the garage until I was old enough.

My sister's record when she got her driving licence wasn't much better and it wasn't too long before even her boyfriends, who were normally as daft as brushes, would not go in the car with her. She tried to take Sprocket for company instead, but even he wasn't too keen. She was always more interested in what was going on around her and she could come back from a trip knowing exactly what was for sale in all the shops she had been past, and how much they cost, and in which colours they were available! When she was involved in a multiple car pile-up, however, the family rallied round with genuine concern – until we read the witness statements. Wendy had not been caught up in a typical concertina effect. She had actually arrived on the scene five minutes after the original incident and ploughed into the stationary vehicles while the other drivers were exchanging their documents! Of course it should be stressed that she is an impeccable driver now – although it should also be noted that she drives a Volvo …

The 50cc engine in her bike, the maximum size of engine for a 16 year old, was a bit tame for me so I managed to come across a salvaged accident-damaged engine from a Kawasaki AR80, which was modelled on a racing bike and had a nose cone fairing, whereas the AE50s were modelled on dirt bikes. But the engines were exactly the same size and were easy to switch so I ended up riding a six-speed 80cc bike – disguised as a 50cc by restamping the engine number – that was at least capable of approaching the speed limit. I think the five-speed 50s were actually more dangerous because you could see a lorry coming up your arse but the bike wasn't quick enough to get you out of the way.

The single biggest event in growing up for most kids must be shagging but for me it was becoming road legal and I counted down the days until March 25 and my 16th birthday. For weeks I had worked on the bike, making sure that everything looked perfect for the big day. I went to bed really early the night before so that I could be up at the crack of dawn to meet my mate, Kevin Goodwin, a pal from school who had turned 16 a couple of weeks earlier and rode an unrestricted Yamaha FS1E. So imagine the dismay when I threw open the curtains to find that it had been snowing all night! That wasn't going to deter me, though, and we must have covered more than 300 miles during the day. Although the engine was 80cc I had not had a chance to find a suitable exhaust, so my maximum speed was probably 50mph but that didn't diminish that feeling of being mobile. I'm not sure my parents ever saw me again after that day.

At the age of 17 learners were able to move up to 125cc bikes but you could also take your full test at that age. Dad could not pay me a fortune for working at his shop but he did promise that if I continued to put the hours in he would let me use a Kawasaki GPZ500S when I passed my test. So there wasn't much doubt that I would take my test at the earliest opportunity. I passed part one, an aptitude test held in a school playground, on the Saturday morning of my 17th birthday, and passed part two, assessment by a guy with a clipboard who could only see you go round a couple of corners from where he stood, on the Monday.

I was out on it the minute I had the certificate in my hand. In today's terms a 500cc twin-cylinder is not very powerful but this had four times the horsepower that I was used to and I could not believe how fast it was. I rode it at every opportunity, literally until I had run out of money to fill up with petrol. And I think I kept Dunlop in business during that period because the cool tyre to have was the Dunlop Arrowmax. I'm not even sure how good they were but I do remember that the front tyres lasted three times longer than the rears, an indication of the amount of time I spent pulling wheelies.

If there was a downside to the GPZ500S it was the brakes. There was a single disc on the front, which wasn't the end of the world because the bike was quite light. But in the rear was a drum brake which was as receptive as the handbrake on a car. So if you got your wheelie a bit wrong and needed the back brake you would bang back down as you couldn't feather it like a disc-pad brake.

Not that I spent much time thinking about the brakes. The shackles were now off – I was road legal and it was time to spread my wings. And my first real trip on my bike was to prove to be a life-changing experience.

4

Tourist Stalker

It was Sean's idea to invite me along on the trip to watch the Manx Grand Prix, and I am grateful to this day. Something changed inside me during that week on the Isle of Man. I returned knowing that one day I would want to try my hand at road racing. I did not think for one moment that I would ever make my living as a racer, as I couldn't see much further than my next motocross race at the time. But I had caught the bug.

I had been to the Isle of Man once before, a day trip with Mum and Dad to watch the TT when I was around 7. We must have spent more time on the ferry than on the island and it rained nearly the whole time, so most of the racing was cancelled and there wasn't really a lot else to do. A day trip must have seemed like a good idea at the time to my dad, who was admittedly a bit 'out there'! I had enjoyed some great family holidays throughout my childhood, although we didn't always travel in style. For instance a two- or three-day drive in the back of Dad's Ford Capri next to my sister, down to Denia on the east coast of Spain and not too far from Benidorm, was a bit of an ordeal. But I did discover Fanta orange, pinball and how to swim – but only underwater as I struggled on the surface for some reason. I had always been really jealous when Mum and Dad headed off with a couple of pals on their bike trips around Europe, Mum on the back of Dad's 1000cc Suzuki Katana. But this trip to the Isle of

Man was the first time I had been away without Mum and Dad. It was a coming of age. The other lads were a bit older than me and I promised to ring home every night, which allayed their fears somewhat, although Mum squeezed in one-too-many 'Now, you be careful' on the morning we set off for Heysham.

We could just about make out the island in the distance when we set off on the ferry. Four hours later it was exactly the same size. 'Any danger of turning the wick up on this engine?' I thought. The first trauma of the trip was leaving my pride and joy in the hands of the guys chaining the bikes up below decks, but they did not leave a scratch. The second trauma was sharing a boat with all the foreigners who were beginning to whiff somewhat and had things crawling out of their beards, having spent days on end reaching the ferry on their bikes. They nearly all wore Rukka jackets, adding weight to the theory: You look a fucker in your Rukka! The only other waterproof jackets around at the time were the waxed ones made by Belstaff, now a designer label. But they smelt the minute you bought them. At least you got a couple of weeks out of a Rukka before you stank.

I have known a few riders who have gone to live on the Isle of Man and I always imagine it to be a bit bleak and quiet, especially in the winter. Obviously, their tax return at the end of the year might make up for these downsides! But, when I look back, I would say that I have enjoyed every minute I have spent there, on this and subsequent trips. We stayed at a quaint bed and breakfast, made all the more welcoming by the landlady's daughter, who had long blonde hair and big rockets and who made it worthwhile getting up for breakfast each morning.

Along with Sean came his boss Graham Clifton, who behaved with Sean exactly how my dad did with me, and Graham's best friend, Charlie Bamford, who owned clothing shops. His daughter was stunning and was always up with the latest fashions from her dad's shops. I had many an impure thought as I cycled past their house on the way to school. Charlie liked a pint and was riding a brand-new Yamaha FZR1000 Genesis. This was not a bike that you wanted to be riding after a few beers, so he was happy to have an extra pint or three and swap with me. I was never too interested in drinking, and certainly not at lunchtime when there was a chance of riding his bike in the afternoon. With my limited experience on the road this was probably the equivalent of me now riding the 200bhp bikes that I now race. But at the age of 17 caution did not really come into it and I was only too happy to help Charlie out.

My enduring memory of the week is doing lap after lap of the TT circuit. At the Manx GP there is no equivalent of the TT's Mad Sunday, when the roads are closed off to cars and bikers have free rein of the course. Nor is there the TT hustle and bustle, so you could just take your chances when it was quiet, always looking out for the mad Germans who forgot they should be on the other side of the road. I had watched a bit of the TT from the top of Bray Hill during my fleeting visit as a kid but I don't remember experiencing the thrill that I did as an adolescent. I don't think kids properly appreciate the excitement or dangers. But every nerve end was tingling when I came over Bray Hill for the first time on Charlie's bike and it didn't take long before I was tucked in behind the fairing, thinking I was Joey Dunlop.

I was quite respectful when I was on his bike and didn't try too many tricks, although my GPZ500S caught him out when he first had a go on it. We were approaching a left-hand hairpin, almost covered by a canopy of trees and therefore slightly damp in the morning. Charlie had no experience of the anchor-like rear drum brake and, as the rest of us cautiously took the racing line into the bend, Charlie hurtled past, facing the wrong direction, eyes like saucers, the front end hopping, back wheel locked and his foot down trying to keep himself upright. He had obviously tried the notorious rear drum brake for the first time and, when nothing happened, had pushed it so hard that it locked. Luckily, he was still so drunk from the previous night and his reactions were so bad that he wasn't able to overcompensate so he somehow managed to stay upright.

Soon the various landmark sections, such as Quarry Bends, Signpost Corner and the Gooseneck, became second nature. I enjoyed the Gooseneck because it was the start of the 'no speed limit' section and, without the trees and houses and villages, it felt as though I could have been on a short circuit. But Ballaugh Bridge was special. Over the previous few years I had improved over the motocross jumps and the natural progression was to starting jumping a road bike, although there weren't too many opportunities near home. The other lads had told me about the bridge and, while I was a bit daft, I wasn't completely stupid. So, while I had been on the gas over the mountain section where there is no speed limit, my first approach to the bridge was not at warp speed. Then with each successive jump I pushed the limits further and even started to break the unwritten rule of never riding the circuit in the wrong direction. Faced with a thirty-seven-mile round trip to get back to the bridge, I preferred to opt for a one-mile detour to try another jump straight away. When I ripped the belly pan off my bike on one landing and followed that up by nearly wearing the pub wall, I decided it was time to ease off a bit.

Spectators crowded into the pub next to the bridge just to see idiots like me go airborne, and a cheer went up for the more spectacular efforts. I remember bumping into some guys towards the end of the week who had obviously noticed me in action. 'Yeah, we noticed the FZR1000 all right. It took us a few days to realize there was someone riding it, though. We thought it was just a T-shirt tied to the handlebar at first,' they laughed. I must have looked tinier than ever on a bike that size. 'You're a fearless little bastard, aren't you?' the guy added, probably thinking I was actually a bit of a prat.

Then the races started and the adrenalin immediately began to flow as soon as the Red Arrows roared overhead, while we watched from the other side of the Gooseneck. I was in complete awe when I later watched the top racers of the day go over Ballaugh Bridge. Whenever we went out after that I would try and replicate what the racers were doing, modifying my lines through certain sections, and I knew it was taking me a lot less time to do a lap, even if I was held up by traffic lights in Ramsey. So when an old guy on a Honda 400 Four took me by surprise at one bend and overtook on the inside, I readily accepted the challenge to keep up with him. The Honda 400 Four, with four exhaust outlets coming down to one along the side, was not really a sports bike, more of a 'sit up and beg' bike. They were crap even when new and this guy was on an old ratter, so I passed him easily on the straights, although he was prepared to scrape his footrest in order to take me back going into the corners. The race was well and truly on. We obviously cleared off from the rest of my group and I eventually had to stop to let them catch up, while I caught my breath. They were pissing themselves.

'Could you not see that he had an Isle of Man number plate? He wasn't even in leathers – he was probably just going home from the office. He has been doing this route for the last forty years. You were never going to stay with him,' laughed Graham. It was maybe my first taste of road 'racing', and the Manx had already made a lasting impression.

Although there wasn't the same pure buzz as at a closed-circuit race, this was certainly a spectacle and one which helped shape my career in racing. There is still a part of me which wants to race at the TT. When I see the on-board footage from the race I invariably change my mind, but it's hard to ignore the kind of thrill that makes the hairs stand on the back of your neck. Having said that, I remember seeing my pal Terry Rymer set off from the start line of the North West 200 road race in 1996 and I was genuinely worried for him. And I don't know whether I would want members of my family to have those feelings, so I don't suppose I will ever take the chance to race there.

When I returned home I was keen to hone my new-found skills on the local roads. I used to enjoy riding on one particular stretch of road between Nottingham and Ripley, and on the way home from work one night I did not realize I had been chased by a police car from the outskirts of Nottingham, through the centre of town and halfway round the ring road. They only caught me when, still not realizing I was being followed, I stopped at a set of traffic lights. It was a full-scale Sweeney operation as their car swerved in front of my stationary bike to block my escape route. They had assumed from the speed I was going that I had nicked the bike.

'I cannot believe that you managed to negotiate that miniroundabout back there. There were sparks coming off your centre stand. Have you any idea what speeds you have been going at?' asked the copper.

'Er, around 35 miles an hour?' I politely ventured. This was one time when I knew that I was not going to be able to pull the wool over someone's eyes.

'Try 80 in a 30 zone. And we could add reckless driving, dangerous driving, and driving without due care and attention. What have you got to say for yourself?'

I did not even understand most of those phrases and was shitting myself. 'I'm going to need some soap-on-a-rope for my prison stretch,' I thought.

'I know this sounds silly but I have been working late and I am really late for my tea. My mum always panics when I am late and I am out on my bike,' I suggested. It was the right thing to say as their mood appeared to relax immediately and I was eventually only charged with the speeding offence, their reason being that I was only a danger to myself as there wasn't much on the roads.

Out came my school uniform for the court appearance. I had not worn it for two years but it still fitted perfectly, in fact it probably still fits me now. I was none too confident about the outcome. After all, I had nearly tripled the speed limit. Luck was on my side, though – again! A lady magistrate heard my case and was obviously impressed that I didn't want my poor mum to think that I was late for tea because I was under a bus. I obviously said all the right things because Dad gave me a furtive 'thumbs up' from the public gallery when the bench went into recess to consider my punishment, as if to say, 'You are going to be all right, youth!' To this day, whenever I am in court, Dad comes with me as a kind of lucky charm.

Still, my heart was in my mouth when she returned. 'Obviously we are not going to ban you, Mr Walker ...' Result! Although how I had escaped a ban was by no means obvious. I was given three points and fined £160 – another result. I had been panicking since the night of the offence about the existing nine points on my licence from the Derbyshire County Council van night out. I could have been banned only a couple of months after passing my test. But those points had been back-dated to the date of the offence and had just expired. So, having also recently changed address, I was able to take a clean licence to court.

Dad was as relieved as I was, so there was no bollocking this time. I had possibly just reached the stage where I was a bit too big for a clip round the ear. He was never a great disciplinarian but I did get a clout when I stepped out of line and it was always no more than I deserved. Deep down, though, he is as gentle as a lamb, and knowing that I might have upset him was enough of a punishment. More often than not he would just go through the motions of taking me and my sister upstairs on the pretence of giving us a good talking to. Mum would be egging him on, saying, 'Go on, John, you go and sort them out.' Once upstairs Dad was more likely to requisition our sweets for the week, which was far worse than a whack on the arse.

He was, however, a little less forgiving when it came to pain. This first became evident in my second year of motocross racing. During the morning warm-up of one meeting I was going round a corner on the inside of a slower rider and my foot, still on the foot-rest, hit the underside of his foot-rest. I had never broken any bones before so I didn't realize anything was wrong, except that my foot was hurting like hell. I definitely wanted to avoid a trip to the St John's Ambulance van but also wanted to take my boot off to see what I had done.

'Oh, what's the matter with you? Stop moaning, you big puff,' Dad said. 'If you take your boot off now you won't get it back on for the rest of the day.' So that was that. I hobbled my way through the rest of the day and finally, in the car on the way home, I managed to wrench off the boot. It was like something from *The Nutty Professor*, when Buddy Love suddenly turns back into the fat guy – my foot instantaneously swelled up. Clearly something was not right but I did not want to go to hospital and risk being put in a plaster cast, which would have kept me off my bike for ages. So I took a couple of paracetamol and borrowed one of Dad's trainers so that I could go to work the next day. The crack in my metatarsal was still visible when I went for my first X-ray a year or so later, when a trip to hospital was unavoidable.

I was racing in the 125cc experts' class and my good mate Simon Hayes, who had started riding later than me, was coming quickly up through the ranks. It was fairly obvious that some day soon he was going to be a very good rider. Every rider has a rival they want to beat, whether it is their brother, their team-mate or their best mate. So I was desperate to postpone the inevitable defeat at the hands of Simon for as long as possible. We were racing at a good old-fashioned little motocross track called Sturston Fields, just off the road between Belper and Ashover, on a lovely sunny day. Simon was two places behind me in the early stages of the opening race of the day when I went over a rutted jump. As I took off my foot hit the top of the rut and was thrown off the foot-rest, folding under the bike when it landed.

I was in agony, but there was no such thing as stopping halfway through a race, especially with Hayesy breathing down my neck. The guy behind me overtook on the next lap and then Simon came past. I finished the race in pieces but, because I had stayed on my bike, neither my dad nor Simon believed there was a genuine problem.

'There's nowt wrong with you, you big puff,' Dad said again. Did he have to keep calling me a big puff!? He didn't actually say, 'It's only because Simon beat you for the first time,' but I knew that was what he was thinking. I could imagine him confiding to my sister: 'I don't know what our Chris is bothered about. It was only a matter of time before Simon beat him. He's a real talent, that lad.' He might have thought differently if he had known Simon was having a go on my sister at the time!

Again my boot had to stay on for the duration of the meeting and I finished further and further down the field in the next races. This was a new pair of boots, however, and Dad had bought them two sizes too big so that I could 'grow into them' – as dads do! That made it difficult to know exactly what was happening down there, although I could tell that something was squishing around when I put weight on that leg. What a shitty day. Firstly, my leg was black and blue and killing me. Secondly, even if my dad had now accepted that I had actually run over my own foot, he certainly wasn't letting on. Thirdly, Simon Hayes had smoked me!

On Monday morning I was hobbling pretty badly, but still turned up for work. By Tuesday I could barely walk, but still turned up for work.

I wish I hadn't turned up for work on the Wednesday. For not only was I in absolute pieces, I was provided with some fairly alarming information by a welder who helped out at my dad's shop, Ian Coulton. He was known as Yooby, because all anyone said to him as a naughty kid was, 'Now, you be good!' His real nickname was Ditch, which I imagine had something to do with where he spent most of his time as a sidecar passenger. He actually once built a sidecar to attach to my Kawasaki 100, which me and a friend, Gary Beresford, known as Benny because he wore the kind of woollen hat that Benny from *Crossroads* wore, were supposed to race on New Year's Day at Buckland Hollow. It was not the prettiest or the safest thing out there and Benny trapped his hand getting in, shat himself and refused to ride in it. So it was down to my dad, still pissed from New Year's Eve, to fill in. He was obviously too big for it and had to kneel down for the whole race. It was another of those irreplaceable father and son times when he was more my best pal than my dad.

Yooby clearly had a screw loose and could pull the biggest wheelies I had ever seen on the road outside Dad's shop. He also claimed to know a fair bit about injuries, as well as sidecars.

'You want to get that looked at, young 'un,' he said. 'You can die if it's broken and bone marrow gets into your bloodstream.' Bone marrow? I had only ever heard of bone marrow in connection with dog food, and the prospect of Pedigree Chum coursing through my veins did not appeal. I was now petrified that I was going to lose my leg, and Dad finally realized that it might be an idea if I was to go to hospital. Yooby took me there the following morning and I was quite excited by my first X-ray and quietly pleased with the result. There was a definite fracture and I was given an appointment at the fracture clinic for the next morning. In the meantime they put on a back slab support and bandaged my leg up but, strangely, there was no mention of bone marrow poisoning!

By now Dad must have been starting to feel quite guilty as he took time off work to take me to hospital on the Friday morning. The specialist showed him the X-ray but Dad could not work out where the break was. (Nowadays he can spot them before the specialist because he has been so many times with me.)

'You can see that he has snapped the bottom of the tibia clean off
– a bit like removing a limpet from a rock,' said the surgeon.

'Does this mean I have to come back soon, doctor?' I asked naively.

'You are going nowhere, young man. You should have come in a
lot earlier. We are going to operate as soon as possible so we will keep
you in overnight, you will have nil by mouth from midnight and we
will screw it back on as soon as possible tomorrow,' he said.

My arse fell out. I went from being quite smugly content that I had
a genuine injury to feeling physically sick. And now Dad was feeling
extremely sheepish. He returned that day with a little portable telly
with an in-built VHS player for me to watch during my stay on the
ward, which was actually quite good fun. The guy in the bed on the
left did not like the strawberries and cream that his wife was bringing
but did not dare admit it, so I was more than happy to dispose of
them. The guy to my right was a nutcase who lashed out and swore in
his sleep, which kept us all amused. I think they call this Tourette's
nowadays. In the other three beds, one bloke had fallen off a ladder
and two had crashed their bikes, and I was everyone's best mate
because of the telly, even though I made them watch *On Any Sunday
2* time and time again. I think the nutter started shouting, 'So Kenny
cut his own and won first time out,' in his sleep in an American drawl
after listening to the film for the tenth time.

I don't actually remember going down for the operation. Maybe I
have blanked it from my mind because I was panicking, but I do
remember coming round to see my leg throbbing just like Tom's thumb
after Jerry had hit it with a hammer. There was also a section of garden
hose coming out of my ankle, attached to a vacuum that was sucking all
the pus and gunge out of the joint. (It was actually more the size of a
McDonald's straw but felt like a garden hose.) I could cope with the
pain in my ankle during my six-day recovery but the tube really irri-
tated me because my skin was inflamed and itchy at the entrance. I also
had to carry the jar when I hopped to the toilet, because there was no
way I was peeing in one of those jars they provide.

My whingeing about the tube finally paid off. The doctor pulled a
classic 'What's that over there?' manoeuvre and, while I stared blankly

at where he was pointing, he yanked the tube out of my ankle. He then had to peel me off the ceiling. I very nearly passed out, and when I stopped whimpering I sulked for the rest of the day and refused to talk to anyone. Apparently they pull it like that so that the friction burns the skin edges and helps to seal the hole. When it was time to leave hospital a fibreglass cast was fitted below the knee and came complete with a Velcro-attached shoe, in which I looked a proper wand.

Once home there was only one thing on my mind – could I ride my bike with my cast on? I made straight for the garage, swung my cast over and found that, as my toes were poking out the end of the cast, I could squeeze them under the gear lever. Phew! I was supposed to wait two weeks before putting any weight on it so I did leave it a week before going out on the road.

The operation had been a painful lesson, but we now knew that it was probably best to play safe with future injuries and have them checked out at the hospital. Early on in the following season I was leading a 125 expert race, which didn't happen very often, when my hand hit one of the posts and fetched me off the bike. I went to pick the bike up but when I grabbed the handlebar I could feel a stone in my glove. I tried to shake it loose but nothing dropped out of the glove so I climbed back on to finish the race, trying to ignore the stone. When I took my glove off at the end of the race I immediately saw that my knuckle had been snapped off and pushed through to the palm of my hand. I had been gripping the bars with the loose piece of bone for the remainder of that race. But there were still two races to go.

'Well, we have come all this way, you might as well ride this afternoon and then we will go to hospital on the way home. Your mother won't even have the tea on yet,' Dad suggested. By now we knew the dance at the Accident and Emergency department. If you went in the middle of the afternoon it was full of footballers who had strained their hairstyle, or drunks from the pub. It started to clear around tea-time, which was much more convenient for us, even if it meant riding in two more races minus one knuckle and using the clutch with one finger. All riders become experts at dealing with broken fingers, which usually involves nothing more sophisticated than strapping two fingers of the glove together and carrying on racing. The only suitable treatment for this fracture was to push the floating bone back as close to the original site as possible. If you look at my fist now you can see I didn't do a very good job, but at least I was able to keep racing. Missing a race was sacrilege. It was as though we were all on £100,000 a year and our lives depended on it, not just pursuing a daft hobby.

There were some injuries, however, which needed immediate medical attention. A couple of years after breaking my left ankle it was time to even things up on the right leg. I was racing at Warsop Sandbowl in the 125 championship class and was going round the outside of another rider during morning practice. He was on the normal line for the corner, and as I stuck my leg out it got caught in his wheel between the chain and swinging arm. I was dragged off my bike and the other rider went over his bars. As his bike dropped, my leg was twisted underneath it and I heard the snap. I have never been in so much pain. I'm no Nancy, but I screamed out loud. The track is in a quarry so my screams were amplified and the red flags immediately came out as the marshals rushed over carrying spanners, chain splitters and hacksaws. My leg was still wrapped around his bike but the attempts to free it were straight out of a Laurel and Hardy movie. The spanners did not fit the bolts. Then the chain splitters broke. Then the blade on the hacksaw snapped. So up steps an old geezer who insisted on attempting to lever my leg free with his – wait for it – umbrella.

It was at this point my screams went up a decibel or two. 'Daaaaaad, get them off me. Do something, for fuck's sake,' I cried. Dad, as ever, was the calmest of the bunch and managed to take the swing arm bolt out at the first attempt, as the bloke whose bike it was looked on in horror as it was pulled apart before his eyes in order to work me free. This fracture was very similar to my previous ankle injury, but this time the bone was not displaced and so I just had the normal six weeks in plaster rather than an operation.

Of course I was not the only one to suffer injuries. My mates had their fair share of broken wrists and collar bones. But we also had the occasional reality check when our injuries, which seemed serious to us at the time, paled into insignificance. First, a member of the motocross club, who none of us knew very well, died in a microlight accident. Then, coincidentally at Warsop Sandbowl again, Craig, the brother of one of my friends, Graham Overton, got a jump wrong, landed on his head and slipped into a coma. Craig, who was just starting to motocross whereas Graham was already quite accomplished, was the kind of guy you looked up to at that age. He had a cool job as an undercover police officer and carried a concealed gun in a holster under his jacket. I did not know him as well as Graham, who became a close mate. But, although we carried on after he was taken off in the ambulance unconscious, everyone was very subdued and shocked for the rest of the day as the whispers about the extent of his injuries circulated.

I could not begin to imagine the worry that Graham and the rest of the family were experiencing while Craig was in hospital. At that age you tended to assume that everything would work out for the best. If you did assess the risks too carefully, you would probably not have turned up the following week, or certainly not have had a chance of winning. Thankfully Craig came out of the coma, and although he has not been able to resume his career he is still a larger-than-life character and always full of beans, if not quite the same guy as before the accident.

It was not long, however, before the dangers of riding a bike were brought much closer to home.

5

Social Stalker

I had always seen my dad as some kind of infallible superhero. Whatever the crisis, he remained strong, calm and sensible and kept his sense of humour. To see him helpless and immobilized in a hospital bed, on a drip and in obvious agony, almost broke my heart. He had never seemed so vulnerable and I never want to see him like that again. I still find it difficult to think about.

I had returned home from an afternoon motocrossing with my mates at Ripley Pit Hills. We had moved back to Nottingham from Ripley a year earlier, essentially so that Dad did not have to drive my sister as far to college in the morning after she had given up on her motorbike for safety reasons. It took a year to sell the Ripley house, and almost as soon as we moved Wendy promptly jacked in college. Dad was not amused.

Mum's car was not in the drive at home, which was strange in itself. 'Dad's had a crash. I think he's in a bad way. He's in the Queen's Med but Mum says not to go,' said Wendy as soon as I came through the door. It was obvious she was in a real state but, being my older sister, she was trying to keep it together. There was no way I was going to stay away from the hospital so I jumped on my bike, still covered in shit from motocrossing, and set off immediately.

Dad spent most of his spare time watching me motocross but on rare free weekends like this one he liked to keep up with the road racing scene and had taken the chance to ride to Cadwell Park to watch John Reynolds and Co. in action in the British Superbike championship. He, like me, did not have his own bike but on these occasions would borrow one from the shop and take it out for a spin. He had recently taken a Yamaha OWO1, which everyone was raving about, in part exchange. It was a beautiful machine, with a close-ratio gearbox, and would have cost a fortune to buy because it came with all the trick parts. He was actually riding this bike when we went out together on the road for the first time, a trip to our club night which would have taken three quarters of an hour in a car, but took us nine minutes. I could not believe how smooth and fast he was and I could not keep up with him unless the traffic held him up. It's a fair assumption that he was going to put the bike through its paces again during that ride to Cadwell.

But before he even had the chance to get off Mapperley Plains and build up any speed, a car pulled out of a petrol station and straight into his path. There was nothing he could do to avoid it and the impact alone snapped both his wrists. He also damaged his pelvis and some bone was chipped from his knee. As the surgeons pieced him back together in Nottingham, bone was grafted from his hip to repair the knee and both wrists were held in place by external fixators. Dad was no moaner, and that is probably how I have ended up being pretty tough. But the plaster casts, fitted on his arms before the fixators, had been applied so tight that they cut off his circulation and he was in obvious agony. With both hands out of action, though, there was little he could to help himself or ease his own discomfort. In fact there was very little he could do for himself for months afterwards, including wiping his own arse, which was not to my mum's liking.

Once her sense of humour returned she got her own back by giving his fixators the odd ding with her fork or spoon at dinnertime.

Even to this day Dad still has trouble rotating his hands and uses this as an excuse why he can never put his hands in his pockets to pay for anything. (Just kidding. He is actually one of the most generous people I have ever met.) It was also really uncomfortable for him to ride a bike from now on, especially a race replica. He occasionally took his crosser out when I went for an afternoon with my mates but he could not ride it as aggressively as he once had because his wrists would not bend properly and would inevitably break again if he crashed. He still has an off-road enduro bike in the garage, but it is used less and less nowadays. Yet he told me at the start of this year that he wanted to buy a Suzuki Hyabusa, his thinking being that at 200 m.p.h. he could make it to all my races in England this season within two hours. Right-oh! The passion is obviously still alive deep down, and part of me wanted to buy him the bike. But I also want him to still be around.

A more fundamental effect was on the business. He was in his mid-40s, the healing process was a long-drawn-out affair and he was forced to spend a lot of time away from the business with medical appointments. This was even worse because it was such a difficult time for the bike industry. So, with his son also costing him the national debt in crash damage, it was no real surprise that he decided to close the business down a couple of years later. In other circumstances he would probably have wanted me to take over the shop, but I was still too green to take on that responsibility. So Dad went into semi-retirement for a while, sold the family house and then started to fit CCTV cameras to properties, satellite TV systems in mobile homes or reversing cameras onto dumper trucks, which he does to this day. In fact he and Mum are still a partnership as Dad is too lazy to drive anywhere, so she drops him off where he is working. If she can't help him out she takes the dog out for the day or goes shopping before picking him up again in the afternoon.

By the time of Dad's accident I had been winning races in the expert class at club level for a year or so. Or, if I wasn't winning, I crashed trying to win. There was an expert class in each of the 125, 250 and 500cc categories. The 500cc bikes were harder to ride, so almost everyone, and especially the younger lads, stuck with their 125cc bikes, which made for really close, cut-and-thrust racing, although occasionally there was someone on an old Husaberg four-stroke, which sounded like a cannon going off when it backfired going into a corner.

Anyone who wanted to progress from expert club level had to compete in the national AMCA championship – a British championship for amateurs which took you to events from Cornwall to Wales to Scotland. The AMCA championship comprised the best three or four expert club riders from each region, ours being the North East Midlands championship.

My first race at this level was at some dusty shithole down south and was another baptism of fire. You now had to qualify for the actual races, so everyone who made it into the race was virtually at the same high standard. If you missed a gear at club level you could get away with it. At championship level three or four bikes would come straight past you. What's more, instead of being fifteen minutes long the races were now nearly twice that length. I crashed so much that year it wasn't funny. Again, at club level you could crash, remount and still finish in a reasonable position. Here a crash effectively meant the end of your race, and even a bad start left you struggling to make ground through the field. The worst bit was going to my local club night on the Wednesday and explaining to all my mates, who were used to seeing me on the rostrum, that I was quite pleased with my twelfth place. The whole experience was a massive wake-up call and I realized that if I was going to take this racing lark seriously I would have to make the effort to improve my fitness, strength and stamina.

I already did a fair amount of mountain biking, and when my legs were not in a cast I tried the occasional run. But to build my upper body strength swimming seemed to be the logical choice of exercise. Dad had swum for Nottingham in his school days but unfortunately he did not pass on this ability. Let's just say I am no Man from Atlantis. The only stroke I could effectively use for any distance was breaststroke, as any attempt at the crawl resulted in a lungful of swimming pool. What I lacked in ability I made up for in effort and got into a routine of swimming sixty-four lengths, equivalent to a mile, every morning before work. At that time of day there were only two other categories of swimmers in the pool. One was the Johnny Weissmuller, who used three strokes per length and completed twice the number in half the time it took me to swim my mile. The second was a swimmer you never wanted to get stuck behind in a lane – the dreaded granny. On a good day she would leave a kind of oil-slick in her wake from the make-up that had dissolved into the water. On a bad day, and this bad day put me off swimming for a long while, it could get a lot worse. Bear in mind that this was early on in the morning. No matter how hydrated you are, the first piss of the day is always the darkest and smelliest. Multiply that by a factor of five for old ladies. Now, to give her the benefit of the doubt, this old dear probably had no idea that I was catching her up. And she had probably pissed in the pool and got away with it every day for the previous sixty years. But on this particular morning she emptied her bladder just as I bobbed under on my breaststroke and I was hit by a wave of warm filth. I came up spitting and spluttering and, treading water and waving furiously, I shouted over to the attendant.

'Urrgh! She's just pissed right in my face,' I coughed.

'Shush! Don't make a scene. She probably didn't mean it,' whispered the spotty lad.

'Don't make a scene? Don't make a fucking scene? I think you would make a scene if Nora Batty had just peed in your mouth,' I growled as I hauled myself out onto the side and sprinted into the shower.

Swimming lost its appeal after that incident, but I now have an even more valid reason for staying away from public baths. After contracting Bell's Palsy I can't close my left eye properly and have to wear the kind of goggles that 'Moon Eyes' Cooper wore while beating the likes of Ago and Hailwood at the Race of the Year at Mallory Park. I look a bit pervy in normal swimming goggles, let alone these bad boys, and I would forgive anyone for assuming that I was lurking underneath the surface just to check out the birds' back ends. It's a lot safer sticking to a cross-trainer and press-ups these days.

But the best training for a motocross rider is to ride motocross bikes. I don't think that anyone outside of the sport appreciates how much effort every single rider puts into a race. Even the guy at the back of a club race, whose knees are shot to bits and who is too fat to fasten his race pants and proudly displays his builder's butt crack, gives it absolutely everything.

Having reached championship standard I started to receive more support from Kawasaki, and they provided me with a 250cc bike so that I could build up my strength on this bigger bike whenever I had the chance to go back and compete at club level. I used to be on my knees after three races. Now I was forcing myself to compete in six races a day, not only doubling the effort but also doubling the chance of wounding myself. Someone as accident prone as me was unlikely to finish any day unscathed. If I had won the first five of the six races, I was sure to receive a rock in the eye during the sixth.

The other way to improve my chances at championship level was obviously to work on the performance of the bike. I didn't lead an expensive lifestyle as I didn't go clubbing or drinking, so I could spend most of the money that I earned on my racing. Apart from all the routine maintenance and engine rebuilds, which I did myself, to try and find that little extra I experimented with a few things such as a Pro Circuit exhaust. Colin Harrison, the Pro Circuit importer, was always keen for me to try out the latest developments and then even keener to charge me for them afterwards.

I did not set the world alight in my first few races at championship level, but I was never too far out of the top ten. Then I started to have the occasional flash in the pan, when I made it into the top five. Again I could imagine my dad muttering to anyone who might care to listen, 'About bloody time too! He might actually make it after all these years – make it to the end of the race without falling off or breaking something, anyway!'

Week in, week out, I battled it out against the usual suspects: the Bradley brothers, Rob Aston, Aled Humphries, Sean Grosvenor and Danny Wilkinson, a well-built bin man from 'facking Landen'. This was pre-wheelie bin days so you can imagine his upper-body strength. Danny was sponsored by Roy Emberson, who still runs teams, and rode a Yamaha YZ125. Being stronger, he always had the edge whenever the track was bumpy or demanding. It was also an obvious advantage to be able to dab his foot down, especially in the wet, while I couldn't even touch the floor still.

The best conditions for me were a tacky track. In these conditions a knobbly tyre would leave a perfect imprint on the surface. We arrived in Stroud for an AMCA race after a week of rain, followed by a day of hot sunshine. The track was perfect and I felt unusually confident after a good morning practice session. Sure enough I made it into the lead and was holding off Danny and the others reasonably comfortably, until it started to piss down. The track was clay-based and in an instant became an ice-rink. When the yellow flag with a black cross came out, signalling one lap to go, I could see my dad stood next to the blue van which contained the lap-scoring old dears. He was gesturing furiously to indicate that the pack was catching me. Quite how he accurately communicated 'Get a move on, you little bastard' with hand signals I'm not quite sure to this day, but the message was clear. By the final corner, a slippery off-camber left-hander with no berm, they were right up my arse. So, within a few metres of clinching my first championship win, what did I do? You guessed it – I crashed. But the rain had made the surface so greasy that my bike slid over the line, closely followed by me on my backside. Danny blasted through behind me but the result stood and I punched the air in celebration, still lying in the middle of the track. What's more, the win left me in second place overall for the day so I also won my first AMCA championship trophy. I couldn't wait to take it back to a club night, after so long of justifying my twelfth places to my mates.

We had not reached the point in my racing career when performances on the bike had a direct impact on performance off the bike, but there was a new girl on the scene. Anita was going out with another rider, a bit of a Joe Average on a bike. But this bloke's group of motocross mates, who were all a bit older than me, were the cool kids that I looked up to at the time. They were mental, but in a 'breath of fresh air' kind of way. You would find these guys down at the Colwick Sidings, disused railways sidings on the outskirts of Nottingham, tearing around and jumping from one side of the sidings to the other – the kind of antics that now regularly feature in motocross stunt videos. They were not supposed to be there, but they were not doing any harm.

I was particularly friendly with one of the group, Tim Booth, known as Millet because he always wore clothes that looked like they were bought at the Millet chain of outdoor shops. Then there was Sean Woolley, The Bull. He was strong as an ox and emphasized his size by wearing about four layers of shirts. His other strange habit was painting his shoes instead of cleaning them. He made us late for many a night out because we had to wait for his shoes to dry. The Bull was incredibly brave (mad) on a bike and was awesome at jumping the sidings. And there was Jim Foulkes, aka Jimmy the Lizard. I'm not sure whether this nickname came from his reptilian skin or because when he rode a bike his head wobbled around as if he had no control over it. He also wore one of the fashionable Arai lids with a really long peak, and on full wobble it made his head appear twice the size of his body.

Rob Meek, a front-runner in the British championship with the likes of Jamie Dobb and Paul Malin, was also one of the gang. He was always the kid to beat in our area, extremely fit and strong, and went on to win the Weston-super-Mare beach race. Millet was also friendly with Jamie Gamble, who was my best man at my wedding this year, and Steve Spray. Steve was the real local hero. Although John Reynolds was from the Nottingham area, Steve was from Westdale Lane, and you can't get more Nottingham than that. The fact that he rode a JPS Norton, a British bike sponsored by a British company, made him even more popular in local circles.

Another member of my close group of friends was Phil Scales, a welder by trade, whose younger brother Simon was also into motocross, and whose youngest brother, Dave, was a butcher and competition angler. I have never been keen on fish and would not have dared look at the kind of fish he was catching if they were in a tank, let alone at the end of my rod. Phil was one of the bravest riders I have seen on a motocross bike and was very animated in everything he did, illustrating any story with expressive hand gestures or a wide range of vocal tricks. Phil was to affect my life in a huge way.

You had to watch your back when you were in the company of these lads. I started going down to the sidings with them and eventually agreed to meet them at the pub with my motocross mate, Simon Hayes, another young-looking midget who also struggled to get served. Simon finally plucked up courage to go to the bar to ask for a Coke for us both. The next thing he knew one of the others came up behind him, grabbed the bottom of his legs, lifted him up and boosted him straight over the other side of the bar. The landlord wasn't too willing to accept 'boosting' as mitigation for Simon being on the wrong side of the bar and booted, another technical term not to be confused with 'boosted', him out of the bar.

Another of their favourite tricks was 'coning'. If you lived anywhere near roadworks you were a target for coning. This was best carried out when you needed to be somewhere in a hurry first thing in the morning as you would wake up to chaos outside your house, with motorists angrily trying to find their way out of the detour that the lads had set up by arranging a line of cones straight up your drive. Coning was most effective on people who had drive-through drives.

Anita continued to knock around with this group after breaking up with her boyfriend. I had admired her from afar for a good while, but the thought of making a move had never entered my head as she was maybe four or five years older than me and much more experienced. Over the past few years I had been out with a couple of girls from school but neither lasted too long. Kerry was very pretty but I had to finish with her when I couldn't afford a Valentine's Day card. I then went out with a girl called Katy for a bit longer but she was a vegetarian – which is always an issue.

So I was more than ready to be taken advantage of when Anita gave me a lift home in her Volkswagen Polo one night after the pub. A peck on the cheek turned into a snog and the snog could have turned into whatever I wanted it to be, but I was a bit conscious that the curtains of the living room might have been twitching. Surely I wasn't going to pop my cherry in a Volkswagen Polo Estate on a cold winter night with my mum watching? Common sense prevailed on that occasion. Until then I had only ever stared at Amanda Smith's rockets in total awe. Although I did manage to undress Katy it was pitch black and I have already said that I am scared of the dark, so not a great deal happened. So, after years of having only ever seen a motorbike stripped naked, I was finally about to tamper with a bare woman and part the watercress. As far as I was concerned Anita and I were as good as married. And it was nice to be around an older girl who could show me the ropes, both socially and in other areas too. I even discovered that women were also supposed to enjoy it too!

But I didn't let girls get in the way of my enjoyment of bikes, and one of the perks of working in the shop was being allowed to ride some of the bikes that were on sale. And I needed no second invitation when Dad said I could borrow the oil-cooled GSXR750M, complete with a Micron four-into-one exhaust, to deliver a staple gun to Sean Childs, another of my motocross mates who had just bought a new seat cover. It was a mid-October Friday afternoon and Sean lived just round the corner, so I decided to cut through the side roads to miss the evening traffic. The bike sounded fantastic, and as I approached a crossroads I remember blipping the throttle as I changed down from second to first, thinking I was Kevin Schwantz.

And then I woke up in the gutter.

6

Stretched Stalker

'How embarrassing can it get? I can't believe I have been knocked down crossing the road to the paper shop. Someone I know must have seen me,' I told myself as I struggled to take everything in. The last thing I remembered was walking to the local shop early that morning to buy a copy of *Trials and Motocross News*, just so that I could see my name in the final standings for the season.

Slowly I started to become more aware of what was really happening. It was dark and there were lots of flashing lights, so it couldn't be morning. Something wasn't right. There were lots of people fussing around me. I was lifted onto a stretcher and placed in the back of an ambulance. Someone gave me an injection. An oxygen mask was put on my face. A blanket was placed over me. I could not feel my leg. I peeped under the blanket. It was still there but did not look right. I could wiggle my toes, though. No blood, either. That was a relief. And then I woke up in hospital.

I had no recollection of what had actually happened. My mind had blanked everything after I had changed down the gears to approach the junction and, judging by the description of the carnage, I was definitely mistaken in thinking that I was going from second to first. It was more likely to have been fourth to third and my brain was probably quite correct to have no memory of stopping at the crossroads. I had been side-swiped by a car as I went across the junction and flung over the handlebars. My shin snapped as it hit the opposite kerb. The bike smashed into a lamp-post, which bent in half and fell onto two parked cars. The bike then bounced over a garden wall and into a shed.

It was no surprise then that they took a blood sample at the scene to check whether I had been drinking, which of course I hadn't. It had obviously been my fault but there was no reason to prosecute – the injuries and insurance bill were punishment enough. The bike was on the works insurance and it was fairly obvious that it would be the last time I was ever lent a bike by the shop. The driver's car, two parked cars (one a write-off), one GSXR750M (write-off), one lamp-post (write-off) and one garden shed (in need of serious repair) probably amounted to around £100,000. And I had ripped my jacket! And we had lost the staple gun!!

I was lucky to have escaped with a fractured tibia and fibula, especially as I was only wearing jeans, trainers and that padded jacket. Miraculously no operation was needed and I was allowed home after an overnight stay. It was one of those rare occasions I actually wanted to stay in hospital longer, because I realized I was in for a world of doom when I returned home. I guess Dad didn't really believe that I could not remember what had happened and he was a firm believer that there was no point crying over spilt milk, as far as injuries and illnesses were concerned. Likewise, I never received too much sympathy from Mum. So it might have been nice to expect a bit of TLC from Anita, but she usually sided with Dad, as they gelled really well, and she probably did not believe me either because she had seen me crash my motocross bike a million times.

The full leg plaster had to stay on for eight weeks and then a half-leg cast was made for another month, which included Christmas. I'm still not sure whether Dad was taking the piss when he bought me a pair of Reebok pumps for my present, knowing I would only be able to wear one of them for the foreseeable future. I'm sure I was a nightmare to live with during that first week off work, especially for my mum, who had to endure a constant barrage of 'Mum, any chance of a cup of tea?' 'Mum, how about some crisps?' 'Mum, is there any left-over turkey for a butty?' 'Mum, are you there? Hello, is anyone there?'

I was very good at sulking when I wasn't receiving attention or if none of my mates had been round for a few days. Also, the pain was more noticeable when I was bored. So the knitting needles came out to scratch the itch down the plaster. Then I started to pull at the cast – anything to keep me occupied – only to be hit by the smell. I needed to be around people, and although I now enjoy disappearing off alone on my mountain bike for hours on end I do still like to be around people when I am home.

Fortunately, being in a cast did not keep me off work for long as I had recently started to help out in the front of the shop on the sales side. While it was difficult to work on a bike while in a cast, it did not prevent me from sitting behind a desk. I must have looked something like Inspector Clouseau in a full body cast after falling out of a window, but this look was a winner with some customers. OK, it was not the best advert for motorbikes for the nervous mum who had finally been persuaded to buy her precious son a bike for his 17th birthday. But it brought serious respect from the serious biker. I was probably a bit of a natural on the sales side, as I loved to talk bikes with anyone and everyone. Plus I had realized that making just enough money to pay for new pistons and rings for my motocross bike probably wasn't the most ambitious of career paths, so the chance of earning a bit of commission appealed. I was satisfying my hunger to work with bikes, just with clean hands now!

I was, and still am, a quick healer, and once the cast was off my focus was immediately on getting fit for the new motocross season, which was only a couple of months away. My leg was very skinny but the most pain came from trying to mobilize the knee joint and ankle joints. A programme of physiotherapy was suggested but it did not push me as hard as I would have pushed myself. So I was soon back riding my mountain bike and in the swimming baths, albeit outside the peak times for old ladies.

Having fought my way back to fitness over those first few months of the year I was doubly determined to make a real challenge for the championship in 1993. And, for once, everything seemed to be falling into place. I was up with the front runners throughout the first half of the season and then the two championship leaders, both Welsh and with names that couldn't be pronounced, let alone spelt, broke their collar bone and wrist respectively and were out for a good few races. This was my big chance, and the next race was at one of my favourite tracks, Abergavenny, which was very fast and right up my street. I didn't really fancy staying overnight in Wales so I loaded up the works van on the Saturday night and set off at the crack of dawn with a great mate, Stuart Haywood. His polite nickname was Stuey but everyone called him Anus. Stuey worked as a Saturday lad at the shop and was known as Anus because he never got off his arse to do anything. If asked to clean a bike he would dutifully clean that bike. But he never thought about maybe cleaning the one next to it as well. His daytime job was labouring on the roads, so he looked like he worked out at the gym every day and lived off fillet steak. In reality all he ever ate was bread, potatoes and chips. In fact I have seen him order jacket potatoes with chips, and apparently his Christmas dinner was once chips, sausage roll and a lump of cheese! I ate everything I was supposed to eat, did not smoke and still was no taller than 5 foot. We always tended to be behind the clock for these long trips and he drove like a nutter to get us there on time.

As expected, the track was billiard-table smooth, just like riding on the road. Maybe there was a message somewhere in the fact that I always did better when the conditions resembled road racing? Sure enough, I got the wholeshot, straight into the lead, at the start and led until the chequered flag – one of only a handful of wins at championship standard. Another couple of similar displays in the next two races and I would be leading the championship with just four rounds to go. Dad had also made the journey over and was peaking.

'Shit hot that, youth! Now try and stay on the thing for the rest of the day,' he said.

That might have been the kiss of death. Instead of the wholeshot, I made the worst possible start to the second race, but the track was still pretty smooth and I started to make my way back through the field. Going into one corner I put my foot down into a rut but then, coming out of the corner, I could feel my boot wobbling around. 'Bollocks! I've got another twenty minutes to get through with my boot undone,' I thought.

I looked down and my boot was fastened tight. It was my leg that was loose. When it had twisted in the rut the tib and fib had snapped in exactly the same places from the road accident. I had obviously not given the bone enough time to heal properly. Even I knew that I would not be able to finish the race with one leg, so I slowly rode to the nearest post, leant the bike against it and swung myself off to sit on the grass. By chance, the post was not a million miles away from where Dad had been watching and I could see him ambling over, hands in pockets and looking a bit puzzled. The nerves had obviously been damaged by the previous break and, although I felt sick and extremely pissed off that I had blown my championship chances, I was not writhing in agony. It was more of a warm, numb sensation. So to my dad it probably looked as though I was just taking a breather – like you do mid-race!

'What the bloody hell is going on? How come you have stopped so early? You won the first race and could have won that one,' he said. At least that's what I assume he was trying to say. It all came out as one long frustrated, garbled rant.

'I have broken my leg again,' I replied calmly.

'What do you mean you have broken your leg? It looks fine.'

'Dad, believe me, I have broken my leg. Look at the angle of it!'

'Here, let me have a look,' he said, taking hold of my leg in both hands. 'OK, maybe it is broken,' he admitted when the two halves of my leg moved in different directions, something which did not exactly ease my discomfort! The fact that we had been spotted by the local Civil Aid volunteers was worse than the pain. All I knew of the Welsh was from schoolyard Englishman, Scotsman, Welshman and Irishman joke stereotypes. I now know they are a friendly and welcoming bunch of people but I wasn't too keen on letting them get their sheep-handling hands on me. A large middle-aged woman led the cellulite-charge down the hill from their ambulance and she built up so much momentum that there was a big doubt whether she would be able to stop in time. The last thing I needed after Dad's clumsy manipulations was to be wiped out by this human steamroller. She overshot by a few yards, so catastrophe was narrowly averted.

The bandages had to be strapped over my boot because it's hard enough pulling a motocross boot off a good leg, never mind one that was swaying in the breeze. Then I was stretchered up the hill to the ambulance, which gave me time to think that I really did not want to spend the next week recovering from the inevitable operation in a hospital in the middle of Wales, miles from home and with no visitors. Any amount of pain would be more bearable than that prospect.

'Come on then, Boyo, you're off to Abergavenny General,' said Ms Civil Aid.

'Actually, we don't live far from here. I will have him at the local hospital in next to no time. You have all been very helpful, thanks,' said Dad as he loaded me into the back of his car while Anus packed up the van. Cushions were placed under my leg to keep it elevated and we set off on the three-hour journey back to Nottingham. There was no point in caning it home because half an hour wasn't going to make much difference, but I felt every single bump in the road. Dad talked to me all the way to the Queen's Medical Centre in Nottingham, probably to make sure I had not passed out, and we knew the drill there so well that we headed straight for the wheelchair area.

'Now, Chris, I think you have been incredibly stupid not going to the local hospital in Wales,' said the doctor. 'Your leg has swollen badly in your boot so we will have to cut it off,' he said.

'What!? You are going to cut my leg off?' I screeched.

'No, cut the boot off, not your leg!'

It was time to bring out my puppy-dog eyes and play on his sympathy. 'But now you are here you are in safe hands and I don't think we will need to operate. I am going to try and manipulate it back into position,' the doctor added.

Fortunately it was not a compound fracture and there was no blood when the boot was removed, but the leg was throbbing badly now. And I knew I was in for serious pain when they sent out a search party for the prettiest nurse in the hospital. It was a long search on that particular night, but when she arrived to hold my hand everyone knew that, at the very least, I would have to pretend to be brave in front of her. Nevertheless when he pulled down on my foot and twisted the leg back into position I did emit the longest F-word in history. It was officially timed at sixty-seven seconds, I think. To give the guy credit, it felt right straight away and he did not need a second go. I could not have been as skilful with Lego, never mind legs. With the bones back in place, the pain was not as bad as I expected after such a trauma, again probably due to the previous nerve damage, and I was kept in hospital until the swelling had reduced enough for me to have a full plaster cast fitted up to the groin.

In the meantime Dad had been carrying out an equally difficult exercise – breaking the news to Mum. 'That's it now, I've had enough. We can't keep going through this every two weeks. You are going to have to find something different to do,' Mum said when I returned home. It was no hero's welcome but I was prepared for the onslaught and knew that silence was the best policy. It would blow over. I had more pressing concerns: how on earth was I going to cope with another four months in plaster? I have always been restless after twenty minutes in the same spot. I needed mobility.

Luckily Big Colin came to the rescue. Big Colin was so called because his name was Colin and he was pretty big. He was a regular customer at the shop and, when he saw my predicament, agreed to lend me an old automatic car while I was in plaster. I could just about work the two pedals of an automatic with my right leg if I contorted myself into the correct position. My tip for anyone who rides a motorbike is to have an automatic car for just this reason (and maybe fractures to the left arm too!). Of course it was illegal to drive in a full leg plaster cast but that was not going to deter me.

I attended the fracture clinic at the Queen's Med every two weeks to check by X-ray that everything was progressing nicely under the cast. Six weeks into my recovery I drove myself there in the automatic, swung myself out of the driver's seat and hobbled down to the clinic on my crutches for what I expected to be a routine appointment. This time a few people were called to come and look at the X-ray.

'Chris, I'm afraid that the bones are healing with a bit of a kink so we are going to have to reset it. If we don't do it your leg might end up being even shorter than it was before,' the doctor said, adding insult to my injury. Resetting didn't sound too bad. I knew that they didn't like taking the cast off and putting a new one on, as it usually put the healing process back a few weeks. Whatever they needed to do must have been important, or they would not be resetting the cast.

The doctor brought out a tool that looked like a motorized pizza cutter and got to work cutting a V-shape out of the back of the cast. 'That's not usually how they cut the cast off,' I thought. Then, without any warning, he took hold of the cast above and below the cut and snapped the leg into place. 'Ah! Now I know what resetting means,' I realized as I fought back the screams. 'It means re-breaking! And they didn't even go and look for a pretty nurse to hold my hand.' Everyone at the fracture clinic quite naturally assumed that I had been given a lift to the hospital or had come in an ambulance. So, after plastering over the existing cast, they packed me off with a packet of anti-inflammatory tablets. I was in so much agony that I could barely focus on finding the car and I realized that driving was out of the question, so I throbbed and nauseated away in the car for about three hours until I was back in control of my senses.

Despite missing the end of the championship my early results had been good enough to clinch fifth place. The top five from every national championship automatically qualified for the international IMBA series, for which my expenses would be paid. I had been desperate to qualify for this for years but did not have to wait that long for my first taste of international action as I was asked to take part in a special invitation event in France in October. My cast came off just in time to do a few local races and there was never any question whether my leg was strong enough. I was 'young, dumb and full of cum' and knew that I was never going to achieve anything by wrapping myself up in cotton wool. What's more, I was on a mission – a road trip with the boys.

Apart from the trip to the Isle of Man, my only other road trip had been with Phil Scales and Anus to watch the Paris Supercross, probably the biggest indoor motocross event in Europe. It was a last-minute thing, organized when Jamie Dobb asked if he could use my KX250 as his spare bike for a race at the NEC. It was actually a bit of an honour to be asked by him and he agreed to arrange three tickets for Paris in return of the favour. It was Phil's first time abroad and I picked him up at the crack of dawn, only for his dad to answer the door stark bollock naked, which is not what I needed at that hour. Then we went to pick Anus up straight from a party. He spent the whole drive down to Dover fast asleep in the back seat, catching flies with his mouth wide open. I'm not entirely sure he knew he had been abroad by the time we got back to England. And I wished I hadn't leant Dobbie my bike for the NEC Show. He got a fast third gear jump all wrong and, instead of landing on the down ramp, the frame of the bike landed flat on the apex of the jump. The impact squashed the foot-rests into the frame, popped the radiator guards straight off and Jamie's groin flattened the tank, with very painful consequences. Let's just say that he has since fathered two lovely kids, so the remnants of his tackle are obviously working OK!

For my race début in France, Anus came along with a guy called Brendan Orrick. For once I had not been responsible for his nickname so I had no idea why he was called Ossie. I just knew that he was a handy lad to have on board for a trip which had plenty of potential for trouble, as any Boys on Tour trip has. Ossie worked at a small engineering company round the corner from the shop and, first through mountain biking and then through motocrossing, had become a good friend. He was also a nutcase. His passion was boxing and he had a typical boxer's nose, which a certain type of girl definitely went for as he was not a bad-looking bloke. He fought competitively at local amateur nights, but his showcase event was the huge annual Goose Fair in Nottingham. Until a few years ago this was a traditional fair, complete with Bearded Ladies, Snake Woman, the Wall of Death and Mouse Town, a miniature room full of mice doing their own thing. Now it is a typical modern fair with dodgems, if you are lucky. Another feature of the Goose Fair was the live wrestling and boxing bouts. Local lads with a good few beers inside them paid a fiver to get up and box and the winner took home the pot. They could also fight the resident beasts that travelled around with the fair and Ossie always chose the biggest, meanest, hardest beast of all – and invariably gave him a good fight, although I don't ever remember seeing him win. My only brush with boxing is my weekly boxercise session at the gym, and a photoshoot for *Superbike* magazine I once did, sparring with a journalist and top bloke, Gus Scott, who was tragically killed riding at the Isle of Man a couple of years later. It is a sport I enjoy, though; I watch the American TV show *The Contender* and most of the big fights.

Ossie was equally fearless on a bike and pretty fast, although I am not sure he ever knew how he was so fast, and when you have absolutely no fear it does not really matter. You could tell him to try any jump and he would be off, flat out in third gear, regardless of the inevitable outcome. During one trip to Santa Pod to watch the drag racing we wanted to move from one end of the strip to the other and Ossie set off flat out down the field, clearly not realizing that he was on his ZXR400 and not a motocross bike with knobbly tyres. So when he eventually touched the front brake, down he went and slid for what seemed like miles. Luckily the grass was quite soft and he picked himself up with just a broken mirror and indicator, and a green stain stretching from head to toe, to show for it.

Me, Anus and Ossie set off for France in a Renault Trafic van and arranged to stay the night in a Calais hotel that my dad knew, which was near to the police station and therefore ideal for safely parking a van containing two crossers. The race was taking place the following night at an outdoor supercross track, not a million miles away from Calais. This would allow us to make our way down there the next day in plenty of time for a good look at the track. So after a quick change of clothing and a shower we set off into town to find something to eat. Had we planned a big night out we would probably have ended up in a crap gay bar frequented by the many Frenchmen wandering around with jeans that were too tight and Lacoste jumpers tied around their shoulders – you know the look. Instead we stumbled across a pizzeria which, by the time we finished eating, was rocking.

OK, there were one or two Frenchmen wearing jeans that were too tight and Lacoste jumpers over their shoulders, but it was also packed with fanny. It felt like a mini *Cheers* bar, where everyone eventually knew your name, wherever you were from. A couple of beers turned into a shed-load of beers and one pizza turned into three as the midnight munchies took control. Before we knew it we were absolutely wankered.

And then one of the Frenchmen with the jeans and the jumper decided to touch Ossie's arse. It was not a smart move and the Frenchman suddenly had his jumper over his head while Ossie gave him a good hiding. It was all a bit messy and the mood turned abruptly ugly. We scarpered, closely followed by an army of French shirt-lifters. Having paid little attention to where the hotel was, we were forced to take refuge down smelly back alleys or behind any crap French car that we could find. We managed to avoid the effeminate yet angry mob and finally stumbled across Hotel Maurice, thankful that it was so close to the police station, for our own security rather than that of my bikes. It was an old-fashioned hotel which had obviously seen better days, but was still pretty posh. I was desperate not to knock any of the ornaments over as we staggered up the staircase. Ossie and Anus were not particularly big drinkers, but I had still not progressed beyond a glass of milk at my girlfriend's and so a full night on the piss was just unheard of, especially the night before my big international racing début.

Our room was a sorry sight in the morning, and we slowly combined the fragments of our memories to piece together the events of the night. We then realized that the tiny distance between Calais and the track on the map was actually more like 100 miles. My pal Graham Overton and his brother, Craig, who had been in the coma so many years earlier, were making their way down there on their road bikes during the day and travelling back straight after the event, a marathon trip all in one go. Our own little posse arrived in time for a walk around the track, which helped the sobering-up process before the early evening practice session started. Still a bit drunk from the previous night, I set off like a bastard, set some good qualifying times and finished first and second in a couple of heats. The residual alcohol killed any nervousness about my début and leg, which I can still feel to this day when I have a hard landing on a motocross jump. By the start of the final for my class, late in the evening, the hangover started to kick in but I still managed to finish third, qualifying me for the grand final for all classes – at 2 a.m. in the morning. By then I was in bits. This event was the first time I had ever raced in the dark and taking off on a table-top jump that was covered in shadow, or going through the hoops, something I struggled to do in daylight, was a whole new experience and demanding enough for a healthy rider. In the grand final I went straight over the top of a berm and finished outside the actual boundary of the event, having to find my way back onto the track through the surrounding trees and bracken. I finished way down the field but, while the other four or five English lads gave a good account of themselves, none of them had as much fun as we had. The life of an international racer is always viewed as being very glamorous and, don't get me wrong, there is a lot to enjoy and appreciate. But the constant travelling can sometimes wear you down. This trip, however, had shown me the fun that can be had when you spontaneously let your hair down with your mates in a totally new part of the world. It had not turned me into an alcoholic, but I returned realizing that it doesn't hurt to have the occasional beer now and again.

I had obviously developed a taste for the lifestyle and top-flight action, but little did I know that the race in France would turn out to be my last competitive motocross race …

7

Stalker Hits the Road

Monday nights in the Nottingham summer were spent at the Grey Goose, nicknamed the Mucky Duck. Hundreds of bikers descended on this pub, rock music from a live band blared out across the car park, people stood chatting next to the burger van and all the lads pulled wheelies up and down the road, trying to impress the girls. It must have worked for me.

The other pub we often visited, just around the corner from the Grey Goose, on Westdale Lane where Steve Spray lived, was called the Westdale Tavern. It did not take long for me to clock the leggy blonde working behind the bar, who reminded me of the girl who worked in the guest house on the Isle of Man, but without the big boobs.

'I don't half fancy her,' I told the boys.

'You don't want to bother with her,' they told me. 'She's a right miserable sod – she doesn't talk to anyone.' She didn't look miserable to me and I guessed that the others had tried their luck and got nowhere. Sure enough, when I went to the bar for a drink she started talking to me straight away.

'Hiya, are you all right? I saw you down the Grey Goose the other Monday night. My best friend's boyfriend, Shrew, has a CBR600 and works in a bike shop. I'm Lisa,' she said. 'Check you out,' I thought. 'She's gorgeous and she knows her bikes.' We began to chat on a regular basis and it didn't take long for me pluck up enough courage to ask her out. There was just one problem – I hadn't quite finished with Anita. We had not been getting on too well for some time. She was all for settling down but, while I thought I might have wanted that too for a brief period, my loins were telling me different. But I was working on the principle that you don't trade in your old car until you have test driven a new one.

My first date with Lisa was a romantic trip to a – you guessed it – motocross race, at Elsworth. I was not racing because I was still recovering from my accident that summer and my cast had only just come off. I picked her up after sneaking the same maroon ZXR750 on which I had been to Scarborough out of the shop again and, always keen to impress, treated her to a Little Chef breakfast on the way. We had a great day, she was lots of fun and it helped that she loved going really fast on the bike. It was clear that I had to do something about Anita so that I could see her on a regular basis. It was a difficult time because Anita had been so supportive during my motocross traumas and injuries, and she was very friendly with my mum and dad. But sometimes the head has to rule the heart and I grasped the nettle.

Just before our trip to France for the motocross race I had decided that I couldn't keep taking Lisa out on different bikes that I had 'borrowed' from the shop. And, after that fateful carnage-creating day the previous year on the GSXR750M, I knew there was no point in asking Dad whether he would loan me one of the bikes permanently. If I'd had a good week at work and not dropped a bike off the ramp or knocked anything over in the showroom he would still begrudgingly let me use a bike for special occasions, but it was also becoming increasingly obvious that Dad was winding the business down and I needed my own transport. It was time to buy my own bike. And maybe I could kill two birds with one stone.

The best place for checking new bikes is the Motorcycle Show at the NEC in Birmingham so I booked a room for us both at the Metropole, with less than honourable intentions. I had been through all the pleasantries of meeting Lisa's mum and dad and, although I was in essence a gentleman and she was pretty choosy, I did sometimes leave for home at the end of a night out 'cutting glass', as they say. So the thought had obviously crossed my mind, and this first night away together seemed the perfect opportunity for the evil deed.

Anyway, cutting to the next day like they do in the movies, we had a good look around the show and in particular the stand of Bat Motorcycles. In those days motorcycles were relatively more expensive and there were not too many of the smaller and cheaper Japanese imports around, apart from the Kawasaki ZXR400. But Bat were one of the biggest importers and displayed a huge selection of these smaller bikes like CBR400RRs, NC30s, etc., which probably cost around £3,000 compared the £6,000 you needed for something like a ZXR750. The one that caught my eye was the GSXR400N, in the classic Suzuki colours of white and the two blues. It was in my price range and Lisa also loved it, so I made my mind up there and then.

While this may have been one small step towards independence, I was still a long way from making any giant leaps. So when Mum and Dad went away on holiday I went to stay with Lisa's parents rather than look after myself, which I am still not too good at doing to this day. She also lived on Westdale Lane, just around 100 yards from Steve Spray. Millet lived just up the hill on the left in a house bought from Jamie Gamble. So it immediately felt like a home from home, close to my group of mates. The intention was to stay for a couple of weeks until Mum and Dad returned from holiday. I ended up staying for four years!

Lisa's mum, who worked for the council, and her dad, a painter and decorator, could not have been more welcoming. I did not realize at the time just how useful it would be to have a prospective father-in-law whose garage was full of paint thinner, but more of that later. All of a sudden I became the son they never had. Lea often came home from his day's work to find that I had snaffled the meat and potato pie that had been cooked for his tea, leaving him with a plate of beans on toast. I could imagine him thinking, 'Not only is he sneaking down the corridor to tamper with my daughter during the night, he's eating my bloody tea as well!' But he was too much of a gentleman to say anything. I have always been lucky enough to get on with the parents of my girlfriends and my pals.

Another step towards more independence, and making a career of my own when the shop closed, was when I was offered a job as a salesman at a Volvo garage, after being forced into a shirt and tie for the interview arranged by Big Colin – the first time I had been dressed up since my last court appearance. Luckily, another job as a mechanic at a car MOT garage, which would allow me to carry on racing at the weekends, came up in the nick of time.

I still popped home to Mum and Dad's on a regular basis because, although I was living at Lisa's and kept my clothes there, my base and bedroom were still at home. So I was able to borrow the van that Dad had kept from the shop whenever I needed to, although my new bike was our main mode of transport. We often disappeared for a ride with Ossie and another guy who I had met through the shop, Carl Gretton. He had set up a computer company just at the right time for that industry and was making good money. Before the shop closed I sold Carl a race replica ZXR750K and actually joked with him that I would like to race it one day. It was effectively the same bike that John Reynolds and Brian Morrison were racing, the equivalent to Yamaha's OWO1, but not the same telephone numbers price to buy. It had an adjustable swing-arm pivot point, slightly thicker forks than the standard bikes that I had been riding, flat slide carbs and a Termignoni four-into-one exhaust. It was a bit of a bastard to ride, and for some reason Carl was just not cut out for it. So he decided to get rid of it before it got rid of him and said that I could have it on the cheap, as he would get a better deal on his new ZZR1100 if he did not have to trade this one in. And he told me that he wouldn't be offended if I needed to sell it the following year to fund my motocrossing, which was a possibility.

I had been a ZXR750 man for the last few years and Carl's machine looked, sounded and felt like a race bike on the road, so I fell in love with it. The offer proved too good to refuse so Lisa and I decided to sell the Suzuki to a pal after just a few months' use and buy the Kawasaki between us. It was a single-seater but we fitted the sub-frame and foot-rests off a twin-seat model straight on for around £200 from a breakers. It was the best road bike I have ever owned and we went everywhere on it.

The maiden voyage was to watch my mate Sean Balls in action at the Plumb Pudding meeting at Mallory Park on Boxing Day. I have never been so cold and it didn't help that our bike was rattling because the cam chain adjuster did not keep the correct tension. Taking the tank off in the car park and trying to fix this with blocks of ice for hands, while Lisa stood shivering in her cat boots and black leggings, was not ideal. But we had a great day. It was the first time since Dad had road raced that I was close to the action. It was his last race on his RGV250 before switching from the Formula 400 class. He had a good couple of races, supported by Graham Clifton and Charlie Bamford, Sean's equivalent of the Big Lads who now follow me racing. It was the same old motocross camaraderie, but in a road racing setting.

It all hit me when I got home: those magical days on the Isle of Man; watching Whitham doing his stuff at Scarborough; my ability on flat motocross tracks. Was somebody trying to tell me something?

It was also becoming apparent that, after Dad closed the business, Kawasaki would no longer support my motocrossing and there was no alternative local dealer in the area to turn to. In the past I had owned one 125 and the shop had been loaned another 125 from Kawasaki, which served as a spare bike but was rarely used for anything other than spare parts. Kawasaki also provided a 250cc bike directly. To carry on at British championship and IMBA level I needed two bikes, each costing around £4,000 each, not to mention a van that could take us all over England. Even if I had the bikes, there was no way I could afford that much money and I did not want to drop back to just doing the regional championships and club motocrossing. It was a bit of a no-brainer. It was time for a break from the motocross scene.

Sure, I soon missed going up to The Desert with my mates but I didn't miss certain aspects of the annual preparations for the motocross season. After a week's work as a mechanic, spending the evenings trying to wash your bike with a bucket and sponge because all the jet washers were frozen was 'just not your mate'. It also was nice not to have the commitment of racing every weekend, although that novelty quickly wore off. Instead we spent a couple of Sunday afternoons in the pub, but I soon thought, 'Any danger of some excitement around here?' It had been fun to have road bikes to play around on over the winter and satisfy my bike-lust, but there were drawbacks too. When I collected the GSXR400 from the dealer in Ashby-de-la-Zouche I had to ride home in the snow in November. Then we bought the ZXR750 at Christmas time and the ice-cold ride to the Plumb Pudding meeting confirmed that this was not the most sensible form of transport for that time of year.

I also missed just being around the shop. It was a great place to hang out, for anyone connected with bikes. My mates used to drop in just to pass the time of day and I made some great friends like Durk, Ossie, Anus, Phil and Carl through the shop. Without the focal point of a motocross race meeting every weekend, the only way we got together was the occasional ride out on our road bikes. It was almost as though my social life had been suspended along with my racing.

I suppose it was obvious to my close friends like Sean that I was already becoming restless and needed something new to occupy my spare time. And it was him that gave me the push that I needed to make the decision to give road racing a go.

'You should forget motocrossing and start road racing before you miss the boat. You know it's where your heart's been for a while. And you have had so much time injured lately. I know you are worried about the expense but the Formula 400 class doesn't need to cost the earth. You don't need a big van, you only need one bike and it doesn't need to be the latest, greatest thing for club level racing. Believe me. You would be good at this, I reckon. All you need is a decent RGV250 and you will be on it,' he insisted.

I agreed, Lisa agreed, even Dad agreed, and there was no turning back, although walking away from motocross was still a bit of a wrench. This had been my whole life since the age of 14. I might have become jaded by the racing, but I would never tire of the bikes. Road bikes are beautiful machines, but the best feeling in the world is being out on my crosser with no stopwatches, no TV cameras monitoring my every move, and no coppers or speed cameras. It's just pure fun.

And motocross racing breeds a certain type of person. When I return to take part in or even just watch a local club motocross race nowadays, I still bump into the same lads who were starting out when I was finishing. They all need to earn a living and they could probably do without being mortally wounded every weekend. But there are no prima donnas and there is never any of the shamming you would find on an amateur football field. There is no pressure to turn out in hail, wind or shine and no pressure to achieve certain results. They do it for the pure love of the sport. And that spirit always shines through.

I still have a garage full of twin-shocks and I suppose I always daydreamed, while I worked on the bikes at my dad's shop, that I might one day own a bike shop of my own. I guess it still is a bit of an ambition. In an ideal world it would be a motocross bike shop, as this remains my true passion, although that would probably not be financially viable. (And I suppose I will have to think of a name other than Stalker Bikes!)

Starting out on a whole new discipline of motorbiking was not something that daunted me. I already knew, through keeping tabs on the careers of Sean and John Reynolds, that a smooth progression from motocross rider to short-circuit racer was definitely possible. Sean was starting to make a name for himself on the road-racing circuit, having competed at AMCA championship level during his motocross days, as I had. JR had raced at the same motocross meetings when I was a boy, riding 250cc bikes while I was still on 80ccs. We both rode a Kawasaki and shared some sponsors, so our paths did occasionally cross in those days. He made it to international standard at motocross, which was no surprise as he was incredibly smooth and fast. Then he disappeared off the scene to race his dad's Velocette in a Classic series. This opened the door for him into road racing proper, and when he secured the Team Green ride it was easy to keep track of his progress through the *Dealer News* magazine and also on the television. I spent many an hour polishing the same tank with my eyes glued on John's races and I'm sure I remember him posting the first sub-fifty second lap of Mallory Park.

Motorbike racing was big on TV in those days and, having grown up watching the likes of Barry Sheene, there was a whole new bunch of up-and-coming British riders to aspire to. Foggy had just missed out on the 1993 World Superbike title and Terry Rymer and Trevor Nation were big names on the domestic scene. Ron Haslam was still very much a force in British motorcycling, running Team Great Britain. But not for one second did I ever think I would make a living out of racing bikes. To be honest, it had never really occurred to me that you could make a career out of racing. I never thought to ask the likes of JR about that side of things, although today's kids can't wait to ask me how much I earn. The world of professional motocross racing had also seemed a million miles away from the standard I had competed at. I was aware of the Jamie Dobbs and Paul Malins of the professional world, but at that young age you don't really consider the financial side of the sport. I was just happy to gasp in amazement when Jamie Dobb turned up at coaching sessions run by his brother, Julian, at their house and jumped 50 feet over our heads.

A more achievable and immediate road racing goal was to try and reach the same standard as some of my other mates. Millet was winning club races and Jamie Gamble, a big guy but very capable, was far from making up the numbers on a Sunday afternoon on his GPZ1100. The local hero, Steve Spray, was already a British champion. (But I have to stress that by no means did I ever dream of being the next Steve Spray! It transpired that he had tried to tap into Lisa a few times before we got together, but she hadn't been interested. He was a bit of a legend on that front and made the most of his time with the John Player girls while he rode for JPS Norton. Let's just say that I am still a few brolly girls behind him.) So there was plenty of incentive for me to mean business from the word go. First I needed a bike.

Sean and Graham had already indicated that an RGV250 was the way to go for starting out in the Formula 400 class. I would be up against the odd ZXR400, FZR400 or GSXR400, but the 250s retained an advantage at most tracks because of their nimbleness. It helped that Whitham had also raced an RGV250 although, worryingly, everyone used to shout 'Hail Caesar!' to him wherever he went because every time he shut the throttle off it seized up and chucked him off.

We soon spotted an RGV250 that had already been raced for sale in the *Nottingham Evening Post*. We went to look at it straight away at the home of the owner, a Geordie with a larger–than-life smile but who looked in a bit of pain. On his wall were lots of pictures of him in his orange racing jacket with his knee down. He was obviously very proud of his racing, as all racers are, but it took a while for us to realize that his discomfort came from a broken arm and that he was wearing a cast under his sleeve.

'Now, Chris, I want to make sure you realize that this is not just any old road bike. This can bite back, so you would have to be very careful on it,' the bloke said. I could see that Dad was thinking that this bloke would never make a salesman.

It then became clear that his latest crash had resulted in an ultimatum from the wife: 'Either the bike goes or I do!' That was probably why he had advertised it in the local paper and not *MCN* – because deep down he did not really want any buyers.

The bike was not the most handsome I had ever seen. Instead of a proper paint job he had decorated the fairing with coloured square and triangle stickers, and it looked a bit of a mess. But it seemed to have everything else we had been told to look out for if a bike was going to be competitive; race-kit pipes, carbon cans, a steering damper, a carb kit and ignition kit. The suspension was standard but set by Maxton, another good sign. It was good to have Dad with me, because I had probably made up my mind to buy it before I got there. But he agreed that it seemed to be the right choice, especially when we knocked the bloke down from £3,000 to £2,450. I have seen him at a few race meetings recently and he is still embarrassed that he warned me to be careful when I started racing.

I was happy to leave a deposit there and then. Lisa was also quite excited about going racing, so she was happy for us to put the money from the ZXR750 towards the racer. She was now a qualified hairdresser and had a job at a local salon and was soon able to buy a little Vauxhall for getting around in. Dad had kept a van so we would be able to use that for race weekends. And when you live in motorbike circles it's never too difficult to find someone who is willing to buy a decent, well-maintained bike at a decent price and I soon sold my Kawasaki to a pal. I was all set – new girlfriend, new passion, new bike. It was time to turn a new page in the Chris Walker book.

8

Seaside Stalker

'I've bought one, I've bought one, I've bought one,' I shouted down the phone to Sean. I had already cleared a space in Lisa's dad's garage and the first job after picking up the RGV250 was to try and remove a lot of the hideous triangles and squares off the fairing, as well as adding my racing number, which was 28 in those days. It was one of the first numbers allocated to me in a motocross race and I must have done well because I kept it for a while. For weeks, if I wasn't polishing the bike, I simply stared at it in admiration. I could not wait to ride it, but of course I could not take it out on the road because it wasn't registered. That alone wouldn't have stopped me but it also ran with a total-loss ignition, which meant that the battery only lasted twenty minutes or so, as it doesn't charge itself when running. So I tried to focus on obtaining the fundamentals like new brake pads, a paddock stand and tyre warmers. The tyres looked OK because they still had tread and that was good enough for me. There was a little money left over from the sale of the road bike but I did not want to go crazy on new equipment because the bike might still have turned out to be a turd. But, before finding that out, I needed to get myself back up to speed.

I was a bit conscious that, coming from motocross where the straights are quite short, I did not have much experience of racing at flat-out speed. And it had been a while since I had been out with my old motocross chums. So before I had a chance to put my new race bike through its paces, me, Anus and Phil Scales decided to enter the Mablethorpe Beach Race in Lincolnshire, staged on a flat speedway-style oval with two longish straights, where I could really open the throttle. Quite a few decent riders still take part and the Honda British Superbike boss, Neil Tuxworth, is a former champion there about fifty times over! Adam Marshall, the son of multiple British road-racing champion Roger Marshall, and Ben Wilson, a current British Superbike rider, were also regular front-runners. To say we were under-prepared was an understatement.

My only other experience of beach racing had been the Weston Beach Race, which I first attended when I was around 16 years old to watch Sean race. The scale and atmosphere of the event blew me away. Around 500 people, riding their motocross bikes, trikes, quads and motorbikes with sidecars, were there to compete on the three-mile beach circuit at Weston-super-Mare, near Bristol. It features a one-mile straight along the beach and two miles of riding in the dunes and over man-made obstacles and jumps. It was exciting, but also frustrating for me to watch the action from the sidelines. So, having seen Sean do a great job and having had so much fun, I decided to give it a go the following year. I added a couple of years onto my age – it's normally the opposite way round for road racers – so that I could enter on a KX100, because I was still not big enough for a 125cc bike. I walked the track on the day before qualifying to get an idea of where I might be going, but that turned out to be a waste of time. During the first qualifying session I jumped one dune, expecting there to be a 10-foot drop on the other side, only to be greeted by a 40-foot sheer fall. I bounced off the bike at the bottom and knocked myself momentarily unconscious. I was discovered by Paul Malin of all people, a professional international motocross racer and one of my heroes, who plonked me back on the bike and gave me a push to start up again. I was still not too clear where I was and it didn't help when the first person who passed me was a guy in a motorbike sidecar wearing a gorilla suit. The next rider I encountered was a bloke who had tied a blow-up doll to his arms and legs. When he moved his own limbs the doll followed suit, always with the same startled mouth-open expression. I was seriously wondering whether the blow to my head had done some lasting damage, but I now know it's normal for the Weston.

Despite this I managed to qualify, but a huge digger – the race was always sponsored by JCB or Caterpillar – had changed the course again overnight by creating another dune, the size of a house, just around the first corner. A couple of the legends made it over the dune first time and maybe another forty riders were able to drag their machines over, while the rest of us queued impatiently, the fumes from 450 revving two-strokes burning the back of our throats and stinging our eyes. When I did eventually make it half-way up someone knocked down the fence and everyone charged round the bottom of the dune. 'That's not right,' I thought, although I fought my way back to finish just outside the top fifty, which was not bad considering the front-runners were on 500cc machines. I have been back a few times since – the main race is now restricted to motorbikes but attracts an even bigger entry of around 1,000. My best finish was nineteenth out of 1,080, again pretty good bearing in mind the winner was multiple world motocross champion Stefan Everts, an indication of the quality of rider, and gorillas, it has always attracted. I'm desperate to compete one more time and finish in the top ten.

The Mablethorpe Beach Race was an entirely different kettle of fish. I think we expected it to be a walk in the park after Weston and motocross racing. After all, how difficult could a straight-corner-straight-corner circuit be, basically an oval like speedway but on sand, especially one as flat as a billiard table? Yet the scrutineering alone proved to be taxing enough. We had not changed the gearing or jetting but our biggest mistake was to turn up without having fitted lanyards, cords which are attached to your wrist and the bike to make the engine cut out should you crash so that the bike does not ride off into the crowd or, in this case, the man and his dog who had braved the fierce winds whipping in off the sea to come and watch. They let us off this oversight on the condition that we would not be allowed to enter without lanyards if we turned up again. Then it was time to be debriefed.

'Do any of you riders like whalies?'

'Whalies? What the fuck are whalies?' I whispered to Phil.

'I think he means wheelies,' Phil replied. 'There might be a competition for the best one.'

'I'll ask you again. Do any of you lot like pulling whalies?' Our hands shot up.

'NOT AT MABLETHORPE YOU DON'T,' he bellowed. Our hands dropped immediately. 'We've had wankers like you lot here before. Before you know it you've looped it out and the ambulance has to leave the beach and the races are delayed and the tide comes in and the whole job's ruined. No whalies, all right?'

Although we did not shame ourselves in the first practice session it would have been nice to have had more than three laps. It was obvious we should have changed the gearing and jetting for the longer straights, but although Phil had an early crash we seemed to be gradually getting the hang of it. I was just a bit conscious that, apart from Anus who was on a shit bike and didn't care, we stood out as 'having all the gear, no idea'. I didn't want anyone to think we were flash, so in the holding pen for the first race in our category I tried to strike up a conversation with the bloke next to me. He was wearing a yellow National Coal Board oversuit, duct-taped around the waist to stop it flapping, and NCB wellies, ribbed down the front with steel toe-caps. His Kawasaki was also yellow, so it must have been as old as his jacket, and was so corroded that he had obviously never thought to wash the salt water off over his many years of racing there. His helmet looked like it was made out of polystyrene and his AGV goggles were scratched and steamed up, hiding the fact that he already had his race face on.

'It's my first time here, mate. Got any tips?' I asked.

'Yeah, try these two. Stay on and stay out my fucking way,' he growled, before setting off for the start line.

I was a bit put out but Anus and Phil, who both heard his answer, pissed themselves laughing all the way to the start line. I pulled up to the elastic tape and waited patiently for the rest of the riders to join me on the line. It wasn't easy to see the red elastic against the red sand, but after my last attempt to be constructive I wasn't about to say anything. They eventually arrived next to me all at once, and after a few seconds the elastic went up. I let the clutch out and my back wheel just dug a big hole into the sand and I went down rather than forwards. The others cleared off down the straight while I sat on my bike wondering what had happened. I knew something wasn't right because I could suddenly touch the floor. They were all experienced enough to know that you don't sit in one spot before the start because your bike gradually sinks into the sand. Anus and Phil must have been on drier sections of the start line, or not as daft as me. I managed to push myself out of the rut and soon got into my stride, working out that I needed to go into the corners fast, slow down mid-corner and then fire off out again. Phil's idea was to go flat out all the way round without ever shutting off, and his growing oval might soon have touched Holland if the sea had not got in the way. Anus couldn't get his bike to go fast enough to get sideways, so he was happy to keep to the smooth inside line. I finished fourth or fifth in that race, but by the fourth race I was on the pace of the miserable old NCB git. 'I'm having you in the final race,' I thought.

Phil had taken a starting position right on the outside nearest the sea, which was starting to come in at the end of the afternoon, making the sand on the outside of that straight very hard. I opted for the inside line and got a flyer. I was going into the first turn flat out and out of the corner of my eye saw NCB man turning in. 'There's no way you are getting in front of me this time. This is my line,' I thought and kept the throttle open. I hit him so hard that his bike, which must have caught a rut as the track was now starting to cut up, cart-wheeled off into the distance. The warning flags came out but did not affect either me or Phil, who took the lead exiting the turn leading onto the sea straight. He was running wider and wider but still hooking up through the gears as he hung off the bike, road-racing style. Then the biggest wave of the day crashed in and grabbed hold of his front wheel as if someone had stuck an iron bar in it. Phil was flipped over the top and looked like a big stone being skimmed over a flat pond. With each bounce he lost a bit more clothing and when he finally came to a stop, face down in the water, he looked like Robinson Crusoe washed up on a desert island in his shredded rags. I thought he was going to drown until I saw him pick himself up and shake the seaweed out of his ear. It was clear that they don't stop the Mablethorpe Beach Race for anything, and luckily NCB man was too beat up to beat me up when I finished on the podium. A few weeks later we decided to buy our lanyards and prepare properly, and I had three wins, a second and a third to finish first overall. Having escaped without maiming or upsetting anyone on that occasion we decided to quit Mablethorpe while we were ahead. And, anyway, the weather was starting to take a turn for the better. It was time to go road racing.

Sean told me that the practice days on Wednesday afternoons at Mallory Park were due to start and that I should apply for a racing licence from the East Midlands Racing Association, EMRA. I agreed to meet Sean and Graham there and set off with Carl Gretton in support. He had become a good friend of the family and got on well with Lisa, Ossie and the gang. He was a little bit older than us and certainly more intelligent than all of us put together, but I think he got a bit of a buzz from escaping his sterile office atmosphere to revel in the petrol-rich paddock. Nobody knew at such an early stage of my racing where it all might be heading, but Carl was pleased to know he helped start me off by selling the ZXR750 to us at such a good price.

I was able to splash out on a new set of Kushitani leathers complete with knee sliders from the Hein Gericke store in Nottingham, who told me to buy a tight fit because they would 'bed in'. That's bollocks! The joints might loosen but leathers never stretch. The boots felt like a pair of slippers but, having previously been happy riding on the road in a padded jacket, jeans and trainers, the leathers were so alien and uncomfortable. It was completely opposite to big baggy motocross kit, where everything is comfortable apart from the boots.

Once I had signed on at the hut, paid my £25 and placed the little sticker on my helmet it was time to go out in the 125cc–400cc group. I can't begin to explain the feeling of anticipation as I started her up ready for the first ride. I had been building up to this moment for weeks, and Mallory, as it was in those days, proved the perfect place to learn how to ride on a short circuit on such a beautiful sunny day. There was no Edwina's Chicane on the back straight or Charlie's Chicane around Gerard's, so a lap was simply down start-finish into Gerard's, down the back straight into the Esses, up to the Hairpin, through the Bus Stop and round the Devil's Elbow. But there was too much going on under my helmet to take everything in. It was my first time on a race bike, the first time on a race track and the first time I had my knee down. Riders do get their knees down on the road, but rarely need to. I had never felt the urge to go round and round a roundabout until I finally had it down, and I only had little legs so my knee had further to go than everyone else. That was always my excuse, anyway! The session was over in a click of a finger and I was buzzing. Nobody came past me throughout the whole twenty-minute session and I managed to catch and pass quite a few other riders who were not wearing the novice's orange jacket, many on bigger bikes, too.

'You did really well. You looked fast straight away. It's not a motocross track though,' said Graham. 'Your back end was sliding, back wheel locking and the front end bouncing. It looked like you had nicked it.'

OK, I might not have been the smoothest rider out there – and I'm still not! But, by being a bit brave and a bit daft, it seemed I had been going pretty quick. They put a stopwatch on me during the next session and my times came down and down. Then, in the third and final twenty minute chunk, Sean followed me out on his TZ250 which he was due to race in that season's Supercup championship. It was also one of his first times on that bike, but after three or four laps he had still not come past. Then I spotted a yellow bike in pieces in the gravel trap in the middle of Gerard's. My immediate thought was that I might have been in his way and caused the crash through being too slow. In my own mind I had been going pretty fast, but maybe everyone had just been saying kind things because it was my first go. It wasn't the case; Sean had actually gone into Gerard's a bit hot and lost the front, but he was unhurt.

I hadn't realized that Sean and Graham, having seen me ride on the Isle of Man several years before, had put the word out around the circuit for people to keep an eye out for me, and there seemed to be a bit of a buzz when I came in. I genuinely did not think I had done anything special. It had all seemed so instinctive. I guess that born racers are born racers, whether on four wheels, two wheels or two feet. Some people are born thinkers or performers, but I was a born racer. Since the age of 14 I only ever knew one speed when the flag went down – flat out. And I would like to think I have maintained that attitude ever since.

It was a huge buzz and I could not believe I hadn't tried road racing earlier. But I had still not even considered taking part in an actual race. The last thing I wanted to happen was to turn up some-where and be blown away by everyone. My plan was to gradually pick up speed and, when I knew I would not be a danger to other riders and was closer to the proper lap times, I might then think about giving racing a go.

I did not have to wait long for my next outing. Carl had been bought a gift of a day at the Yamaha Race School at Cadwell Park run by Mark Phillips, who inevitably got stuck with the nickname Captain, although he was definitely not a member of the Royal Family. Carl invited me and a few mates to come along and join him on the Saturday straight after the Mallory outing. This was ideal for me as I would be riding a FZR400RR, one of the four-strokes that I would eventually be competing against on my two-stroke. It was also a good opportunity to learn another circuit. Always thinking ahead!

My instructor was a guy called Mick Corrigan, a down-to-earth bloke from Sheffield who later helped put James Toseland on the map, who gave us the usual lecture before we all took to the track for the first session. 'There are only a few rules. Just follow me and don't stop in the middle of the track, don't pull wheelies and, above all, don't fall off,' he said.

I didn't know whether he was a good, bad or indifferent racer but these guys did this for a living three days a week so they knew their way around Cadwell like the backs of their hands. In the first session we concentrated on braking markers, peeling points and aiming for cones at the apex and exits of corners. I might have already thought I knew the fundamentals, but it helped to introduce these new elements of discipline into my riding. We were all probably going flat out, but you could tell that Mick was just playing with us.

At the end of the four sessions the instructors filled in a sheet about each rider, marking us for things like braking, cornering, throttle control, style and confidence, ending with a summary comment such as 'Don't bother coming back'. Mick refused to believe that my first time on track had been just three days earlier and his written comment about me was: 'This lad should start racing – now!' I have kept the sheet to this day. After just two outings I was now champing at the bit to try my first race, and the report sheet gave me even more incentive to revise my planned start date – you guessed it – the very next day!

EMRA held a five-round championship at Mallory and it just so happened that the first round was the very next day. Mick's comments prompted us to make a few last-minute phone calls and secure a late entry. It was clear that everyone around me was just as excited as I was. Lisa was one hundred per cent behind me and, while Mum was naturally worried – the word she would use is 'whittled' – she never showed it apart from saying Mum-like things such as 'Only go fast enough to win!' Dad was obviously keen, but not unconditionally. Having raced himself, he was aware of how quickly the costs could spiral. It was one thing to race at club level on a £3,000 RGV250, but it was a completely different matter to compete in the British championships, needing a £15,000 bike and a big caravan. There was also an unspoken understanding that, at this stage, I would not race on road circuits.

Sean, Graham and Carl obviously knew about my first race, but apart from telling a couple of other lads such as Ossie, Phil Scales and Anus, I did not want to shout it from the rooftops. I'm like that when I play golf. I really enjoy it but I know that I am crap and I know that everyone watching me on the first tee knows that I am crap. And that's why I hardly ever play. There was no way that I wanted to invite a big gang only for them all to see my arse kicked. I have never been a cocky person, and to this day tend to have conservative expectations so that anything else is a bonus.

Short-circuit riding at this level did not compare with the physical exertions of riding a motocross bike, but the speeds involved meant that I had to concentrate twice as hard. So, having absorbed everything I had been told during the day like a sponge, I was mentally drained when I got home from Cadwell and I slept like a log on the Saturday night. I woke up on the Sunday morning with that feeling that can never be matched – race day.

I did not know too many people at Mallory apart from Sean's gang, but everybody was really friendly, especially when I collected the orange jacket that every novice has to wear. One of the first people I bumped into in the paddock was Mick Corrigan. 'I see you took my advice to start racing as soon as possible,' he laughed. There were quite a few novices at this first race of the season, so I did not feel too much out of my depth. Even the scrutineers, who looked like they could have been scrutineering since the days of BSAs and Nortons, offered friendly advice like 'You should lock-wire that sump bung, lad.' I don't think they have actually ever failed anyone but they did insist I have a dog-tag for my name and blood group, so Lisa's first job was to make one out of cardboard and a shoelace.

There was no limit on the number of classes that I could have entered, but I did not want to face fifteen races on my first day, and not just because of the entry cost. So I settled for the three races in the Formula 400 class, for two-stroke 250s and up to 400cc four-strokes. All the orange jackets had to start from the back and, as I pulled up to my slot on the eighth row of eight, I could not believe how different it felt to the start of a motocross race, when forty bikes all in one line aim for a 10-foot space, and if you don't make it that space in the first handful then you can't expect to escape unscathed. This seemed a lot more civilized, and I pointed my bike at a slight angle, plotting my path through the field. The races only lasted six laps, which meant six minutes at Mallory, so there would be no time to muck about.

Without TV cameras, and being so far back on the grid, nobody would have realized if I had let the clutch out while the starter still had the Union Jack flag raised, but I was not about to cheat in my first race. Even so, it felt as though I had set off a couple of seconds early and it actually seemed that some of the riders didn't realize it was a race. It didn't take too long before I was up there with the more serious front-runners. During the morning practice session, having been on a 400cc bike the previous day, my 250cc bike felt light and twitchy and difficult to control. A couple of laps in, when I began to settle a little, I realized that it was a lot more nimble in the corners, although I couldn't match the power of the 400s down the straight. But I was still making progress and before too long I was up to third, then second, and then found myself leading my first race. It developed into a two-way dice with a guy on an FZR400, and the lead changed hands several times. I led at the start of the final lap before he came back past me going into the hairpin on the last lap and there was no way back.

Far from being distraught, I could not believe that I had finished second in my first race. It might only have been a club race, but everyone has to start somewhere and I was already looking forward to race two, knowing that I would not have to start at the back of the grid. At some meetings your start would be determined by selecting a peg and it was helpful to know the guy holding them, as a nod and a wink would give you an indication of the best peg to choose – I quickly learned to never turn down any form of underhand help. And the general suspicion must have been that something underhand was going on, because everyone wanted to have a look at the bike to check that I wasn't cheating, as always happens when someone wins convincingly out of the blue.

The script was similar for the next two races and I ended up battling with the same guy on both occasions. But now I realized that I had to pull a bit of a gap before the final hairpin in order to make sure his speed advantage did not count. It was close on both occasions but I managed to hold him off and won the second and third races. I returned to the paddock to a big kiss from Lisa and I could tell that Dad was really proud. He did not say much, but was probably thinking, 'Why the hell have we wasted so much time and money on motocross?' In the back of his mind would have been the fear that five races down the line I might tip the bike upside down and I might suddenly need to find another £5,000 from somewhere to start up again. But even Dad, whose heart had always been in road racing rather than motocrossing, forgot to fret for the rest of the day.

And I could not get my breath. I was hooked on road racing for life.

9

Spongelike Stalker

I had not dared think any further than that first race meeting. It might have been a disaster and I might have been forced to return to motocross racing. But now I was suddenly engulfed by the idea that we were going road racing for good. Carl Gretton offered to pay for me to enter the final newcomers' race of that first meeting at Mallory, but I was more than satisfied with my three trophies and £50 winnings. We stopped off for a celebratory beer in the pub at the circuit and immediately started to map out the rest of the season, while Carl explored ways in which his company could pay for my race entries for the rest of the year.

My next race would be in the Shell Oil Clubman's Championship, which was held at a number of circuits around the country. I tried to plan my days off work so that I could learn as many tracks as possible at their practice days. This wasn't an easy job as some races were a fair distance away, such as Penbury, a small but exciting little circuit in Wales that used to be a venue for F1 testing. So I occasionally entered local club meetings too. It's a shame that those practice days do not really exist any more. I have no idea how much it costs to rent a track now because I am wrapped up in the closeted world of factory teams, and the cost of our track time is usually shared with other teams. But most of the spare time at circuits is now used for track days, when people ride their own bike for the thrill of it. I think this probably results in fewer people taking up racing, as previously the only way to enjoy the thrill of riding at a circuit would have been to obtain a racing licence and take part in a practice day or just go racing, encouraging those who found they had a talent to take up the sport more seriously.

I'm often asked why I took to road racing so quickly. The honest answer is that I don't know. Maybe it was because I had been scooting around on two wheels almost as soon as I was on two feet. Then as a teenager I had access to the fastest machines around, courtesy of the shop. And it's inevitable that, on a fast machine, you will ride as fast as you can on the roads, within reason. I also took road racing more seriously, although I did not have any dreams of fame or fortune. The simple fact was that, while you could fall off a motocross bike two or three times a day and get away with minor bumps and bruises, road bike crashes hurt a lot more and could do more lasting damage. So the extra preparation and application were essential.

My first couple of Shell Clubman's meetings went much the same way as the first, with me winning Rider of the Day at one of them. I won a helmet for this, which was a good job because the fuel can fell over on the way to the next race, filling my normal helmet with petrol. I would have been as high as a kite if I had not had this spare one. People soon started to notice my results but I did not get carried away – that's not in my character. After all, this was still only club level and I had won championships at higher levels during my motocross days. However, at least I now knew I could win races and maybe challenge for the championship, so I did everything possible to give myself the best chance. I stepped up my training regime and was willing to take any advice on board.

Everywhere I went for that extra little bit of track time, whether it was Snetterton on a Monday afternoon, Cadwell on a Tuesday evening or Mallory on a Wednesday afternoon. I bumped into a young lad called Lee Dickinson, who wore Marlboro Racing leathers and rode a Yamaha 125cc GP bike. He was obviously having the time of his life and often grinned across at me if we were side by side, flat out down a straight. He might only have been on a 125, but he could do faster lap times than the Formula 400 bikes and it was obvious that he could ride.

Over the next year or so Dicko took me under his wing and became one of my lifelong friends. He now owns a TV aerial and satellite installation business and still races one of my old bikes in the MRO championship, while his brothers, Joe and Mitch, race in British Supersport and motocross respectively. I must have appeared so naive to him. I didn't know that brake pads became glazed and needed replacing as often as possible. I had been happy to leave them in until they were totally worn out. The same with tyres; if it still had some tread then it was good for another three races in my book. It was not a case of the blind leading the blind, because nobody in our posse was in a position to lead. Instead we learnt from our mistakes – and there were plenty.

My right-hand man was Tim Quinn, better known as Que. He was a salt-of-the-earth council glazier and was best mates with Guzzi Kev, one of the mechanics at Dad's shop, so named for his love of doing up old bikes like his Moto Guzzi. Que also liked to trick up his bike, an immaculate oil-cooled GSXR1100. He spent far more time adding a special new swinging arm or polishing the frame than he did riding it, and I'm sure it has only done 3,000 miles to this day. Que had a straight side-parting that looked like it had been whistled into place each morning and Dicko insisted he must have been born with this hairstyle, he'd had it that long.

Que came along to watch one of my first races out of interest and also became hooked. He was no race mechanic but he was mechanically minded and was more than happy to help out, fetching tyres and doing some of the more mundane work on the bike. His only condition was that I would always check what he had done before I went out on track. He had obviously picked up on one trick of the trade, to wipe any tyres that had come straight from a new mould with a rag sprayed with contact cleaner, to take off the extra shininess. Unfortunately Que sprayed WD40 onto the rag, the equivalent of wiping oil onto the tyre. Luckily we spotted his mistake before I went out but he had ruined a brand new set of tyres and, at around £200 a go, he felt bad enough to offer to buy me a new pair.

However, he did take his role very seriously and in the early days did not go out for a beer before my races, although he had a bit of a reputation for liking a pint – and a fight. I don't think he went looking for trouble but he would not shy away if trouble found him. Que was from the old school; having grafted away all week he liked to let his hair down at the weekend, and his girlfriend Amanda despaired at some of his alcohol-fuelled antics. For instance, his local Chinese takeaway owner snapped into Bruce Lee mode after Que told him that his chicken chow mein was too 'wubbewy', jumping over the counter to beat the crap out of him with a bamboo stick. Another night he arrived home from the takeaway carrying two brown paper handles, not realizing that his takeaway sauce had spilled and the bags had dropped off. Then there was the time he leant next to the heater in the chippy for too long and was not aware that his Crimplene trousers had turned crispy. By the time he had staggered home they had fallen apart and he was effectively wearing a pair of tattered Crimplene shorts.

We once went out together the night before a race at Cadwell. Ossie was also there but had managed to crash his bike during the two-mile ride from the track back into Louth, adding a large hole to the grass stains that were still on his jacket from his spectacular 'off' at Santa Pod. He needed a beer or two to take his mind off his ripped knee but he did not need reminding the next morning because we duct-taped a red cross on the white roof of Anus's mini. I was making my one bottle of beer last the night, but did not mind Que having a few. After all, he was not a paid mechanic and his responsibilities on race day were pretty basic. He disappeared to the bogs after about five pints, and after around half an hour I realized that he hadn't come back. I thought I had better go and see if he was ill. Apparently Que had seen the local boxing champion doing a bit of shadow boxing in the mirror and overheard him brag that he could break the nose of anyone in the pub.

'I bet you twenty quid you can't break my nose,' taunted Que. And that's when I came in to find him semi-conscious, stretched out on the floor.

'What happened?' I asked.

'Never mind what happened. Is my nose brock?'

'It doesn't look like it,' I said.

'Well that cunt owes me twenty quid then!'

Snetterton was the first circuit I hadn't managed to visit in advance of a Shell Clubman's race but my confidence was growing after a few decent results. And it couldn't be that difficult to learn a new circuit during a race meeting. Or could it? I crashed at the first corner of my third lap of the first practice session. I went into the 100 m.p.h. corner a bit fast, ran wide onto the slippy stuff, touched the front brake and lost the front. The bike cart-wheeled into the field and I followed it, sliding along on my foot, wrist and elbow for what seemed like an age. This was not like crashing a motocross bike – it really hurt. Even on rock-hard ground there was always a bit of give when I crashed a crosser, plus I had all the body armour. Picking bits of hay out of my visor and stones from my boots was a true reality check for me. It was all the more sobering because it had been so long since I had crashed a road bike. I was badly shaken.

Dad wasn't there to see it but his words of warning were ringing in my ears: 'It's not like crashing a crosser, you know. It's going to hurt when you come off. And you won't get away with turning up at meetings with no spares.' He was correct on all fronts. One look at the bike and I thought it would never race again. Having now had a bit more experience of crashing, I know that the damage often initially looks worse than it actually turns out to be. All it needed was a new foot-rest hanger, front fairing, screen, bar and lever, probably costing about £400 in total. This was the first day of a two-day meeting and I was desperate to get back out there, so I set about trying to 'mackle' the bike up. But I still did not know too many people in the paddock and so could not source all the parts. I was also battered and bruised, with a possible broken wrist. The final nail in the coffin came when I realized the damaged end-can would affect the performance of the bike so there was no other option but to head for home. I was furious with myself. Lisa bought me an ice cream to cheer me up!

Luckily there was a two-week gap before the next race, time enough to piece myself and the bike back together. So far it had been good fun because we were always running near the front. But this break gave me a chance to become a bit more serious and organized, as I had always been when I was motocrossing. I went to breakers' yards to stock up on a few spares and Lisa and I got to work cutting out new red and blue triangles and squares to stick on the new front fairing. After realizing that the old ones took an hour to come off, we had decided the easier option was to stick them back on. It still looked awful but it was better than having to spend more money on a paint job. At last I looked like a real club racer with duct tape holding my leathers and holes in my boots.

A couple of breakdowns also spurred me to work a bit harder on preparing the engine, which was not too difficult for me because the V-twin of my Suzuki was effectively like a couple of the little 125cc engines in my crossers. So I already knew how to gain that little bit of extra performance, which I needed at the faster tracks like Snetterton for the higher standard Shell Clubman's meetings, where the 400cc bikes came into their own. One option was to buy flat-top pistons, which is how I first became involved with the Padgett's dealership in Batley, Yorkshire. With Clive, Don, Peter and Alan, I reckon nearly the whole of Batley was in some way related to the Padgett family, a famous name in British and Grand Prix racing circles.

Clive Padgett knew all the bits that I needed and was keen to help out with advice on getting the most from my bike. I decided to spend a bit of money on things like cylinder heads with spark plugs at a different angle, making the combustion chamber a better shape. So I went into the next race meeting, again at Mallory, feeling in better shape with matching cylinders, new cylinder heads and the correct thickness of head gaskets. I was bound to have lots more power.

The engine seized senseless during the first practice session. I had been maintaining my own bike for ten years and hardly ever had a problem. I could not work out why it overheated until Sean found me taking it to pieces back in the paddock and scratching my head.

'You did bleed it?' he asked.

'Err, no,' I said. 'Nobody told me I had to bleed it.'

'Hello! Anybody there?' he laughed.

I was used to putting the water in the radiator after stripping down a motocross engine, and topping it up when a few bubbles came up after kicking the engine over for the first time. All you then needed to do was check the levels after it had been hot. I hadn't realized that, with a much bigger radiator in the RGV and an extra cylinder, the radiator needed bleeding in a couple of places otherwise water did not reach one of the pipes. Luckily I had kept all the old parts and quickly fitted them back on so that the day would not be completely ruined. But the bike was still as flat as a turd. The battery had been damaged in the crash at Snetterton and, although the bike started properly, there was not enough voltage to keep the engine running correctly. It would not have mattered which new engine parts I had used, after all.

I managed to finish the races but was not up with the leaders and started to realize that I was fighting a losing battle trying to make a 250cc competitive against 400cc machines. Although I managed to sort out the problems over the next few weekends and return to winning ways, it was costing me a fortune as I needed new pistons almost every week because the skirts were cracking, on top of all the day-to-day expenses such as new tyres and the travel. I was still on a mechanic's wage, and something needed to give. The obvious solution was to trade the RGV250 in for a more reliable 400cc bike, which would be instantly more competitive and would not need as much money throwing at it for maintenance.

Mick Corrigan was often at the race meetings and had been following my progress after spotting my name in the results section of *MCN*, when I had been Rider of the Day at a Shell Clubman's meeting. He had two Yamaha FZR400s and told me that the yellow one was for sale for £4,000. I had only paid £2,450 for the RGV and the difference seemed like a fortune at that time. There was no way I was going to fork that much out without having a go first and so I took it for a spin at a damp practice day at Cadwell. I was extra cautious because I had been told: 'You bend it, you mend it.' Once I became used to the fact that it was a bit more cumbersome I developed a real feel for the bike – and it felt so much faster. There was no going back, especially when half the paddock showed an interest in my old bike because I had been winning races on it. I sold it to my mate Tim Booth for a small profit at £3,000, and when Mick knocked £400 off his asking price it was suddenly much more affordable.

It felt like I had stepped up to the next level, although there was still a lot of hard work to do because it was obvious there were still better riders around. At motocross I could make up time with bravery and stupidity. As long as I had a new knobbly rear tyre and a clutch that did not slip then I had a chance of winning a motocross race. Road racing was a far more exact science and the likes of Dicko helped bring me up to pace with the black art of set-up. I was facing a very steep learning curve if I was to compete with the very fast lads like Mark Townsend and another of my biggest rivals, a young lad called Scott Smart.

Scott's talent alone was enough to place him under pressure to do well, but the fact that he was the son of former Ducati legend Paul Smart (I still have a Paul Smart replica Ducati in my hallway) and nephew of Barry Sheene added to the weight of expectation on his shoulders. Scott's trick paint job, a black metallic look with flames down the side, complemented by a cool set of leathers, added to that aura. It was the same in my motocross days; you always wanted to beat the bloke with the mint bike. He might not have been as fast as the guy with the brown bike that had not been washed for three weeks, but that did not matter. Scott had smoked me at Snetterton when his FZR400 had a clear power advantage over my 250, but he was not at my first meeting on my new bike at Cadwell because he was based in the south and did not attend some of the more northern meetings. It was another two-day event and it took me a bit more time to get up to speed on my new bigger bike than I had anticipated, although I was quickly developing a new riding style to suit the bigger bike, braking in a more upright position and getting earlier on the gas on the exit from corners. At the end of the six races I was definitely riding faster than I had ever done on the RGV and I thought the new bike was the bollocks.

Ten minutes into the next meeting at Mallory I thought it was a load of bollocks. I heard a rat-a-tat-tat and, after limping back to the paddock, we discovered that the big end had gone. In simple terms it had blown up. 'Where's that Mick Corrigan?' I immediately thought, and it was probably a good job that he was not within reach or earshot. I had bought this bloody thing to cut down on the maintenance costs, not increase them. People had warned me that some sellers would strip the trick bits off the bike before delivering it to you. And the thought that Mick might have done just that flashed through my mind. But Mick was obviously not like that and when I cooled down I realized that it was not his fault at all and I started to focus on practical issues like how I was going to afford a new crank. It would also have to be fitted in the engine by someone because, although I knew a two-stroke engine inside out, building a four-stroke racing engine from scratch was out of my league.

An old guy called Peter Tomes, a genuine gentleman, saw us packing up for the weekend and said he had been keeping an eye on my progress. His son, Steve, raced in the Formula 400 class and Peter had already worked on my engine when it still belonged to Mick Corrigan. It was clear that over the years he had come to know, in his old-school way, exactly what made a four-stroke work and he offered to help if I took the engine along to his house, near Ambergate in Derbyshire. I was always a little concerned when I dropped an engine off with him because he looked so old that I might not get it back unless he got his skates on! Luckily he had a second-hand crank available and offered it to me for £100 when it was probably worth five times that amount. Once that was fitted the whole disaster had cost me not much more than £300, although I was starting to understand how so many people find themselves in financial trouble through racing. It was a good job I didn't smoke or drink or kick back for two weeks on a beach holiday or I would have already been destitute.

After the new crank was fitted by Peter the bike did not miss a beat for the rest of the season. And I did not fall off once in winning nearly every EMRA and Shell Clubman's race, including the rematch with Scott Smart at Snetterton, which was mega. Our paths hadn't crossed too often, but whenever they did we enjoyed a good tussle, both taking wins off each other. Those were the moments that made it rewarding for all the people – my parents, Lisa's parents, Carl, Que – whose constant support made that first year such a whirlwind of enjoyment, as I tried to absorb everything there was to know about my new world like a sponge. Unknown to me, Carl had already taken that support to a new level.

10

Limitless Stalker

Carl Gretton had been working on a secret master plan for my future racing. After I bought the FZR400 I did not have the same need for so many trips to Batley to see Clive Padgett, as the reliability was a lot better than my old Suzuki. But we still valued his advice and Carl decided to pay Clive a cloak-and-dagger visit to ask about my next step.

'The sooner you get Chris on a proper race bike the better,' said Clive. 'I have some Honda RS250s left over from last year. They are a bit more expensive than the Yamaha TZ250s but they are faster and come with spares kits.' Not many people were riding them at that time; Nigel Bosworth in the British 250cc championship and a few well-known riders on the road racing scene like Joey Dunlop, Steve Hislop and Ian Lougher. But all these riders had a lot of support with special race kits from Japan, which were worth a fortune.

Towards the end of that first season of road racing Carl told me that we still owed Padgett's some cash for the stuff like brake pads or spare numbers that we bought from their truck at the meetings. He suggested we should travel up there in the van to pay it. It did not occur to me that we could send a cheque, or travel in Carl's 911. When I walked into the showroom there was a bike on display and everyone was beaming.

'Here's your new race bike,' said Carl. I grinned like a Cheshire cat and didn't know what to say. The surprise of it all helped quash any reservations I might have had about the new bike. Only the factory-supported riders seemed to be winning consistently on the Hondas and I was a bit worried about their running costs. Should Carl have taken Clive's word at such face value? Was he just trying to flog him some leftover stock? Knowing Clive as I do now, he would not have sold it to us unless he thought it would bring results. But this seemed to be a big leap of faith, although it turned out that Carl had also spoken to my dad. All those doubts disappeared when I got the bike back to Lisa's. It was a work of art and I did not want to ride it in case I damaged it. It felt so light, even to sit on.

Nobody outside my family had ever shown me such generosity before. It was now clear that my racing had become Carl's passion too. He had been to watch me motocross but was obviously not as captivated as he was by the road racing scene. His business was doing well and this was his release from sitting behind a desk in front of a computer all day. Carl was a naturally generous person and derived his pleasure from seeing that everyone else was enjoying the experience. His thinking was that if I did well on this bike then there was a chance that I might be noticed by one of the bigger teams, because it was unlikely that our little posse would be able to step up to the British championship on our own. Sure, some people had already shown an interest but it did not take long for me to realize that once people pledge their financial support you are unlikely to ever see them again. It still happens to this day, never mind when I was starting out. Others were happy to supply product as a favour; AGV gave me a couple of helmets, which turned out to be a result when I ruined my favourite Arai helmet when a jerry can of fuel spilled into it in the back of the van. The team was supported by leathers manufacturer Texport, and Putoline, who had helped me out during my motocross days, were happy to provide my oil in return for a sticker on the side of the bike. That was about all the exposure they could expect at the level I was at, apart from the occasional picture in the *Nottingham Evening Post* or a mention in *Bike Sport News*.

My main sponsor, for better or for worse, was Bridgestone tyres. The Suzuki had come with Avon tyres and, although there was not a lot of choice of compound or size, the rubber was really soft and they seemed to do the job. When Bridgestone, who were relatively new to the sport, offered me free tyres there was only one option as tyres were my single biggest expense. I did not know whether they were good, bad or indifferent but almost immediately I started having the odd crash – the kind when you wonder what has happened before having any idea that anything was happening! The Avons used to be rubbed up after races, whereas the Bridgestones didn't show any sign that they had been working. The Yamaha FZR had also come with Avons but when I developed trouble steering I switched briefly to Bridgestone again. This brought the same issues with rear grip and so I finally opted to pay once more for the proven Dunlops, while Bridgestone went away to work on the problem.

My results in the Formula 400 class were good enough to qualify for a national licence and enter a couple of national races on the Honda in the 250cc class at the end of the year. Bridgestone again offered to provide their slicks for free. Slicks? Hold on a minute, nobody mentioned I would be using slicks! Surely all the grip came from the tread? I was crapping myself, yet everyone was telling me that slicks were just the same to ride on as treaded tyres but with lots more grip, so I should be able to go round the corners a lot faster.

So that's exactly what I tried to do during the first morning warm-up session at my first major meeting, the Race of the Year at Mallory, a one-off national-standard event that did not count for any championship. Nowadays it is held at the end of the season because it became too much of a distraction for the riders competing in their major ongoing championships like the Supercup. The race is open to all sizes of bikes and it was a bit of a foregone conclusion that Jamie Whitham, riding the Moto Cinelli Ducati that he raced in the World Superbike championship, would walk away with the £5,000 prize money. It was a big moment for me to be in the same race as one of my all-time heroes and I was a bit gutted for him when he crashed while in the lead early on, Matt Llewellyn going on to win the race.

I was also up against all my 250cc heroes such as the Vincent brothers, Jay and Max, who were so fast around Mallory that rumour had it they lived there, and the reigning champion, Nigel Bosworth, who rode the same bike as me – well, kind of – and was immaculately turned out. Apparently a few of the other riders had been winding him up, saying that there was a new kid on the block who was going to kick his arse. I had not said a word – that has never been my way. I have always tried to get on with the other riders, adopting the attitude that we are arch enemies with helmets on and pals (usually) with helmets off. Bosworth actually came over to say hello and he had obviously been watching my progress in light of the ribbing he'd received. He didn't give too much away but it was very flattering because he was enormously experienced and I still have a lot of respect for the guy. I have done the same thing with young riders, trying to encourage the likes of Craig Jones when he was coming up through the Junior Superstock ranks. It's nice for them to know that their efforts and progress are being appreciated.

I had only raced my Honda a couple of times before the Race of the Year, and even before tackling slicks for the first time I was having loads of trouble with grip. It was a minefield. One week I had no grip but then I had loads for the next race. How was I to know that when you moved the eccentric adjuster of the single-sided swinging arm, to tighten the chain after changing the gearing, the ride height would change by up to half an inch? The higher the ride height the better the steering is, but only at the expense of grip. This revelation, when it was eventually pointed out by Dicko, was one more step up the ladder in the dark art of race bike set-up. I had just assumed that I needed a new tyre every race, so the prospect of being provided with free Bridgestones definitely appealed again.

After a couple of laps of morning warm-up for the 250cc race I needed more than new tyres. The back end came round on me going into Gerard's and I saw the bike cart-wheeling into the gravel. Of course, like all racers, there was no way that I was going to blame myself entirely, and when we examined the tyre there was a band of roughness on the edge. It would not have lasted a full race as it was clearly too soft. Bridgestone were not present at the race so Dad wandered off down pit-lane to check what tyre Bosworth was using and buy one for the races. Back in the paddock it was all hands to the deck repairing the damage. The scrutineers did not recognize the bike when I took it to them before the race. At the start of the meeting it had been white but, with metres of duct tape holding the fairings and screen together, the bike was now almost pure silver. I blagged other bits like foot-rests and handlebars from around the paddock but was worried that the flattened tank would not hold enough fuel for a twenty-lap race. This was not an ideal way to start my first big race in such a competitive field and I was still annoyed about smashing up the bike for the first time.

I managed to qualify on the second row for the 250cc race and, after a pretty good start, found myself in the top three. The new rear tyre had loads more grip. Then Bosworth crashed going into the Bus Stop and I was in second place in my first national race. This was too good to be true, but the excitement did not last long. On the same lap I went into the hairpin too hot and lost the front. Clearly the grip from the Bridgestone front did not match the level of grip from the new rear because we all know it could not have been down to rider error, could it!? I was spewing as I pulled the bike off to the side of the track, especially when the race was red-flagged a couple of laps later. There was not too much fresh damage from this slow crash so I had another chance for glory in the Race of the Year itself. When the lights went out I released the clutch as normal but the bike went nowhere. I was devastated but it was again down to an element of my own naivety. I had not noticed that my clutch plates were worn and did not know that dry clutches, another new feature for me on my Honda, were prone to overheating and excess wearing, especially when used for two starts in reasonably quick succession.

I still get in trouble from my mechanic, Les Pearson, for being too harsh on the clutch on the start-line. 'We'll never get two starts out of it if the race is stopped,' he says. When they look at the data it shows that I let my clutch out a little with the back brake on but I think that my trademark good starts are as much to do with my motocrossing background as any special technique. The safest place at the first corner of a motocross race is at the front and I guess I just carried that mindset into my road racing.

It was not just the bike that left Mallory a bit dented. My confidence had taken a bit of a battering too. I had gone from hardly ever crashing my RGV and never crashing the Yamaha to crashing the RS250 twice in one day. But I started to gain a better feel for the new bike by entering the 250cc races at the same meetings where I was still competing in the Formula 400 on the Yamaha. And, despite starting the Shell Clubman's 250cc championship two thirds of the way through the season, I still managed to finish third.

The next big event was a national meeting at Brands Hatch. On top of the national racers a few of the top riders, such as John Reynolds on his Padgett's 500 GP bike and Ian Simpson and Phil Borley on their Nortons, were appearing in a special unlimited race, so it was a high-profile event. I did not even dare approach JR in the paddock in case he did not remember me.

Bosworth was out before me in the Saturday practice session and was so fast that I couldn't get my breath. I followed him into Paddock Hill Bend and was convinced that he was going to run off track. But he just flipped the bike on its side, hit the apex, spun the rear and cleared off down Paddock Hill. 'I'll never be able to do that,' I thought. I had felt pretty comfortable at Mallory as I had been there every Wednesday for the previous six months and only Gerard's was particularly technical. Now I had to cope with the banked start-finish straight and braking into Paddock Hill in a dip with the corner hidden from view. I was a fish out of water and qualified something like twenty-fifth out of thirty. I finished outside the top fifteen and out of the points in the race and was completely disheartened. It was just the same feeling that I had experienced when making the jump from senior to expert or from the AMCA to championship level at motocross. This was a big reality check. I actually nearly fell off my Yamaha for the first time during the Clubman's race later in the day. 'I can't actually ride one of these yet,' I realized. 'There is more to this than being a bit brave and a bit daft.'

I started to spend more and more time in Dicko's company and he was only too willing to help out. As we became increasingly wrapped up in our bikes it meant that his lovely-looking girlfriend, Jenny, and Lisa played second fiddle, which neither was too happy about. But I was focused on how I was going to move up to the next level and realized that no longer could we pitch up with our Renault Trafic van, a few spares and a paddock stand. We needed spare pistons, spare rings, different jets and a choice of tyre compounds. Things would have to change for the following season.

I wrapped up the Shell Clubman's Formula 400 championship with races to spare and was delighted to have won this title, and the EMRA championship, and finish third in the 250 Clubman's in my first season. But I was already focused on the final race of the year, another one-off national standard event at Donington. Again there was a host of big-name entries. Ron Haslam was competing on one of his Team Great Britain bikes, with James Haydon in the line-up after completing his Supercup season. Adrian Clarke, Steve Sawford and Ian Newton joined Bosworth and the Vincent brothers in a talent-crammed grid.

It was six weeks or so after the Brands Hatch débâcle and I was still a broken man, anxious to put the set-up and tuning knowledge I had gained during that period to good use on a circuit that I knew much better. I was excited, nervous and pensive, especially because this was a good time of year to impress anyone that might be looking to support riders for the following year. Back on the newly improved Bridgestones, I gradually built up speed during practice and qualifying, to the point where it was humanly impossible to go any faster. I qualified in twenty-seventh. The gap seemed even greater than it had been at Brands. I know now that improvement can always come from a combination of the rider and the bike, but this gap seemed too big to ever bridge.

'You are twenty-seventh. What should we try?' asked Que when I came in for a sip of water. Dicko and Padgett's were not there to offer advice during the middle of a session.

'I'm buggered if I know. I'll just go back out and try harder,' I said.

Even though I improved to around twentieth fastest during warm-up I would be starting the races from so far back on the grid that I might as well have been under the Dunlop Bridge. I could hardly see the lights. But then it absolutely pissed down for the rest of the day. I bumped into a guy called Richard Slynn, better known as Trick, who worked for a 125cc rider who used Bridgestones and went on to be Dicko's mechanic.

'You'll be all right on the Bridgestones in the wet. Just put your tyre warmers on them for an hour before the race and take it easy on the out-lap. You will have more grip than anyone out there,' he said. The last time I'd heard something similar I was upside down after three laps, but I did not know any different because I had never been on wet-weather tyres of any kind, as everyone was on intermediates at club level in the wet or the dry. There had been a few wet races during the year and my policy was no different then to what it is now in the wet: you go faster and faster and you will either end up near the front or fall off.

I could just about make out the lights in the distance through the murk, and after they went out there seemed to be somebody upside down at every corner. Before I knew it, I took fourth place at the old hairpin. It was a long old race but I managed to stay out of trouble. The tyres were like chewing gum and I passed none other than Ron Haslam in finishing third. Now a lot of people were suddenly sitting up and taking notice, having maybe thought that I was a bit of an idiot after qualifying twenty-seventh. It perhaps set them thinking that maybe my bike or my tyres were not up to scratch, and people always say that wet conditions are a great leveller. That's probably not as true now, with the onset of traction control. I actually hate riding in the wet, especially when everyone assumes 'Oh it's wet, it's Walker weather.' Sure, I have had a lot of good results in the wet and that's again probably due to my off-road background. A motocross bike never stops weaving and sliding so you are never scared when you lose control for a split second. Using the camber of a motocross track or riding on wet grass helps you gain an immense amount of feel for the grip of your bike.

But I have made some daft mistakes in the wet, too. Out-and-out speed goes out of the window and an element of chance is bound to creep in. If you squeeze the brake a fraction too hard in the dry you will have a 'moment' out of the seat or maybe run a bit wide. Do that in the wet and you are off, so you ride on a knife edge for the whole race. It's extremely rewarding at the end, if you finish, but give me a dry race any day. Having said all that, I genuinely believe that this one race gave me the leg up to where I am today.

A win in the Formula 400 race capped it off and my two bikes stood proudly in the garage with their podium rosettes. It was also a great day for the people who had come to support me. This included a Royal Visit from my mum, my dad and his mate, Smithy, and my sister and baby niece, Kristy Boo. Anus and Phil Scales had been joined by Mick Pales, a southerner who had moved to the Midlands to work for Central TV as a stage hand. He was a mad keen bike fan and always looked in the programme to support riders from our area, such as me or Dicko, or anyone from near his home town of Borehamwood.

'I fackin lav you, I do,' he said, hugging me after the race. His short brown leather jacket, black jeans and Cockney accent made Phil mistake him for Barry Sheene and, although the resemblance was minimal, Mick, who became a regular member of the posse, is still in my phone as Bazza.

My performances in that first year earned me a trial for Team Great Britain. I had already decided not to spread myself too thinly in 1995 and concentrate on the 250cc championships, so I sold my Yamaha to Millet, who did pretty well on it the following year. There had been a queue of people wanting to pay £5,000 for it but he was a mate, and had bought my Suzuki, so I dropped the price for him. I still made a profit because it was a good little bike and was in great condition because I hadn't crashed it. Sticking with my Honda RS250 meant that I would be racing a 1993 model for another year but that would not be a big disadvantage, as the newer 1994 and 1995 versions of the RS250 were not radically different.

There were two places for 250cc riders and two for 125cc riders at Team Great Britain. Yamaha supplied the bikes and the ACU provided some of the funding, along with a collection of other sponsors, and the aim was to bring on up-and-coming British riders. The selected riders were then asked to contribute around £5,000, which I suppose was a way of guaranteeing that you were committed and willing to put your neck on the line. Ron Haslam was the mentor and still rode one of the bikes at certain events. I remembered Ron and his brothers coming into Dad's shop when I was knee-high and from then I had followed his fortunes on the Pharoah Yamaha TZ750 and the Elf Honda in GPs. I was still pretty much in awe of anyone with any kind of reputation but especially genuine legends like Ron.

The trial was held at Donington, where Ron still has an affiliation. He initially followed you round and watched you ride your own bike. Then you were asked to ride one of their bikes and I was a bit taken aback when the gear lever fell off. The gear lever never fell off my bike. Somehow it just didn't feel as comfortable, or even as fast, as my bike. Ron then had a go on my bike and I could tell he was quite impressed with it. It was an invaluable experience to pick up tips from him but I came away wondering whether I really wanted to ride a bike that did not seem as fast as my own – and pay for the privilege. The job wasn't necessarily given to the fastest man on the day, but I decided not to push it even if I was on their shortlist and then worried for a good while whether I had made the right decision.

I had been approached by an outfit called Team No Limits. It was run by a couple of boffins and it was obvious that what they didn't know about race bikes wasn't worth knowing. Bridgestone were interested in coming on board as their tyre sponsor and the team would pay my entries and tune my engines. Team No Limits were supported by Texport, so I would receive a shiny new set of leathers through their UK representative, Dave Pickworth. It didn't get any better than that, I thought. They left their numbers and asked me to contact them if I was interested. Padgett's had also shown an interest but Clive had been off round the world supporting John Reynolds in GPs, so it did not seem as attractive a proposition, as I did not know exactly what level of support I would receive from them, if that relationship was to continue with John or any other rider.

Team No Limits were attending the annual test at Albacete in Spain early the following year and I agreed to ride for them there, along with Dave Wood. I jumped at the chance, not only to get to know their strengths and weaknesses but also to ride in a new country and at a new circuit. They had also entered a few races in the Ducados Spanish championship, a strong national championship that served as a natural feeder for GPs. Kenny Roberts's junior Yamaha team competed in it, as did Harold Eckl's Aprilia 125cc outfit. The first race in this championship was also at Albacete, the week after the test, so the plan was to stay out and maybe even do the second round of the Ducados championship at Jarama. This was another huge and exciting step for me.

We had to get to Spain under our own steam and the trip would have meant too much time off work for Que, so Carl came along to share the driving with Bazza. This was the first time Bazza had been involved at that level. We either sailed from Portsmouth to Bilbao or Plymouth to Santander, but the sailing time was similar and the smell was the same, essence of sick! It was particularly strong near the fruit machines, because people could not tear themselves away to go and be sick over the side or in the toilets. The outward journey was thirty-two hours, including two nights and one day, and the return was twenty-eight hours, with two full days and one night to pass. There was a cinema (big telly), disco (jukebox and floor), gym (clapped-out exercise bike) and a swimming pool (no bigger than a bath and nearly as dirty as the Penbury hotel), but the cabaret took the biscuit. I took the same boat last year and, eleven years on, the same people were playing the lead roles in *Grease* – and it wasn't John Travolta or Olivia Newton-John, I can tell ya!

I was a bit pissed off when we finally arrived and went out on track. Apart from the shit paint job in the team's colours, these two Nutty Professors had tinkered with my bike and it did not seem as fast as before. From the official lap times it was clear that I hadn't closed the gap since the end of last season, despite all the work on the bike over the winter. I rang Dad to tell him after the first day.

'It doesn't surprise me. I've never had a bike tuned yet that went any better,' he grumbled, as ever only happy when it was raining! I sort of agreed. I usually make my mind up about people pretty quickly and these guys seemed odd to me. We were just not on the same wavelength. But it was still good to familiarize myself with the guys I would be competing against in that year's main 250cc British Supercup championship and also the lesser National Cup, which was held over fewer rounds and featured only one race compared to the Supercup, which had two races per meeting. They were all there: Bosworth and Max Vincent on their Hondas, Jay Vincent and Steve Sawford on their Yamahas, and Jamie Robinson and Ian Newton on Aprilias that were missiles at top speed but not too easy to ride. I also got to know a few of the guys in the 125cc championship, like Robby Freer and Mick Lofthouse, who tragically lost his life at the TT the following year.

I chipped away at my times over the three days of the test but still had problems with grip at the rear. A few of the other British lads were also staying out for the first Ducados rounds, and most, having driven their race trucks down, were camping. So we spent the week having barbies or venturing into town to find somewhere serving English food, or at least an English menu, as I had never been too adventurous with food abroad. Unfortunately we did not find anywhere that did cheese boats!

The early practice and qualifying sessions of the race weekend at Albacete were again a bit hard work for me because I was now also being blown away down the straight. I was told not to worry because most of the competition was on last year's 250cc GP bikes. Even so, I was determined to put in a good performance in the final qualifying session so that I had a reasonable position on the grid for Sunday's races.

With ten minutes remaining I pulled into the pits to fit a new softer and stickier tyre and was hoping to leap a few places further up the charts. The exit of pit-lane at Albacete is quite close to the end of the start-finish straight and riders are blind to what is happening on the straight behind them. So a marshal stands at the end of pit-lane to act as a traffic policeman, waving riders through when the coast is clear and slowing them down when someone is braking for turn one. He waved me straight through and I was about to tip into the corner when I was smashed into from behind. The marshal had not noticed the guy approaching and he was left with nowhere to go but straight into the back of my bike at 60 m.p.h. He glanced off me and his bike was a right mess, but although I was sent cart-wheeling and banged my head and wrist there was not much wrong with my bike except a bent lever.

Despite the agony from my wrist I picked it up and set off back to the pits, realizing that I could take a short-cut back after a few more turns. Bazza and Carl were not expecting me back so quickly and when I saw that they were not at the garage I banged the lever back into position and exited pit-lane again, hoping to still record at least one flying lap on the new tyre. At the end of the session I was eager to see if I had made up some ground on the others but found that I was not even on the charts. Then a Spanish official appeared at our pit to tell me to report to race control. I was sure that they were going to blame the crash on me so I was looking for some TV cameras to prove that the marshal had waved me through. I had never been in trouble at a race meeting before and I was really panicking. Obviously I did not have a clue what they were trying to tell me in their thousand-words-a-second spit-babbling Spanish, so I went in search of someone who also spoke English. I was told that they were accusing me of cheating by taking a short-cut back down pit-lane, where the transponder still worked and recorded my fastest lap time of the meeting even though I had not completed a full lap.

It was so frustrating. It felt like being branded a criminal and I was choking back the tears. We had all stayed on an extra week, and my dad and Que had arrived to watch that very morning only to find I had been disqualified. I desperately tried to explain about the crash but their minds were made up – I would have to miss the race at Albacete but would be allowed back for the second round at Jarama the following week.

I woke up the next morning still sore about their decision but my wrist was even sorer. It had swollen badly overnight and I had actually fractured the scaphoid bone in my wrist. There was no way I would have been able to hold onto the bike, even if I had not been disqualified. There was little chance of it being right for the following week either, so the boffins from Team No Limits said it would be best for me to head back to England, having first cheekily asked whether they could put someone else on a bike I owned at Jarama! I was beginning to realize that Team No Limits was actually Team Not Right. I had never felt comfortable in their company. I was experiencing all the intensity that goes with being part of a team, without actually being a fully fledged team member. Also, there were none of the upsides in the performance of the bike that you get from being in a well-run team. I suggested to my dad that we might be better off starting the season on our own, without their help.

So the signs for the start to my second season were not good: I was off the pace; had decided to go it alone again; and had a broken wrist one week before the start of the British championship.

11

Wild Stalker

We needed a Plan B – and quickly. I knew that we would be out of our depth in the Supercup if we tried to go it alone. And if I was to have any hope of being a contender that year, we definitely needed the support of an experienced racing outfit. I remembered the interest that Clive Padgett had shown in me towards the end of the previous season, and they didn't come any more experienced than the Padgetts. So, on the eve of the season, I went cap in hand to see whether Padgett's could still provide any support.

Clive came from a long line of racers but his own career came to an abrupt end when he suffered a bad arm injury in a crash. He is a typical no-nonsense Yorkshireman who is far happier conducting business over a pie, chips and peas supper in his local than in a sterile office atmosphere. You always knew exactly where you stood with him, and while he might not have promised the world you knew that he would deliver on the promises he did make. To this day I don't think I have come across anyone more up-front and honest in racing. When you took into consideration that Padgett's owned the Honda and Yamaha race franchises, had already won British championships and had run John Reynolds in GPs, it was a wealth of racing know-how that we badly needed to tap into. And I could not have asked for any more from the deal he offered.

'This is what we can do. You pay your entries, supply the fuel and tyres, and we will pay for your running costs and any crash damage. You will have to start off on the bike we sold you. As soon as a 1994 bike, which is hardly any different from this year's model, becomes available you can use that and we will add a few race bits. The better you do, the more goodies we'll add. How does that sound?' Clive said, before throwing in a big old Mercedes van which had more than enough room for all my spares and tyres.

I almost bit his hand off. This was my first real stroke of luck on my way up the racing ladder. It was a dream deal at such a late hour. What's more, I was now part of the extended Padgett family. While his dad oversaw the whole business, Uncle Don ran the Isle of Man dealership and oversaw the racing operation, his brother Alan owned the Autorama Kawasaki dealership next door to their Batley head-quarters, Clive looked after the racing side and his two daughters tore around the workshop on their toys, oblivious to the fact that they were running over the fairings of JR's Grand Prix bike. I was immedi-ately made to feel part of the set-up and appreciated. It was now down to me to repay some of the faith that he had shown.

My first outing of the year was for a national race at Cadwell and the first obstacle I faced was to pass the scrutineering. It was too early to remove the cast from my broken wrist, and if the scrutineers had noticed they would probably have referred me to the doctors, where I would have been asked to do a few press-ups, which would have been impossible. They would not have been bothered how much pain I was in, just concerned that I was not going to cause an accident and injure another rider – I have seen it happen on a few occasions since. If a championship is at stake the officials sometimes turn a blind eye to it but, although I was desperate to impress from the word go, that would not have been a good enough reason for them. However, I managed to keep my arm out of sight from them and passed the scrutineering without any hitches. I still have a picture from that meeting which shows that I could not even pull my leathers down over the cast far enough to fasten the zip, so it was clearly visible at the start of the race.

Riding the previous season's bike, now with a Padgett's paint job, I struggled in the race. I did not have the necessary feel for the throttle and was probably pushing too hard to compensate when I went into the left-hander at the bottom of the mountain. As I flicked the bike right and cracked the throttle open the rear end lost traction and it spat me off. I'm not sure of the exact drop between the top and bottom of the mountain but I went so high that I could see people in the grandstand at the top of the mountain. 'This is going to hurt,' I thought. Amazingly, despite putting my broken wrist out to break the fall, I didn't suffer any new injuries and my wrist actually felt a bit better when I picked myself up.

Maybe the cast wasn't the only factor affecting my control of the bike. There was a slight improvement when it came off for a practice day at Oulton Park, and then Padgett's delivered the 1994 bike in time for the first Supercup race at Donington. It was almost exactly the same as my old bike, except the forks and shocks were better and the airbox, not present on the older models, provided more torque and grunt. So the bike was a lot faster but, strangely, more difficult to ride. I was sideways and losing the front everywhere. This was not going to plan. I felt a bit out of my depth again, and with not much idea of a way forward. Having picked up trophies willy-nilly the previous year, I faced fighting it out for the minor places again. There was no point making excuses, especially to the likes of Que, who was giving up his spare time to sleep in a van and spend his weekends spannering for me. I have never been one to tell fibs to explain poor results – you owe it to your team to be honest, even when the chips are down, because otherwise you end up going round in circles trying to find a better set-up. So the only option was to get my head down and try to ride round the problems.

Then, during a practice session for the next race at Mallory, I remember passing Ian Newton on the brakes into the Hairpin but then being sideways again going into the Bus Stop chicane. I clipped the hay bales on the inside of the bend and they bounced back out in front of Ian, who had to brake hard to avoid them. Ian was very experienced and had one of the best-looking bikes, and wives for that matter, in the paddock. He rode ex-factory Aprilias that were a genuine work of art, faster than the Hondas but not as easy to ride at some of the more technically challenging circuits. But I don't think it was just the paint job he was scared for when he came to find me after that session.

'Chris, here is a brand new Dunlop slick rear. For fuck's sake use that in the race or you are going to kill someone. You might have a chance of winning, too, because you will never get anywhere on those Bridgestones,' he said. I wasn't sure whether he had spotted something in me that he wanted to nurture, or whether he just genuinely feared for his life. Whatever his motive, it worked a treat. I was immediately up near the front of my second Supercup race, battling against the usual contenders like reigning champion Jay Vincent and his brother Max, Jamie Robinson, Nigel Bosworth, Gary May and Ian himself. All I had hoped for at the start of the season, having made a bit of a mark towards the end of the previous year, was to carry on making progress. So to find myself immediately mixing it with my heroes – and on the podium for both those Mallory races – was more than I could have dared wish for.

The grip from the Dunlop rear that Ian Newton gave me was a real eye-opener, although the Bridgestone front, which had been fine before, could no longer cope with the extra grip at the rear. It was clear that, apart from their wets, they were not quite ready for the 250cc class, which has always been Dunlop's domain, even to this day. But all of a sudden I was earning a bit of prize money and, although part of the agreement with Padgett's was that I split any winnings 50–50, I reckoned that the improved results would still enable me to pay for Dunlops for the rest of the season. It helped that my two main rivals in the Supercup, Ian Newton and Jamie Robinson, did not do too many national rounds, so there was always a chance that I would pick up the £500 first prize for those races, boosting my tyre budget for the next Supercup round.

It also helped Padgett's budgets that I only crashed the bike twice all year – at the same corner and on the same practice day at Knockhill. It was the first time I had been to the circuit and, although it was more car than bike friendly in those days with big gnarly kerbs, I immediately clicked with the track. It was so much fun to ride, until

I came off at the hairpin and broke the foot-rest hanger and put my head through the screen. The damage was minimal so I was soon back on the bike – until I came off at the hairpin, breaking the foot-rest hanger and putting my head through the screen! What a tool!

We were staying at the same place where Scott Smart was with his family. Scott's sister, Paula, was beautiful and often brought her 16-year-old mate with her to the races. I would be lying if I said I didn't have the odd impure thought because they wore the shortest skirts imaginable, although I was still scruffier than a scruffy thing in my fake Timberland jumper and jeans that were tighter than the ones British Superbike racer Tommy Hill still wears. But I still found Paula really easy to get on with and I became very friendly with the whole family over the years. What's more, I won one race and broke the lap record on the Sunday, Scott winning the other ahead of me, so I found myself spending more time with the Smarts!

With my Supercup campaign now on track and going to plan, the other big race on the radar was the Race of the Year at Mallory, with a chance to put last year's clutch problems on the start line well and truly behind me. The thought of being in the same race as John Reynolds, on his Reve Red Bull Kawasaki superbike, for the first time was a big thrill. JR is up alongside Niall Mackenzie as being one of the nicest, straight-up racers you could meet. But when he was racing he did not get too chummy with the other riders. It was probably because he would find it too difficult to stuff it up the inside of a rider in a do-or-die manoeuvre on the last lap if he was too close to them. So I didn't really get a chance to see him until he took up his position on the front row of the grid – with me in pole position.

I couldn't get my breath after the final qualifying practice. It had been a shitty weekend but the track was basically dry, with just a few damp patches, for the final session and I knew I had done a pretty fast lap, certainly the quickest I had ever been around Mallory. We did not have timing screens in our pit but someone told me that I had done a 48.999, so I rushed up to the offices to check on the official sheets. I bumped into Matt Llewellyn, the winner the previous year, who was staring at the sheets and scratching his head.

'That's not right – a bloody 250cc bike on pole against superbikes. Gotta hand it to you, though. That's some going, lad,' he said.

By the time of the race the weather had taken a turn for the worse again and it was pissing down by the start. I had already done a few wet races in the Supercup during the year and, with help from Clive, had a decent wet-weather setting for the bike. With just a few clicks here and there, a bit of preload off the front and rear, and a slight drop in the ride height, the bike was soft and forgiving – just how I liked it. Clive was a great help all year with bits of tips. He was even known to pop the tank up and change the jetting on the start line occasionally.

I was also now pretty comfortable on the Dunlop wets. And, although this was a lot wetter than I had ever raced at Mallory before, I managed to take the lead and only JR was able to stay with me for a while. After swapping the lead a few times JR eventually had to retire when his visor fogged up, leaving the way clear for me to win the race, lapping everyone up to fourth in the process. To this day it is the only time a 250cc bike has ever won the Race of the Year. JR caught up with me afterwards and said: 'I really didn't want to be going that fast in the wet round here. Well done, Chris – that's some achievement.'

All that was left for me to do was to go and collect my £5,000 cheque from the organizers. I had never even owned a car worth that much, let alone won it from one race. So it was a bit of a shock to open the envelope to find that the prize money was down to just £1,000 this year. Someone explained that the rest of it had probably been spent on tempting John Reynolds to interrupt his World Super- bike campaign to race there. And after I had split the money with Padgett's there was barely enough left to cover my costs. But I was not there for the money – the sense of achievement was more than enough reward.

Back in the Supercup championship I was a regular challenger for the podium and claimed my first win at Snetterton. Outside of motorbike racing circles there was not too much media recognition, but the 250cc class was the main support class for the British Super- bike championship. You could tell it was popular – even more so than the 600s, who only raced once at each meeting – because there were no queues by the burger vans when we were racing. I still think the 250s should race at British championship level and it's probably one of the reasons we are struggling to produce top MotoGP riders. The MotoGP bikes still behave more like the 250s than superbikes and, with a few exceptions, it's usually the guys coming up from 250cc GPs that make it at that level. Occasionally our races were also televised and, challenging for third place in the championship mid-way through the season, I must have been creating a good impression.

Only the previous year I had taken Lisa to the Grand Prix at Donington, barely four or five months into my racing career. We had bought normal punter tickets and so were not allowed anywhere near the pits. The closest we came to the paddock was poking our noses through the mesh fencing, trying to spot some of the big names like Mick Doohan. 'I'm going to be in this paddock soon,' I joked with Lisa.

A bit sooner than I realized! Clive was obviously pleased with my progress and, behind the scenes, was pushing the organizers of the Grand Prix series, IRTA, to give me a wild card ride in the British GP. And he obviously carried a fair amount of influence, having raced John Reynolds in the previous year's 500cc championship, then Eugene McManus and a Japanese rider, Toshi Arakaki, this year. I, on the other hand, did not even know what a wild card was.

'Chris, I've managed to secure you a ride in the British GP,' Clive told me.

'Yeah, right-oh! Pull the other one,' I smiled.

'No, seriously. It's a wild card ride. They give them to the best local lads each year to help boost the crowds. Jamie Robinson and Jay Vincent have got one too. Your entry fee is covered by the organizers and Dunlop will provide the tyres. It's a no-brainer – you are doing it,' he said, as if I needed some persuading.

Within a few weeks I was at Donington for a public relations day with Padgett's two 500cc riders and a few other teams. I was a bit puzzled to see the Padgett's team wheel out JR's 500cc bike from last year and even more surprised when I heard the noise it made when they warmed it up. 'Rather you than me,' I thought. I thought wrong!

Clive waited until the last possible moment, to stop me from getting too nervous, to tell me that I would be going out on the 500cc bike before my 250cc. I nearly shat myself.

I came in after five laps and the cameras from *East Midlands Today* and Central TV were thrust into my face before my eyes had a chance to refocus. A 250cc was the sweetest bike to ride – the ultimate racing machine where the chassis and brakes outperform the engine. Sure you could still crash through carrying so much corner speed, but you rarely got into trouble from the power of the bike. To jump on a 500cc bike with 180 bhp, the same brakes as my 250cc and no better handling – let's just say it would have been an eye-opener, if I had kept them open!

I could not wait to get back on my 250cc bike, but even that was different in preparation for the GP ride. However well I was riding we were not going to compete with the regulars unless we tried to keep up with them technically. You look at Eugene Laverty in his first season in 250ccs this year. I think he is an exceptional young talent but he is only ever going to look OK until he is on the same machinery as the front runners. So we had to try some new parts, which actually made the bike harder to ride. Up against new riders on new machinery, however, it was difficult for me to tell what was lacking.

Then Clive dropped the bombshell. I had been given an entry into both the 250cc and 500cc classes. It was up to me to decide which race I wanted to compete in. My head said the 250cc race, because I was having such a great year in that class. But my heart found it hard to turn down the 500cc opportunity, despite my lack of experience.

'Listen, Clive,' I said. 'You have got me this far, so I will do whatever you think is for the best.' He let me know his decision the day before the first qualifying session.

'OK, lad, I've decided. You're doing both!' I had been having enough trouble sleeping, and that was when I thought I would only be in the 250cc race. Now I was in bits, and that's probably why he left it so late to tell me.

I had coped pretty well with the extra press interest in the build-up to the GP. The series was a bit in the shadows of World Superbikes in Great Britain at that time, because Foggy only had to look at a Ducati to walk on water in the eyes of the fans and grab all the headlines. Although a few British riders were in that year's Grand Prix series, nobody was really making a mark in the wake of Niall Mackenzie, Rob McElnea and JR. So everyone wanted to make the most of the interest created by me making a début at that level so soon after I had started to race. People did not expect too much, especially when they knew I would be in two classes, one of which was totally new to me. To this day I think I am the only rider to have competed as a wild card in the 250cc and 500cc races at the same GP. But I was still conscious that I did not want to raise expectations – nobody wants to arrive like a Jensen Button in a blaze of publicity and then do nothing. So I played everything down, stating that I would be peaking if I made it into the points.

In fact I was peaking from just wearing my IRTA photo-identity pass and rubbing shoulders with some of the people in the paddock. It seemed like one big circus: all the lorries, hospitality units and colour. I was amazed by the number of tyres lying around, and as the weekend went on I asked to keep some of the discarded new tyres that would do very nicely for me at British championship level. I went out of my way to spot Doohan, and this time I was on the same side of the paddock mesh fence as him. Kenny Roberts and Kenny Roberts Junior were there, as was Kevin Schwantz, plus the likes of Norick Abe – all guys I had only ever seen on telly or read about in magazines. Thursday was the Day of Champions, an open day in the paddock. So I was interviewed on stage and, whilst most people did not know who I was, they were obviously behind me and the other wild cards, Jamie Robinson and Jay Vincent, who had been there and seen it all before. It was obviously a very proud time for my dad and Lisa, although both were also very level-headed and did not show it too much. The only other person the nerves really got to was the other half of our Laurel and Hardy duo, Que.

'Does this mean I am a GP mechanic?' he asked me, excitedly.

'Yeah, I guess it does, even if it's only for one weekend,' I said. 'And I suppose that makes me a Grand Prix racer!'

Que was in pieces with worry that he might make a mistake, although Clive's presence helped calm us both down. Clive had missed a few GPs during the season to come and help us out at the British championships. This was either because he thought there was a chance of me winning the title, or that he thought we were completely useless without him. Even with the continued help of Dicko, who was to all intents and purposes a rival in the 250cc at British level, although you would never realize it off the track, there was still a hell of a lot of work to get through preparing the bikes and I had to work flat out in the garage on top of the riding. So, if Clive had not pitched in at British championship meetings and said things like the gearing needed changing because it wasn't revving high enough in second gear, my head would have been spinning. However, with me as the third Padgett's rider in the 500s and competing in the 250s on my own machine, the GP paddock was awash with Padgett's bikes, and before long Que and I felt a bit more at home.

I was excited every time I went out on the bike, and I don't think my nerves really settled until Sunday evening. For a Supercup meeting I was barely on the bike for two hours in total over the weekend. All of a sudden I was riding four hours a day and my hands soon started to blister, although I did not feel too tired physically. Half that time was spent battling with that beast of a 500cc bike, and it was difficult to swap between the two. Every time I flicked left down Craner Curves I thought the 500cc was going to swap ends on me. And the words of Uncle Don Padgett were always ringing in my ears. 'They are not cheap things to mend, tha knows. That John Reynolds cost us a bloody fortune down the years, throwingt' thing downt' road.' I had one slide off at McClean's in a practice session, but thankfully not much damage was done.

I also had to get into a different mindset on that bike, thinking well ahead of every move. For instance, coming out of Goddard's I was halfway into Redgate and needing to brake before I even had time to think about getting my head down behind the screen. I had got to know Phil Plater and the guys at Dunlop well over the year so they helped me out with the best rubber they were allowed to supply, although they could not provide the same stuff as the top riders. What I didn't know didn't bother me. What did worry me was when one of the top riders like Doohan came past, smoking his rear tyre and shaking his head. He was not trying to tell me that I was a wanker, just that as a wild card I was expected to clear out of his way. My immediate reaction was that they all thought I was a cock and that I was slowing them all up. But I have done it since with wild cards; it's just a way of making sure that they know what to do in future. Even so, you still get the occasional one who will mess up your one and only flying lap during qualifying, and that's worse than if he had run off with your missus!

Yet, despite all this, I didn't disgrace myself and qualified seventeenth out of about twenty-five for the 500cc race, with the top fifteen scoring points in the race. Everyone was excited but I was actually still a bit down about my performance on the 250cc. The others carried more corner speed, braked later and were on the gas quicker. 'Any danger of someone slowing down,' I thought, 'or it raining, perhaps?' As luck would have it this was probably the only British GP in history to be dry for all three days. The gap between me and the front was probably not much different than in the 500cc class, but I qualified down in twentieth out of thirty in the 250ccs.

My race day nerves were not helped when, on the warm-up lap of the 250cc race, Max Biaggi nearly knocked me off. I was happily bedding in my tyres at the left kink after Starkey's Bridge before heading to Schwantz Curves. He came up my inside as I tipped in and there was no room for two bikes, so he was forced onto the dirt. 'Check you out. In a bit of a rush, Nobby?' I thought. I needed binoculars to see the lights from where I was on the grid, and the depth of talent in the line-up was unbelievable. But I soon settled down into a good race with the guys at my level and held onto a place on the final lap with some do-or-die braking into the Foggy Esses, as they are now known, to finish in eighteenth. I was disappointed to be outside the points. Wild cards are forgotten by the next round unless they make people sit up and take notice by finishing in the points. Still, everyone was kind and complimentary although there was no time to take in their comments. Still sweating and dying for a drink – knowing nothing about hydration or nutrition at that stage I probably had two cans of Coke for breakfast – I barely had time to clean my visor and add a new tear-off before I was off out to join the grid for the 500cc race.

I was not exactly gasping for breath when I arrived on the grid, but certainly breathing heavily after my 250cc race exertions. When I took my helmet off I looked like I had just completed the Paris–Dakar, whereas all the legends were fresh from their massages or pedicures, or whatever it is that legends have before a race. It was not the ideal look for the biggest shop window of my career. In front of me was a sea of bikes occupied by the biggest names in the sport: Doohan, Criville, Barros, Cadalora. 'I really should not be here,' I thought.

Clive tapped me on the shoulder and said, 'Don't worry, lad. You will score points in this race – I'm sure of it.' That was easy for him to say. I had only been on the bike for a few hours and, although I have never been one to be de-tuned by a crash, the slide during qualifying had not exactly helped my confidence. Still, in the first few laps I managed to pass a few people, although riders also passed me as everyone cagily jockeyed for position, knowing that a mistake in those early stages could cost them the race. After lap five I was on my own – with a lonely twenty-eight laps to look forward to. A couple of crashes or retirements edged me further up the field and before I knew it I was behind Eugene McManus in fifteenth place and set to score a Grand Prix point. I could sense the support from the British crowd and there was certainly no shame when Doohan eventually lapped me on his way to winning the race. In fact I have a picture of me behind him around the Melbourne Loop, just after he came past. There I am, on a two-years-old YZR500, knee-sliders taped on because the Velcro had worn away, and on track with Mick Doohan with my knee down. As soon as I saw the picture I thought, 'I'm framing that bad boy!'

I was 'hanging' when I finally got off the bike. There were big hugs all round, especially from Dad, and everyone seemed to have forgotten that I didn't score points in the 250cc race. Que was chuffed to bits, Bazza and Dicko, who had both helped out over the weekend, were proudly wearing their Padgett's team shirts, and we had a big team picture taken next to the bikes. It was used on the front of the sport section in *MCN* under the headline: 'Walker Makes His Point'. The *Nottingham Evening Post* also carried a big colour picture on their back page. So Clive was obviously delighted with the exposure they received in return for the money they had spent on running the extra bikes. And there was no need to worry about finding a beer to celebrate. I was riding for Padgett's, so right next to the cupboard for spares and wheels was a cupboard for beers and bacon, to make the butties with.

Looking back, that day brings a tear to my eye. I guess not even the likes of Valentino Rossi has scored points in a Grand Prix just eighteen months after racing a road bike for the first time. Still, I took it all very much in my stride. In the front of my mind was the realization that I now had another huge gulf that I needed to bridge if I was to reach that standard on my 250. But not even in the back of my mind were there yet any thoughts that I might one day make a living out of this sport.

12

Starstruck Stalker

There was hardly time to catch my breath after the Grand Prix before Clive planned another adventure: my first road race abroad. The destination was Assen, a former road circuit in the north of Holland, dubbed the Cathedral of Road Racing. I was going to take part in their round of the European 250cc Championship, which was held as a support championship for the World Superbike series. This had always been a popular round for British fans to visit and, with Foggy flying high in that year's championship alongside the likes of Jamie Whitham and John Reynolds, there was sure to be a great atmosphere.

The atmosphere in our van, setting off on the long drive to Assen with Que and Dicko, together with Jay Vincent who was coming along for the ride, was a combination of Brits on Tour and quiet determination. I had already competed in one of the European rounds at Donington earlier in the year and had not set the world alight. Jamie Robinson won that race and was also travelling to Assen to race. He was desperate to make it into the 250cc GPs the following year and this was a natural stepping stone, so he wanted to do well. I was quite worried about racing on a new and technically challenging circuit without having been there in advance. But it was comforting, on arriving at a paddock which felt just like being back in GPs, to find that the British contingent were again very supportive and appreciative of my efforts at the GP.

Dicko had been to Assen before and had warned me that it rained for every race. So, in preparation, he brought a special new yellow rain visor, which was supposed to improve visibility in the wet. The first half-hour practice on the Friday was dry, so I used the session to find my way around and try and sort out my gearing. Sure enough, it looked like it would rain for the second half hour, so Dicko persuaded me to use this new visor. I was getting faster and faster, but halfway through the session riders suddenly started to drop like flies. Ian Newton snapped his bike in half out on the fast section and Robinson also crashed, while many of the other riders were pulling into the pits. I pulled in at the end of the session to be greeted by huge smiles from Clive, who had travelled out for the race, and the rest of the crew.

'You're third fastest, chief,' said Dicko. 'Did you not know it was raining?'

The visor had worked so well that I had not even noticed that the track was now really damp, and I had managed to stay upright on my slicks. The weather deteriorated as the day went on, and although the track was drying before the start the race was declared wet so it would not be stopped if it rained again. I was joined on the front row by Jamie Robinson, some dude on an Aprilia who was older than my dad, and the Italian rider, Luca Boscoscuro. Everyone had set out for the out-lap on wets but, having found so much grip from my slicks in the morning qualifying session, on the grid I decided to change my rear to an intermediate – halfway between a wet-weather tyre and a slick. The only problem was that our intermediate had not been on a tyre warmer for too long, and it was virtually cold when the guys put it in. Still, I was confident that it would last the race on a drying track and I tried to get as much heat into it as I could on the warm-up lap before it started to rain again halfway round. Every time I tipped the bike over I thought I was going to crash. I was going to be in deep shit.

When the lights turned from red to green I snaked my way down to the first corner and was down to tenth by the third turn. But the shower had been brief, and because the whole circuit is banked or cambered it dries a lot faster than most. The riders on full wets immediately started to struggle and I picked them off one by one, soon passing Jamie Robinson, whose back wheel was spinning so much that he looked like he was doing doughnuts for the crowd. I briefly battled for the lead with Boscoscuro, who was also on an intermediate. After Boscoscuro cleared off the old dude on the pink Aprilia just managed to pip me for second place as he was faster in certain sections where circuit knowledge was invaluable. It was a great feeling to be on the rostrum for a European championship race – until I saw the picture. The Dunlop cap, probably still with the cardboard inside, came down over my eyes and made my ears stick out. Then I was given a bunch of flowers to hold. I would have forgiven anyone for thinking that I had learning disabilities.

By the time we left the circuit for our long-awaited night out in Assen we were probably well on the way to needing a stomach pump. The British lads were all staying out to watch Foggy and Co in action the next day, so after finishing off the champagne we cracked open a few tinnies as we showered in the Padgett's GP truck, which we had been able to use to bunk down in because there was no Grand Prix round that weekend. It sounds very flash but was in actual fact not much better than the horsebox that Rob McElnea later used for his Cadbury's Boost team in the British championship. So, prize money in pocket, probably enough to buy a round of Heineken, I set out with Que, Dicko and Jay Vincent for my first night out abroad since that memorable escapade in Calais. It was a rare chance for the racers to let our hair down because we usually packed up to go home on the Sunday. And it was the first time I had been out with Que, who had a bit of previous for liking a beer, when neither of us had to worry about how we would feel the next morning. Dave Jeffries, who was John Reynolds's team-mate and who lost his life at the TT a few years later after becoming one of the all-time great TT riders, was heading into town for a meal and gave us a lift in the back of his pick-up. Que spent the journey leaning on the fifth wheel, the connector for his motorhome trailer, and was covered in grease long before things started to get really messy.

Assen was buzzing with British bike fans and, so soon after the British GP, we were recognized by a few who bought us beers all night. We had made the schoolboy error of not having anything to eat and before too long our parents would not have been proud of us. The only flashpoint came when some Dutch guy thought it might be fun to take the piss out of Que for wearing two earrings – not a wise move. But even that passed off without too much of a skirmish as we dragged Que off to some seedy nightclub. Now that I have been to Holland a few times and have my eyes wider open, I guess everyone else in the club was smoking spliffs, but I barely knew what a normal cigarette looked like. Jay was in full flow buying round after round of sambucas and tequila slammers, until Que tried to stand up and knocked all the glasses off the table. The bouncers gently escorted him off the premises and I knew that I didn't need any more to drink, so I followed him out onto the street and we found a bench where he could sit and puke.

'Thish ish the lasht time we'll be able to do thish,' he said, as I stroked his head, which was now resting in my lap. 'You will be off doing shtuff and I will be left behind.'

'What are you talking about, you daft bastard? We got this far together – I'm going nowhere without you,' I said, trying to sound sensible in what was our first real moment of bonding, as he spewed on my shoes at ten-minute intervals. The truth was that, in his state in the centre of Assen at 2 a.m. on a Sunday morning, I was going nowhere with him! Needless to say we struggled to hail down a taxi because Que could only remain upright while I was propping him up. Then some English-speaking locals suggested we join the queue at the main taxi rank and I managed to man-handle him across town.

When we reached the front of the queue I opened the back door of the next taxi in line and pushed Que inside, but as I climbed in he was already being dragged out the other side by a couple of Dutch policemen. They then reached in and hauled me out the same door and straight into the back of one of their vans. I was shitting myself, especially because they were growling away in Dutch, a language in which people sound like they are going to spit at you at the best of times. Even Que seemed suddenly semi-conscious. At the station we were marched to the front desk.

'You English hooligans! Every year we have the same trouble from you. It's only ever you English,' he shouted.

'Surely this can't just be over that argument over the double earring in the pub,' I thought, as they prepared to throw us in our cells. But their way was not to take away your belt and laces. Here you were stripped down to your underpants.

'Chris, shay fuck all. Tell the fuckersh nothing,' Que yelled as they dragged him away.

'What do you mean, tell them nothing? There's nothing to tell. I was on the rostrum of a European championship race a few hours ago,' I thought. This was like a normal Friday night out in Heanor for him – but I was ready to squeal like a pig! Que was not ready to take this treatment lying down until, from my cell, I could hear him being shoed to within an inch of his life. At least it meant that he could not hear me sobbing the hours away, especially when I found out why we were actually there. It was nothing to do with the argument in the pub. Some local woman had been mugged and tampered with earlier in the night by two English blokes. Quite how a small lad with blond curly hair and a bloke wearing two earrings, who had always defied description, resembled their suspects I will never know. And it must have been even harder to round up some similar-looking blokes before they dragged us out of our cells at 5 a.m., still handcuffed, for an identity parade in front of the woman, who was on the other side of the one-way glass. All the stories about miscarriages of justice flashed through my head and I imagined being left to rot in some stinking Dutch jail for the rest of my life.

But there was no word of apology when we were eventually turned loose on the outskirts of town. Que looked a mess: still covered in grease, sporting a few bruises and handcuff marks, carrying one shoe and his trousers hanging down because the police had lost his belt. We had no idea what had happened to Dicko and Jay, and there was no chance of finding a taxi at 7 a.m. in the morning. So by the time we limped back into the paddock morning warm-up had started for World Superbikes. We had already sworn not to let Clive know anything and luckily he had already headed back to England.

However, we also agreed to be very selective about anyone we told, and I'm not sure my parents know about that night to this day. In any case, Que disappeared into the truck and was not seen for the rest of the day. It turned out that Dicko had indeed given someone a bit of a pasting in a doorway following the earring dispute, and that might have been why the police were so keen to accuse us of the other incident. That wasn't my only stroke of bad luck. John Reynolds had been injured in a nasty crash on the Saturday afternoon and Ben Atkins had been considering letting me ride the bike in the World Superbike race – if he had been able to find me!

Back home, Padgett's were true to their word in improving my bike as my results started to improve. New carbs gave me a bit more drive and grunt and Ian Newton and I were closing the gap on Jamie Robinson in the Supercup. His Aprilia was either a missile or parked at the side of the track, whereas my bike was totally reliable. Steve Sawford and Jay Vincent were also going well, but had both suffered through crashes or breakdowns and had lost touch with the top three. With two or three rounds remaining, but with a fair chunk of the season left, we were keen for as much track time as possible and I entered the next European championship race in England, on the full circuit at Brands Hatch. I had only been there once before and this showed when Jamie Robinson cleared off to win, while I was down in seventh or eight, which was frustrating because I was either up his arse or even in front of him in British championship races. However, the weekend was memorable for different reasons.

I had been staying with Scott Smart for the weekend. His parents lived near Brands, so I rang to ask if he knew a hotel in the area, half hoping that he would invite me to stay. Not only was this preferable to sleeping in the back of Dicko's van, but it had the added advantage of placing me in close proximity to Scott's sister, Paula. They might have been wise to me, though, because the room I was allocated was up on the tenth floor, and next door to Paula's grandad, Frank –Barry Sheene's dad. He might have been 300 years old but he still had the hearing of a wolf, so there was no point trying to sneak across to Paula's wing of the house, even if she had wanted me to.

Come Sunday night, I expected to head off home but had heard a lot about the legendary Brands Hatch post-Superbike parties. Needing a beer to drown my sorrows after the race I popped into the hotel at the circuit, where all the big hitters were staying and already beginning to fill the bar. Foggy and his entourage were there, as were Troy Corser and Scott Russell and a few other top World Superbike riders. Some spoke to me, some didn't, but I got talking to Niall Mackenzie, then in his final year in GPs and at Brands to do some TV work. I had never really bumped into him before but we got on like a house on fire and the Bacardi and Cokes started to flow. I was only used to drinking beer so this went straight to my head, and as the night went on and only the hardcore were left standing we were out of our trees and giggling away like school kids. We then realized that neither of us had anywhere to stay for the night. The only option was the back of Dicko's van, as he was in his caravan with his girlfriend.

Niall was driving a mint Honda NSX two-seater and we set off in it, expecting to drive through the circuit to the paddock until we discovered that the main gate was locked. Not wanting to risk driving over the limit on public roads, he then set off, flat out and throwing in the occasional handbrake turn, through the public car parks towards the paddock. We then discovered the paddock gates were also locked. There was no option but to climb the fence and, still giggling away, we both ripped our jeans on the mesh. To avoid freezing to death I had to cuddle up in the back of van with a Grand Prix star I had met only five hours earlier and who, just two years ago, I had been cheering on from the grass next to the exit of Schwantz Curves, having drawn him in our group's sweepstake.

Neither of us was exactly bright-eyed and bushy-tailed in the morning because we had laughed and giggled ourselves to sleep, but the night had been a real eye-opener for me. This was the first time I had socialized with professional riders, and it was as though someone had thrown a switch. Not only do they get to race bikes, they get paid to do it – and they like a party. This was the job for me. Working as a mechanic in an MOT garage was not exactly a job for life and my lack of qualifications ruled out being an airline pilot. Now there

Left Butter wouldn't melt…

Above With my sister, Wendy, on my dad's Dot Demon at a weekend scramble.

Above The start of my two-wheel addiction at home in Ripley.

Above My first-ever trophy – I wasn't fed until I won one.

Right The only time I have caught crabs – honest!

Above Mucking about with Dicko in the paddock at Snetterton.

Left Clive Padgett making his customary last-minute checks on the Donington start-line before my one and only 250cc Grand Prix in 1995.

Right Deep in thought with pal James Whitham.

Below Getting a lesson from Mick Doohan in my first-ever 500 GP at Donington in 1995.

Left The moment I met Rachel on the Kawasaki stand at the NEC Show in 2005.

Below One of the best feelings in the world – power-sliding my crosser.

Above Big air!

Left I'm lower than lino after my title hopes went up in smoke at Donington in 2000.

Below Bashing fairings with Neil Hodgson at Oulton Park in 2000 before it all ended in the gravel trap and then in court.

Above A celebratory burn-out with my team-mate, James Toseland, after the final race of the 2003 season at Magny-Cours.

Right Suffering from Bell's Palsy at the official test in Valencia, 2002.

Above King Carl jumped over the pit-wall at Valencia to salute Stalker's first-ever podium for the Petronas bike in 2004.

Above A welcome break from superbike action at a local motocross event in 2004.

Below A typical Stalker start at Ollerton in 2006.

Above Nobby the dog, my furry son.

might be some light at the end of the tunnel. Could I really become a full-time motorbike racer?

Padgett's obviously thought so, because they had already set the ball rolling to try and secure me a place in the 250cc Grand Prix championship. But before I could even think about that, on the back of my performance in the British GP, they offered me the chance to partner McManus and Arakaki in the forthcoming Czech Republic Grand Prix on the 500. There was a natural break in the Supercup season and I had a comfortable lead in the British National Cup, so this was not going to disrupt my domestic efforts. I did not need much persuading.

Padgett's provided me with a Japanese mechanic for the weekend, and because Que could not get time off work I asked Dicko to come along so that I would have a familiar face working with me. The three of us set off in the smaller of the Padgett's trucks, another noisy glorified horse box. There was not much chance of sleeping on the way because the living quarters were separate from the cab, but the saving grace was that there was no tachometer, so we could maintain a steady 70 m.p.h. However, for someone like me with the attention span of a 3 year old the 2,000-plus miles journey was torture. I had no fingernails left by France and by Germany my face was covered in spots from eating fast food and having my hands around my face all day. Our only amusement was asking the Japanese guy to say things like 'This chicken is wubbewy,' 'Welease Wodewick' or 'Awound the wagged wock the wagged wascal wan.' He had the biggest thighs I have ever seen on a man and it turned out that his previous job was as a kick-start tester for Honda. Quite how he ended up living in Batley and working for Padgett's I will never know. He spent the whole journey barefoot and digging wax out of his ears with a wooden stick. Nice!

As lovely and reliable as the Padgett's were, stuff like the correct paperwork for crossing borders was never going to happen. We had been warned we would be asked for a carnet when entering the Czech Republic and had Padgett's T-shirts and caps at the ready for bribing the border guards to let us in without the necessary documents. As we pulled away from the crossing they were all already proudly sporting their new kit. Within a quarter of a mile we came across a huge building at the side of the road, with bright flashing neon lights announcing 'Girls, Girls, Girls'. A couple of hundred yards further on was another massive brothel. Everything along the road was 'Sexy': Sexy Motel, Sexy Disco, Sexy Burger. Although I had been to Holland, we had not seen any of the sights of the larger cities like Groningen or Amsterdam, so this was a real eye-opener. Dicko and I were peaking and I couldn't wait to ring home and tell my dad. We had no intention of stopping, though, because I would have shat myself if I had gone in one.

'If you get a good result on Sunday we can treat ourselves on the way home,' laughed Dicko.

I was actually in no physical shape after that trip to tackle my second GP at such a technically difficult circuit as Brno. But after just jogging round the circuit, another former road circuit set in the undulating countryside outside the town, I was hooked on it. It was so wide and the television pictures did not do justice to the undulations. It was also nice to see a few familiar faces in the paddock: Niall Mackenzie was there and an Irish guy called Jim McArdle, who was running the Maxwell 250cc team. The Padgetts were also out in force. Uncle Don went to all of the rounds, not exactly as a team coordinator but overseeing everything and making the legendary bacon butties. He was the Padgett's Café. Clive had been spending more and more time with me at the British championships and he also came out for this race.

Despite all this support, it was clear from the word go that I was out of my depth there. On such a wide track the natural racing line was not necessarily the best line, as you had to think two corners ahead. And while Dicko knew a million times more than I did about motorbikes he was used to working on 250ccs and was a long way from being a proficient GP mechanic. The Japanese guy's English was far from perfect and this limited his usefulness, although he could sometimes make his point. After the first practice session he came into the garage with the timesheet and stood next to me as he examined it. He slowly read down the first batch of names – Doohan, Cadalowa, Bawos – and when he didn't find my name he glanced disapprovingly across at me. He ran his finger down the next ten names and I received the same frown. He finally discovered my name near the bottom of the sheet. 'Ahh, so! Change "l" for "n" and here you are: Wanker!' Thanks a bunch – it was no way to kick-start my weekend!

I tried everything to learn the track as quickly as possible, but really struggled with the chicanes. And if I tried to follow a fast rider I would no doubt pick one that was four seconds a lap faster, so I nearly ended up on my ear a few times trying to keep up as they blasted away out of the corners. It also took a while to get used to the way the team worked. After an hour-long morning practice session Uncle Don walked in with sustenance for us riders: not an energy bar or fruit, but a tray of bacon and egg butties. 'Come on, lads, you'll feel better after getting one of these down tha necks,' he bellowed. Then, during a stinking hot afternoon qualifying, Arakaki came into the garage and had forgotten to prepare himself a drink. Uncle Don, still sporting a bright yellow stain down his team shirt from where his egg yolk had dripped from his bacon butty in the morning, had the solution – to offer him a sip from his warm can of Stella. Arakaki gulped it down, probably thinking it was some fancy isotonic concoction.

My frustrations got the better of me when I pulled into the garage during one session, ready to go out on a new tyre, only to find that Dicko had forgotten to plug in the tyre warmer. 'For fuck's sake! This is a Grand Prix, not a fucking club race,' I shouted, before blasting straight back out on my old tyre. It's not often that I lose my cool and it's nearly always when I'm struggling, but I was able to laugh about it with Dicko that evening. I qualified on the fourth row of the grid, which was not embarrassing but was not where I wanted to be after scoring a point in the British GP.

Overnight Clive managed to secure a couple of tyres that Luca Cadalora had discarded after just a handful of laps, and these made a big difference in the morning warm-up session. I broke into the top fifteen on the timesheets and started to feel excited about the race again. Then, on the sighting lap, the bike developed a horrible rattling noise. I pulled the clutch in, let the clutch out, changed up gears, changed down gears, but it would not go away. I was flapping when I arrived at the grid, as I did not have a spare bike. Dicko popped off the fairings and discovered the culprit straight away. A screwdriver, which had gone missing two days earlier, had obviously been left in the belly pan and the plastic handle had welded itself to the exhaust. This calmed me down but the vibration was still there on the warm-up lap and the bike felt like it was going to seize at any moment. I did not dare take my hand off the clutch for the whole race, especially when chucking it into one of the fast corners like turn one in third gear, as the corner entry speed of the two-strokes was incredible. At the end of the race, in which I finished eighteenth, it was discovered that one of the main bearings had gone and was spinning around in the crank case. Nobody moaned about the result but I felt that I had been capable of better. More importantly, I was about half a second a lap down on the sort of times that IRTA had told Clive I should be targeting.

I needed something to take my mind off the weekend's racing so it was good to bump into Niall Mackenzie, who told me that he had arranged to meet Rob Mac at a hotel in the centre of Brno called Hotel Bobby. Apparently there was a decent restaurant, a nightclub downstairs and a strip club upstairs. This did not surprise me because there was even a strip club in the paddock at the circuit. Me and Dicko were peaking in anticipation, not just at the strip show but also at the thought of a decent restaurant. Czech food had not exactly floated my boat; every meal is like Sunday dinner – but shit. After a decent pizza, Rob Mac paid for the four of us to go into the strip club. Bearing in mind the only Czech girls we had bumped into had been working at a MacDonald's and had hairier legs than me and Dicko put together, I was not expecting too much.

Out came two nuns, in full habits and with big wooden crosses dangling from a chain around their necks. I instantly froze, as though I had a full body hard-on. Then they undressed each other and started to kiss and lick one another everywhere, before using the crosses in a way that God had certainly not intended. I could barely move my eyes to check that Dicko was as transfixed as I was. I tease Rachel to this day that I have never seen better-looking naked girls, except her of course. They might not have had the biggest rockets, but they were perfectly formed and I thought things could not get much better. But then, when the nuns had dressed and left the stage, out came a little blonde in all the stunt gear: stockings, suspenders and a big feather boa that she used to hook a bloke from the audience, smaller than me – in height – onto the platform. The size of his cock was a clue that he was a plant in the audience, or maybe all Czech men are blessed in that way. But, although this was not as big a turn-on – there was too much male for my liking and it became a bit seedy when he started to shag her arse off over the bar – I was still mesmerized. When the show was over we all wandered, dazed, down into the nightclub, which was rocking by now and full of more gorgeous Czech girls on the dance floor. It was difficult to focus on the girls, though, because Mackenzie was wearing a trick new pair of Nike trainers, with fluorescent DayGlo laces, and all you could see were these laces bouncing up and down. The energy that these guys had was incredible. It was as though, after being so professional and focused all weekend, they needed a big blow-out on a Sunday night before returning to the normality of pressure and fitness regimes on the Monday. The night served to reinforce everything I had thought after Brands Hatch. If there was the slightest chance that I could become a professional motorbike racer, I was going to grab it with both hands. The Czech nuns had made up my mind! I have raced in the Czech Republic many times since then and it never disappoints.

The journey home, before the invention of Red Bull and never with the correct change for a piss in the various countries we passed through, was never-ending, although it did provide enough time to talk about the nuns over and over again. The only highlight was when the Japanese guy, who had seized the chance for a kip at the back and thought we had stopped for good when we came to a halt at a toll barrier, got out of the truck wearing just his boxer shorts and holding his ear pick. We drove off, leaving him yawning and puzzled until he realized he needed to chase us a couple of hundred yards down the motorway to keep us happy.

Back in England it was time to get my head down and concentrate on trying to win the Supercup. The next race was at Cadwell, a circuit which suited bikes like mine with a bit more torque. I desperately needed a good round. Sure enough and typical of Chris Walker's luck, as you will discover as the story unfolds, the bike let me down for the first time all year. Granted, I'm lucky to do what I do and lucky to be here in some ways, but this was just the first of many instances of my luck running out when it really counted. At the halfway point of the race I was challenging for the lead and the bike was really flying. Now I know that your bike is never faster than just before it is about to seize. I was tipping into the fast first corner and the bike locked. I just managed to grab the clutch in time and, after a small slide, ran off down the escape road, which was more like a motocross track. I managed to keep it upright but the con rod had snapped and come out of the front of the crank cases. Even worse, Robinson had won the race and my championship challenge was all but over. With another race left, however, I was desperate to carry on battling even though I didn't have a spare engine.

Nigel Bosworth was still supported by Honda that year and I knew that he had a spare engine so I asked if I could borrow it for the afternoon race. 'You are welcome to use it,' he said, 'but don't expect too much. It's really bog standard.' It was then all hands on deck to fit this new engine and switch a few of the trick parts from my engine. The bike was ready just thirty minutes before the start of the afternoon race and I managed to finish third, beating Bozzy in the process. It's always easy when a new kid appears on the block, as happened with Casey Stoner at the start of this year in MotoGP, to attribute his success to better machinery. But Bozzy treated me with a lot more respect after that result. This was important to me because a rider I still looked up to now knew that my previous results had not just been down to the bike. It was still mathematically possible for me to win the title at the final Supercup round at Brands, but Robinson only needed to finish the races to clinch it, which he did. I had two great results, third and second, and finished second in the championship, which was pretty unheard of in just my second season of racing. But I could not help thinking what might have been if my bike had not seized at Cadwell, as I was less than 25 points behind Robinson in the final standings.

All that was left to do was to wrap up the British National Cup at Donington. The meeting also featured a special Shell International Race with most of the top British Superbike riders like Steve Hislop, who had just won the Supercup title in superbikes, his team-mate on the Devimead Ducatis, Ray Stringer, Michael Rutter, Jim Moodie and Matt Llewellyn, and also two of the big names from World Superbikes, Aaron Slight on the Castrol Honda and Simon Crafar on another factory RC45, the Rumi Honda.

Clive managed to blag us a space at the back of the Devimead garage because we did not take up much space with just one bike and a few spare wheels. Our practice day was Friday and race on Saturday, whereas the international race boys practised on Friday and qualified on Saturday before two races on Sunday. I qualified on pole for our race and then watched the others in action. Hizzy was up in the top three or four but had injured himself during the week after falling downstairs at home, maybe in the aftermath of his championship celebrations. You could tell he was uncomfortable on the bike and overnight on Friday he decided not to continue for the weekend and suggested to his boss, unbeknown to me, that I take his place. So I turned up for my race on the Saturday and could have been knocked over with a feather when the Devimead boss asked me whether I wanted to take Steve's place for the rest of the weekend.

'You are joking, aren't you? Course I want to, but you had better ask Clive,' I said. Clive was fine with it, as the two race days didn't clash and I basically only had to stay upright in my race to clinch the title. So I sat on Hizzy's bike and it immediately felt perfect; all that was needed was to swap the gears to the road bike way of one down and five up. Most racers have them one up and five down, but some including Chris Vermeulen, Max Biaggi and John Reynolds, for example, have them the way I do.

There was only a matter of minutes before the morning practice started so I rushed into my leathers and was just about to head off down pit-lane when Hizzy's mechanic, a great bloke called Martin Bennett, who went on to become Whitham's mechanic in World Superbikes with Suzuki, gripped my arm. 'Those are Hizzy's lucky fairings. He has had them on all year, so don't crash it,' he said. My arse fell out.

Even on my out-lap I could tell that the thing was a missile: a bit heavier in feeling than my 250cc, but the fast and flowing character-istics of Donington helped. I built up speed in my first two laps and started to push. I went into Redgate, got on the gas and short-shifted from third up to fifth, flicked it left down Craner Curves and dropped back down to third for the Old Hairpin. Maybe I went in too fast or leant it over too far for a superbike, but the front end folded and, in slow motion, all I could see was gravel, sky, gravel, sky, gravel, sky. Bits of Ducati were flying past me and I looked up to see Hizzy's lucky fairings smash into smithereens. I was unhurt but a bit dazed and bewildered, as I had forgotten what it was like to crash. While limping to the tyre wall I spotted his dashboard, which looked pretty expensive, so I thought I had better salvage something. I did not dare make my way back to the garage as I had never crashed anyone else's bike before. When you crash your own you know you have a bill waiting, but not a bollocking. So I stayed put for the rest of the session, refusing a number of lifts from riders who were cruising round. When the van came to pick up what was left of the bike I climbed in the back with it and was locked in pitch darkness during the drive back to the pits. I could hear people telling the driver which garage I was in and then the doors opened to bright sunshine. It was like Steve McQueen being let out of the cooler, and I braced myself for the angry reception.

Martin was the first team member that I saw. 'Great job, Chris!' he said, patting me on the back. 'Great job? I have just totalled your bike,' I thought, trying to detect any sarcasm in his tone. 'You are on the front row behind Slight and Crafar – not bad for three laps,' he added. It was my get-out-of-jail-free card, and nobody mentioned the damage. Clive was a bit concerned that I would be OK for my own race but I had escaped with just a few cuts and bruises and I won the National Cup race to clinch the title, which I suppose is my one and only national title. I had also been entered into an open race that afternoon, riding my 250cc against the bigger bikes. I also managed to finish on the rostrum of that race, won by Matt Llewellyn, so it was turning into a dream weekend, with a bit of prize money thrown in for good measure.

By the next morning I was very nervous and it didn't help that it had rained heavily overnight and was wet for the morning warm-up. 'Don't fall off, don't fall off,' I kept telling myself throughout the twenty-minute session. Towards the end, as I braked into the Esses, I heard an almighty noise behind me before a Castrol Honda came spinning past. Aaron Slight had lost the front end and missed me by inches. This did nothing to ease my already frayed nerves. But the track dried out and I made a fantastic start to the first race. Slight and Crafar played with us for a couple of laps before clearing off and I then ended up in a terrific battle for third place with all the top British superbike lads. On the final lap Jim Moodie made a big move to dive underneath me at the Esses, but after what seemed like an eternity fighting for a podium position there was no way I was going to give it up on the final lap. I let the brakes off and leant in towards him, forcing him to sit up. All I then needed to do was to ride defensively through the Melbourne Loop and Goddard's and there I was, in my first race on a superbike, sharing the podium with Slight and Crafar, although unfortunately the Michelin cap fitted as badly as the Dunlop one and my ears stuck out the sides again. The bike broke down on the warm-up lap for the second race of the day, which in one way was a relief because it was unlikely that I would have been able to improve on third place and probably, knowing my luck, would have crashed again.

I had crammed a huge amount into my first two years of racing. Sure, I should have started sooner; you only have to look at lads of 15 and 16 who are winning 125cc GP races now. But my schooling in race craft had come in my motocross days, so I knew how to hold a defensive line or how to chase someone down in front. And the Supercup was a real cut-and-thrust class, so I learnt a lot from some very experienced riders. I suppose I had also already developed a bit of a distinctive style. I was never dangerous, but I was perhaps a bit looser than most and I have always preferred it when the bike moves around underneath me. People say that I look on the edge. I guess I am because I am always riding as fast as I can, but I don't think I am on the ragged edge. I know my limits. That style has probably been a factor in my popularity, as the crowd can see that I am always giving everything. Maybe my style already suited superbikes, where you tend to stop the bike mid-corner and then fire it out, more than 250cc bikes, where my aggression was not conducive to carrying optimum corner speed. My outing in the 250cc GP, when the likes of Biaggi were coming round the outside and tearing off a rip-off mid-corner, was an indication of that.

So, knowing that I was now committed to trying to become a full-time racer, I had a big decision to make about where my future lay for 1996 and beyond. And it proved to be a decision that shaped my racing career.

13

Spicy Stalker

Within a few months I was a full-time professional bike racer. It sounds easy but, as ever, there were a few sleepless nights before and after the decision about what to do for the following season. I was already aware that Padgett's were trying to secure a 250cc Grand Prix slot for me, although it was not a foregone conclusion. Competition was tough for places on the grid and Jamie Robinson had already claimed one spot, so the organizers were not desperate for another British rider. It was also unclear which bike would be available if I was accepted, as it was down to Honda where they allocated their factory bikes, as well as the trick race kits for other teams. It all seemed a bit up in the air, and although I wanted to do a season in GPs this was a nagging doubt. Padgett's were also unable to pay me any kind of wage and I didn't fancy having to do a paper round to pay my direct debits during the months I wasn't away racing. Any prize money would go to the team and I wasn't in a position to start demanding money from leathers or helmet manufacturers. Even when I eventually learned that Padgett's had secured a slot in 250cc GPs after all, and with the best race kit, I did not regret not taking the opportunity.

My mind was set on another career path. I had raced at Grand Prix level on 250cc and 500cc bikes and not been particularly competitive. But in my first outing on a superbike I had beaten some of the best of the British riders and only finished behind guys who were winning world championship races. Something seemed to have naturally clicked and there was another exciting opportunity beginning to take shape.

Bridgestone, who knew that I wanted to move on to bigger and better things, told me that an American team, Erion Racing, were on the look-out for up-and-coming riders. The team was formed when brothers Craig and Kevin Erion went their separate ways to form Two Brothers Racing and Erion Racing respectively. They raced two riders per bike in two-hour races in the Supersport 600cc and Formula Xtreme classes, but also had plans to move into superbike racing. I travelled alone to the team base in Anaheim but was met by Kevin, a typical American – boisterous and friendly, not 30 stone in weight. We travelled in a big Rubber Duck Truck all the way to the Firebird International Raceway in Phoenix, Arizona, where the team was running the rule over a number of riders. We never actually warned any fellow truckers about any 'smokies in a plain brown wrapper' – a cop car to you and me – but it was real '10-4 good buddy' territory.

They wanted to see me on both bikes and I was excited about my first time on a 600. But it was set up for race shifters, one up and five down. They were reluctant to change it because it was likely that any team-mate I might have would ride this way. It was one of only a couple of times that my road preference has bitten me on the ass, but there was no way I could change at this point. Also, it didn't handle as well as my 250 so I struggled in comparison to the guys with more experience of these bikes.

In Formula Xtreme, for bikes of any capacity, the rules allowed 900cc Fireblades to be converted into 1150cc machines. I had never been on a bike with so much power – it was the bollocks. It had ridiculous horsepower and torque, with Wilwood brakes which helped make it really ridable. A lot is made about the safety of American circuits and, yes, there was a brick wall along the drag strip start-finish straight. But if you came off there at 180 m.p.h. a brick wall was going to be the least of your problems. And when I came round on one of my first flying laps, rear wheel spinning and smoking up, broad-siding onto the straight, Kevin's eyes lit up. I could tell he was thinking: 'We want this lad on that bike.' I finished one of the quickest riders there, including the guys who had raced the bike the previous year, and Kevin told me that they would be considering me for a ride, once their plans were firmed up.

The whole trip was like a dream come true. I met the head honcho of Honda in the USA, was taken round the Honda factory and saw all Jeremy McGrath's motocross and Supercross bikes. On the night before I was due to leave I was invited to the birthday party of Miguel Duhamel, the reigning Supersport champion on the Smokin' Joe's Honda. I remember thinking he was around 70 at the time, so he must be approaching 90 now!

Back at home I received a call from Kevin, telling me that they wanted me to ride for them, but in the Supersport and Formula Xtreme championships. Riders often participate in more than one class in America, reducing the costs for the team but also making the most of the limited number of rounds for themselves. Honda had not come up with the extra money to compete in the most prestigious class, the American Superbike championship. When they finally did, a few years later, Erion Racing went on to win the superbike championship pretty quickly with Kurtis Roberts. I have often thought what might have been if I had accepted their offer and taken a low-pressure ride for two years in the States. It was an attractive package and nowadays riders like Ben Spies cannot afford to leave America for the world championships because the money is too good over there. But I have never based decisions on the money on offer, and by this time I had been presented with two more options to race in the British Superbike championship.

The first came from the Devimead team, who had parted company with Ducati and wanted to run a Kawasaki team with me and Steve Hislop. It was flattering to be considered for the same team as the reigning British champion. However, it was one thing to run the Ducati 916, the best superbike around at the time, but a different kettle of fish to create a competitive race bike from something that came straight out of the crate with a number plate on. It just didn't seem to add up.

My other offer came from Hoss Elm, of Ducati importers Moto Cinelli, who had previously run Jamie Whitham in World Super-bikes. He was an Iranian bloke with a wooden leg, the result of a motorway car accident, who seemed pretty businesslike. His big fat cigars smelt fantastic, at any rate. I knew him from working in the shop and along with many others thought he was friendly, but a little eccentric. His plan was to run Whitham's world championship bike from the previous year in the British championship and had promoted a great guy called Eric MacFarland to run the team. Hoss was talking to a number of other riders, including Terry Rymer. He was also offering me £20,000 a year, an offer that I could not refuse and more than I had ever dreamed of earning. I had to pinch myself. Two years after starting to race I was accepting a ride with Ducati in the British Supercup. This was like a fairytale. But, while most fairytales have a happy ending, this one didn't.

Soon after the New Year a test was organized for me at Cadwell Park. When I rode Hizzy's Ducati at Donington the bike was already set up for the circuit and the best tyres had been selected. This was the same specification bike, but Whitham's bike was not set up for cold days at circuits like Cadwell Park. It was a beast to handle, but I was comforted by the knowledge that it could be made to feel like Hizzy's had done at Donington. In the meantime, with so little experience on a superbike, I did not have much idea what to do to make it feel better. Even so, I was buzzing after the test, despite finding it very demanding. I probably suffered a few more sleepless nights wondering whether I had made the right choice, but I had made my bed so I had to lie in it. Nowadays I possibly worry even more about similar choices, because I know the consequences of making a bad move.

Two more pieces of the team jigsaw then slotted into place. Terry Rymer, who had raced in World Superbikes for Muzzy Kawasaki and had won World Endurance titles, had signed for the team and was, by all accounts, a top bloke. Hoss had also found a title sponsor in Old Spice, the men's aftershave, which had been old hat even when I was a kid. I think it had become fashionable to resurrect old brands, despite their smelling of embalming fluid. But the mock-up graphics of the bike livery were mint, with the white sailing ship on the side. In an interview with MCN I said that Terry could be the Old and I could be the Spice. We were reminiscing during a recent Eurosport appearance and Terry apparently thought I was a 'facking little cant' for saying this before we had even met.

Since leaving Team No Limits I had continued the relationship with leathers manufacturer Texport and Dave Pickworth, who had become a good friend during the previous season. He took me over to Texport's base in Rimini to size me up for my first made-to-measure set of leathers. OK, they arrived without the agreed white patch on the front and had to be sent back, but they were the bollocks as far as I was concerned. Wendy Bradley at Pheonix, the distributors for Arai, agreed to provide me with a few helmets and talked about the possibility of producing a replica further down the line. I stuck with a bold-looking paint job designed by Paul Farrell, inspired by the Japanese rider Keiichi Kitigawa, which was black with a splash of colour down the side.

Carl Gretton also continued to be as generous and helpful as ever. During the previous year he helped out with any bills that were not covered by my prize money. This year, now that I no longer had to worry about those bills, he again secretly worked behind the scenes on other ways in which he could help. Carl always tended to go large and this time he came up with a massive 30-foot American-style Fleetwood Flair motorhome, which he paid for through his business so that he could entertain his staff and clients at events like the British Grand Prix, providing the kind of thrill for them that took their minds off the fact that they had the dullest jobs in the world. Although Carl and a few others would also stay in it nearer race day, which was great fun, I could now take myself out of the way for the first couple of days of a race meeting and concentrate on the job in hand rather than wasting time travelling to and from bed and breakfasts on a scooter. All of a sudden I was doing all the things that professional racers took for granted and everything was going to plan. Hello! Earth calling! This is Chris Walker we are talking about!

The call came two weeks before the season was due to start and one week before the big curtain-raising official test at Donington. It was from Hoss's right-hand men, Eric. Not only had Hoss lost a leg, he had lost his bollocks somewhere along the line, too. (What is it with me and these fuckers with one leg? More of that later!) Eric told me that Hoss, in his wisdom, had decided to pull out of the project. If someone could be found to buy the team then he would recommend that I still have the ride; if not, the job was fucked. I was spewing and *MCN* rang me for my reaction before I had the chance to cool down. I was as green as grass as far as the press went and I basically let rip, calling Hoss and Moto Cinelli all the names under the sun. Hoss hit back, claiming that I had been out of breath after five laps at Cadwell Park. OK, I might still have had a bit of puppy fat, but I had given up work before Christmas and spent the rest of the time preparing for the new season, running, swimming and working out at a new gym. Although Cadwell had been an eye-opener, I was fully confident that I could recreate the set-up and form that I had found on Hislop's bike just months earlier.

The whole slanging match became very messy and when I read *MCN* I thought: 'Oh no! Did I really say that?' I did not regret what I said, just the way I said it. It was understandable, though, because it looked as though I was about to miss out on the best British championship for years. Rob Mac had brought Niall Mackenzie back from GPs and Jamie Whitham back from World Superbikes to ride for his Cadbury's Boost Yamaha team. Hislop was on the Devimead Kawasaki, Reynolds was back from World Superbikes with Reve Racing, Ian Simson and Jim Moodie were on Hondas, and there was some good new talent emerging. Plus, I had given up the chance to go to 250 GPs.

This was my introduction to the big, bad world of motorcycle racing. The further up the ladder you climb, the more time-wasters there are. Not the grassroots guys, or the riders themselves, but the blokes who control the purse strings. So far I had only dealt with the Padgetts or Dave Pickworths of the industry, who delivered on their promises. But I soon started to learn that the money side is often all fur coat and no knickers. I guess I am still bitter towards Hoss Elm, because he let me down and nobody likes that. Riders are called all the names under the sun if they ever leave teams in the lurch – and rightly so. But nobody ever seems to kick up the same fuss when the rider is the victim.

However, out of the blue I received a call from Robin Mortimer, brother of the racer Chaz Mortimer, who was willing to buy the team off Hoss. Robin owned a Ferrari dealership and had raced cars himself. He sat me down at his home, introduced me to Jim McArdle, who I had already met while he was managing a 250cc GP team the previous year, and tried to find out how I still felt about the whole thing. He agreed with a lot of what I said, but gave me a bit of a lesson in what to say and what not to say publicly. Obviously the whole situation was making Old Spice a little uncomfortable. He was quite up front that nothing would be easy and that we were already behind the competition, explaining that the bikes which had been bought from Hoss needed a lot more attention than he had expected. Ducatis required a lot more expensive spare parts than their Japanese equivalents, especially crank cases that had to be replaced every 2000 km or so. An engine would basically last a couple of race meetings, and I guess that Robin thought the bikes would be ready to go racing, when in fact all the engines needed an overhaul. Robin even found that the necessary parts weren't available from Moto Cinelli, proving that Hoss must have known that he was not going to race long before he told any of us.

An experienced engine guy, Stewart Johnstone, was brought in to rebuild the engines from second-hand parts, and some experienced guys like the sombre crew chief Rob Tolton and Chris Anderson were drafted into the team. Part of me felt really bad that there was no place for Que, especially after our drunken heart-to-heart in Assen. But this was now my career and neither of us knew enough about a Ducati to provide any technical input to the team. Que was just so happy that I had the chance to take my career to the next level. There was no way he was going to stand in my way and he continued to attend a lot of races as a pal, which was important in what was to become a tough year.

The new teams were out in force for the official test at Donington, all proudly wearing their new team gear, except for me in my flawed leathers. Rymer was fast straight out of the box on a cold opening day and found the bike easy to ride after being on the four-cylinder Kawasakis for so long. Mackenzie and Whitham were also on the pace immediately, on the factory Yamaha Belgarda bikes from the previous year's World Superbike championship, and it was soon clear that the season was going to be all about Yamaha versus Ducati. The Yamahas were quite nimble but did not have the grunt of the Ducatis, and were therefore quite well suited to the tight British circuits. My first day came to an abrupt end when oil leaked from the clutch onto the back tyre, although I narrowly avoided a crash on my first day at work.

The opening round of the season was also at Donington on the following weekend. Whitham and Mackenzie immediately started to set new lap records and were faster than the World Superbike guys had been there. I was fourth in race one and then found myself in a race-long battle for a podium place with Niall in the second race, after he made a mistake at the Esses and lost touch with James. I would pass him into the Old Hairpin, then he would squirt back past on the way up to McLean's. We were pretty evenly matched going into Redgate and swapped places there. On the final lap I got the better over Niall going into Redgate and pulled away through Craner Curves and had a début second place in my grasp. Going under Starkey's Bridge and around the Schwantz Curves the rear let go and I had the biggest crash ever. Again the bike was in pieces, and although the damage turned out to be fairly superficial I was rattled. I was distraught to miss out on the podium place, but the result gave me a lot of heart that I could mix it with these guys straight away.

Next up was Thruxton, a circuit I had only been to once before. There was moss growing through cracks and big craters in the Tarmac. It looked like a five-lane section of the M1 in places, with over-banding joining the various bits of track and former airfield runway together. At superbike speeds the bumps were horrendous. I struggled during qualifying and never really worked out how to ride there, with higher gearing needed for more corner speed. It just didn't suit my aggressive style and still doesn't, as I have never had good results there. Rymer had not been present for the two days of qualifying. The uncertainty at the start of the season forced him to also accept a ride for Suzuki in the World Endurance championship. His race was on the Saturday so he was able to get to Thruxton in time for the Sunday races. I had qualified on the second row of the grid but Terry jumped straight on the bike and finished fastest in the morning warm-up session. 'I want his set-up,' I thought. As it happened my set-up did not matter when my chain snapped the second I let the clutch out on the start line. I have seen some horrendous crashes on the start line because there is nothing much a rider can do, except tiptoe to keep his bike upright and hope that the twenty bikes behind miss him. I was on the outside of the grid, which helped the others avoid me on this occasion, but that kind of unreliability proved to be a sign of things to come.

14

Frenzied Stalker

Terry Rymer had become like an older brother to me and took me under his wing from day one, providing pointers at the end of the day if I was struggling. He also gave me tips to improve my training regime and constantly had a dig at me for being a bit chubby, probably a stone and a half heavier than I am now. I don't think I ate a biscuit all year without him noticing. He was also critical of the fact that I did not like to wear a back protector. His way of persuading me that it might be a good idea was to punch me in the back at every available opportunity and say, 'It will hurt more than that when you fall off.' I didn't need to fall off; I finished every race weekend black and blue from Terry's punches. I eventually gave in and he gave me a small, thin Kushitani protector, which I used for years until it was swiped at Monza. Only an Italian would nick a second-hand sweaty back protector.

You always aim to beat your team-mate, but even though I had beaten Terry at Donington I wasn't often in the same league. Like Mackenzie and Rob Mac, he had an aura about him and was confident in everything he did, including grabbing a bird's arse and getting away with it, something he schooled me in very early on. We had a lot of fun on the Old Spice promotional days, organized by a lady called Jane Rose. She had a tough job keeping us in check, standing in a Boots store for the day in team gear with a race bike. While she squirted customers with Old Spice, Terry and I would disappear for ages wandering round the shops or having a coffee. I panicked that I would get in trouble but Terry was worldly wise in these matters. I suppose our punishment was receiving an endless supply of Old Spice, which I still have in cupboards to this day because not even my dad would take it.

One of the PR duties was in Northern Ireland before the North West 200, the famous road race around the streets of Portrush, Portstewart and Coleraine. Terry was actually racing but the team had decided, for whatever reason, that they wanted me to concentrate on the British championship. Maybe there were only enough funds for one rider and they thought it was too much of a risk to throw me in at the deep end of road circuit racing. But I was encouraged to stay on for the races, maybe to gain some experience for the future. Terry had somewhere to stay over there but nowhere to hang out during the day and said he would pay for me to take my motorhome so he could use it as a base. That seemed like a good excuse for a road trip with Dicko.

We headed off up the motorway to Scotland, dreading the 90 miles of single carriageway before Stranraer and the interminable crossing with the ferry on quarter throttle to save money. With the turn-off to Stranraer a few miles away I decided it would be a good idea to hand over the wheel to Dicko and go for a pee. With the cruise control on there was no need to stop while we switched over. It did not actually matter when I chose to go, either on a motorway or a windy road, because once I was in the toilet Dicko would start to swerve so that I peed all over myself and the walls. So I cleaned myself up afterwards and took the chance to put the kettle on the back gas ring. As I waited for the whistle to sound on the kettle I noticed that we were approaching the Stranraer turn-off.

'Off at the next junction, Dicko,' I said.

'Yeah, right oh!' he replied, as I went back to check on the kettle. I looked again and we were just yards from the junction.

'Dicko, this fucking turn!'

He veered off to the left but had forgotten that we were on cruise control, which did not switch off until you dabbed the brake. The motorhome was nearly on two wheels and I lunged towards the cooker, mouthing 'kettttlllle' in slow motion. I missed the kettle and smashed my chest on the corner of the table. As I landed the kettle fell off, pouring boiling water all over my feet.

'All right back there, chief? Good job you reminded me, I nearly missed that one,' said Dicko, oblivious to the carnage in the back. I was gasping for breath on the floor, unaware that I had broken two ribs, and was peeling the burnt skin of my legs off the lino. What's more, we didn't get a coffee until Stranraer.

Mind you, Terry could easily have finished the weekend with injuries far worse than mine. The team had pushed the forks further through the yokes to increase stability, not taking into account that the brake hoses were now going to be a bit on the short side, especially when the front wheel was in the air and the forks were fully extended. During practice Terry was braking from 180 m.p.h. down to 50 m.p.h. for the tight left into Metropole and back onto the Seafront. The constant stress on the hoses had obviously weakened them and they just blew off when he hit the brakes, leaking brake fluid onto the front disc in a cloud of smoke. I have never seen anything like it. Terry was frantically pumping the front brake, but with no response, but then he had the presence of mind to change quickly down through the gears while jamming on the back brake. He snaked towards the barrier, still at speed, and miraculously managed to guide the bike through the tiniest of gaps in the fence onto a slip road. He is very lucky to be with us today – through no fault of his own – and this is the one incident that has put me off road racing. I was scared for him and he must have been shaken for the rest of the weekend because he backed off a bit for the races.

On the last night everyone headed to Kellys Complex in Portrush, a massive nightclub with different music on many floors and packed with pretty young Irish students from the University of Ulster, in nearby Coleraine. Having had such a sheltered upbringing I was now beginning to see a bit of the world and experiencing the temptations that most lads do at the age of 17, not 24. With Lisa at home, I never had any intention of straying but I had not suddenly grown wings, either. I was no angel and neither was Dicko. But on this night we had no luck with the Irish. By the end of the night we were well and truly wankered and had tried to ship into almost every girl with a pulse, with embarrassing results. I had somehow been placed in control of a car for the night; I think it had been lent to Terry by the organizers, as racers are always extremely well looked after in Ireland. It seemed like a good idea for me to drive back to the paddock, although I have to stress that I have not driven over the limit since. And technically I was not driving on the road, because two wheels were always on the kerb. Dicko had wound his window down and was lifting up the skirts of girls as we drove past. Somehow we managed to persuade three girls to accept a lift back to the paddock, on the promise that there was beer in the motorhome – a blatant lie. Dicko squeezed in between two of them in the back seat and, through the mirror, I could see him rubbing his hands in glee. He was no stud muffin, but he certainly had more experience in these matters than I did. I did have a game plan, though, and showed the other girl around the motorhome like it was a four-bedroom semi-detached, finally arriving at the bedroom and closing the door softly behind me. All was going smoothly – even my broken ribs and burnt feet had stopped hurting – until I discovered she was wearing tights. Now that's not right when you have been dancing away in a sweaty club for four hours.

'Where are you going, Chris?' she asked, as I slipped off the bed.

'Just checking that your two friends are OK,' I said, opening the door to find Dicko snogging one and groping the other's tits. 'Yeah, I think they are in safe hands,' I whispered back. But the moment had been lost and there was an even more sobering moment when they all asked for a lift back to their digs.

The PR duties came thick and fast back in England, too, and the team asked me to attend the annual *Performance Bikes* Frenzy weekend. The magazine pushed the boat out once a year and hired a track for punters to ride round on Saturday, have a few beers at a party on the Saturday night, and ride again on the Sunday if they were in any fit state. I was just expected to do a few laps each afternoon, jump the Mountain a few times and pull a few wheelies. I was borrowing a red

3-series BMW company car from Carl Gretton for a few weeks at the time – probably the fastest thing I had driven – and had placed a Ducati sticker in the rear window. Although I wasn't late, I was in a rush to arrive as usual and was nailing it along fast country roads that I knew quite well from going to the Mablethorpe Beach Race. When I shot over a blind crest at about 90 m.p.h., out of the dazzling sunlight appeared a cop with a radar gun. There wasn't even a chance to brake and through the rear-view mirror I could see him spinning in the road before wiping the dust-storm that I had created out of his eyes. I was in the shit – so I pinned it.

It would be pretty obvious to him that I would be heading for Cadwell, so I turned off the main road only to come to a dead end. My heart hadn't raced as fast since the last time I had been chased by the cops on my bike. The only option was to turn down a gravel track, not ideal territory for a lowered-suspension sports car. I skirted around the edge of Cadwell for about fifteen minutes before I found a way in through a farm field gate and edged my way towards the Old Spice truck. I was parking up, thinking I was in the clear, when the cop leapt across the bonnet Sweeney style, dragged me out of the car and pinned me up against it. He didn't handcuff me but he might as well have done and the commotion had attracted quite a crowd, including the rest of my team, who were pissing themselves laughing.

'Maybe next time you want to drive like a maniac you shouldn't carry a sticker in your car window telling me where you work,' he said.

'I'm really sorry, officer. I never drive like that normally, but you can see all these people were waiting for me,' I pleaded.

'Better late than dead,' he said. What exactly does that phrase mean? I wasn't planning on being dead – I just wanted to arrive a bit sooner. He charged me with speeding and failing to stop and I was told to appear at Louth Magistrates, but not to drive myself there as a ban was expected. At the courts I bumped into Malc Wheeler, from *Classic Bikes* magazine, who had been contesting a parking ticket.

'Their mood is ugly, Chris. You could be looking at soap-on-a-rope for failing to stop,' he warned. With Dad as my lucky charm, my school uniform out of the wardrobe and a smart new haircut, butter wouldn't melt in my mouth. But the cop had really churched up his statement: 'I heard the engine, revving to a considerable degree, from almost a mile away but was still amazed at the speed of the vehicle that appeared like a bat out of hell. The confident young driver was wearing fashionable sporty sunglasses ...' It is fair to say he was not on my side but I switched to full-on brown-nose mode and told the lady magistrate how much the public and sponsors were depending on me and that I never liked to let people down. When the bench retired I got the customary thumbs up from Dad. 'Shit hot that, youth,' he mouthed from the public gallery.

'Obviously we are not going to ban you, Mr Walker,' said the magistrate. I nearly leapt out of the box when I was fined £300 and given six points. I was even allowed an extended period to pay the fine. Malc Wheeler was handed a harsher penalty for parking on a single yellow in Louth.

The journey to that *Performance Bikes* Frenzy wasn't the only frenzied action of the weekend. After eventually making it out onto the track in the afternoon I needed a drink at night to settle my nerves. David Pickworth had brought his wife Serena and Lisa down to stay at the Admiral Rodney in Horncastle, where a few of the *Performance Bikes* lads were also staying. It was also the night of the 100 m final of the Atlanta Olympics, where Linford Christie had a good chance of gold, so there was quite a buzz about the place. After our meal we settled in the bar and the hotel set up a portable 10-inch television so that those willing to stay up until 2 a.m. could watch. Lisa and Serena went to bed, which was just as well because a group of girls from the wedding upstairs descended on the bar. One stood out from the crowd, but for all the wrong reasons. She wore a stunning red dress and had a nice body, but the rest of her was very manly; big hands, a fuzzy top lip and a strong jaw line. The Lady in Red – or was it Laddie in Red – also came to watch Linford and his Lunchbox, which barely fitted on the 10-inch screen, and we realized she also had a slight speech impediment. When it was her round David cruelly asked for a Becksh and I asked for a shpritzer, although neither of us were drinking these drinks. And when she asked David his name, the first thing he could think of was Mishter Becksh.

There were more restarts to the 100 m race than at a round of the British Superbike championship at Mallory Park and I was starting to get bored – and drunk. So I sidled up to Dave and jokingly asked: 'Are you going to tamper with her or what? Because if you don't, I will.'

'No, no. If anyone's going to it will be me, thanks very much,' Dave replied, coming over all defensive. When the bar started to clear after the race, eventually won by Donovan Bailey after Christie was disqualified for two false starts, Mrs Becksh invited us both back to her room and looked even more hideous with all the lights on. Neither of us had form for spit-roasting, so I collapsed on the bed, pretending to be unconscious, as Mrs Becksh climbed onto David's knee on the chair. She started to kiss him and rub his crotch, while David was keeping one eye on me keeping one eye on him.

'I can't do thish in front of your friend,' she said. 'I don't know you from Adam.'

'We don't know whether you have an Adam's apple,' I thought. 'Or a lunchbox for that matter!' Nevertheless their petting became a bit more frantic and I had to pretend to choke in my sleep when she uttered the immortal line: 'Are you aroushed, Mishter Becksh?' David managed to stay composed and hitched up her dress, revealing the biggest pair of apple-catching knickers, which he then slid partially down. I could not resist. I wet my finger and slid it between her arse cheeks and she seemed to like it, albeit thinking it was David's finger. David could still see me out of the corner of his eye and was struggling to contain himself. Luckily, she sat up quickly, rearranged herself and, after asking whether I was all right because I still appeared unconscious, went to the toilet. It sounded like a race horse.

'Dave, I swear she is standing up in there. Let's do one,' I urged. He needed no second invitation and we bolted out the room and back to our own rooms, where Lisa had never looked so lovely. I did not dare go down for breakfast in case she saw me with Lisa and, telepathically, David had also pretended to be too ill to face the food. While the girls ate we packed our stuff and sneaked out of the back door of the hotel as soon as they finished. We did not see or hear of Mrsh Becksh again.

On the race track, our Ducatis were now proving to be consistently temperamental, and after a couple of crashes I was around sixth in the championship, which rapidly turned into the Cadbury Boost Cup, as Mackenzie and Whitham traded wins. Terry was as fast as them on his day but could not compete with their consistency. Yet there were also some circuits where I was faster than Terry. At Snetterton, for instance, it seemed like we were on different makes of bike. I remember the first time I was there, being almost sucked off my 250cc, when Ian Simpson blasted past down the straight on his Duckham's Norton. It wasn't quite the same with me and Terry this year, but his bike was a turd all weekend. I have always gone well at Snetterton – except for the diabolical effort in 2007. There are not many corners, so not much to get wrong, but it's still a difficult circuit to put a fast lap together on. My Ducati had long legs and took a while to get up to top speed but it did like the fast circuits and I managed to catch and pass Terry during the race for the first time in the season. When a couple of front runners retired or crashed, I came home in second place – my first podium at Superbike Supercup level.

Robin tried everything he could to help us maintain that level of performance, but he could not invent parts or the budget for the parts. He did, however, pay us promptly and it took a long while for my first pay cheque to sink in. I had only ever seen cheques for £5,000 if I had sold a bike, and I was careful not to go out and fritter it away.

Meanwhile Terry had been offered a few rides with the Lucky Strike Suzuki team in the 500cc GPs, replacing Daryl Beattie, who had lost some toes in a bad crash. Again he suggested that me and Dave Pickworth travel with him to the next round, at the Nurburgring in Germany, so that he could use my motorhome as a base, but also so that I could spend a bit more time in the GP paddock. Terry had heard that a Swiss-owned team based in France, Elf 500 Roc, which was also sponsored by Pepsi, had mysteriously dropped their rider, Adrian Bosshard. The team was owned by a mega-rich Swiss guy, Michel

Metraux, who flew in to the races in a private jet with his son. The team ran a Swissauto-designed V4 engine that was built to run in sidecars, for Rolf Biland among others, and solo bikes, while Roc, who had worked with Wayne Rainey in the past, designed the chassis. There wasn't a more powerful engine out there, although the delivery was not the easiest to handle. The other rider was Juan Borja, who had some impressive results like tenth in their début race in Malaysia.

'It's an impressive team,' said Terry. 'Dave can speak German. Why not get him to ask them if you can ride at the British GP?' The team obviously did a bit of homework, and by the time we were home they had offered me the wild card ride at Donington.

I did not want to go behind Robin's back so I let him know as soon as I got the offer. I think he was beginning to feel like Tom Hanks in *The Money Pit* and knew that times were hard for our team. So he did not want to stand in the way of this opportunity. I also wanted to try and arrange a ride on the bike before the GP and we managed to arrange a test at Mallory on the Wednesday of Grand Prix week.

It was difficult to get used to riding a two-stroke again after being on the Ducati, and twisty Mallory probably wasn't the ideal choice for such a powerful machine. Although the engine was a bit brutish, the power was usable and the bike steered well as the settings were all infinitely adjustable. It was a beautiful bike to look at too, especially compared to the Padgett's bike, which had not been especially handsome. There was no gravel rash on the fairings for a start. It also helped that we were running Michelin tyres, which I was used to from the superbike championship. The team made me feel very welcome and spoke much better English than I expected, and probably better than me.

Over the two days of qualifying at Donington I was always around the top fifteen, so there was a chance that if a couple of the others crashed or broke down in the race I might be on for a top ten finish. With ten minutes of the final qualifying session remaining I was not too far behind Borja when the team called me in to fit a qualifying tyre.

'Look, I have never used one of these before. Are you sure it's wise at this late stage?' I asked.

'Don't worry about it. It's just softer rubber with more grip, so you can go faster everywhere,' my tyre technician explained. Faster everywhere? My arse!

That seemed pretty straightforward, so after my out-lap I hooked on the back of one of the faster riders down start-finish and, sure enough, everything seemed so much easier. I was braking later into corners and getting on the gas sooner out of the corners. I was able to select a higher gear through Craner Curves and the bike turned into the Old Hairpin much more easily. I short-shifted from third through to fifth, flipped the bike left under Starkey's and … suffered the identical crash that I had on my Ducati in the first race of the season – except much faster. I cart-wheeled across the grass like an acrobat and almost ended up in the tyre wall, which is a huge distance. Every time I landed I bashed first one wrist, then an ankle, then the other wrist and finally the other ankle. The visor of my helmet was ripped off and it seemed like an eternity before I could catch my first breath. As I hauled myself up onto my feet, I spotted a piece of Old Spice Ducati fairing in the grass, as if I needed a reminder of my identical crash there earlier that year. My whole body was swollen and nobody really knew whether I had broken anything, apart from the bike of course, by the time I left the circuit to rest and ice my injuries at home. I just knew that I had thrown away the chance of a third-row start and would now be starting the next day's race from the back of the fifth row of the grid.

I did not sleep a wink that night because I was in so much agony and I walked to the Clinica Mobile the next morning as though I needed a shit and had not made it to the toilet in time. Dr Costa told me that nothing was broken, but I had sprained both ankles and wrists. My right ankle was so bad that I could barely move it at all and the team had to change the position of the gear shifter so that my foot would fit underneath. I wanted to save any painkillers for the race so I went out on the bike for morning warm-up before any injections and was barely able to ride round. I have never had a tattoo, but it felt as though I was having one when they gave me about sixteen injections in each ankle and a dozen in each wrist and forearm just before the race. Add in the various painkilling concoctions and I barely knew what planet I was on. I could not even tell whether my gloves were on, although I did not let them know that because the officials would have stopped me from racing. I was in agony when I finished the race, just outside the points in sixteenth. Although I was furious to learn the hard way that the extra grip from a qualifier was not always a good thing, the team seemed pretty upbeat and impressed that I had even bothered to go out. David appeared to have built up a pretty good relationship with them over the weekend and the team boss thanked me for my efforts, adding: 'Maybe see you again soon.'

On the Monday morning I felt as though I had been thrown from a speeding train in just my underwear. And there was no Clinica Mobile to provide me with painkilling injections. The plight of the Old Spice team didn't help my mood, either. Robin Mortimer was still being a star, now ploughing in some of his own money when it turned out the Old Spice title sponsorship deal was not as big as first thought. Terry had also been racing at the GP and, after taking the opportunity yet again to remind me that his back protector had prevented even more injury, he then told me that he was under pressure from Lucky Strike to concentrate on GPs and quit the Old Spice team.

'If you get the chance, Chris, take it. The Old Spice thing is going to go tits up. You might get a bit of a knocking if you leave now, but you won't get any thanks for hanging around. You've got to look after facking number one,' he said. By now Terry was a good pal and, not only was he a wise old bird, he also had my best interests at heart. It was all becoming a bit disheartening until I received a phone call from David Pickworth.

'I've had a call from the team,' he said.

'Yeah? What does Robin want now?' I asked.

'No, not that team – the Elf team. They want you to do the next Grand Prix in Austria because they don't think they have seen your full potential. There might be a chance of a few more rides after that, too,' said David.

15

Collared Stalker

I was very keen to do everything above board, as Robin Mortimer had paid my second instalment as promised despite the cash problems of the Old Spice team, so I immediately rang to inform him of the offer from the Grand Prix team. Initially he was not too keen on the idea, because he knew I had already been injured once and thought that further mishap might affect his team's performance in the British championship. He also wanted to know whether I was going to be paid by them – questions I had not really wanted to ask until I had his permission to accept the ride. 'Listen, Chris. I have already said that the last thing I want to do is stand in your way. I have been a racer myself and know that these opportunities don't grow on trees. Just remember who is paying your wages, OK?' he said.

So, after a couple of weeks' recuperation, I drove to the A1-Ring in Austria with David, who had by now become a bit of a wingman, performing some of the roles of a manager without taking any percentage. Lisa, Mum and Dad were all travelling out later in a private plane, part-owned by one of Carl Gretton's mates, Phillip Lyons. Although I was still a bit sore, I was perfectly fit to race a bike and even managed to jog round the track, a wicked circuit set on a big hillside, on the Thursday. I also gave the team a bit of a hand in setting up the garage and I don't think they were used to seeing a rider on his hands and knees duct-taping the carpet to the floor. Towards the end of the day I also blagged a newly released KTM Duke supermoto to ride the circuit on so that I had a bit of an idea of where to go in the morning session. I spent that first day trying to hook onto the back of other riders and learn the circuit as quickly as possible. The team were also trying to iron out a few remaining teething troubles with the ignition, so I was sent out for one session wearing a rucksack on my back containing data-logging equipment. It wasn't a full-on back-packer's rucksack but I must have looked odd to the likes of Doohan, especially when I got in his way yet again and was on the receiving end of more shakes of the head and hand gestures.

My benchmark was Jeremy McWilliams, who was riding for a privateer team but had a decade of experience, and I managed to qualify just behind him on the fourth row. I was fairly pleased with my performance before a huge thunderstorm hit the area late on the Saturday afternoon, flooding many of the garages. The circuit had also recently been re-landscaped and the rain washed some of the new grass onto the track, together with a lot of chalky stone. At one point it looked doubtful that there would be time to sweep it clean for the Sunday races. However, there was beautiful sunshine in the morning and although the track was still damp and dirty in parts I was able to switch to an intermediate tyre after ten minutes on a wet in the morning warm-up session. By now the team owner, Metraux, had flown in on his private jet and was watching from the garage, where David was asking him and team manager Serge Rosset about plans for the rest of the season. We knew that the team had been reasonably impressed by what they had seen. I was not quite as fast as Borja, but was not far behind, and his bike was one step ahead of mine in development.

'We could offer Chris £10,000 to ride for the rest of the season,' Metraux told David.

'That's only what he is on now,' David replied. 'If you offered £15,000 it might make all the upheaval that he will suffer a bit more worthwhile.'

At that point I went back out on the intermediate, just ahead of Doohan again down pit-lane. After a couple of laps I was puzzled that Doohan had not come past me. I knew he was still out on track and behind me because I could see his pit board. Then I caught and passed Luca Cadalora. When I returned to the garage at the end of the session I looked up at the screen and saw my name at the top, ahead of Cadalora, Scott Russell and Doohan. I couldn't get my breath, and I have kept the original sheet to this day.

'OK, it's a deal. We will pay him £15,000 for the rest of the season,' Metraux told David, before I had a chance to lift my visor.

The team were delighted and Randy Mamola, working as a roving reporter for TV, made a point of coming up to congratulate me. 'Good jarb,' he said, in his distinctive American accent. By the time of the race the track was clean and bone dry, and the advantage that I had gained on the level playing field of a damp track had disappeared. But I still managed to finish fifteenth behind McWilliams and score one point, not bad for my second time on the bike and my first time at the circuit. On the drive home David and I discussed the awkward topic of how to break the news to Robin, because the next British race was the following weekend. I was also worried about the effect it might have on my mechanics. But, if I found that journey uncomfortable, it was not half as bad as the discomfort that Lisa and my parents were feeling. It might have sounded posh to say they were travelling in a private plane, but in fact the thing was a shitter and developed a problem with the hydraulics in Austria. Their take-off was delayed for ages and by the time they reached Tollerton Airfield it was dark – and Tollerton does not have landing lights. They circled round and round while the pilot tried to alert someone. Finally they found a bloke in the local pub to ride his motorbike down the runway, his tail-light guiding the pilot in. Even my dad, who is normally fairly unflappable, thought that his end had come.

Back home, with the Old Spice bikes becoming ever more fragile, Terry had quit to join the Lucky Strike team on a permanent basis. So my decision to leave as well was not exactly what Robin wanted to hear. And Old Spice did not want to be seen to be losing their bright, but sometimes daft, young prospect without a fight. So Robin set about suing me and Terry for the money we had already been paid under breach of contract. I argued that I had been training and riding for them for a full half year, which was all I had been paid for. On top of that the bikes had not turned out to be what was promised when I signed the contract.

I was introduced to a solicitor, Richard Ratcliffe, based in Kent. He agreed to work for free on this occasion, on the basis that I used him in the future. Richard was not your stereotypical solicitor because although he was well-spoken and on a different intellectual plane he could also talk at my level. Since then I have nearly always taken his advice, the exception being when he suggested I buy a flat in London to rent out. But I was still living with Lisa's parents and if I was going to buy any accommodation I wanted to live in it. If I had taken his advice I would probably be able to retire from bike racing now! At that time, however, I was still not exactly flush and Richard managed to secure Legal Aid. People assume that all bike racers are paid the same as Michael Schumacher but most of my wage was eaten up by things like insurance and running costs for the motorhome. After a couple of months of legal toing and froing we agreed to disagree and the matter was settled out of court. The only people to benefit were Robin's lawyers, and there had been no need for the legal action. The team was better off without us and our wage bill. They struggled on, sometimes with one rider and sometimes with two, including Matt Llewellyn and Scott Smart among others, but struggling to make the points by the end of the season.

The next Grand Prix with the Elf 500 ROC team, in the Czech Republic again, was important for me to show everyone that I was not just there to make up the numbers for the rest of the season. I also needed to prove to myself that I had made the right move. I set off for Czecho in the motorhome with David. Soon after leaving the ferry David decided that he could not wait for a shit, but when he went to the toilet he discovered it was so full that he would have needed to lift himself up on his hands to fit any more in. We realized that we could not carry on without emptying the shit tank, which would start to 'chuck up' and stink if we went much further. So we pulled into the next services in the middle of nowhere in Belgium. It seemed fitting somehow that we nearly always emptied the tank in Belgium, which was good for little else except beer and chocolate. (Oh, and maybe the odd motocross rider like Eric Gebours, Goerges Jobe and Stefan Everts and his dad Harry! I have also since got to know a cool Belgian, Pluto, who works for Ohlins in the World Superbike paddock, so I had better be careful what I say.)

It was now late at night and we struggled to find a drain large enough to empty it into and, having parked next to a steep grass verge, we decided to just empty it there, hoping that it would run harmlessly down the bank. Smaller motorhomes, like the one I have now, have a cassette that can be pulled out and taken to a toilet. It always amazes me how many fans still want to stop you and shake your hand and ask for an autograph while you are clearly carrying a waste cassette which is still warm, although we have a golden rule now that the toilet is only to be used for number ones. Anyway, I drew the short straw. First I had to attach a pipe to the outlet before pulling a lever that would first empty the shit tank, then pull the grade waste lever, which served to flush out the tank with the used shower water. Unfortunately I didn't attach the pipe properly, and when I pulled the lever it dropped off and the shit, mixed with Blooloo and toilet paper, just poured out underneath the motorhome, splattering my trainers.

'Urrrgh! It's gone everywhere underneath us,' I shouted as I clambered back in. 'Quick, drive off before anyone notices.' Just then there was a knock on the door and I fully expected it to be the services officials, wanting us to clean up the mess or turn the music down from the big fuck-off speakers that I had fitted when Carl delivered the motorhome. Instead I opened the door to a couple of Dutch guys, smoking big reefers.

'Hey guyzh, can we join zhe party. You have zhe muzhic, we have zhe pot and zhe beerzh,' one said. I could see a big 20-foot pool of shite beginning to circle around their feet, but they were too stoned to notice. There was only one thing for it. I slammed the door shut and shouted: 'Drive!' David hit the accelerator while the two guys were left to wonder what they had said, and what the funny smell was. It was pure comedy genius – until we arrived at the paddock in Brno the next day. We pulled up next to Doohan's massive American Eagle motorhome and got out to the kind of reception that Pigpen always receives in *Peanuts*. Shit had been splashing out of the open shoot all the way through Belgium, Germany and the Czech Republic and was freeze-dried all down the side of the motorhome.

The team was trying a new type of engine with a balancer shaft which Borja crashed during practice. He was too injured to race so the new engine was fitted in my bike and it did not run right all weekend. I also struggled to adapt to it and had no team-mate to help me with a direction. I was in legal shit at home, in literal shit in Belgium and in a whole world of shit in Brno when I struggled to finish in twentieth place. It felt like I had jumped from the frying pan of the Old Spice team into the fire of the Elf team.

There was only one thing for it – a return trip to Hotel Bobby, where Rymer was conveniently staying. It's a fair distance from the centre of Brno to the circuit so Terry said that me and Dave could stay in his room. Obviously, the initial plan was to revisit the Czech nuns, but a real party atmosphere developed in the club downstairs. Dancing girls were performing on raised stages, which turned into showers as they stripped off. Then, during a break for the girls, a bunch of Jeremy McWilliams's overweight Irish mates leapt up onto the stages for their version. It wasn't quite the same as watching the nuns, but equally good value. The security men did not see the funny side, however, and a big fight broke out between the locals and half the GP paddock.

I was at the bar talking to Terry's team-mate, Scott Russell, who is too smooth to move. A local bloke landed next to him, probably after a dig from Terry, and Scott casually tipped the drinks off a metal tray on the bar and whacked the bloke over the head, like it was just an every-day occurrence in a sleepy Georgia bar. The bloke's eyes were rolling in their sockets and you just knew he was seeing stars, while Scott simply carried on the conversation as though nothing had happened.

Back in the room it was decided that the twin beds would be allo-cated on height. As Terry is the tallest rider ever to have lived, with the possible exception of Will Hartog, and as Pickworth is well over 6 foot, there was not much debate over who got the couch. We were helping ourselves to a few more drinks from the mini bar and laughing about the bar-room brawl, when Pickworth decided to get out of bed and go for a pee, dressed only in his boxer shorts – probably Armani. Rymer, who is as daft as a brush, waited until Dave shut the door to the toilet and, giggling away, quickly revealed his plan. When Dave came out of the toilet we pounced and bundled him out of the door leading onto the corridor, which we had already opened.

'Call security. There is a strange man on our corridor wandering round in just his pants. He must be some kind of weirdo and he should be thrown out of the hotel,' said Terry, on the phone to reception. I was literally crying by now.

'Come on, let me in, you wankers. The joke's over now,' pleaded Dave from the corridor. Then everything went quiet for ten minutes until there was a faint knock on the door. We weren't sure whether it was Dave or security so we looked through the peephole to find Dave, stood with his arm round two gorgeous minters, dressed as scantily as he was. Dave had gone massive! They were sharing a double room with their friend, who had pulled in the bar and had asked them to make themselves scarce while she was having her hip knocked out. They had thrown on lightweight Kagool jackets over their underwear and had presumed that the same thing had happened to Dave. We sat around on the beds having a laugh for about half an hour before Terry, obviously flagging after the races, dropped a bombshell in his Cockney accent.

'Look, lavs. Are you going to put out, or fack off?' With that he switched the light off and pulled the sheets over his head. My chin hit the floor. And the girls facked off! But Dave's efforts in turning that situation round earned lasting respect from us all.

The next round was at Imola. I loved Italy and it's probably the only country where I have raced that I could consider living outside England. And I loved Imola, too: a fantastic old circuit in the middle of the town with loads of history and atmosphere, a bit like Monza. The Italian crowds love their bike racing and whenever any rider from any country in any class came out of their garage the horns would blast away and the fans would chant their name. I was starting to feel a bit more like a GP rider. The track suited me as well. It was fast, bumpy and off-camber, a bit like a British circuit but three times as long. Even the weather was favourable and the on-and-off rain of the two days of qualifying made the difference between our bike and the factory machines less apparent. For most of qualifying I was knocking on the door of the top ten, making me pumped and confident for Sunday's race. More showers in the morning created a drying track for the race, but after a great start I made a mistake at the first corner, leaving me mid-pack. Going into the second of the chicanes, before climbing the hill, I was bumped onto the painted kerb. This was my first lesson that rain and paint is not a good combination. The rear broke traction instantly and the bike flipped me into orbit. I landed like a sack of spuds, shoulder and belly first. The bike went spinning down the track so I immediately went racing after it and tried to lift it out of the gravel and get back on. It was then that I realized that my arm would not move and that there was a horrific pain in my shoulder. When the marshals arrived I was already pale, dizzy and, before I knew it, in the back of an ambulance heading for the Clinica Mobile to receive the diagnosis of my first broken collar-bone.

Dad was typically sympathetic: 'We've come all this bloody way and didn't even get to see you do a lap. And it's bloody raining. I told you it always rains in Italy.' Luckily, the team were more understanding and arranged for me to fly home, as well as offering to look after my motorhome until the next race at Catalunya. Back home the race was on to be fit for Spain. I had been told about a guy based in Ipswich called Brian Simpson, the physio for the Ipswich rugby team, who used a new laser treatment for healing broken bones. I now just refer to him as Laserman but a lot of riders call him the Bone Welder. He now uses all the latest techniques, such as the Hyperbaric Oxygen tanks, and although some people are sceptical about how effective his methods really are I believe in him and you cannot help but feel better just through his positive thinking. If you tell him when you need to be fit for, he will make you fit for it. It wasn't all that expensive either at around £30 per session – the petrol down there cost more. Within a week he had me doing press-ups with a broken bone, which was amazing because I couldn't do them before breaking it. In truth, there was never a chance of me missing the race and giving another rider the chance to get his foot in the door.

The Catalunya GP, in Montmelo but near Barcelona, threatened to be just as disastrous as Imola. The collar-bone was actually still really sore and perhaps affected my control of the bike more than I let on at the time. I was again learning a new circuit, one that I struggled to get to grips with. Every corner seemed to be more than 180 degrees and went on for ever, on a bike which didn't really like to complete a corner but instead wanted to be under-steered and run wide. And the qualifying session gave me a lesson in how cruel the 500cc two-strokes could be. I had completed just one timed lap when, at the end of one of the longest straights on the European calendar where the bikes reached 200 m.p.h., the engine seized. Absolutely nothing happens as fast as when a two-stroke seizes with your head on the tank, flat out just before the braking area. I went into a tank-slapper and managed to pull in the clutch, but could not stop because there was no engine braking. If I had let the clutch out the back wheel would have locked. So, when I hit the gravel I grabbed the front brake and squirmed my way towards the tyre wall, tipping the bike over just before it made contact. Coincidentally, Clive Padgett was out at this corner spotting for Jay Vincent, who was doing a good job on the 250cc ride I had been offered, and he gave me a lift back on his scooter.

'You were bloody lucky there, lad,' he said. I didn't need telling. I went straight back out on my spare bike and almost immediately locked the front going into the downhill left-hand hairpin. It was a hard crash and fortunately it was my head that took the big whack, not my collar-bone. But the bike landed on my hand and chopped the end off the middle finger of my glove. Luckily, the glove had slipped off slightly, so my finger remained intact, otherwise it would have been badly squished at best. When I arrived back at the garage the team told me to take Borja's spare bike out. At the same corner I forgot that Borja's gears were set up for race shifting, whereas I used road shifting. I crashed again. I was so embarrassed that I told the Spanish marshal to take the long way back to the pits because I didn't want to face the team. I qualified next to last, so someone must have had a worse session than me, which was hard to believe. When Borja came back into the garage he noticed that both my bikes were missing.

'You have problem?' he asked.

'Yeah, the engine seized and I crashed the other,' I replied sheepishly. Then his eyes turned to the empty spot where his bike should have been. He looked slowly back at me.

'You crash my bike too?'

I nodded.

'Cabron!' he muttered, which I am reliably informed means 'dickhead' in Spanish.

The problems did not end in qualifying. Three laps into the race one of the plugs broke and the bike was running on three cylinders. Sometimes it would kick back in and revert back to four, but I actually found it easier to ride with just the three working, and my lap times were not much different. Other riders were clearly also struggling with the circuit, and although I virtually just rode round for the rest of the race I managed to finish fifteenth and secure my second point of the season. Again the team remained very kind and encouraging – I was certainly not the first person to have fallen off that bike. And I think they again appreciated the fact that I was riding through the pain barrier. But I did not feel that I was fulfilling my potential. This was not why I had given up my British championship ride, and the odd ray of sunshine, like the result in Austria, was beginning to fade. I guess it was another of those gentle reminders that motorcycle racing always provides. When these trials and tribulations arise you just have to get your head down and get over them.

However, there was not much chance left to rectify these particular problems. With just two rounds of the GP season remaining I was told that I would be riding in Brazil, but not in Australia, where the team thought it would be better to use a local wild card, Marty Craghill. Maybe they thought it was a cheaper option, or maybe they thought that another new circuit, while I was still suffering from my collar-bone injury, might prove another difficult test for me. I was a bit disappointed not to be completing the season, but very excited to be going to Brazil – until I checked in for my flight, with Brazil's national airline, Varig.

I had only once been out of Europe before, so did not know the difference between economy class and business. I was allocated the middle of five seats in cattle class, sandwiched between two fat, sweaty, chain-smoking Brazilians. Yes, believe it or not, you used to be able to smoke on flights. Until then the word Brazilian had only meant a mint bird with a shaven haven. There were certainly none of them on this flight, and on a seat worn through to the metal and with a broken collar-bone it lasted forever. I was so sick – not travel sick but smoke sick – that landing in Rio de Janeiro completely passed me by. Then I was hit by the intense heat, followed by my first taste of jet-lag. I have always suffered outbound, whatever the time difference, but am usually fine on the return journey. I wish it was the other way round because you can still be groggy come Friday morning practice sometimes. But after ten minutes staring out of my hotel window onto Copacabana beach I felt much better. This was where the true Brazilians hung out, and they were all playing beach volleyball. I had an overwhelming urge for a spot of sunbathing. The whole country seemed to be on the beach and I don't remember ever seeing anyone do any work during the whole trip.

I was travelling on my own for the first time, although by now I knew Borja pretty well and knew most of the mechanics by nickname at least. Borja was a bubbly character and a good team-mate and I knew that I would be able to hang around with him for the weekend. A few of the other riders, like Jeremy McWilliams, were already down on the beach there with their families, as many took the chance to take them along for a spot of holiday beforehand. It would have worked out cheaper if Lisa had come because I was caned on the cost of phone calls home twice a day.

Borja perhaps noticed that I was a bit nervous being out of Europe for the first time and was keen to wind me up with stories about the shanty-town dwellers blocking off the big tunnel leading to the circuit and robbing all the trapped drivers at gunpoint. At least I thought he was winding me up, until I heard that it had actually happened the previous week and there had been doubts whether the GP would go ahead. It was obviously a dodgy place but we did not see any trouble the whole time and I always felt safe. Even the bike felt more comfortable as they had made progress with the balancer shaft and had cured the vibration problems. My main problem was coping with the heat. When you popped your head up from behind the screen at the end of the straight in the braking area, it felt like someone was blasting ten hairdryers into your face. Bear in mind that I only ever reluctantly revealed my pale, pasty skin to have a shower once a day. So I was not ready for these intense conditions, although nowadays I love the heat and struggle when it's colder.

It was another circuit with long, hanging corners, but I managed to reduce my qualifying time by nearly one and a half seconds on one flying lap, admittedly on a new tyre and with the help of a tow from Loris Capirossi. But it was a long, hard race and, although I managed to finish seventeenth, it probably exposed the fact that my shoulder was still not quite ready for race distance. I guess that vindicated their decision for Australia, but neither bike went on to finish that final race. It was a blow to finish my season on a low, but maybe also a timely reminder that I needed to return to Britain to thoroughly learn my trade before thinking that I was ready to compete effectively at Grand Prix level.

16

Staaaaalllllkkkkker

I realized that opportunities back in Britain would be limited. Not only were rides scarce but teams are sometimes a bit nervous about taking on a rider who has failed to finish the previous season with his team, whatever the justification. So I needed a shop window. At the end of the previous season, as part of the agreement with Padgett's, I worked on their stand at the NEC Show in November, and I agreed to do the same again this year. These days, teams start to plan their line-up midway through a season. For instance, only this year John Hopkins announced his move to Kawasaki with more than half the season to go. But the merry-go-round did not tend to start for the British championship until well after the season had finished. So, with all the top team bosses at the NEC, it was a good place to be visible. I knew that Padgett's were happy with Jay Vincent's performance in the 250cc GP series, so there was no point going down that route – and I have never been the type to step on anyone's toes.

When Rob McElnea, the Cadbury's Boost Yamaha boss, came over to the stand, I expected it to be to reminisce about the Czech nuns. His two riders, Niall Mackenzie and Jamie Whitham, had walked away with first and second spots the previous year, especially when the Old Spice Ducati results had started to tail off. Niall wanted to stay and defend his title but Whitham felt he had unfinished business in World Superbikes and was in talks with Suzuki.

'Look, Chris, I am going to be honest with you. Yamaha does not have a massive budget for the British championship. And we have had to spend some money to keep Niall with us, so there is nothing left to pay a second rider a wage,' explained Rob.

'I'll need something,' I said. 'Otherwise, how am I going to be able to do a professional job and train properly?'

'I realize that, but there are lots of positives. You will be on exactly the same bike as Niall, an evolved version of the bikes that the factory Belgarda team used in World Superbikes last year. You will be on a bonus for any podium position, and you can keep any prize money. And I'm sure that Yamaha will help you out in other ways. If you can make some money on your leathers and helmet deals you will be able to make a living. Plus it's a great opportunity for an up-and-coming rider,' he said.

'But what if James doesn't get the Suzuki ride? That would leave me with nothing.'

'Don't worry about that. I'm his manager and I will make sure it happens,' said Rob. Over the course of the next few days at the show I spent a lot of time with Rob and Whitham. James was a keen mountain biker, who had only recovered from cancer at the end of 1995, and invited me to join him and his mates on a ride in the Peak District. He had always been a fitness fanatic but had stepped it up a level since his treatment. James arranged for me to borrow a trick ex-demo, hard-tailed bike with front forks, but I could see his jaw drop when I got out of my car. While he was wearing all the gear – tight-fitting tops and leggings with a padded arse – I was dressed in a pom-pom hat, Kagool, Lisa's tracksuit bottoms tucked into my football socks and a pair of trainers. As soon as we left the car park the very first section was a long, steep climb up a rocky hillside.

'Look at him go!' shouted James as I set off at a decent pace, although I was still trying to work out the gearing. He followed, simply hopping over any obstacles that I had to ride around. It took around two hours to reach the pub for lunch, and the hour listening to James was worth all the discomfort of the morning. Anyone connected with motorbike racing knows that he is one of the funniest men in the sport and can hold counsel for hours with his stories. At the end of the break my legs had seized up and felt like fag ash – 'café legs', as we now call them. Plus my arse was now like a baboon's after a morning's hard riding. And it probably wasn't all that wise to have had a pie and chips eatathon, plus a couple of pints of Guinness, although the sustenance might well have kept me alive during the afternoon.

As we set off back the weather quickly closed in and the heavy rain turned to hail and then to sleet. The crotch of my tracksuit bottoms was soon between my knees, and the knees were scraping on my trainers. I had to sit sideways with my buttocks on the saddle so that my arse didn't hurt so much and I covered my face with the fingers of one hand to stop the hail from hitting me. I could not begin to imagine how the guy wearing shorts was feeling. 'Any danger we might get back to the car soon?' I thought. Whit was cycling on ahead and waiting for us at the gates but, with the car park now in sight about two miles below, I carried on at the final gate whimpering, 'I can't stop. I will die if I do.' Whit was pissing himself but it was on that day that I realized I needed to step up my training. And, when I swapped an old motocross bike for a MuddyFox mountain bike, I was committed to a new fitness regime. I think James was quite chuffed when, a few years later, I blew him away on a ride up an Austrian mountain, because he could take some credit for my improved fitness.

I carried on motocrossing as well, of course, and this was a good way of seeing Terry, who had remained a good mate even though we had moved to different teams midway through the previous year. He brought some mates up to join me, my dad, Dicko and a few others on a two-day mission at The Desert, the disused sandy quarry near Mansfield – an official unofficial venue for crossers. Unfortunately his mate Dean, who ran a cleaning business and was obviously known as Clean Dean, only lasted the first fifteen minutes before breaking his wrist. Conditions were perfect on the second day, wet enough to lean the bike over on a knobbly tyre but not too slippy.

'Right, we're not leaving here until we get our facking knees down,' said Terry, who was always up for a giggle. It was all right for him – he was so tall that his knees were almost touching the floor when he was upright. But I have never had so much fun, going faster and faster around an oval we had created until I finally did manage to touch my knee down. Unfortunately, it did not slide like it did on Tarmac, but dug in instead and twatted me off the back. The next challenge was to ride facing the wrong way, just like in the *Crusty Demons of Dirt* video. It was a fantastic couple of days.

By the time that Whitham's ride with Suzuki was confirmed I had managed to negotiate a deal with Arai and David had persuaded the Italians at Texport to provide him with some free suits that he could then sell to help me out. Rob Mac had also arranged for me to work as an instructor at the Yamaha race schools at Donington and Cadwell. Only two years earlier I had been paying to go to one of their training sessions. They paid me over the odds for that work because of the promotional value and credibility they gained, but it was actually like being paid to go out with my mates. So many of the people attending were guys I used to motocross with or lads that I had sold bikes to from the shop.

Another of the perks of joining Yamaha was that they promised to loan me an ex-demo YZF 1000 Thunderace for the year and two YZ125 motocross bikes for me and Niall, whose base was still in Scotland although he rented a place in the Midlands for convenience. So he asked me to go and pick them up and keep them at my house and was quite happy for me to choose my favourite. I thought it would be a good idea for me and Dicko to go and test them out at The Desert before I chose my bike. One was a bit prettier than the other so I rode that, at one of our favourite spots there, next to a bit of a lake. This was just after the release of a popular motocross video, *Moto XXX*. One of our favourite stunts on the video was when the lads hit a big pond, similar to our lake, flat out in top gear on their CR250s. They had enough speed to skim over the top of the water before gradually losing power at the other side.

'Fuck it,' said Dicko. 'Let's have a go. You'd better do it, you are better than me.'

'Yeah, I'm up for it. They are not our bikes, after all,' I said. We found a flat run-up area facing the corner of the lake, which was about waist deep in the middle. It was about 50 metres across and I needed to build up enough speed if I was going to make it across. I reached about 60 m.p.h. in sixth gear when I touched the water: straight in, straight across and straight out the other side.

'Chief, chief! Do a bigger bit,' Dicko urged me. By this time a few people had spotted what we were up to and a small crowd had gathered. I rode at the lake from a different angle and added another 10 metres without any problem. To try any further I would have to find another entry spot, and with a longer run-up. But I didn't notice the slight ledge just before entry. I hit the water with my front wheel slightly in the air and when it came down, 20 metres onto the lake, it just dived in, flicked me over the top and the bike submarined while I pond-skated to the other side. It had been like hitting concrete. My chin-strap was ripped off, my goggles were nowhere to be seen and there was water in my watch. Bits of white and blue plastic were floating around while just the end of the handlebar grip stuck out of the surface of the lake, surrounded by bubbles. 'Wahoooo!' cheered the crowd. By now it was turning dark and the temperature had plummeted. As I waded in to pull the bike out, the crowd were suddenly nowhere to be seen. I dragged the bike out and tipped it upside down to drain the water, but there was no way it would start. So Dicko had to ride twenty minutes back to the van for a bike strap and, while towing it back, the bike eventually fired and remarkably ran like a dream. This was now going to be the bike for Mackenzie, just in case. Niall came down for a go the following week and I didn't realize that the water had caused the engine to momentarily lock hydraulically. This weakened the con rod, which came out of the side of the crank case after just ten minutes. Niall did not know anything about the underwater expedition, or that I swapped the bikes back when Yamaha replaced his engine. He was not the type of bloke to worry about stuff like that, thankfully.

Niall turned out to be everything I expected and hoped for from a team-mate. Having two professionals like him and 'Too Tall Tel' Rymer to look up to in those early years was invaluable. It was as though I was being instructed by two Jedi Knights. Niall was a lot smaller than Terry and looked more like a bike racer. He was extremely fit and, because he often stayed at his rented place, I spent a lot more time mountain biking with him and a few of the mechanics. He taught me a lot about training regimes and eating more healthily, too. I guess I went from being a boy to a man in that year. Niall was also very good with the fans, and never missed an appointment or autograph session. And he never moaned about these responsibilities, at least not within earshot of anyone who mattered. I always remember him telling me: 'You are supposed to arrive at a signing session, not be there waiting.' He was right; there is nothing worse than waiting around like a knob for the public to turn up – it's much more exciting for them if you build the anticipation and turn up a few minutes late.

I can also honestly say, hand on heart, that this was the only time in my career when my bike was better than any other in the race, except for my team-mate. At places like Snetterton, with long straights, they needed a separate lane for the Yamaha. John Reynolds was a force on his Ducati at certain tracks, but Michelin did not have as much experience of British circuits as Dunlop and struggled with consistency. At the start of every race I knew that I had a chance of winning, and this was a world away from the pitiful finish to the previous year in Brazil. But you are only as good as your last race, and in my very first meeting with the Cadbury Boost team I finished second behind Niall. I had Rob Mac to thank for my change in fortunes. He knew that he had the best bike, the best team set-up and the best rider in Niall; the only thing he did not know was exactly how good I was. I suppose I had developed a bit of a 'win one, bin one' reputation but Rob took time to try and smooth my rough edges with gems of advice like concentrating on short-shifting through the gears in order to improve grip. And it did not take long for me to repay that faith in the second round at Oulton Park, although, as you might now imagine, not without drama.

Both days of qualifying were wet but the first qualifying session on the Friday was on a greasy track, as slippy as I have ever known it at Oulton. After just a handful of laps I was behind Terry Rymer, now riding for Colin Wright at Kawasaki, going down into Knickerbrook. He touched the brakes and went down instantly – one of those poetic crashes where the bike goes straight on while Terry slid for ages on his back before slowly bumping up onto his feet in the gravel trap. I was also struggling for feel from the new Carbone Lorraine brake pads, which were slow to heat up in the wet. Three laps later I yanked on the brake and did exactly the same thing as Terry and at exactly the same spot. But, while Terry slid on his back, I slid on my belly, which was starting to grow through all the Cadbury's Boosts that I was eating. The chocolate started to taste like gravel trap by the end of the season! I hopped onto my spare bike to finish the session and was met at the holding pen by Rob Mac.

'Those brakes are shit in the wet. I want something else for this afternoon,' I moaned, walking back to the garage down pit-lane.

'Stop right there, Chris. That was your fault. You were trying to go too fast too soon and you can't go blaming anyone else for your mistake,' he said firmly, but so that nobody else could hear. Rob was second to none as a man manager, and did not say another word about it again. I immediately wanted to hit the rewind button and take back what I had said and I was upset that I had obviously upset him. I have never been big-headed or jumped up, but my results were improving on the bike and I wanted to do even better. Occasionally, though, you need to be brought down to size and I probably had the bollocking coming.

The final qualifying session was even wetter but there was more grip because wet-weather tyres are designed to cope with standing water and not a greasy surface. I was anxious to make amends for the morning and set about trying to build up my pace. I instantly felt more comfortable and, sure enough, the brakes started to work better. I could not believe how fast I was going through Cascades. With ten minutes remaining I was in the top five but was desperate for a front-row start because Oulton is a difficult circuit for passing moves. The forecast also predicted dry races on the Sunday and I had no set-up in the dry, although the team were confident that the previous year's data would see us right. I went past the chequered flag and my pit-board said P1, although I did not know whether the fast guys in the rain, like Michael Rutter and Ian Simpson, were already finished. I was on pole position for the first time in a British superbike race and did not sleep a wink.

I led the first race from start to finish, although JR pushed me all the way. Normally those races last for ever but this went by in the blink of an eye and I loved every second of it. Rob and the lads were all leaning over pit-wall to cheer me home and I felt as though I could walk on water, lapping up the Lap of Honour in the back of the parade car. Again, I was brought back to earth with a bang. A big bang. The biggest bang of my career so far!

It had been a weekend of firsts: my first real bollocking, my first pole position and my first race win. So it was fitting that I should cap it off with my first near-death experience. I got the holeshot again but JR was right up there, just as in the first race. As I came over the lip to drop down towards Cascades the front wheel went light but I must have hit the brakes at the same time, so the front folded – at 130 m.p.h. The bike gripped, spat me off, flipped 180 degrees and hurtled upside down. It was actually underneath me as I flew, facing the wrong way, for the best part of 50 yards. I have seen a picture of me trying to look over my shoulder to see where I was going to land. At first glance the crash looks nasty enough, until you realize that I was travelling in the wrong direction. Yet at the moment the picture was taken the only visible damage to the bike was a splinter coming from the screen. It was to get a lot worse. And so was the damage to me. I landed on the outside kerbs of Cascades, first on my ankles and then my back, so I was again thankful for Terry's advice about the back protector. As the marshals placed straw bales around me and what was left of the bike it seemed like an hour before I could take a breath. Because I had landed backwards my helmet had been forced forward and broken the bridge of my nose. A bit of bone had been chipped off one ankle, similar to my motocross accidents, and the other ankle was badly sprained. Two ribs were fractured and my little finger was also broken. I was in a bit of a mess. *MCN* carried a big spread of my weekend – the win and the crash – and there was a picture of me sat on a bench in the medical centre looking very dazed, while Lisa tried to clean me up.

Big Colin was also there watching and, after the medical centre allowed me to go, he took me to hospital. Once all the breaks had been diagnosed and my finger and ankles strapped there was no point hanging around to see if they wanted to keep me in for further treatment and we sneaked away. At that point the only thing in my mind was being fit to race as a wild card at the World Superbike round at Donington the following week. But back at home I got worse before I got better. I spent the best part of forty-eight hours in bed, dragging myself out for the first time when Dicko called round to see me. I made it to the bottom of the stairs before passing out and I woke up on Lisa's mum's couch, having peed myself. Luckily she was out at the time! Even I had to admit there was no way I would be ready to ride in a couple of days, although I managed to limp along to Donington to support Niall. In hindsight, I should have stayed in hospital as it turned out that my kidneys had also received a battering. But I would have a second chance at Brands Hatch later in the year and the focus switched to getting fit for the following week at Snetterton.

I visited the Laserman two or three times and the ankles started to feel a bit better. The sprained one was actually more painful than the broken ankle but Brian strapped them so that I would have enough support but also enough flexibility for riding. I could now cough and laugh without passing out (or passing water), my finger had been broken so many times as to no longer matter, and my nose looked no worse than it did before the Oulton crash. More importantly, Snetterton was the perfect circuit for an injured rider; the least physically demanding on the calendar with just the two straights and four corners. I was all set for the challenge – and had a massive crash at the Bomb Hole within ten minutes of going out on track.

The Bomb Hole was not a good place to crash in those days, and tended to make a mess of bike and rider. There was not a lot of run-off before the tyre wall, made from tyres that had been around since God was a lad and were harder than a brick wall. I lost the front on the exit of the corner, where there was a bit more run-off, and I thought I had avoided causing too much damage to the bike – until the carburettors flew past me. 'Rob is going to kill me,' I thought. I bashed my feet again but they actually felt better afterwards. I guess a lot of people were interested to see how I was going to react after the big crash at Oulton, because a few riders are never the same after a big one. That kind of thought never entered my head, and still does-n't. And in one way it was good to have a crash so soon afterwards, because I knew there was nothing to worry about with my existing injuries. The rest of the qualifying went a lot more smoothly and, after problems with the rear floating into corners in the first race, Rob made one of his demon tweaks for the second race and, on a damp track, I won my second race of the season pretty comfortably.

By now I was in the thick of the title race, second behind Niall and thirty points ahead of JR, with Sean Emmett, Jim Moodie and Terry also having the odd good result. And I was earning more in prize money and bonuses than my previous year's wage. But I found that I was struggling to make the switch from the 400cc bikes at the Yamaha race school to my superbike at race weekends, so I stopped working as an instructor to concentrate on my racing.

The team was a joy to work for, and every week I travelled to their Scunthorpe base to go mountain biking with the lads, and often round to their houses for a bite to eat. At races Niall and I had an agreement that the slower rider in any qualifying session would make brews for the rest of the team in the living area of the race truck, a converted horsebox but now without the hay. It was a pleasure to make the boys a brew, just difficult to take straight after being slower than your team-mate. Even when the title race started to hot up Niall continued to help me out where he could. He was always confident that, whatever my package, he would still be able to win. And when I did beat him he was happy for me because he knew that I must have deserved it. Rob Mac never stopped trying to bring me on as a rider, either. Whatever he suggested always made sense and was often more beneficial in the long-run than a quick-fix change to help cover up a problem. If something he suggested did not work he was the first to accept it. There was a great family feel to the team, something I have only ever found elsewhere with Italian teams, although I was never too sure that I understood their jokes.

Rob arranged for the team to have a big presence at that year's TT – the ninetieth anniversary of the event. It was the first time back on the Isle of Man for me since I had started racing and I was very excited about going back. We had a week of PR duties, such as being at the Ramsey Sprint with our Cadbury's Boost horsebox and, always conscious of costs, Rob had booked a twin room for me, him and Niall. The beds were allocated on size yet again – and I still lost – so it was the floor for me for a week. Rob had organized to use a Yamaha road bike between the three of us and his mate had also come up with a Triumph Speed Triple Challenge bike, with big handlebars and a noisy exhaust, which we could also use. I rode it back from his mate's with Niall and Rob leading me what seemed to be a long way back in their hire car. As we turned onto the promenade I could see the punters spilling out onto the roadside from the massive Bushey's Bar on the front. I slipped the Triumph into second gear, popped the clutch, lifted the front wheel and wheelied from coming into sight of the bar all the way down the front until I was out of sight. Niall and Rob just pulled over and pipped their horn to urge me on. They had known that I would not be able to resist a stunt. Unfortunately I landed the front wheel almost on the big toe of one of the many coppers looking out for idiots like me. He smashed me on the arm with his truncheon and I raced back to the hotel, dumped the bike and turned my jacket inside out, crapping myself that he would try and take the punishment further.

Later on in the week we went out for a lap of the circuit, Niall on the Yamaha and me riding pillion with Rob on the Triumph. He had competed in the TT before and was fairly sensible for the first half of the lap. Then we stopped for some chips and Rob decided to have a rare pint – and then another. Niall and I looked at each other nervously. I'm not sure whether it was the beer or just his natural racing instinct which pushed him over the edge for the rest of the lap. Going into the Gooseneck he had the front foot-rest down, the exhaust down, the back foot-rest down and my feet down. Although we made it back in one piece I have never been on the back of anybody's bike since.

Another free weekend in the British season coincided with a gap in the World Superbike calendar and Whitham had organized a big enduro ride in Wales with the Geraint Jones School. I had never really been on an organized ride and knew that a lot of the paddock would be there so I wanted to make sure I had the right gear. I still had an enduro bike but it was not road legal so I rang James to find out what I could get away with. He told me to just stick on a back light and a registration plate, so I nicked my dad's FUK 1T plate. The registration wasn't legal, but it would do for a laugh. Instead of asking James everything in one call I must have rung him five times to ask what kind of jacket or bag I might need, so I assured him that I wasn't a stalker. On the night before the ride I rang one last time to check I had the right boots.

'Sorry to bother you. It's Chris again,' I said.

'Staaaaallllllkkkkker,' he laughed down the phone. And if Whitham thinks he has invented a nickname, rest assured everyone will get to hear about it. Believe me, it's not easy when your new girlfriend's granny's first question is: 'So why do they refer to you as a stalker on the telly?'

It just so happened that, at around the same time, I was attracting the attention of a real-life stalker.

17

Stalked Stalker

Jean was harmless enough. She was clearly a bike nut, probably in her late forties, but by no stretch of the imagination a handsome woman. Not after drinking all the beer in Belgium would I have found her remotely attractive. Initially she would simply come up to me in the paddock and give me a hug or a peck on the cheek. And I have always known that it doesn't cost anything to be polite and friendly; I also think it makes you feel better about yourself. So I would ask how she was doing and, over time, learnt that she was a nurse who still lived with her mum. Then she began to hand me envelopes containing the worst pictures ever taken, always through a fence and out of focus, and always on an in-lap because that was the only time she could catch the whole bike in the shot. But there was no harm in accepting them and appearing to be grateful. I knew that she gave similar pictures to other riders, but I did not realize that I had become the object of her affections.

I do not remember ever giving her the phone number at Mum and Dad's, but soon she started to call. I was not home much but once or twice was there when Mum and Dad were out and answered the phone. The conversations were brief and more than a bit awkward, but essentially all she wanted to do was to say well done or wish me luck. Then, and again I have no idea how she obtained my address, letters started to arrive. They were not love letters; she just asked about Lisa or mentioned that she had met my granddad at one of the races. By this point I was beginning to realize that this was all a bit abnormal. Then came the crunch letter.

> *Dear Chris*
> *I know we have only known each other a short time but I just wanted to give you something back for all the enjoyment you have given me over the years.*
>   *All my love*
>   *Jean*

The envelope contained a cheque for £500. This was an awful lot of Cadbury's Boost bars, and more than I received for a race win. But, just like stealing sweets from a kid, I also knew that you did not accept money from old dears. So I just threw the letter and the cheque in the bin and left it at that. Four weeks later Jean came up to me in the paddock.

'Hi Chris! How are you? I haven't seen that cheque go through my bank yet,' she said, cheerily.

'Look, Jean. I don't talk to you because I want your money – I talk to you because you come and support me and I class you as a friend,' I said.

I do not have many regrets in my life. But that sentence is one of them. From that day on she stalked me good and proper. I had to change my mobile number twice as she became more and more obsessed. She befriended my friends so that she could be in my company and spent a lot of time with my granddad, who came to a lot of races in those days. When he told her that he lived in Dartmouth – surprise, surprise – that was where she was going for a holiday. He must have told her to pop in for a brew, which she did – and stayed for a week. My granny was on the verge of moving out of her own home! But I never felt physically threatened, so there was little I could do about it but try to ignore her and hope that she would go away.

There was no point telling Lisa what was happening. And anyway she had her own new obsession – horses. She had learnt to ride as a girl and her older sister had always owned a horse. Lisa had also become very friendly with Jamie Whitham's wife, Andrea, who also owned horses, as did all his sisters. Rob Mac's wife and daughter had about five between them too. I felt like an extra in *The Horse Whisperer*. It was at a time when I was finding myself busier and busier with training and PR duties, so when Rob Mac's wife, Sharon, offered to sell us Star, their three-legged nag, it seemed like a good idea. Star was actually a beautiful beast and came with new Dunlops (horseshoes) and a Recaro seat (Stubben saddle). But owning a horse was not like owning a motocross bike. When a bike breaks down you can stick it in the garage and forget about it. When a horse breaks down it costs £1,000 at the vet's. That's after you have bought a horsebox to get it there. And that's after you have bought a new 4×4 to tow the horsebox. Oh, and not forgetting that horses don't eat Cadbury's Boosts. They eat polos and apples. And neither Trebor nor Granny Smith sponsored bike-racing teams. Still, a friend called Carl Willoughby, known as Hollywood because he loved jet-skiing and modelled himself on Scott 'Hollywood' Watkins, had a livery at his home and allowed us to keep Star there on the cheap. Soon Lisa was spending less time at the races and more time eventing. So, looking back, I guess it might have been the start of us drifting apart – just around the time that *MCN* decided to step up the brolly-girl scene a notch with the creation of the Babe Squad!

The British championship was going well but I had been looking forward to the Brands Hatch round of the World Superbike championship ever since missing out on Donington. Rob, Niall and the rest of the team were also excited to be competing against the World Superbike elite like Foggy, Aaron Slight and the factory Yamaha boys, Scott Russell and Colin Edwards. Correction, make that the factory Yamaha boys, Scott Russell and Chris Walker. Rob Mac broke the news to me the week before the event.

'Edwards is taking the chance to have some reconstruction work on his knee after his recent crash, so he will not make it to Brands. They want one of our riders and I think it should be you. Niall is happy with it. He has had his chance at world level and has no aims to go back there. He recognizes that this could be a big chance for you. Obviously I would prefer it if you were riding for us, but I really think you should accept the ride,' he said.

I didn't need too much persuading. The positives far outweighed any negatives. It would be my first chance on a bike capable of winning races at world level, and with a factory team with the best choice of tyres. The downside was that I did not have much experience around Brands on a superbike. Although the factory bike would be essentially the same as mine, it was bound to feel different. The pressure also started to mount immediately. A wild card can stay pretty low key in the build-up, but *MCN* wanted to make a big thing of my factory opportunity and I did a load of interviews that week.

I was shitting myself when I arrived at the circuit to find myself in such a professional set-up. No horsebox here; the factory team had two big race transporters. I was made up with my shiny new leathers, with Yamaha on the back in gold, and new matching boots from Alpinestars. The bike looked lovely, too; everything just oozed factory. I was buzzing, especially when I was invited to the same signing session at the Kentagon Bar as all the stars like Foggy, Corser, Russell and Slight, the guys I looked up to in superbikes. OK, not everyone in the crowd knew Chris Walker, but they gave me a little cheer all the same. I also discovered that the guy who produced the Cadbury's Boost merchandise, Tim Clinton, had made a special Chris Walker T-shirt for the event, with a picture of me looking over my shoulder as I came in on an in-lap. All of a sudden I was signing shirts with my name on – I was buzzing. I had obviously become more used to attention from the fans during that season. Niall was immensely popular and respected, and James Whitham has always been one of the most popular riders, so the team was already a firm favourite. Wherever Niall went for autograph sessions at the British championship rounds, I tagged along and was usually asked to sign my posters at the same time. I guess people had also started to appreciate that I always gave 100 per cent. I might be lying fifteenth but, through my busy style on the bike, I still looked faster than the guy leading the race. I am sure that Clinton probably spent more money producing the T-shirts than he made from selling them at Brands that year, but it all added to the pressure and expectation.

I didn't actually like the factory bike as much as my own. It was faster, but all revs and no grunt. The power characteristics were not as progressive as mine and it also steered differently. Maybe I put too much pressure on myself for the first race, my first World Superbike race. As a winner of British championship races I was expected to do a lot better than as a GP wild card. But Brands was still a circuit that I didn't know too well and I struggled to get used to it and came eleventh, while Niall was third behind Frankie Chili and Scott Russell. The second race was wet and I was a lot closer to the action, finishing tenth, seven seconds behind Whitham, although it could have been higher because I dropped back after wearing the back brake pads out. The team were quick to point out that there was also a thumb brake, but I had never used one before and wasn't about to start in a wet World Superbike race as I would have ended on my arse without a doubt. I have tried thumb brakes since and still not mastered them. Nevertheless, Rob and the factory team were delighted, and to almost make the top ten in both races was a huge achievement. It also earned me the chance of more rounds, when Edwards's recovery was further delayed. It would have been easy for the team to pick a local wild card each time, but Rob was fighting my corner, even though he was running the risk of losing me for the future.

Luckily for me the next few rounds were all at circuits that I had already been to. First up was the A1-Ring in Austria, where I had raced for the Elf team. While I was keen to repay the faith shown by Rob and the factory team, I did not want to risk future rides by pushing too hard and throwing the thing down the road. The results, twelfth in the first race and tenth in the second, were similar to Brands so everyone seemed happy enough and I kept the ride for Assen. Again, while I did not set the world alight, I did not disgrace myself either with a tenth and a ninth, although I was amazed at how different the circuit seemed on a superbike, having previously only been there on a 250, when I thought it was the fastest, widest track around. Now the straights seemed half the length and the track half as wide – no different to riding round Cadwell on a 250. I was happy with another racing milestone, beating Whitham for the first time in race two. OK, he was given a ride-through penalty for jumping the start but you do not lose much time at Assen because you miss the final chicane when pitting. It was also great to spot a few Walker T-shirts in amongst all the Foggy fans over from Britain, making me feel accepted as a competitor on the world stage.

I knew that, even if Edwards was still not fit to return for the final two rounds in Japan and Indonesia, Yamaha were unlikely to take a British wild card over there, so my final chance was at Albacete, where I had tested at the start of the 1995 season. But first there was the penultimate round of the British championship at Brands. Niall was in a strong position to win the championship and I was now in second place, with Michael Rutter challenging me for the runner-up slot. Two good results and the championship would go down to the final round at Donington. That all changed when, like a prat, I fell off on the final corner of the final lap of the first race at Brands. It was a slow crash but, as ever, my first thoughts were to get back on and finish the race in the points, as the marshals rushed to help pick the bike up.

'The front brake has snapped, Chris. You can't get back on,' yelled one of the marshals, as more and more bikes came round to finish their race.

'I can see the chequered flag. Just get the fucking thing started,' I shouted. I managed to get back on and blast down the straight to finish eleventh for a few points – and then remembered I had no brakes. With Paddock Hill Bend approaching I jammed down the gears and had both feet on the track to just stop myself going straight on into the gravel. But the damage was done and Niall only needed to finish the second race to take the title, which he did with a win. There was no chance to join in his celebrations because me and Dad needed to pack up straight away and head for the next World Superbike round at Albacete, our first road trip together.

It was like taking your son with you. I'm sure Dad pretends to be useless when Mum isn't around, because I know that he isn't actually useless at anything. But I am also sure that adults spend their first fifty years learning and then forget ten years' worth of stuff every successive year until they are like kids again at 60. First he left the connector at Brands while packing the power cable away; then he stuffed all our ironed clothes, still on their hangers, into an overnight bag when we left the motorhome below decks on the ferry; and, of course, he forgot to pack his toothbrush. Despite all this it was a mega trip and we made it to Southern Spain on the Tuesday, in time to spend an afternoon in Benidorm, about an hour away from Albacete. So we parked on the outskirts and hopped on my scooter to ride into town for a walk on the promenade. It was pretty hot so Dad suggested that we have a quick half a lager before finding a pizza. I'm not really a fan of Spanish food, although I will eat paella as long as it doesn't contain rabbit. It's just not right when you have owned one as a kid! I agreed to one beer, but was conscious that I was racing in a few days' time.

'Oi, Walker, you ignorant git,' came a shout from another bar while we wandered along the front looking for somewhere to eat. It was Foggy, who was with his team-mate, Neil Hodgson, and mechanic Anthony Bass, known to everyone as Slick. I didn't know too much about Carl but had been impressed at Assen when he invited me up to the top of the Ducati hospitality for a coffee and chat. I knew the PR demands on the top riders at a race meeting and it was good of him to spare me the time. I didn't know too much about Neil, either, except that his nickname was Hair Gel Hodgson and that his manager, Roger Burnett, was known as Roger Hairnet. But after a few more lagers we were all getting along like a house on fire and Dad was probably peaking that he was chilling out with Carl and Neil. Again it proved to me that most of the racers were just 100 per cent down-to-earth blokes, who could nevertheless ride the nuts off a motorbike. The evening turned into a bit of a bar crawl and, without any tea inside us, me and Dad were starting to struggle. When we bumped into a few girls from Neil's home town, Burnley, I was relaxed enough to get quite friendly with one while still being aware of a few disapproving glances from Dad. While he might not have been Lisa's biggest fan he was still a bit old school, so I sneaked off to the toilet for a little while, where I discovered, with the lights on, that more make-up was definitely required!

We left the group, with Foggy pleading that we had not seen him in Benidorm in case his wife, Michaela, found out. Even multiple world champions are scared of some things, then! But I was too pissed to ride the scooter and Dad did not know where we were, so I jumped on the back while he took the helm. Maybe the Spanish cops spotted that we were not wearing helmets, or maybe Dad was on the wrong side of the road, but a Guardia car started to give chase and Dad suddenly sobered up enough to disappear quick smart down the narrowest of alleys. The car could only stop at the entrance, blue lights flashing away and cops hurling warnings at us as we sped away, somehow found the motorhome and sheepishly hid the scooter away for the night. I was annoyed with myself in the morning for having a hangover so near to a race weekend, even though it was three days before I would put my leg over a bike. (But Foggy and Hodgson must have had bigger hangovers!) It might be starting to sound like I was drunk all the time but I have probably only mentioned the few occasions when I did let my hair down. And I always punished myself afterwards with kill-or-cure exercise, so I loaded Dad up with bananas and tackled a mountain on our push-bikes on the way out of town. It was cure for me and almost kill for Dad when his front tyre blew on the way back down, just after I persuaded him to try 'no hands'. 'You are a little twat, you are,' he grumbled, when his heart-rate eventually settled. 'You shouldn't be encouraging me to do stuff like that – I'm nearly 60, you know.' Precisely – you'd think he would have known better!

I struggled all weekend to find a rear tyre with enough grip around Albacete's long corners and had to opt for a hard compound for the race. The first few laps were awful and the rear was snaking around, but gradually the grip improved. People describe it as the tyre coming back to you. The leaders had cleared off but I was around tenth, and closing in on a group of five or six by around a second a lap. If the race had lasted another couple of laps I would have been on course to pass them all. I finished in tenth, but this was one of the few times when I had made progress during the race, rather than starting well and slipping back, so with a few more points from another eleventh place in the second race Yamaha seemed fairly chuffed with my efforts over the four rounds.

Again, though, there was little chance to reflect as we headed straight back to England for the final round of the British championship at Donington. Whitham's team were on the same ferry, along with a few British fans, so spirits were high as we set sail. Mine improved even more when we went for dinner because the young Spanish girl that was serving spotted my Yamaha shirt and asked me how the races had gone. It was difficult to tell exactly how handsome she was under her chef's hat, stained apron and shiny complexion from serving hot food all day. But Maria was very friendly and I was caught off guard when she asked me if I would take her to that evening's show on the boat. I had already seen their version of *Grease* too many times over the years, so I could not work out why someone who did the crossing several times a week wanted to go again. But we agreed to meet at nine o'clock although I still wasn't sure about the whole thing. I didn't want to sit through the show yet again if she turned out to be a minger. So I turned to Dad for a rare bit of fatherly advice.

'Just wait around the corner and, depending on how she scrubs up, either do one or tuck in,' he said, obviously having given up on any pretence to be disapproving. It turned out he had a bit of form on blind dates, having once left a cinema halfway through the film when the girl wouldn't snog him in the back row, and abandoning another girl on the way to Skegness because she was moaning about how fast he was riding his bike.

So I picked my spot to spy on Maria and couldn't get my breath when she turned up. She was drop-dead gorgeous, her long dark curly hair still wet from the shower and wearing a skimpy little white dress that barely covered her butt cheeks. 'Let's show John,' I thought.

I walked into the bar with her on my arm, and Dad's jaw hit the deck. After a few beers she was joining in with the Suzuki lads and having a laugh with Dad. Luckily the girls that Maria shared with were working on a different crossing so Dad did not have to put up with me apple-tarting in his face all night in our cabin. When I crept in early the next morning he did not say a word. He didn't need to because his look said it all: Check you out, youth! I knew that what had happened was not right but – how does the saying go – 'what the eye doesn't see, the heart doesn't grieve over'. I think that most people go through that phase. I had never had the five years – or twenty-five years, for some people – of going to clubs until I was sick of partying, and all of a sudden I was living anything but a sheltered life. My team-mates were married and so obviously didn't participate but would go to great lengths to encourage me. So I was getting it out of my system a bit later than most! My first taste of Latino Love was pretty memorable and Maria provided this still naïve young man with another lesson during this year of learning with Rob Mac and Mackenzie. If there had been any danger of me trying to forget it, Maria rang me a few weeks later when I was wandering around the Dirt Bike Show with Lisa and my Dad. Mobile phones were still as big as me in those days and it was before the caller's number was displayed on the screen.

'Ola, Chris love. It's Maria. I love you,' she said. My arse fell out. 'I remember you tell me you from Nottingham, the land of Robin Hood. Well, you never guess, I now visiting some friends at Nottingham University.'

'Dad! There's someone on the phone for you,' I said, hurriedly handing him the phone and guiding Lisa to another stall. I think the penny dropped with Dad, and he quickly rang off.

Needless to say the phone stayed off for the next few days, although I didn't need to go to those lengths because I could barely speak when I arrived back in England. Whether it was a bug from the beast from Burnley, the beauty from Bilbao or the bacon from the boat, or a combination of all three, I was as sick as a pig. Ironically, Rob Mac had often said during the year that I was a smoother rider when I was injured, so he was not too worried about my chances for Donington. I had already clinched second place in the championship but all riders like a strong finish to the season and I had not kept any food down for days. Over two weeks I lost a stone and a half and I have only ever put half a stone back on, so it probably did me a bit of a favour. But, although I was drained of energy come the race weekend, the team had made a slight but transformational set-up tweak at the front to help the bike steer lighter. I qualified on pole and won the first race comfortably, followed by a rostrum in the second. It was a fantastic way to finish the season and I was so pleased that I had repaid Rob Mac's leap of faith. You generally find that the young lads who are shown such faith, such as Johnny Rea or Tommy Hill, will eventually come good. So I thank my lucky stars that Rob had spotted that bit of something in me and put me on the same bike as the reigning British champion, because it had been a gamble for him and Yamaha at the time. OK, I had not received a wage but I had earned good prize money on top of my sponsorship deals and had put myself in a position to command a decent wage for the following year. Or so I thought!

I had no real intention of moving anywhere, because I had so much fun with the team and on such a brilliant bike. And then Rob dropped the bombshell that, as they were keeping Mackenzie on, there was still no decent budget for a second rider. Their best and final offer was £15,000, yet I had won nearly as many races as Niall, finished second in the championship and had been offered £20,000 by Old Spice the previous year, having only sat on a superbike on one occasion. But I was not in a strong bargaining position because many other riders would have jumped at the chance of riding that bike for nothing. It took the wind out of my sails and I had no option but to look around to see what else was available.

The best alternative offer came from the Total Kawasaki team, managed by Colin Wright. I had come across Colin some eight years earlier, when he was running Kawasaki Team Green in the Motocross World Championship, with Kurt Nicholl, and also overseeing test days that Kawasaki ran when launching new motocross models at Chippenham Wild Tracks. And, perhaps not surprisingly, he gave me my first ever bike bollocking. I had been invited to the test day through the shop and was given a brand spanking new KX125 to take out. But after three laps the throttle came off in my hand and I had a huge crash in one of the hidden spots of the track. I didn't want to face the music so I managed to bend as many bits as possible back into place before sheepishly handing it back and quickly wandering off.

'Hey, you, you little cant. Don't bother coming back on one of these days again if that's the way you are going to treat our bikes,' he growled. 'You could at least have told us that you crashed it.' But that's Colin; you always know where you stand with him and I have never had a problem with that. If he is happy with you, you know he is happy. And if he isn't, you know he isn't. But once he has said something he doesn't bear grudges and moves on. Unless you do it again, that is.

The team's riders that year had been Terry Rymer and Iain MacPherson. It had been MacFearless's first season in superbikes and the Kawasaki had been increasingly competitive, with Iain taking a win at Knockhill. He was staying on but Terry was moving to Paul Denning's Crescent Suzuki team. Paul had finished racing and wanted a big push to take the team to the next level. So here was a chance to join a team as a number one rider, as I had finished four places higher than Iain in the championship. If I stayed at Yamaha I would always be in Niall's shadow. Even if I beat him the following year the bike would probably have taken most of the credit. At Kawasaki I still had the chance to challenge for the title but would have to stand on my own two feet and develop the ZXR750 from scratch. Colin had also assembled a great team for this purpose. Stewart Johnstone was chief mechanic and one of the best in the business. I was also introduced to my number one mechanic, Les Pearson, who went on to become my crew chief for the next four years. And he is the best in the business. I was also keen to stay on a four-cylinder bike, which I found easier to ride than the Ducatis.

OK, the profile of the Total Kawasaki team would not be as big as at Yamaha. And the offer was not telephone numbers higher. But it would be enough to cover my costs and, importantly, look at buying a house so that me and Lisa could have a better chance of making our relationship work. It was still a big wrench to leave Niall, Rob Mac and the team, but Colin was very understanding about my dilemma – he allowed me forty-eight hours to make my mind up!

When the deal was announced a mock-up picture appeared in *MCN*, with my head superimposed on the body of someone wearing a set of Kawasaki leathers and holding a bag with a big pound sign on. The headline read: 'Walker signs big money deal with Kawasaki.' This was published the week before the NEC Show, where *MCN*, as the new title sponsors of the British Superbike Championship, were attempting to make a big impact. This included the bevy of beauties known as the *MCN* Babe Squad, wearing *MCN*-branded hot pants and cropped tops. Some were young, some a little older, some daft, some not-so-daft. But they all had two things in common: they were minters and had read the piece about my 'big money deal'. I was about to enter the big bad world of popularity among the fairer sex – but for no apparent reason.

Kawasaki had me at the show for the full ten days, staying in a hotel ten minutes from the NEC. It was a good chance to get to know the main men at Kawasaki, and also a few of the girls. On the final Saturday night a big bunch of us, including Kawasaki staff, a few members of the Yamaha team and as many of the Babe Squad as we could rustle up hit Birmingham's New Street for a big night out. With a few alcopops inside them some of the *MCN* girls were even more approachable. There was Zoe from Newark, and Debbie from Birmingham. And then there was a half-Italian girl called Olivia Masi from Cheshire. It was all quite innocent, although we did swap numbers. A world of hurt ensued.

18

Kneecapped Stalker

Taking that first step onto the property ladder felt like taking the first step towards being a real adult. I didn't tell Lisa at first, because I didn't want things to spiral out of control until I had found somewhere suitable, with real character, and had secured a mortgage. I also wanted to buy it on my own, as Lisa was just making her way as a self-employed hairdresser and didn't need the burden of a mortgage at that stage of her career. On a cycle ride around Sherwood Forest – every house I have ever owned I have found while cycling – I came across a quaint village called Ollerton. It was a tiny place, with a couple of pubs and a watermill, and I spotted a cottage for sale at the end of the main street, with wooden shutters on the windows and what looked like a witch's hat on the garage roof. I rang for the details there and then and it was just about in my price range. So I went to view it on my own and it was perfect, like a little Munchkin house. Two cottages, formerly the houses of the village policeman and fireman, had been knocked into one and the old wooden beams had been retained. The garage had been used to stable the fireman's horses and the witch's hat was a vent to take away the stench of the horse manure.

Securing a mortgage was not easy. The bank did not accept Cadbury's Boost wrappers as proof of income, but after showing my contracts and bank statements I eventually proved that I did have an income. So it was time to break the news to Lisa. On the day of completion I suggested we drive over to Ollerton for some tea in one of the pubs and then, while walking back to the car, I stopped at the cottage and put the keys in the front door.

'What the hell are you doing?' whispered Lisa. 'The owners will hear you, you idiot.'

'I am the owner,' I said, opening the door into the cottage. A tear immediately appeared in her eye and she was lost for words. 'I have bought it for both of us,' I assured her. At last we could move out of her mum and dad's home and build a home together, and Lisa set about the task with relish before we moved in.

The house was also in a great spot for launching into my winter training regime on my mountain bike, right next to Sherwood Forest, Rufford Park and Clumber Park. I would set off for 40-mile off-road round trips, armed just with an Ordnance Survey, emergency food and my mobile. I also made a big effort to become part of my new Kawasaki family and it was great to discover that Colin and the boys were just as sociable as the Yamaha team. We arranged a day's motocross bonding near Easingwold, where Stewart Johnstone, the crew chief for both me and Iain, lived. This was also close to the home of my number one mechanic, Les Pearson, in Tollerton, so we went out for a beer the night before. Dicko came with me and we gelled really well with Stewart, Les and a few of the other mechanics. I remembered having a go at people who wore Wolf motocross gear – which we called Wilf gear because you looked a bit of a Wilf in it. But I remembered little else when I woke up the next morning looking like a unicorn after, apparently, face-planting the pavement on the way home. The lads must have been thinking: 'What have we ended up with here?' And I didn't know where to put myself when Les turned up for the motocrossing kitted out from head to toe in Wolf gear.

The team organized an outing on the bike at Knockhill and my initial impression was good, but also that we there was a lot of work to do. It was not as good as my Yamaha from 1997, although I knew we had a team capable of making further developments and teaching me more about setting up a bike. Then the first major test was at

Cartagena in Spain, where all the main teams were present. Niall Mackenzie had been joined by Steve Hislop in the Yamaha team and both were instantly on the pace. Me and Iain were in and out the pits, doing twice as many laps, playing catch-up, and so the team decided to use the new specification engine on day two. It had more torque, power and top speed but the bike was now a monster to ride. The Boost team stopped after the third morning but we finally got the bike dialled in and I beat first Hislop's and then Mackenzie's times in the afternoon. I left Spain, with one week to the start of the season, as the fastest rider. You could tell Colin was peaking because his gnashers were constantly on display.

I picked up where I left off at Brands, qualifying on pole and just beating Sean Emmett to the race win, my first at Brands. A third place in race two meant I was leading the championship. But, before resuming the battle for domestic honours, Colin entered me as a wild card for the second round of the World Superbike championship at Donington. I was pleased that he had taken the calculated risk, to give me more experience and track time on the Kawasaki. The most memorable part of the weekend came during morning warm-up on Sunday when Foggy came past me out of McLean's. He looked over his shoulder and nodded at me, before standing up on his pegs and wiggling his arse. I had not spoken to him since Benidorm and it was a special feeling that he had made the effort to have a laugh with me. On the warm-up lap of the race I always tried to be first back to the grid, not only to warm my tyres but also to get into a racing frame of mind. Carl came up to me afterwards and said, 'Fuck me! I thought the race had started early when you came flying past.' When he signed me for his team years later he asked if I still always tried to win the warm-up lap. Little did I know that I would never be high enough up the grid to even win the warm-up lap on his bike!

I finished the Donington World Superbike races just outside the top ten but the results at Brands had gone a long way towards easing my nerves about the switch from Yamaha, although I knew that I would have to fight for every result in such a strong British Superbike Championship field. Troy Bayliss had arrived on the scene on the back of a sensational one-off ride in the 250 Australian Grand Prix for Lucky Strike. He had already been turning heads with his performances on a superbike in Australia and was head-hunted by the owner of GSE Racing, Darryl Healey, who brought him to England, put him up and became his manager. He was a great bloke: horizontally laid-back off the track but a terrier on it, and as tough as old boots. He was capable of winning races, as was his team-mate, Emmett. James Haydon and Terry on the Crescent Suzuki won races, as did Michael Rutter and Matt Llewelyn. The Cadbury's Boost boys were obviously always a threat – when they were not clashing on and off the track. For whatever reason, Niall and Hizzy did not get on and even collided on the final lap of the Snetterton, allowing Terry to pick up the race win in front of me.

I was having no such problems with my team-mate. Iain was a great laugh and very easy to get on with. It helped that he was the only team-mate I have ever had who was smaller than me – by a good inch. He was struggling in his second year with the team, though, and as lap times came significantly down in 1998 Iain found it hard to make that step. It's never easy when one rider is faster than his team-mate because the bosses are bound to ask questions. Colin Wright was perhaps not the most sympathetic of team managers, although he would provide a shoulder to cry on when necessary. But, after he had dished out some advice, it was then your job to deal with it. Iain had certainly been handed a bit of a Colin Wright 'tune-up' after the first few rounds and their relationship suffered because of it. For me Colin was another big part of my racing education. I guess I was at a stage when, like any adolescent, it's easy to fall in with the wrong crowd and pick up bad habits that stay with you for life. Colin did not allow that to happen and taught a rider to respect those working around him. It was a bit like going to finishing school.

His team philosophy was work hard, play hard. If the lads knuckled down and finished their work, they would be the first out on the beers. If the work was not finished, they would have to stay until it was done. One of the first times we were able to let our hair down was during a team PR appearance at the Beaulieu Bike Show in

Hampshire. On the Saturday night we ended up in the only decent nightclub nearby, the Zoo and Cage in Bournemouth. This had two separate areas, each with different music, and the tequila slammers started flowing. Colin was on form, doing his party trick of wiggling his stomach like a belly dancer and shouting: 'Not baaaad for a fackin' firty-eight year old!' Colin and Stewart are as thick as thieves when drinking but Stewie had to disown him on this occasion, while me and Iain headed into the Cage section, which was a bit quieter. It was a good move because I had never seen bigger boobs on a barmaid, all pushed up and almost fully exposed by her low-necked top. They were also at face height for two midgets, especially when we stood on the metal foot-rest running along the bottom of the bar.

'She ish lovely, by the way,' slurred Iain, who was a bit more drunk than I was because, being a Scotsman, he wasn't turning down any of the drinks being offered him. He said 'by the way' after every sentence, by the way.

'I bet you a tenner that I can feel her boobs,' I said, knowing that a tenner to Iain was like £100 to anyone else.

'Fuck off, by the way,' he said. I stood back on the foot-rest and beckoned the barmaid towards me. 'I have just bet my mate here £10 that I can feel your boobs. Here's £20. Get us two tequila slammers and you can keep the rest if you will play along.' She winked at me, served the drinks and then leaned invitingly forward. I put my hands straight down her top and scooped them up for what seemed like a lifetime but was probably only a couple of seconds.

'No way. That's not right, by the way,' grumbled Iain, handing over his tenner. It had obviously cost me £4 but it was the best £4 I have ever spent. We were all second hand in the morning. I tried to run it off with an early-morning jog before going back to the show, Colin was also decidedly rough, but Stewie was, as ever, brand new. Iain turned up at 3 p.m., just when we were all packing up to go.

After two more podiums from the second round at Oulton, I was momentarily knocked out of my stride at Thruxton when it became clear that Jean had taken her stalking to a new level. I woke up on race day, had a good stretch and pulled back my motorhome curtains. Fuck me! Jean was staring straight at me from the window of her own motorhome. She had somehow obtained a pass for the paddock – if you actually needed one in those days – and parked directly next to me. I yanked the curtains shut again and tried to stop shaking. David Pickworth, who still often stayed with me at race meetings, had to check that the coast was clear every time I left my motorhome for the rest of the day. Jean had also obtained a sidekick by now, another middle-aged obsessive nicknamed Two-Litre Rita, after her estimated breast capacity. She drove a car that looked like it had just come from a set of *Pimp My Ride* and always painted her fingernails in the colours of the rider she was 'following' at the time.

While Jean's attentions were unavoidable, and definitely not welcome, harmless flirting with Olivia was also inescapable. She worked at a few of the rounds and also did some promotional work for Kawasaki. She was pretty and I enjoyed her company, but I did not realize I had any kind of chance because she acted similarly around a few other blokes. When the penny eventually dropped and I did realize I was in with a chance, I had no inclination to act. Lisa and I were setting up home, renovating bits of the house whenever we saved enough money. I still did not see an awful lot of her because of that bloody horse and it's a good job I'm not the jealous type because she might have found a horse's head on the pillow! But at least we now had our own space and could do the homely things that most couples do.

Perhaps, after the shock of seeing Jean, it wasn't too surprising that Thruxton was the only round when I did not make it onto the podium before travelling to Oulton again for round six. I struggled to dial the bike in throughout the weekend and had to battle with front-end chatter, especially through Cascades. I wasn't a million miles off the lead in the first race but fighting to stay in touch when, going into Cascades, the bike let go when I cracked open the throttle. The Kawasaki was not the fastest machine out there but the grip was immense, so when it let go it let go big. I always preferred very loose-fitting leathers but this sometimes meant that the knee cup would work round to the side of the leg, and my kneecap landed directly on the Tarmac. It instantly swelled to the width of Colin Wright's head and I was in agony. At the medical centre the British Superbikes doctor, Toby Branfoot, who has put my good pal Mark Heckles back together a couple of times, drained a dark brown goo out of my knee with a needle which seemed to be as thick as a McDonald's straw. I don't like needles at the best of time but this made me feel sick and faint, just as I started to hear the rain fall on the medical centre roof. I hopped around until race two, not wanting to show the officials that I was struggling to walk in case they tried to stop me riding.

The wet conditions were the last thing I needed, because you do not lean the bike over as much in the wet and you stick your knee out more for stability. But my knee had almost no flexibility and I rode the whole race virtually upright, yet managed to finish seventh. Stewart and Les had to lift me off the bike at the end and I was in tears from the pain. An X-ray at the hospital revealed that my kneecap had shattered into seven pieces like a plate. The doctor told me that I would be in a full leg cast for six to eight weeks and Dad said that I looked at the doctor like he was from another planet. There was simply no way that was going to happen. They put me in a temporary cast until the swelling came down but, armed with X-rays stolen from the Queen's Medical Centre, I went to the Laserman instead. He said that he would have me fit in time for the next round in three weeks – and I believed him.

Unfortunately I would have to miss the Brands Hatch round of World Superbikes but I was now trailing Mackenzie by 48 points and had to focus on the British championship because I could not afford to lose any more ground. Having been runner-up the previous year when I was a new kid on the block, I now wanted to win the title at all costs. And I wanted to keep away the paddock vultures, who are always circling ready for a go on your bike – and your bird, for that matter – at the first opportunity. I cadged lifts from Lisa, Dad and my mates down to Ipswich to see Laserman three times a week for constant lasering and draining of the joint, and the movement of the knee started to return. So I was devastated when Colin rang to tell me that he had lined up a journalist to ride at Knockhill instead of me.

'We are not going to find someone as fast as you so we are trying to get as much exposure as possible. Dan Harris writes for *Superbike* magazine but is a handy racer, too,' Colin explained.

'I am trying to be fit, you know,' I pleaded. 'But you might have to give me a piggy-back onto the rostrum.'

'Yeah, right-oh! All riders say they will be fit, Chris. You just concentrate on your treatment, fly to Scotland on the Thursday and I will make a judgement when you arrive.'

Mum offered a lift down so that I could squeeze in one final treatment session on the Thursday morning before flying to Edinburgh. Mums rule! Brian inserted electric probes into the joint and it worked wonders. The knee was back to about 70 per cent flexibility. He told me that I should be able to race but that the underside of the bone had not healed smoothly and would scrape on the knee-joint. 'You risk having to have your knee replaced in about ten years if you do race straight away,' Laserman warned. Touch wood, it's now nearly ten years down the line and I can run further than I ever could, although my knee does ache after a long bike ride.

I had told Mum that I was flying from nearby Stansted so that she would not panic about driving me there on time, but I was actually flying from Luton. I made the flight just in the nick of time and Colin met me at the airport, by which time my leg had seized up again. But I could tell that Colin was chuffed to see how much progress I had made.

'I'm confident you are fit enough, but let Dan ride tomorrow morning. You ride in the afternoon and if you go quicker than him then you can stay on the bike for the rest of the weekend,' he said on the way to the team hotel. It was nice not to be in my motorhome for once and to be able to spend some time with our unsung heroes, the mechanics: Stewart and Les; my number two, Lee Rynet, Terry Rymer's brother-in-law; Iain's number one, Craig Webb; and Iain's number two, an Australian called Anthony Warnock, known as Skip for obvious reasons.

I was in a lot of pain on the bike but I was straining at the leash and went faster than Dan, who had done a reasonable job in the morning. I did not qualify too well and the first race passed by in a blur – until Colin was carrying me piggy-back onto the rostrum. I had finished second behind Niall. I think I probably won a lot of admiration that day, from the spectators but also my team. Until something like this happens nobody really knows to what lengths a rider will go to try to win. Colin had taken a chance and believed that I was telling the truth about being ready to race. And I think it helped him discover how much success really meant to me.

The soap opera continued the following week at Mallory Park, the television pictures bringing my trials and tribulations to the armchair fans as well as the paying punters. Still using crutches and wearing a special brace that the Laserman had made, I hopped onto the bike and put it on pole position. I normally used the softest tyres available but we were using a narrower rim for the first time, which helped the harder tyres reach optimum temperature sooner. But obviously not as soon as the second lap of the first race, when I flicked the bike into the Bus Stop chicane, the rear end broke traction and I high-sided. It all happened so fast that I was leaning on the tyre wall before I knew what was happening. Luckily, my injured leg had not taken the full force of the fall and I was able to pull myself together, patch myself up and win the second race.

With four rounds remaining I trailed Niall by 79 points but managed to reduce the gap by 30 points with two more race wins at Cadwell, my first double. Niall might have been more of a threat that weekend had I not high-sided at Barn on the first lap of the first race. His bike hit mine as it was spinning around on the track and the underside of my foot-rest sliced into the top of his foot. I ran over to him and could see the blood spurting from the wound. Only a tough old trout like Niall would have got back on when the race was restarted after the red flag I had caused. Two wins, a lap record thrown in for good measure and my nearest rival in hospital – it was a productive weekend!

If only the next round at Silverstone had gone so smoothly. I had seen a ZX9R, the Kawasaki flagship superbike, parked in the garage all weekend but thought nothing more of it until after Saturday qualifying, when I was about to focus on my final race preparations. Colin then told me that *MCN* readers had taken part in a competition to win a Pillion in a Million – a pillion ride on the back of me, Mackenzie and Bayliss. I was not really given any instructions so assumed that the passenger would want to go as fast as humanly possible. I met my winner, told him to bash me on the shoulder if I was going too fast, and set off on my out-lap to get a feel for the bike – a real rocket. On our first fast lap we soon passed Niall and Troy and I had sparks coming from the foot-rests and exhausts through the chicanes. I checked after one lap that he was OK and he gave me the thumbs up so I did one more flying lap and was slowing down on the in-lap when the marshals gestured for me to pull a wheelie. My man had not moaned so far, so I guessed he would be up for it and I accelerated down the back straight, touched the clutch and the front wheel came straight up.

Suddenly his legs were level with my helmet. I had not realized how tired he was after hanging on for dear life for the first two laps and he just couldn't hold on any longer. When I looked round he had disappeared – or 90 per cent disappeared. His flared leather jeans had caught on the handrail and he was being dragged in a 360-degree spin along the track with just his helmet touching the surface. It was like someone had angle-grinded the circumference of his helmet and visor. The leathers then worked themselves loose from the bike and he was left sprawled across the track, so I stopped, flipped the side stand down and ran back to him.

'Quick, get up, or I will get in trouble,' I said, as he grimaced, not really knowing where he was. I helped him back on the bike and held him on until we reached the medical centre, where I could see way too much skin through his ripped leathers for my liking. I had no idea what I was going to tell everyone.

'Where is he?' asked Colin, when I rode the bike back into the garage.

'The twat fell off,' I said, chuckling nervously. Colin had never looked so serious.

'Chris, this is his wife. Is he all right?'

My cheeky grin vanished instantly and I told them that he was in the medical centre, but OK. The least I could do was offer him a new set of leathers, a new helmet and some boots.

'Yeah, but I borrowed these from a mate,' he explained. 'So can I have a set for him, too?' The whole episode had cost me two sets of leathers, two helmets and two sets of boots. I often see the bloke, a lovely guy, at the races and it is still the highlight of his life. He even asked me to sign the copies of his local paper in which it was reported. Needless to say I have never done another pillion ride to this day – and don't intend to.

The thrills and spills at Silverstone did not end there. I was lying second in the first race when I had a tiny crash, weakening the gear lever, which broke off while in fifth gear on the start-finish straight after I had remounted. I was desperate for any points and managed to come home in fourteenth, despite having to slip the clutch in fifth out of hairpins where I would have normally used second gear. So, after I had secured only two points while Niall was fourth, he only needed two decent finishes at the penultimate round at Brands to clinch his third successive title. I had second place to protect, though, and took a 34-point lead over Hizzy into the final round at Donington, where a win in the opening race clinched the runner-up spot again.

After having changed teams, and after suffering a serious injury mid-season, it was as good as I could have hoped for. The team had taken me to the next level of understanding a motorbike, and knowing what I wanted from it. But, having previously seen Rymer and Mackenzie at close quarters, I now knew what it took to be a winner. So I was now fitter, stronger in mind and body, and more focused. I was gagging for 1999 and had no great desire to change teams because I had never had much continuity until then. Sure, I had one eye on World Superbikes and had a brief chat with Harold Eckl, who ran the factory Kawasaki team. But they had already replaced Hodgson with Gregorio Lavilla, although Harold promised to keep an eye on my progress for the future.

Colin then offered me a reasonable hike in wages, which meant there was not too much in the budget for their second rider, as Iain was being replaced. That was fine by me now that the shoe was on the other foot and I was the number one rider! The team signed Warwick Nowland, a likeable Australian who had done well in the World Endurance championship and a few World Superbike rounds. Colin told me that we were also going to be using two factory bikes that Yanagawa and Hodgson had ridden that year.

For once I could go into the winter not having to worry about my future, and a great way to wind down, theoretically, was by accepting an invitation from Whitham to join about twenty of his mad mates on their annual, professionally organized four-day enduro mission through a stunning part of France. Kawasaki had loaned me a KX250 for the year but I had also bought a KTM enduro bike, one of the best off-road bikes I'd ever had. Graham Overton came with me and we were all given a map at the start of the day, which was then attached to a scroll on the handlebars. It wasn't a race – or wasn't supposed to be – but if you wanted to be at the front you needed to be able to ride and read the map simultaneously, while flat out. Soon we were reaching the designated meeting points an hour before the van, and the organizer, Chris Evans (not the ginger and funny one – a hard combination to come by), was starting to lose his sense of humour, having spotted us wheelying through farmyards. But, once we were dialled into the map-reading it was always going to be messy and we were off for the next stage at flat-out motocross speeds.

I took a wrong turn at one point while at the front and was looking back to check that everyone had seen me double back. But I hadn't spotted some tree roots growing above ground and hit them at 40 m.p.h. in fourth gear. The front hopped over but it was as though the back wheel had hit a breeze block. I was thrown over the top, landed on my head and knocked myself out. Whitham arrived to see me struggling to disentangle myself from a barbed-wire fence, with blood gushing from a deep cut on my forehead. Needless to say I took it easy to reach the next meeting point, from where the van took me to a hospital which looked more like a village hall, where a nurse with halitosis stitched my head without anaesthetic and bandaged all my other wounds. I looked like a cross between Mr Bump from the Mister Men and the Elephant Man. At the overnight hotel, as Graham pieced my bike back together, Chris decided I could not ride the next day and I was spewing. But, despite not being able to fit my goggles over a bump which was now hanging over my eye, he weakened in the morning on the condition that I took it easy. My sensible head lasted ten minutes before I was flat out again. And I probably stayed on the bike another ten minutes before I passed out again and – donk! – landed on my head once more.

'This is beyond a fucking joke,' said Whit, who for once lost his sense of humour. 'Get him in the back of the van.' He was not the only one to fail to see the funny side. As everyone packed up to go home Chris took James to one side and told him not to bother booking on the trip again – we were all banned because of my antics. Maybe it was time to refocus on next season's racing.

Above Sticking it up the inside of Yukio Kagayama at Silverstone in 2005.

Above Drenched in champagne on the podium at Valencia in 2005.

Above Assen 2006 – finding the Holy Grail with my first World Superbike win.

Right The aftermath of losing the front end at 100mph on entry to the Parabolica at Monza in 2006.

Below Smoking' – Stalker style.

Above Leading Nori Haga when I used this one-off Cross of St George helmet at Brands, 2005.

Right On the grid with Rachel at Brands in 2006.

Right The Stag Do: (from left) Ben Wilson, Cal Crutchlow, Tommy Hill, Magpie, Stalker, Craig Jones, Fish and Dog.

Above Tying the knot at St Augustine's Church, Flintham, with Rev David Wakefield.

Above The first dance.

Left Consummating our marriage over the bonnet of Rachel's 1967 Fiat 500.

Above The A-team: (from left) Stalker, Dog, Fish, Magpie and best man, Jamie.

Right My mum and dad, John and Christine.

Below Oi, Nobby, that's my spot.

Above Stalker flying high over the Mountain at Cadwell Park.

Above Doing something I love – spending time with the fans.

Above Me and my bro, Les Pearson, the best mechanic in the business.

Right Come on, Stalker!

Above Me and my team-mate Cal Crutchlow as Batman and Robin at the Rizla Suzuki Christmas party.

Above And you thought my right foot was in a strange position!

Left Joining the Honda young guns, Johnny Rea and Kiyo, on the podium at Silverstone in 2007.

Above Mrs Rachel Walker – she's mint, isn't she!

19

Enduring Stalker

The almost inevitable bombshell was dropped as I wandered around the Dirt Bike Show at Donington. The call came from Martin Lambert, the marketing manager at Kawasaki, who had always been brilliant with me.

'I'm afraid this isn't just a social call,' he said, after a bit of polite chit-chat. 'Colin Wright has left to join GSE Racing. And he has taken Stewart with him. We are going to do everything we can to go racing still, but I have to tell you that there is no guarantee it will happen,' he said.

I was speechless. Colin was one of the main reasons I had not looked at too many other options. His style of management had worked for me that year. On paper we should perhaps have clashed, but there was no need for him to be regimented with me as long as I was delivering the results. In one phone call my number one mechanic Les Pearson had become crew chief, team coordinator, chief mechanic and engine builder. And the team, which had previously operated out of Stewie's home at York, no longer had a base. All the plans, such as the ordering of parts for next year, were up in the air because Colin had been asked to leave immediately, and one of the hardest things to take was that I had not been able to talk to him because of constraints placed on him by Kawasaki. I did not blame Colin one bit, and he has gone on to great things with GSE. He would never have been able to achieve that at Kawasaki and, looking back, I am amazed how he ran such a professional team on such a small budget. Maybe that was why we only had a 7.5 tonne truck and fairly average hospitality unit. But I needed to focus on the coming season, not dwell on the past.

The first step that Kawasaki made in the rebuilding process was to employ a bloke called Simon Buckmaster as team manager. I only knew him from the nickname he had been stuck with since his racing days – Simon Backmarker – but I did find him immediately annoying. He had raced in GPs and also World Endurance, where he had lost the lower part of one leg in a bad crash at the Bol d'Or, although it was difficult to tell and even today he still plays squash with his son. From those endurance racing days he obviously knew Steve Hislop quite well, and Simon's first act was to sack poor Warwick Nowland, before he had even sat on the bike, and bring in Hizzy. There was no doubt that Steve was one of the fastest riders in the world on his day – he was a phenomenon. But on other days he needed counselling in a dark room to get him through the session. I couldn't help thinking that the arrival of Steve meant that Buckmaster did not have much confidence in me as a number one rider. Warwick, whose family worked in the legal profession, set about suing the team for breach of contract.

Simon had also worked with the Harris brothers in World Superbikes with Suzuki and did a deal to use their unit in Stevenage as a team base. This meant that Les had to drive down on a Monday morning and sleep in bunk beds in the workshop during the week, along with a couple of mechanics, which could not have been great for his relationship with his girlfriend back home in North Yorkshire. Les had learnt a lot working alongside Stewart during the year and took it on himself to do the engine work, along with a guy from Harris. Les was also given the job of driving across to deepest, darkest Germany to pick up the factory bikes from the Eckl team. I was on the phone every five minutes to find out what they were like but Les managed to disguise his own disappointment. They had a few factory bits, like trick forks and swinging arm, but they were not what we expected from factory machines, which we had assumed would be heaps better than our existing bikes.

The first test was at Albacete along with the World Superbike team and, a little nervous after all the changes, the first task was to get used to my new team personnel and structure. Les was now my crew chief, but still worked on the bike alongside my new number two, Gary Arnold. He was known as Slim, because he wasn't especially slim. Skip was Hizzy's number one mechanic and Graham Brown did Steve's engines, but also worked on the bike. Ralph, Harris's guru responsible for their Grand Prix frames, was also on board. He looked and sounded like Maurice Gibb from the Bee Gees, so I never learned his surname. It was clear from the start that Buckmaster had a very different way of working than Colin. It was also clear that he was more of a Steve Hislop fan than a Chris Walker fan, maybe because I didn't blow smoke up his arse.

And, if Buckmaster and Hizzy had been friends before Albacete, they were best mates after it. I struggled with the new bike and discovered, just as I had found with the factory Yamaha bike, that there was loads of revs but not a lot of torque, so it was difficult to put the power down onto the track. However, on his first visit to the track Steve jumped on the Harold Eckl bike, found a great setting with the help of Maurice Gibb and smoked not only me but the factory boys too. Many people are obsessed with a number one rider having to be faster than his team-mate. I have always found that all to be a bit odd. Nobody is more competitive than I am. But I also like to have a good relationship with everyone around me, including my team-mate. I had learned from Niall and Terry that it was performances over the course of a season that count, not a one-off test, qualifying session or race. So I had never experienced this kind of rivalry before.

Anyway, the tables were soon turned at Cartagena the following week, when I concentrated on dialling in my 1998 bike and went faster than the previous year, and not too far off the rest of the teams. I have since found out that good settings for Albacete rarely work for

British tracks. And when Steve struggled to get close on the factory bike, which had worked so well for him only the previous week, I saw the first signs of his fragile nature.

By the start of the season, Les, who was working every hour available on the engine, had managed to find more torque and I was second in both races of the first round at Brands. Neil Hodgson, back from World Superbikes as team-mate to Bayliss in Colin Wright's INS Ducati team, was fast out of the blocks with a race win and James Haydon took the other victory. James had a reputation for crashing, which was a bit unfair. It was just that when he did crash he did it in style. He also won a race at Thruxton, where again I scored two more podiums and trailed him by 5 points in the British championship. But no sooner had I got into my stride than we headed off to France for a one-off ride in the Le Mans 24-Hours with Kawasaki France. There was no pressure placed on us to take part but Buckmaster thought it might prove useful and there was always the chance of earning a few quid in bonuses.

At the test for Le Mans it was difficult to get used to a bike that had to be set up as a compromise between me and Steve. I liked my bike jacked up at the back, with a long swinging arm length and all the weight on the front. That way the front went where you wanted it to, even if the back did its own thing, and if that happened I would turn to Les or Dunlop for more grip. Steve liked a more sedate setting, with the back end down and the head angle kicked out, similar to the Ducatis on which he went on to later success. I was as sick as a dog on the night before the test, spewing and shitting, sometimes simultaneously. It was probably from eating some dodgy French food, because the French do know how to ruin a good steak or crucify a good chicken breast. And I was amazed that the mechanics tucked into a glass of red wine at lunchtime and our third rider, a French journalist called Bertrand Sebileau, even had a beer before going back out on track in the afternoon.

Come the race I was nervous about two things: riding in the dark, because you needed to know the circuit like the back of your hand to do it well, and riding in wet conditions, because their wet-weather tyres were a bit 'old school' and they did not use tyre warmers. So, of course, after ten minutes of my first night session it pissed down. But as all the other riders went down like skittles – one rider from the other Kawasaki team even crashed in pit-lane – I managed to stay upright and build a two-lap lead. My reward was to be told to stay out there on track as I was now used to the conditions. After two hours on the bike in the middle of the night I came in with my tongue on the top yoke. Our team manager, Christian Bourgeois, who was a bit nuts, came up with a solution: a glass of red wine. Red Bull, maybe, but definitely not red wine. 'In France we call it "late braking"', he laughed.

Hizzy took over from me and set a new lap record in the pitch dark at 2 a.m. It was simply incredible. By morning we still had a healthy lead and my pit board was telling me to slow down. Whitham, riding with Rymer for the Suzuki team, needed us to make a mistake if his team were to have a chance and so he was constantly trying to goad me into racing him. But the last thing I wanted to do was let my team-mates down. Steve, who had a lot of experience of endurance racing, had taken me under his wing that weekend and we really gelled. And to see Sebileau doing a stand-up wheelie over the line in front of his home fans was an amazing feeling. The podium was also a great place to be. Even though Whitham had hit a marshal who, quite rightly under endurance rules, had refused to help him pick the bike up when he crashed, James and Terry were also up there in third. But none of us had as much energy as Hizzy. After the urine sample, scrutineering, prize-giving and a shower, we were on the piss by 4 p.m. I was pissed by 5 p.m. and in bed by 6. I don't think Steve even went to bed.

Mum, Dad, Lisa and Pickworth had been over to watch, but David and Lisa needed to be back for work on Monday morning, so they set off straight away. At a toll booth 100 miles away from the circuit the gendarmes pulled David over for having an illegal radar detector. They confiscated his driving licence and both their passports until he could pay a cash fine of 2,000 euros, which meant David driving all the way back to nick my prize money to pay it.

Back home, Bayliss began to stamp his authority on the title race with two more wins at Oulton, before we broke off for another distraction – the Donington round of World Superbikes. After the first day's qualifying at Donington, my mate Millett rang to ask how Foggy was doing.

'He's eighth,' I told him.

'Bloody hell. That's not too clever. Who's on provisional pole then?'

'Corser,' I told him.

'No surprises there. He's an awesome qualifier,' said Millett.

'So where were you?'

'Second,' I said. There was a stunned silence. I managed to stay in the top eight throughout Saturday, going into their new qualifier format, Superpole. The top fifteen riders each had one flying lap to determine the grid and this was my baptism – not of fire, of snow. It was a freezing cold weekend and I was nervous enough about this new format, which tended to suit some riders more than others. And the qualifying tyre was so cold that I lost a bit of confidence through the faster sections. As I turned into McLeans the first flakes appeared on my visor and Superpole was cancelled halfway through my lap because of the snow. The times stood from the normal qualifying instead and I managed to hang onto seventh place on the grid, which enabled me to get a great start for the first race. I was third after the first lap and held on to fourth place, the first Kawasaki home, ahead of factory rider Akira Yanagawa. This was doing my future on the world stage no harm at all, although I had to pull in midway through race two with a technical problem.

Donington was one of Jean's favourite haunts, as she lived fairly close, not that proximity was ever an issue now she had her motorhome. I had tried being nice, hoping she would just go away. I had also tried being a bit off with her, maybe not appearing too grateful for the pics she gave me and Hizzy. And I had tried to ignore her. But nothing was succeeding in shaking her loose. Lisa was now aware of her and a bit fed up with it, plus the team did not like her hanging around all the time. During that weekend she had managed to attract Les's attention at the back of the garage.

'Chris has been really funny with me all weekend. Do you think he is jealous because I have been talking to Steve Hislop, too?' she asked, in all seriousness. Les told her to hang on a second, went into the garage and brought out a life-size cut-out that our sponsors Total had produced to advertise their oil. I say life-size; it was actually an inch shorter than me, which was a bit of a piss-take when I am only a midget to start with!

'Here, Jean. If Chris isn't talking to you then this might be the next best thing,' he said.

'Oh, I've already got one of those. But what use is a cardboard cut-out to me? I need the real thing,' she said, before showing Les a picture of her at home, kitted out from top to toe in my helmet, leathers, boots and gloves, which had been bought from various charity auctions. There was only ever going to be one way of shaking her off – by leaving the country!

I also bumped into a guy called Geoffrey Money at a few Kawasaki track days, who was just as big a fan. Unfortunately he had a hearing disability and was inevitably christened Deaf Geoff. He did not have the best physique but he was bloody quick on a motorbike, especially when taking his disability into account. Geoff was extremely animated when telling stories of his mishaps on bikes, often caused because he could not hear the engine when changing through the gears. He, too, had bought a replica helmet, similar to today's design with the W effect down the middle, a purple background, initially designed to match the Cadbury's Boost colours, and yellow and orange halves. He owned a Chris Walker replica ZXR750, replica leathers, always had the latest Stalker T-shirt and even named his cat Stalker. He was a legend.

My consistency continued in the British championship, and after round six at Silverstone I was still in second place behind Bayliss. I had not managed a race win yet, as the Ducatis were proving difficult to beat, but I had more than double Hizzy's points tally. Buckmaster, a typical fair-weather friend, did not mess around and gave Steve the flick. I felt terrible but needed to keep my head down and concentrate on the job in hand. I had always found him to be a great team-mate and a great guy, with not a malicious bone in his body. People say that he was maybe fragile or insecure, and perhaps it didn't help that he was pretty isolated, living on the Isle of Man. I know that when the chips are down for me I like to be surrounded by my family and friends.

I was devastated when I learned of his death in the helicopter accident in 2003. He is one of the few people that I have known really well to lose their life, and the hardest thing is to think that you will never see them again. There is hardly a day goes by when someone does not mention his name – maybe talking about his TT exploits or that amazing qualifying lap at Donington in World Superbikes in 2001 – because he was one of the all-time greats. But I like to remember him running to his bike when the flag dropped at the start of the Le Mans race and then giving him a hug on the podium, after he had been instrumental in helping me to my first win at world championship level.

His place was initially taken by Max Vincent, which puzzled me because I did not expect him to be as fast as Steve. Harris had also built a third bike, which Shakey Byrne rode for the first time at Oulton. He had come from a good year in the 600s and I really like him. It was obvious that he was destined to be a fans' favourite. And I guess the next chapter in the story of popularity was written at my next World Superbike wild card ride at Brands Hatch.

It was a red-hot weekend with a massive crowd, many there to see Foggy march towards his fourth World Superbike title, although he had a disastrous weekend with tyre problems. I qualified in tenth and, having missed out at Donington by one place, was desperate for my first World Superbike podium. Hello? Earth to Stalker! On the warm-up lap for the first race the bike cut out at the top of Druids, as though it had run out of fuel. I parked it up and sprinted down the hill and across the gravel trap back to the pits. The crowd were going mental, cheering me on like it was in the 100 metres final of the Olympics. The team heard the commotion and spotted me running back on their TV monitors and the big screens. When the gravel slowed me up it just needed *Chariots of Fire* music to complete the effect.

As I reached pit-lane the spare bike was already running under the control tower.

The race started just as I jumped on and I joined the back of the field when the last man went past. I had made up six places by the end of the first lap and gradually clawed my way back up to tenth. My weakness at Brands has always been Surtees, leading onto the back straight. I used to put it down to riding a 750cc against the 1000cc twins, but I was no better there when I switched to a Ducati. But in this race it did not seem to be a problem and the crowd went wild every time I made up a place around Paddock Hill bend or going into Druids. Normally, as a wild card, World Superbike races seemed to last for ever as you struggled to maintain the pace of the fastest riders in the world. This one went by in a flash and is one of the most enjoyable of my career. The start to race two was a bit more Stalker-like. I was second at the end of the first lap but immediately developed a problem and dropped back through the field before pulling in towards the end. But the whole experience had whetted my appetite to perform on the world stage on a regular basis.

First, though, I had unfinished business in Britain. Four more podiums at Knockhill and Mallory and I had closed the gap on Bayliss to just 25 points with three rounds remaining, starting at Cadwell. Only James Haydon had broken the dominance of Ducati race wins, with John Reynolds and Sean Emmett in the Reve Racing team joining Bayliss and Hodgson in also having made it to the top step of the podium on their Ducatis. It was about time that changed, and I won my first race of the year at Cadwell to close the gap on Bayliss to 18 points with two rounds remaining. It was building up to be a gripping climax to the season – but I was still hungry for World Superbike action.

David Pickworth had been working on *Superbike* magazine to provide enough funding to allow us to compete at Assen, in return for a special feature and some stickers on the bike. Although Buckmaster did not necessarily approve, we argued that the extra experience and track time would prove useful and he agreed as long as it was not going to eat into his budget. It was worthwhile for me, because I qualified in front of both factory riders in sixth and was only passed by Lavilla on the final lap of the first race. Two top tens for a wild card outside my own country would surely help put me in the shop window again.

Speaking of shop windows, me and Dave stopped off in Amsterdam on the way home. After a good few beers and the effects of passive smoking in the coffee bars where everyone was smoking spliffs, we were in the Amsterdam mood and decided to do a lap of the red light district. It was the only time I was even remotely tempted to visit a lady of the night. She was a cute little Thai girl who wore a zebra print bikini, but I could not make my mind up what to do, conscious that a lot of British bike fans would be in the vicinity. After a couple more beers we did another lap and, as at any new circuit, our lap times were coming steadily down, mainly because her curtain was now closed and she was having her hip knocked out. Further down the road the bloke outside the live sex show stopped us.

'You want to see zhe shex show? We have girlzh on girlzh, girlzh on boyzh, boyzh on boyzh, girlzh on midgetzh. We have two seatzh at zhe front – so close you can zhmell zhe cont,' he said. We were on the floor; it was pure comedy genius. A couple of hours and yet more beers later, our fifth lap found us back outside the window of the Thai girl. Before temptation struck I heard a bloke on the other side of the canal shout, 'Fuck me, there's Chris Walker.' Not far behind him was the *MCN* reporter. My arse fell out and we legged it back to the hotel.

Now it was time for the business end of the British championship and my strong finish continued with another win in the first race of the penultimate round at Brands. Bayliss came second but only after his team-mate Hodgson let him through, much to the crowd's disgust. I was up there with Bayliss midway through the second race when my clutch started to slip. I dropped back into a dice with Mackenzie and I am sure that he took pity on me and delayed the inevitable pass. I then started to lose drive on the straight and soon it was like riding with no chain. I coaxed the bike back into the garage, threw my helmet down and shouted, 'What the fuck do I have to do to win this championship?' The Suter clutches had been a law unto themselves all year and this was a devastating blow to my chances. Bayliss now had a commanding lead and there was no realistic way I was going to win the title from there. After being so focused all year, after all the work that Les had put in, and after having fought all year to stick with my 1998 bike despite pressure from Buckmaster and Kawasaki to ride the factory machine, it was hard to stomach that the title was going to elude me for the third successive year – and because of a technical failure. What's more, John Reynolds had sneaked past me into second place. But I was not about to give up the ghost because I knew I would be strong at Donington for the final round.

I pulled out all the stops and won the opening race, which was as much as I could do. But, with Bayliss riding a sensible race, his sixth place was all he needed to clinch the title. I was now also back in second place above JR again and found myself in a battle with him in the second race. Trailing him into the Esses, I remembered a bit of a move he had stuck on me earlier in the season. So I let the brakes off, went underneath him and forced him to pick the bike up. He ran off in the grass and was unable to start it again. But I had lost momentum too and dropped back to tenth, which was enough to hang on to the runner-up slot. John did not make too much of a fuss. He was the toughest rider out there and would probably have pulled the same move. And it wasn't as though I had just taken my brains out and done a Capirossi – when he ran into Harada to take the championship on the last corner of the last lap of the previous 250cc GP season. Having been Mr Consistency all year it broke my heart to finish second again. But a miserable end to the season was about to get worse.

The call came from one of my pals, telling me that Phil Scales had been killed in a road accident. At first I did not take it in because, just months earlier, someone had told me that another rider of a Fireblade, who had been killed in a crash, was Phil and it turned out to be untrue. This time it was real. He had been on his way home to his girlfriend Emma after a day at work as a welder, when he was in collision with a bus that had pulled out of a junction as he rode down a line of nearly stationary traffic. Goodness knows how Emma coped, as her previous boyfriend had been killed on a bike while on the Isle of Man to watch the TT.

I had spent so many good times with Phil: taking him on his first trip abroad to watch the Supercross in Paris; watching him pull the biggest wheelies outside the Grey Goose; motocrossing at The Desert along with Anus. I had vaguely known a few racers who had lost their lives, and also the occasional customer from the shop. But Phil had been part of growing up. He had actually become a very good road bike rider through attending various track days and would have been a good racer if the circumstances had allowed.

His brother called me to ask if I would be one of the coffin-bearers and I told him straight away that it would be an honour. He was laid to rest at home on the morning of his funeral in an open coffin, wearing his leathers. But I did not go in because I did not want to remember him that way. I actually had seen him just a couple of weeks earlier at the Two Wheel Centre, a motorbike shop owned by my friend Terry Connor in Nottingham. He was as funny and animated as ever, and that was the Phil I wanted to remember – someone who had never once upset me or let me down. The music played at the funeral was the Robbie Williams song, 'Let Me Entertain You' – the words on Phil's number plate. From the hundreds who turned up for the service it was clear that Phil had entertained an awful lot of people.

The wake was held at the Grey Goose and there was a book to sign for the family. His favourite film had been *Days of Thunder* and his favourite line was when the team manager told Tom Cruise's character, Cole Trickle, that his rival's aggressive move in the NASCAR race had been fair: 'That was rubbin' – and rubbin's racin'.' I signed the book: 'Rubbin's racin', CW.'

Phil's dad, a lovely old school bloke with big Ron Haslam side-burns, came up to me in the pub, hugged me and said, 'Are you going to win that bloody championship one day?'

'Too right I will. And I will win it for you and Phil,' I said.

And I still mean it – I will win it for him one day.

20

Rollercoaster Stalker

Fasten your seatbelts! As white-knuckle rides go, 2000 was the Big One. Not only was I involved in a titanic battle on the track, my private life was no less turbulent. It doesn't help when you go into the new millennium having just sat through two Christmas dinners.

Earlier in the year Lisa had finished a college course in hairdressing and had taking a job at the college as a teacher, meaning fewer hours for the same money. I went with her mum to the degree ceremony at the Nottingham civic hall. She was all kitted out in her cap and gown, as were the several thousand other students there that day, so it was a bit of a yawnerama, although I did feel proud. The new job meant college summer holidays and she did start to come to more races again, which I appreciated. I fully understood that she needed her own hobby, but the race track can be a lonely place for a rider sometimes and it's important to have someone there in your times of need. You will find that most successful riders often have strong relationships: Carl and Michaela Fogarty, Colin and Alyssia Edwards, Troy and Kim Bayliss, for example.

However, that same teaching job was not available again when the college resumed after the summer and Lisa asked me whether it would be OK to pack in working so that she could continue to spend as much time with me. We were by no means an extravagant couple, although we had recently incurred a small extra expense when we adopted a stray, cool, black female cat that we named Whoopi, after the only cool black female that I knew of, Whoopi Goldberg. So losing Lisa's income was not a big issue. What did become an issue was that as soon as she stopped working, out came *Horse and Hound*, in came a new horsebox and another horse, and suddenly the hobby had become a huge commitment. I actually saw less and less of Lisa as the year progressed and, after bumping into Olivia again at the NEC Show, what had started off as harmless text flirting resulted in me having a lot more Christmas presents to wrap and a really full stomach while watching, ironically, *Only Fools and Horses* after my second Christmas dinner at Olivia's mum's. (I didn't actually eat too much of it because Olivia was a vegetarian and grilled halibut and sprouts is just not right – for a number of reasons.)

At least my ride for the following season was a bit more settled. Coming second in British Superbikes was starting to grate, even if I had been runner-up to Mackenzie, who had been fourth in the 500 GPs behind Rainey, Schwantz and Doohan, and to Troy Bayliss, who went on to become a double World Superbike champion. And while I didn't want to just walk away from Britain with unfinished business, I was looking for a chance on the world stage. David Pickworth was putting a few feelers out in the World Superbike paddock with Harald Eckl and the Alstare Suzuki team, and Rob McElnea arranged for me to test with the Kenny Roberts Proton team on the coldest day I have ever been at a road race circuit. I felt unlucky when the engine seized, probably because of the conditions, and threw me over the screen going into what is now known as the Foggy Esses. But when the same thing happened to the spare bike three corners later going into Goddards something was clearly not quite right. I was later offered a lucrative ride with the team but, having had prior knowledge of a prototype with the Elf team, I thought that I needed more experience before going down that road again, even with such a low-pressure option. Rob was a bit annoyed that my hesitation was based on one shitty day at Donington in November, but I asked for more time to think about it because there were already discussions that GPs might soon introduce four-strokes, and that appealed to me more.

Meanwhile, Simon Buckmaster, having now realized that I could in fact ride a motorcycle, was keeping my ride with Kawasaki open for as long as possible. But I also had other options in the British paddock because David had arranged talks with his pal, Paul Denning, the boss of the Crescent Suzuki team. I had met him before but never really sat down to talk to him and I Instantly felt more at ease with him than I had ever done with Buckmaster, who was often argumentative and abrasive. (I can just picture him now, speed-reading through this book to see what I say about him. Keep reading, Simon!) Paul told me all about the bikes and asked if I wanted to bring Les along. I had become very close to Les over the previous year and had full confidence in his abilities, and it wasn't always that a rider was given the chance to bring his crew chief along.

David thrashed out a deal with Denning while I was shown round the workshop in Bournemouth, the first time he had taken on the role of my manager. I'm not the type of bloke who is comfortable saying, 'I'm Chris Walker and I'm going to win you the championship.' Even if I did think it, I would probably say the opposite. It sounds so much better coming from someone else. But we both felt very comfortable with Paul, who proved to be an amazing team manager, which is why he was later head-hunted to run the Suzuki MotoGP team and delivered their best results for years. Les was to stay in the house in Bournemouth that was rented by the team for all the mechanics, which still wasn't ideal for someone based in North Yorkshire but better than a bunk bed in a workshop in Stevenage. My engine builder was Dave Hagan who, after crashing out after a boozy dealer launch, exposing his dome-like belly, was known as Millennium Dave from then on. My number two mechanic was Dan Sawyer, known to me as Young Dan, who is now Shakey's crew chief. Paul made me feel instantly part of the family and invited me to his home for dinner with his lovely South African wife, Kate, who has still not forgiven me for criticizing her cooking. (How is it possible to ruin a bowl of pasta? Maybe that's why Paul is so skinny!)

My team-mate was John Crawford, known as JC, who had twice won the British Supersport championship for Crescent and had been promoted up into superbikes. We were replacing James Haydon, who had moved to the Reve Red Bull Ducati team with JR, and Marty Craggill, who replaced me at Kawasaki. Like Paul Denning, JC was also into his rally driving, and was a friend of Colin and Alister McRae.

The bike looked handsome in the typical Suzuki dark and light blue and white livery, despite having to accommodate the longest team name in the history of racing – National Tyres Clarion Crescent Suzuki – and that funny GSX-R750 tailpiece. After one lap of our first shakedown test at Croft on another shitty day in February – global warming had not kicked in by then – the bike didn't look quite so handsome. I was riding one of the two bikes that Frankie Chili had used with the Alstare Suzuki team the previous year, and in tight new leathers I didn't feel too comfortable. I turned into the final 180-degree hairpin at no more than 20 m.p.h. but didn't come out the other side. It was not an ideal start, although the damage was minimal.

The first real chance to assess the bike came at Albacete, and I could not believe how good it was. The power-to-weight ratio was superb. It had really nimble handling and felt much smaller than the Kawasaki. We arrived at Albacete a day later than the other teams but at the end of our first day I was fastest, with JC not far behind. It was good that I was already being pushed from within the team. James Haydon came wandering along pit-lane and commented that the Frankie Chili bike must be special. I didn't have the heart to tell him that I was on his bike from the previous season. Although I didn't leave the next official test at Cartagena as the fastest rider, I already knew that I had made the right decision.

I had stepped up my training regime to another level and bought a road push-bike for longer rides. At the push-bike shop I met a good friend, Michael Fish, for the first time. He is a sales rep for Science in Sport, a sports nutrition company who now sponsor me, and was one of the ushers at our wedding. I went to the gym to do more weights, played squash and racquetball, and Suzuki had provided two motocross bikes for the year, an RM125 and a new

DRZ400. I didn't have the kick-start motocross model because I still cannot kick-start a single-cylinder 400cc machine to this day. I had the heavier, middle-of-the-range crosser with a battery and electric start, and an afternoon on this made returning to a superbike bike feel like a walk in the park.

So I was good to go, and the championship line-up was as strong as ever. Bayliss had gone to American Superbikes, but later replaced Carl Fogarty at Ducati, when that horrible crash at Phillip Island finished his career. Mackenzie, after an average year on the Yamaha R7, replaced Bayliss at INS Ducati, while Hizzy replaced Niall at Virgin Mobile Yamaha. Honda had also brought out a purpose-built V-twin for superbike, with Shakey at the helm. Toseland rode the same bike for Paul Bird in the Vimto Honda team, on his return from World Supersport. Oh, and not forgetting that Mackenzie's team-mate at Ducati was Neil Hodgson, whose return to Britain the previous year had not set the world alight. Having now done the same thing this year, I know how difficult it is to re-acclimatize.

Ding, ding! Seconds out, round one! I should have won the first race of the year at the Brands Hatch Indy circuit, but Reynolds stuck it up the inside of me going into Druids on the last lap. I had been struggling with corner entry grip but still didn't defend my line well, although JR was coming thick and fast and we all know that the terrier never gave up. We swapped the rear rim size for the second race and had even less grip, so I dropped down to fifth. Round 1: 1, Reynolds 38 pts; 4, Walker 31 pts; 5, Hodgson 29 pts.

Les went back to the geometry drawing board before the next round at Donington and, although I took a while to get dialled into his changes, the corner entry grip was much better and I qualified well. I was leading the first race when the engine blew spectacularly, caused by a weak valve spring retainer – a £5 part. It became evident they were a bit vulnerable, especially with the high revs of the bike and the profile of the camshaft. It was going to be something we would have to monitor throughout the year. I rode the spare bike for the second race, which I led almost from the start. James Haydon had a poor start but was charging through the field until he crashed at

Coppice, forcing the others to roll off. But I was in front of him and able to pull a bit of a cushion for the rest of the race. Round 2: 1, Reynolds 83 pts; 2, Hodgson 65 pts; 3, Walker 56 pts.

Thruxton has never been my favourite track, although I do enjoy racing there and could pull off some demon braking going into the chicane. I knew it would be an uphill battle, but I have always tried not to be pessimistic. And it wasn't as though the bike was poor around there. As I cruised in after my flying qualifying lap I could see JC going through the Complex and could tell that he was on it. He qualified in pole, which was great for team morale, although his luck ran out for the races. He was eighth in the restarted first, which was red-flagged after his crash with Shakey, who broke two vertebrae and knocked his spine out of alignment. I came home in second, but only after tangling with Hizzy and the other boys on more than one occasion at Club Chicane.

Then I was involved in the kind of draughting second race when you can enter the back straight in third and come out in sixth, which is where I was lying as the race was again cut short when JC's bad luck continued with a blown engine. The Ducatis always had long legs at Thruxton, so Haydon and Hodgson shared the wins. Round 3: 1, Reynolds 112 pts; 2, Hodgson 106 pts; 4, Walker 87 pts.

Time for a breather at the Donington round of World Superbikes. That might have been the theory, but the practice was far different. It was actually nice to take a break from the pressure of the British championship, because the only pressure as a wild card was the pressure you placed on yourself. This year, however, there was even more attention on the British wild cards than usual because Foggy was out of action, leaving a void in the championship which has only really been filled this year with James Toseland leading the way in what has now become a really tough championship again. That year's championship didn't feel right without Foggy, although it's fair to say that the wild cards didn't disappoint. To this day it remains one of my best moments in racing.

Having qualified at the front of the second row I knew that my lap times were capable of challenging for my first World Superbike podium, so I was a bit deflated to finish the first race in fifth, although not a million miles behind the winner, Colin Edwards, and Neil Hodgson in third. Les made a tweak for race two and I felt less anxious than I had at the start of the first. I could also sense a feeling in the massive crowd that something special was going to happen.

I got away with the leading bunch; Chili leading, Edwards second, Neil third, me fourth and Haga fifth. Edwards went down going into Redgate on lap 11. 'That's one less to worry about,' I thought. As Chili pulled away, doing exceptional and consistent lap times, Haga came past me into third two laps later. I passed him back almost straight away going into McLeans. OK, we might have rubbed leathers, even handlebars, and it might have been a bit 'lastminute.com', but it was a fair move. Still, it left Haga shaking his head and he backed off. Anyway, of all people, how could he complain about a Banzai manoeuvre?

For most of the second half of the race Neil and I were involved in a dice for second position. Despite the extra rear-entry grip that Les had found, I was still sideways going into the Melbourne Loop and Goddards. It might not have been the fastest way of getting round the track, but it was the fastest way for me and I could put the front wheel bang on the apex of every corner of every lap. Hodgson, on the other hand, never put a wheel out of line and was riding superbly smooth and fast.

We swapped positions lap after lap. He would pass me down the straight and I would pass back into the Melbourne Loop. He came back at me down to Redgate and I would retake going into McLeans. And all the while we could see from Chili's pitboard that the gap to him was coming down. His tyre was clearly starting to go off and we were quickly catching him with five laps remaining. On the penultimate lap I made a couple of mistakes and allowed Neil to pull a three-tenths gap and I was no longer in a position to overtake. But as we both came round McLeans on the final lap we saw Frankie have the biggest slide. He came out of the seat and landed back on the bike, bashing his bollocks on the tank. It took the wind out of his sails and, as he shifted down, Neil went through into the lead and I was right behind Chili in third. But he had lost drive out of the Esses and I squeezed it up the inside of him into second place. Just two corners to go and second place was mine. The crowd went beserk as we went round the final corner. I had not won the race, but that didn't matter one bit. It was five years since I had first sat on Hizzy's superbike and now, on Chili's bike from last year, I was on the podium of a World Superbike race. I was as chuffed about Neil's win as I was for myself, because he was bouncing back from a tough time on the world stage. And the fact that we had both been pushing each other so hard had kept the pressure on Frankie, causing his tyre to wear out. So we had contributed to each other's success. The crowd invaded the track and it was one of the proudest moments I have ever had in racing. It was also a sign of things to come. If it felt as though I could sometimes walk on water on my Suzuki, and so could Neil on his Ducati.

Neil was quoted after the race saying: 'It's good to see Chris has not changed at all – he's still as dangerous as ever. He's the only man on earth who makes Haga look like a safety-conscious rider!' I had not had much to do with Neil since seeing him in Benidorm. He tended to keep his head down at races and I preferred to spend time with my mates like Dave Pickworth, his business partner Rick Cappella, Graham Overton and a few of my friends who were later to become known as the Big Lads. Neil and I probably gave each other a hug on the podium at Donington but that didn't mean we were suddenly the best of friends, although we weren't enemies either. That all changed at the next British round at Oulton Park.

It was the first time that season when I struggled to find a rhythm, whereas Neil was flying all through qualifying and was on pole. My Suzuki was always a missile off the line and I led the race, although I was still riding like an old woman with her skirt trapped in the chain. The more I struggled, the more aggressive I became, which was probably why my lap times didn't come down and the rest of the field gaggled up behind me. I had a bit of a reputation for being difficult to pass, and I definitely was hard to get round when I was sideways into every corner. The only rider who did manage to overtake was Hodgson. He pulled away to take the win, while I hung on to second from a typically determined Reynolds.

I was very impressed with Neil's display but not too chuffed with my own. So it was straight on the back of my paddock scooter, a Suzuki Street Magic, which Graham rode to make it easier to negotiate the crowds back to the motorhome, where I gave myself a bit of a talking to while Graham made the ham, cheese and tomato butties, with a packet of Pickled Onion Monster Munch – Stalker's regular between-race nibble. It did the trick and I was back to my old self in race two and led for a while before it came down to another two-way scrap with Hodgson. Again we had different strengths and weaknesses around the track and I was stronger going into the banked Shell Oils corner, where it was easier for me to hold a tighter line. We continued to swap places before, with a couple of laps to go, Neil ran slightly wide there and I squirted the throttle a bit more to dive up the inside, touching his leg and unsettling him as I went past.

This continued until the last corner of the last lap. I was leading through Cascades but could hear the grunt of the Ducati behind me. Those bikes seem to make more noise from the front than the back, especially when Ruben Xaus is riding one! I held a tight line coming out of Cascades and braked as late as possible going into Lodge. But Neil had set himself to go round the outside. Wherever I braked, he was going to brake later. When he did finally slam on the brakes, fractionally later than me, he turned straight in towards the apex, leaving me nowhere to go. I could not slow down any faster than I was doing and before I knew it I had smashed straight into his side at 100 m.p.h. Both my feet and one hand were off the bike as it slewed violently from one side to another. Luckily I landed back in the seat as I careered into the gravel, as did Neil. But yet again, no matter how much I tried to dab my feet down and stay upright, my little legs didn't work and I lost the front. Neil stayed upright and rejoined the race to finish fourth, but by the time I had picked the bike up and rode out of the gravel I could only nurse it home for a couple of points in fourteenth. I was livid. If he had just held his line, OK, he might not have won the race, but he wouldn't have been fourth and I wouldn't have been fourteenth, allowing John Reynolds to increase his championship lead.

I stormed into his garage and shouted, 'For fuck's sake, we should have been first and second in that race. What were you thinking?' He didn't say a lot there and then, but was later quoted in the press saying: 'I was still on the straight and moving across to defend the inside line. We both went for the same piece of Tarmac. It was a racing incident. I don't ride dirty.'

But, meanwhile, the marshals at that part of the track had told Paul that they thought it had been a dangerous manoeuvre. He asked them if they were willing to stand up and be counted, which they were, so Paul lodged an appeal. The arguments raged long into the night, but when we left the circuit Neil had been given a 36-second penalty, dropping him to fourteenth. Colin Wright immediately appealed against the penalty and a date was set to argue it out in a courtroom hearing, scheduled for after the next round at Snetterton. Round 4: 1, Reynolds 153 pts; 2, Hodgson 133 pts; 4, Walker 110 pts.

'We are both right at the top of our game,' I told *MCN* before Snetterton, not wanting things to escalate out of control. 'We both want to be winning races and be the top man in Britain. Neil's a great guy and I'm sure he feels the same. Racing's racing.' Deep down I was desperate for revenge, but didn't think that it was likely to come at Snetterton, where the Ducati power advantage was obvious. Yet again the first contest turned into a two-horse race. After JR dropped back I was behind Neil for the whole of the second half of the race, trying to stay close enough to have a go at passing him through the Bombhole or the final chicane, but second place was all I could realistically hope for. If you go into Russell's chicane in second you have effectively lost the race. But for some reason – whether to rub it in or to make doubly sure – Neil looked over his shoulder at me there and missed a gear. I had a split second to squeeze past and managed to keep my front wheel ahead over the line. My team went wild and he was spewing. There were certainly no mutual congratulations on the cool-down lap, although it had been a good, clean, hard-fought race, as fair and square as any race can be between a 1000cc twin and a 750cc four-cylinder bike at such a fast circuit. A couple of mistakes early on in the second race meant I lost the tow with Neil and JR and

I was never going to be able to improve on third. Round 5: 1, Reynolds 194 pts; 2, Hodgson 173 pts; 3, Walker 151 pts.

Maybe we were a little naïve going into the appeal hearing, in front of a few old farts from the ACU. Backed by eyewitness accounts from the marshals we believed that it would be enough to simply tell the truth. But Neil's team had hired a top-notch barrister to spout a load of bollocks and ask questions designed to make me look stupid. We were lambs to the slaughter. 'When Mr Walker collided with my client with two laps remaining the pain in my client's leg was so severe that he thought he might have to retire from the race,' explained the barrister. It was proper *Jackanory* material. But it did the trick, impressed the appeals panel, and his points were reinstated. Round 5.5: 1, Reynolds 194 pts; 2, Hodgson 184 pts; 3, Walker 150 pts.

We were both taken to one side by race director Stuart Higgs at Silverstone and told to cool it, although I still didn't think that I had done anything wrong. I rode the bike as hard as I could in the first race but Hodgson cleared off to win by 6 seconds. We changed everything for race two – all the things you are not supposed to alter between races like offset, springs and wheelbase – to try and make the bike that bit more competitive. And I made a great start but, sure enough, Neil was soon on my tail and pulled alongside me going into the hairpin at the bottom of the back straight. It was a re-run of the Oulton Park incident. When he tipped in I had nowhere to go and ran over the kerb, cut across the corner on the grass and could not avoid T-boning him on the other side. I managed to stay on my bike and went on to win the race, while he went spinning into the gravel. I have never heard a cheer like it. It was as though England had scored the winning goal in the World Cup final, which we all know is never going to happen again. And let's just say that the marshals were a bit lethargic in going to his aid. One told me later that Neil was shouting, 'You bastards are all on his side, too.' But it was now clear that public opinion was firmly in my favour, especially after he had let Bayliss through on more than one occasion to help Troy win the title the previous year. And I had pulled back a good chunk of points on both

Hodgson and Reynolds. Round 6: 1, Reynolds 221 pts; 2, Hodgson 209 pts; 3, Walker 195 pts.

On the Saturday night of the next round, at Oulton again, we headed out in Dave Pickworth's yellow M3 to a bar called Quincy's for some food with the team. Dave was now officially my manager and, unknown to him, known as '10 per cent' to all my mates. Dave and the others had a few beers so I drove back, but we missed the curfew to get back into the circuit and the security men would not let us in. (Maybe it had something to do with my handbrake turn off the back road and into the circuit entrance.) So I just put my foot down and accelerated over the bridge, by which stage some other security men, who had already been alerted, were trying to wave us down. I swung the car onto the grass, looped round the back of the paddock, parked the car behind a truck and legged it back to the motorhome.

When we heard a tap on the motorhome door we assumed that we had been rumbled by security. I tentatively opened the door to discover not a big burly security guard but a pretty girl, wearing a skirt shorter than the one Paula Smart used to wear.

'Hi, Chris! Mind if I pop in?' she asked.

'You better had, it looks freezing out there,' I stuttered. When she was inside and in the light I could see that it was the sister of one of the racers. We all sat round the table and there was a bit of an awkward silence before Graham said, 'Right, me and David are going for a beer in the clubhouse.' 'A beer, at this time on a Saturday night? That's a bit unusual,' I thought, as Graham closed the door and winked at me. The penny had still not dropped.

'You are a bit quiet,' she said. 'Are you not used to girls coming round to your motorhome?'

'No, not really. I was shitting myself when you knocked. We were being chased by the security guards and I thought I was going to get my collar felt,' I said.

'It's not your collar I have come to feel,' she said, before kissing me, sticking her hand up my shorts and dropping to her knees without so much as a by-your-leave! 'Seeya around,' was all she said when she left half an hour later, just before the boys returned to find my face still frozen in a state of shock and my chin on the motorhome floor. This had been a whole new experience for me, and not one that was ever repeated, I have to say.

By morning, it had been blown out of all proportion – the incident with the car, that is. All hell had broken loose and the officials were threatening to throw me out of the meeting, with claims that we had nearly knocked over three spectators. At 9.30 p.m. and in the pitch dark they could only have been Jean and Two-Litre Rita, who wouldn't have minded if we hit them, and Deaf Geoff, who wouldn't have heard us coming even if it had been light. Paul Denning had learned from our appeal hearing that the truth does not always pay with motorbike officials, so we hatched a plan for Pickworth to take the rap as he had less to lose, except, as it turned out, his shoe leather because his car, not him, was banned for the rest of the season and he had to walk in from the circuit perimeters.

There was no repeat of the on-track Oulton drama, although Neil rode like a man possessed in the first race. He stalled on the line, and the officials enforced a new rule that he had to start from the back of the grid. He was leading the race on lap nine! I struggled a bit again in race one but found my rhythm for the second race and managed to hold Neil off by just two tenths of a second. I had closed the gap on the leader of the championship, but now that leader was Hodgson, as we headed to Brands for the second round of the world championship in Britain. Round 7: 1, Hodgson 254 pts; 2, Reynolds 248 pts; 3, Walker 233 pts.

Brands Hatch was another useful chance to alert the main world championship teams and I guess that Hodgson was as desperate to return as I was to compete there for a full season. A powerful bike was definitely an asset around Brands and I was just off the pace of Bayliss and Hodgson in the first race, but still managed to finish on the podium in third, and ahead of Chili on the factory Suzuki, the next stage of evolution of my bike. Hodgson went on to win the second race while I was a lonely seventh, but we don't need to go into that – it's not his fucking book!

The next round of our championship was at Knockhill, somewhere I had always enjoyed racing. I went back this year and the atmosphere had not changed a bit. The weather was always the same, too, and we woke up on race morning to low-lying fog which caused morning warm-up to be cancelled. When the fog cleared the rain came in, and the hairpin had to be swept clear of water in order for the race to start. The track was really slippy but I loved the Suzuki in the wet, perhaps because it had a little less grunt, which can get you into trouble in those conditions. We made a few slight set-up changes, such as lowering the ride height, and I led from start to finish. For much of the race my pit board said between +2 and +5, before suddenly saying +14. Haydon had done a Haydon and disappeared down some Scottish glen. It was my race to lose, which I very nearly did with a massive lead and only two laps remaining, when my feet were off the pegs and I nearly came off. Have a word! Importantly, Reynolds and Hodgson were down in fifth and sixth.

The sun came out during the break, the track steamed itself bone dry, and although I made another great start Hodgson came past and pulled a 2-second lead. My rear entry grip issue had returned, probably because I was using a softer tyre than the opposition. It was affecting me at one corner in particular, but then, with a handful of laps to go, I saw Hodgson suffering the same problem at the same place. But it seemed to be affecting him more and I started to pull half a second a lap. On the penultimate lap I dived up inside him at the hairpin for my first double of the year. I was now in second place and just one point off the championship lead. Game on! Round 8: 1, Hodgson 284 pts; 2, Walker 283 pts; 3, Reynolds 272 pts.

We had already tested at Cadwell so Neil was playing catch-up during qualifying, although he was soon on the pace. I was vulnerable to him on the exit of Charlies and down the back straight, which is where he passed me in the first race to take the win. After a huge downpour between races the majority of riders opted for slick tyres on a drying track. I was in the lead but it was difficult to know how hard to push and my lap times didn't start to come down until Neil took the lead again. I was right behind him until, on the final lap, I flicked the bike right into Charlies, unsettling the rear and going sideways, and lost 20 yards on Neil. Luckily there were two back-markers ahead, including Neil's team-mate Niall Mackenzie, who had obviously chosen the wrong tyre. They held him up and I joined this group going into the one section, under the trees, which had not dried properly. Normally there would be little chance to pass from Hall Bends onwards, and the dry line was only the width of a bike, making it even harder. Neil must have thought a first double win was his, despite the back-markers. But I had not given up yet. Going into the Old Hairpin I let the brakes off and snaked onto the damp track, didn't touch the brakes again until long after the apex of the corner and slid up the inside of all three bikes. My tunnel vision had blocked out any thought of the consequences to my title chances if I had gone down, and my team could not believe it when we reappeared on the straight and I was in the lead. Niall was suicidal and Neil was spewing. But we had now built a strong mutual respect, and we shook hands on the cool-down lap, knowing that it was now effectively a two-horse race. Round 9: 1, Hodgson 329 pts; 2, Walker 328 pts.

Everyone was now pulling out all the stops in the pursuit of the title. I was training like a madman and had put my social life on hold. The team also arranged a test at the next venue, Mallory Park, another of my favourites, to fine-tune our preparations. So the last thing anyone needed was for me to have a big crash coming out of the Bus Stop chicane. Michael Rutter lives within earshot of Mallory and has turned up during every test that I can remember. He was there at the end of the 2006, when I was testing the Rizla Suzuki for the first time, looking at me through the fence like the Grim Reaper because he was also in the frame for the ride. He was at the Bus Stop on this occasion, too, as I messed up short-shifting up through the gears on the exit of the corner. The left-hand side of the tyre must still have been cold because the back end let go so fast. I could see Michael setting off to run to see if I was OK long before I landed. Earlier in the year my boots sponsors, Stylemartin, had produced an advert with the slogan: 'These boots were made for Walker.' That particular pair were now no longer made for riding. I regularly wore through my boots, through either my foot-rest position or riding style, and often just patched them up with tape. This crash ripped off the tape and scraped the nails off my outside three toes, which were broken in the process. I rode again later that afternoon, but didn't gain too much benefit from the test.

So I was a bit second hand going into the race weekend, not helped by a bout of food poisoning on the Thursday. That was down to my so-called pal and Master Chef, Millett, whose house I had been to the previous night for tea, when he decided to experiment with wood pigeon or some other type of game shite. I could not keep anything down and I missed the whole of Friday practice, attached to a drip in the medical centre to rehydrate me. Fortunately Mallory was not the most physically demanding circuit in those days, and although I was still very weak I was able to ride on the Saturday. In the late stages of the race the championship script was followed to the letter: a two-way dogfight between me and Neil. Going into the Hairpin on the final lap I knew that if I braked later than usual I could have sneaked past him, but not without rubbing fairings or touching his front wheel. Maybe my weakness caused a bit of hesitation. Or maybe, after what had happened earlier in the season, I was a touch more cautious than usual. Whatever the reason I didn't try the move and Neil took the win. The roles were reversed for the second race but, importantly, Neil could only finish fourth and I was going to the Brands Indy circuit for the penultimate round of the championship with a 6-point lead. The pressure was mounting. Round 10: 1, Walker 373 pts; 2, Hodgson 367 pts.

The media hype was also building, everyone making the most of the rivalry between me and Neil. There were television ads, extra coverage in the national media and features on Radio 1. More and more people were coming to the circuits and there was a huge air of expectancy. But I was keeping my nerves under control. I knew that the bike would work well around such a compact circuit which suited my rough-around-the-edges style more than the smoother riders, who struggled to get into their flow around the Indy Circuit. After two days of good weather I had a good set-up – and then the heavens opened on race morning. Come the start of the first race there was a drying line again but the race was declared wet. We gambled on a slick rear and intermediate front, but it didn't matter whether I had the right tyre on because I had the wrong head on. As I turned into Graham Hill Bend on the first lap everyone else was still coming out of Druids. I was hell bent on winning and went into that left way too fast and lost the front. The bike slid into the gravel and, although I was able to keep it running and rejoin the race, the engine cover had worn through and oil was leaking into the fairing. After a couple of laps the engine ran dry and seized up. Two laps later the rain came again and, with most of the riders on slicks, the race was red-flagged for safety reasons. We argued that, because the race was declared wet at the start, everyone should be allowed to restart, but the officials stuck to the letter of the law. I had not finished the first part of the race, so was not allowed on the grid for the restart. I had to sit and watch the race from the garage, and it was torture. Rutter won the race, but that fact barely registered because I didn't take my eyes off Hodgson, who struggled home in sixth place to claim a 4-point lead.

The conditions remained wet for race two but I was now on the back foot, as everyone else had a wet setting. But there was no point dwelling on it, I just had to get my head down and win the race. I took the lead when Anthony Gobert crashed out but had no idea where Hodgson was until, accelerating out of Graham Hill Bend, I saw him standing in the middle of the track trying unsuccessfully to start his Ducati. The win was mine and I had stretched my championship lead to 21 points. Even if Neil won the final two races at Donington, another of my favourite tracks, all I needed to do was finish third and fourth and the championship would be mine. All of a sudden I was in bits. Round 11: 1, Walker 398 pts; 2, Hodgson 377 pts.

I had one hand on the cup – apparently. It certainly didn't feel that way, and over the next two weeks I probably only had the equivalent of two nights' sleep. I bumped into Neil while we were setting up our motorhomes at Donington. There was no lingering animosity and we had a laugh about how we had both tossed it down the road at Brands. Then it was down to business and, although Neil was now using Troy Bayliss's factory Ducati 996, I qualified on pole. I had been on the rostrum every round of the season but I still needed this confidence boost and slept much better before the biggest day of my racing career. I have had mixed fortunes in my racing career: great days, tough days, happy days, sad days. This day was wank. One hundred per cent wank.

It started off well enough. Neil won the first race but I was third. The gap was down to 12 points. If he won the second race and I finished fourth I would win the title on the count-back of race wins. But I was on hot coals between the races. Everything on the bike was new for that weekend: cranks, crank cases, pistons, conrods, nuts, bolts, valve springs, valve spring retainers. Even so, I checked and rechecked with Les that everything was in order for the grand finale. He assured me that no stone had been left unturned. Now it was down to me.

I made a great start and was away with Hodgson, Haydon and Reynolds, in fourth place but with a comfortable gap on Mackenzie in fifth. There was no real need to be dicing for the lead, so the team gave me signals to slow down with six laps remaining. So I did a safe, steady lap. Then, when I turned into Goddards, the back wheel locked and I ran a bit wide. Or was I imagining things? No, there was no doubt the bike had less power down the start-finish straight. Then the engine let go through McLeans. A valve spring retainer had broken again. The top had fallen off the valve and into the piston. The engine was chucking oil into the exhaust and plumes of white smoke were billowing out of the back of the bike. What should I do? The bike was still running on three cylinders. If I kept going and enough oil spewed out they might stop the race and take the result from the start of the previous lap. I would still be champion. With four laps remaining I came onto the start-finish straight to see the dreaded black flag with the orange circle containing my number 2. This meant I had to get off the track straight away, so I pulled up at Redgate, leant the bike against the fence and gave it a little pat. Then I took the deepest breath, took my helmet and gloves off and could not hold back the tears.

Everyone knew that Neil was the new British champion, yet it was the most surreal experience of my life. The spectators were applauding and cheering as I walked past, and then the grandstands suddenly emptied. Neil must have crossed the line in second to almost total silence. But I was not there to witness it. I nipped through the gap at Redgate and headed straight for my motorhome. I didn't want to see or talk to anyone, because I knew that I would say or do the wrong thing. I just threw my helmet on the floor, got out of my leathers, put my normal clothes on. And, in a total daze, I just walked and walked and walked …

21

Stalker in Rehab

... and I walked all the way to East Midlands Airport. Cars were streaming out of the circuit but the only lad to spot me was Chris Jones, who was killed in an accident at Cadwell Park five years later, aged just 14. He raced mini-moto at the time and I recognized him because he had once given me a signed photo of himself earlier in the year. It was usually the other way round!

'I can't believe it,' he said and gave me a big hug. 'That was your championship. You will win it next year.'

'Thanks, mate. Appreciate that. But you'd best run off back to your old man now,' I said. I was a broken man and could not face talking to anyone right at that moment.

I found myself inside the terminal and sat down for a coffee, my head between my legs. 'Is it really worth all the effort, hurt and heartache?' I asked myself. I had left my phone at the circuit and had just a few quid in my pocket. If I'd had my passport and a credit card I might have ended up in Timbuktu. I rang my dad from a payphone, just to let him know that I was safe.

'Are you OK?' he asked. 'Do you need anything or want me to come over?'

'No, I'm better off out of the way for a while. I'll come back later to collect my motorhome.'

A few Irish and Scottish fans, on their way home after the races, spotted me and offered their commiserations. They looked as devastated as I was. But for a couple of hours I managed to go largely unnoticed, which is exactly what I needed. When it was dark I wandered back into the circuit and could hear everyone partying in Redgate Bar.

Back at my motorhome I checked my messages on my phone. There were lots from my mates and one from Les, in my phone as Bro, which read: 'Where are you? Worried about you.' Another message, typically insensitive, was from Olivia: 'In Redgate Bar having a beer. Get yourself over here.' It had been on and off with Lisa all summer and this was a time when she had moved back to her mum and dad's home, so she had not been there to witness everything.

I was certainly in no mood to join in any celebrations, so I packed up the motorhome and headed home. I maybe slept for a couple of hours but woke up at 4 a.m. and went straight out on my mountain bike. As the sun came up I was having a full-on greasy spoon breakfast at Limes Cafe. A bloke wandered in and spotted me in the corner.

'Hey, Stalker! I missed the races yesterday on telly. I assume you won it,' he said.

'Just fuck off will you,' I snapped. His face hit the floor. 'Look, sorry, mate, I didn't mean that. I haven't spoken about it to anyone yet. My bike broke down with four laps remaining. Hodgson won the championship.' It was perhaps the first time it had sunk in. Neil had deserved to win the championship – but so had I. We had both ridden the wheels off our bikes that year, above and beyond the call of duty. If ever a title should have been won by more than one rider, this was it. Neil obviously went on to win the World Superbike championship in 2003, so it was no disgrace to lose to someone of that calibre. And I know that, all in all, I am an exceptionally lucky person to have such great family and friends and, coming from a humble background and education, to be doing what I do for a living. Sometimes I have to pinch myself. But when it really counts my luck does seem to have a habit of running out.

I kept my head down for the next couple of days and did not want to answer the phone to friends, press or anyone from the team. To round the season off we were intending to do the final round of the World Superbike season, back at Brands for a second time that year as a replacement for a cancelled round. But that was the last thing on my mind. I had picked up *MCN* on the Wednesday only to see a big picture of Hodgson punching the air in victory on the front page, and not a mention of my bad luck until the sports pages. *MCN* also received a flurry of hate mail for having done a test feature on my bike in the issue before the final race. Readers assumed that those extra laps for the test were the ones responsible for the valve spring retainer failure. In fact the journalist had used JC's bike, but with my fairings.

But I needed to snap out of feeling sorry for myself, so Dad, Les and Graham took me for bangers and mash and a few beers at a restaurant called Sinatra's in Nottingham. We reminisced about the season, laughing at all the incidents which become so insignificant when the season is done and dusted. It was exactly what I needed and it re-chipped me into race mode for Brands.

I arrived at the circuit to find out that a new part for the bike had been sent from the Suzuki factory in Japan – a titanium valve spring retainer. Talk about trying to put the shit back in the horse! But the weekend proved to be the best possible cure. The reaction of the fans was sensational and it was soon clear that I could hold my head up high. I have never seen a queue like it outside our garage for the pit-lane walkabout signing session and I received good luck messages from fans from all round the world, who had seen the television pictures in Japan, South Africa, Australia and Spain. Ironically, Hodgson's bike broke down on the third lap of the Friday morning session. If Sunday's race had been three laps longer I might have been sat at East Midlands Airport, not knowing I was the new British champion. My third place in the first race, with JR winning his first World Superbike race and Neil in fourth, was some consolation at the end of that traumatic week, which still brings a tear to my eye to recall.

There was little time to brood, though, because I was soon faced with the biggest decision of my racing career. Paul Denning knew of my ambitions to move up to world-level racing and came up with a plan for me to race for Crescent Suzuki in World Superbikes. We agreed terms and I signed a Letter of Intent, which was sufficient until the details of the deal with the factory were finalized. Then I received a call from Martin Wilding, known as Wild Thing, who was closely connected with Dorna and Irta, the bodies which ran the Grand Prix series. There had been no decent British hopes since Niall Mackenzie and they were desperate for young British talent. And, with the arrival of four-strokes only two seasons away, superbike riders were a logical option. Neil Hodgson and James Toseland had gone to World Superbikes with GSE Racing, and John Reynolds had already been there and done it. So I was an obvious target. The money was identical to my offer from Suzuki, but I was offered a two-year deal for the Grand Prix ride, on a factory V4 Honda, run by the successful Shell Advance 250cc team. After the two years of finding my feet there would be an option for a further two years on the new four-stroke.

The trials and tribulations of the previous season with Suzuki were still fresh in my mind and I had reservations about their rookie status at World Superbike level. And the potential for the Grand Prix deal was huge. This was the pinnacle of bike racing and it was a chance to take my career to a whole new level. The sooner a rider takes that step up to the next level the better, as James Toseland has done this year despite being criticized in some quarters for his choice of team. Nobody would have criticized him for moving to a factory Honda team, and that was what was being offered me – on paper. What's more I had the chance to bed myself in over two years. Look at the riders who have had similar chances recently: Nicky Hayden, John Hopkins and Chris Vermeulen, for example. They have all gone on to great things. This was likely to be my one and only chance to map a career path leading to a Grand Prix world championship title. I talked with Dad, David and Les, of course, and made my mind up to bite the bullet. Then came the hard part – telling Paul of my decision.

He went berserk. I had tunnel vision to go out and ride a motor-cycle, so I had no idea how much work had already gone into his plans with Suzuki for the following year. Money had been spent on building things like packing cases for trips abroad. But my mind was made up and there was no going back. Paul said that I would never ride for him and Suzuki again. The ructions I caused with Suzuki meant that he was left to run our 2000 bikes in the British championship, not the step forward that he had envisaged. I have already apologized to him, but that's all I can do now. I was a twat and I know it.

Once that trauma was behind me I was ready for a new start, both on and off the track. I had stopped seeing Olivia at the end of the previous season. She had been great fun but I found her a bit materialistic and superficial, and realized there was no future for us. I had spent time with Lisa on and off during the summer but I was so wrapped up in my racing that I became perhaps more selfish than she had ever been with her horses. When I actually travelled with her to a couple of gymkhanas or showjumping events when my season finished I began to feel a bit guilty that I had not made more of an effort, because I am not a naturally selfish person. We had been at loggerheads for not being there for each other, but maybe we were equally at fault. So, a little older and wiser, we had decided to give it another go over the winter.

Obviously it would be difficult for Lisa and my other mates to come to some of the long-haul GPs. So it was great that Honda had offered Les a job, too. And within a few months we were also near neighbours. I had been cycling around a village called Bilsthorpe and, while fixing a puncture, got talking to a gardener, working at an old farmhouse. He was moaning that he would soon be out of work because the owner was selling up, having bought a hotel in the States. Although I didn't really need a bigger house, he needed to sell up quickly so I nicked it off him and moved in during the winter. Les later spotted a house on a new development nearby, which worked out well for him because he went on to marry the sister of his next-door neighbour, the lovely Sarah, who is many years younger and much better looking than him, the lucky bastard.

Until things start to go wrong a rider sometimes does not realize just how important it is to have a good, stable team set-up around him – just like I had at Suzuki. And it soon became clear that the Shell Advance team was not a good, stable team. I did not realize that the Shell Advance 250cc outfit had effectively been two teams in one garage. HRC funded Tohru Ukawa, who was runner-up to Rossi in 1999. The other half of the team basically had very little budget and fielded a variety of riders for next to nothing. This was the team, run by an Australian called Geoff Hardwick, which was making the step up to 500 GPs, with financial help from the organizers promised as long as they secured a top British rider.

There would be two V4s for me and two V-twins for the second rider, Leon Haslam, son of Rocket Ron. He was a star of the future and added to the all-Brit appeal, having made a few appearances in 250 and 125 GPs. Honda insisted on using only qualified Honda Racing Corporation mechanics at crew chief level, so Les was wasted in a menial role while I was allocated a crew chief that I found pretty useless. I could only ever talk to him out the back of the garage because he was a chronic chain smoker. It soon became apparent that my bikes were the ones that Alex Criville had found so difficult to ride for most of the previous year. I had not gone into this with my eyes closed, but the full facts were only gradually revealed. Before long, walking out of the garage to get onto the bike felt like walking the plank. I just knew that it was going to do something bad to me. Right from the start I found the pig difficult to steer, but I was discouraged from making changes.

Mick Doohan had recently retired and had taken on the role of overseeing all the Honda riders. We did not see too much of him, but he did go out spotting on the circuit and occasionally popped into our garage to lend a word of advice. He might tell me that I was moving around on the bike too much at a particular corner, or that I needed to shift my weight a bit earlier in another spot. Early on I did not feel comfortable on the bike and asked if I could have the handle-bars wider and my foot-rest back, to make it more comfortable for the knee I had broken.

'You are trying to make it like a superbike,' said Mick. 'If you were moving from touring cars to Formula One you wouldn't take your seat and steering wheel with you, would you?' He looked at me; I looked at him and then Les; and Les looked back at me and then him.

This was the man for whom the thumb brake was invented because his back brake was too uncomfortable to use after a bad crash. I could not exactly start arguing with a man who had won five consecutive GP titles. I had way too much respect for him and really liked him as a person. But I thought his statement was a bit odd and it proved to be a sign of what I was up against.

These cracks had not started to appear, however, when the fax came through with details of our winter testing programme. There were four tests at circuits like Jerez and Estoril and I would be away from home for a total of six weeks. It was not an ideal scenario when trying to give things another go with Lisa. But I was really excited as I set off with Les, armed with my free Shell fuel card, which became essential during the year as my motorhome probably did about 5 miles to the gallon. We were also lent a map by Leon, which had all the McDonald's highlighted. He is a real athlete now but did enjoy a burger and chips in those days. So we plotted our routes around Europe via Shell stations and McDonald's. David joined us for the first test at Jerez and, together with Les, the three of us were blown away when we saw and heard the bike for the first time. For this test it was not in full livery, just carbon black with a Shell Advance sticker on the side and my number, 8. It was a thing of beauty, a lot more compact than a superbike, and I was immediately in awe, plus a little daunted. The cackle that came from the exhausts when the mechanics started it up was savage.

That test was cut short because of poor weather but I did not disgrace myself during the rest of the six-week programme, although I knew there was work to do on the lap times. It's rare, however, for a rider to make a step up in level and be immediately on the pace. So I was still upbeat when I returned home for a short break before the first race at Suzuka, when I could up catch up with my motocrossing mates and Lisa. I had been away for Valentine's Day but she had given Les a card to give to me and I remember her calling our hotel room on the evening itself, while me and Les were watching the Tom Hanks and Meg Ryan film, *You've Got Mail*. I hasten to add it was the only thing on the telly in English – honest! Bear in mind that the first email

I ever sent was to Paul Denning to try and secure this year's ride, and Rachel had to write that, it was not a film that set my pulse racing.

As ever, though, no preparations for a Stalker season went that smoothly. I returned home to find that some bloke connected with the horse scene, a married man with two kids, had been hanging out the back of her while I had been away. I knew something was not right as soon as I walked through the door, but she denied it when I confronted her. When text messages started to arrive in the middle of the night it was time to act. I rang the bloke, who was one of the thickest men I have ever spoken to, and told him that Lisa had told me all about it. I think he was expecting me to go round and ruin his domestic bliss, or at least stick one on him. But I just wanted confirmation so that I knew exactly where I stood. Having made the same mistakes myself, I would have been a hypocrite to do anything more about it, other than accept that it was the end of our brand-new start together.

The first race of the season was at Suzuka, where I had been once before with Stewart Johnstone in 1998, testing for the Suzuka 8-Hours race for Kawasaki. I loved the circuit but the heat was ridiculous. There was no point showering before leaving the hotel because you were drenched in sweat the moment the hotel foyer doors opened into the furnace. I spent the whole three days clasped to the air-conditioning unit in the garage. Japan is mind-blowing for the first-time visitor, even the first ride from the airport in their taxis, which all look like Lada Rivas. The drivers wear white cotton gloves and the headrests have paper doilies that are replaced for every customer. And the doors spring open automatically when the taxi stops to let you out.

Once out of the taxi, though, you are fucked. The signs might as well be in Braille as their hieroglyphics. Nobody speaks a word of English and everyone does look the same. They say that we look the same to them but at least we have different hair colours and hairstyles. Japanese women all dress like schoolgirls, which is not necessarily a bad thing. And can anyone explain who would buy a pair of freeze-dried, shrink-wrapped ladies' pants that can be found on sale in their shops? I was not too experimental with their food and tended to follow Leon and Ron to the nearest fast-food place. I was not too sure about KFC, though. I have been to Japan many times now and I have never once seen a chicken, so we used to call it Unlucky Fried Kitten. By now we referred to Leon as Una Brau, after the character in the Austin Powers films, because his eyebrows had merged into one. He has sorted it now thankfully and looks quite cool these days.

Qualifying was a battle, as I struggled with front grip as we were clearly not receiving the best rubber available from Michelin. 'You'll be up there with a Stalker start,' urged Les. But he failed to remind me that, having got that great start, I was using carbon brakes, which take some heating up before they work! The result was that I went into the last chicane too hot and took out half the field. Jose Luis Cardoso was the only victim to hurl gravel at me, as well as that Spanish insult that I was now used to: 'Cabron!'

Dad and Graham Overton had made the trip out to Japan and, all said and done, it was a miracle that they arrived at Suzuka Land, the huge theme park containing the circuit, with Dad still in tow. Remember that Dad cannot negotiate his way around Nottingham when Mum is not there to hold his hand, let alone catch the right bullet train from Tokyo Central. Dad was not too chuffed about the crash either. 'What a wasted bloody journey. All this way and we didn't see one lap.' He would have been even more disgruntled if he had known that I had travelled out to Japan with a broken shoulder-blade. Only Les knew, because he was with me up The Desert on our crossers when I didn't land a tabletop jump properly and the bike landed on my back. At least this crash now gave me an official excuse to show how injured I really was.

I was still a bit second hand come the next round at Welkom, South Africa. I have no idea why they called the place Welkom, because that is definitely not how you feel when you see certain parts of the country, like the townships. I'm actually a huge fan of South Africa, but the parts that you are taken to see. At Welkom, however, there isn't a lot to see. It used to be an old gold-mining town but everyone disappeared when the gold dried up. There was not much to do, although Dad, not put off by his Japanese experience, did manage to find some excitement along with a couple of the Big Lads – Dave Hogg, or Hoggy, who ran the Hogsped transport company back home, and his mate, Richard Allen, who was just known as George, because he looked like George Clooney. Dad had been warned about the carjacking out there and had been told not to stop for anything or anyone. Unfortunately Dad took that to include a traffic cop who was flagging him down for speeding in their hire car. The policeman caught up with him at the next toll booth but fortunately accepted his explanation, in return for a small donation! Nothing changes in John's world: he seems to attract trouble when Christine is not around, and especially when he is with the Big Lads.

Before the race I bumped into a bloke called Bill Hunter, a former drag-racing champion from Nottingham. I had actually seen him only a few years earlier in the States, when the Erion team took me to the Winston Drag Racing Finals. I felt a tap on the shoulder and heard: 'Ey up, Bogbrush, what are you doing here?' Bogbrush was one of the many nicknames given to me by Dad, including Bug and Pigswill. Apparently my hair was all over the place in my motocross days and looked like a bog brush. On our van we painted: 'Bogbrush Racing Team – clean round the bend'. I have even seen some Bogbrush banners at British rounds, made by the lads I used to race against, but was never too keen on the nickname sticking. Bill had moved out to South Africa and was after a couple of tickets for the Grand Prix, but I remembered that I still owed him. On one of his visits to our shop, when I was about 13, Mum had let slip that I had a new girlfriend so Bill chased me round the shop, pinned me down and gave me a full-on love bite. Try explaining that to your girlfriend.

The number of right-hand corners at Welkom made it even more uncomfortable for my broken shoulder but I finished the race, and scored one point in fifteenth place. Things were looking up at Jerez, where I was dicing with Carlos Checa for a top ten spot and I remember thinking: 'Fuck me, I have just overtaken Chubby Checa.' Right then I lost the front going onto the back straight. Cracks were now starting to appear in the team's financial structure. 'That will be another $8,000 for a new seat unit,' moaned Hardwick. 'I'm not actually crashing deliberately,' I said. I may have heard a mechanic having the occasional moan about the extra work following a crash, or overheard the boss complaining to his wife, but no team manager had ever said this to my face before. I stayed on during the next race to finish twelfth at Le Mans and we stayed on to test there, which was useful because Michelin also provided a new front tyre that gave better feedback. I was now receiving next to no input from my crew chief but still managed to come up with a better direction for set-up too.

I was excited about racing at Mugello, having gone to watch with Les a couple of years earlier. There is a unique atmosphere at this Italian circuit. Fans take their own engines, anything from a two-stroke to a V12 car engine, attached to gramophone-style horns instead of an exhaust. These would bellow across the valley to the other side of the circuit, where someone would immediately respond with their own engine. Then there were the twelve Vikings riding the stretched-limo equivalent of a scooter. I say riding, but the scooter engine was not big enough to power twelve blokes so they had to scoot along Flintstones-style. It's a crazy atmosphere and spectacle to this day.

As the race started a few spots of rain started to appear and suddenly it was Walker weather. I set the fastest lap of the race on lap 5 and was catching the leading bunch when their hands inevitably came up and the race was restarted as a wet-aggregate race. Again I was up there in the mix when I grabbed my Grand Prix claim to fame – overtaking Valentino Rossi. Apparently, on the television coverage back home, the commentator was just saying: 'Let me repeat that, Chris Walker has just passed Valentino Ro—' when I touched the white line and went down. The only consolation was that Rossi did the same thing at the same spot the very next lap, as I was still picking myself up out of the gravel.

I was still enjoying the challenge of Grand Prix racing, but it was becoming hard work. I had only been joking when I chose number 8 at the start of the season because it looked the same upside down. It was my own fault because I was pushing hard to get further up the field. Most new arrivals to GPs are expected to be bitten a couple of times before making sustained progress. Surely that was why I had been handed a two-year contract. Still, I was looking forward to Catalunya, where I had experience of the circuit. All we needed was a good few sessions to find the right set-up and tyres and I was confident of scoring some decent points.

At the start of my first timed lap on the Friday morning I went into the chicane at the end of the start-finish straight, tipped the bike in right and then flicked it hard left. I did not know that the front sprocket oil seal had popped out down the straight and leaked oil onto the back tyre. The back end let go so fast that it flicked me into orbit. I landed flat on my face on the track, with my arm stretched out. The rider right behind me, Johan Stigefelt, had no chance to avoid me and ran straight over my arm. I was in agony when I got back to the pits and pulled off my leathers to reveal an S-bend in my forearm. 'That's broken,' said Les. 'Get yourself off to the medical centre.' Amazingly the X-ray showed that there was no break, just squashed muscle tissue. I missed a lot of the rest of practice and qualifying and had to cut through my leathers to pull them over the swollen arm on race day morning. But I managed to finish in thirteenth, maintaining the sequence of crash-points-crash-points throughout the season.

If that sequence was to continue I was due to have another crash in the race at Assen. But I did not make the race because I had the crash on the first morning instead – and it remains *the* biggest of my racing career. The backward, downhill, 50 metres launch at 130 m.p.h. at Oulton had been big, but this was massive. I was flat out through the fast right-hand kink on the back section, had good drive on the very outside of the track and was just about to snick it into sixth gear when the back wheel dropped off the Tarmac and onto the grass. The next thing that I could feel was the wind whistling through my leathers and I could hear it whooshing past my ears as though I was doing a parachute jump. I was 15 feet up in the air doing 140 m.p.h. and could see exactly where I was going to land.

I regained consciousness briefly as they carried me from the medical centre to the ambulance, long enough to register my dad's little worried face before I passed out again. Jurgen van der Goorbergh had been behind me and said that I must have passed out when my head hit the grass because my body went limp as it hurtled into the tyre wall. I woke up four hours later in Assen Hospital, wondering why the Thai girl in the zebra bikini was making a beeping sound. Then I came round fully to see that it was in fact a small ginger Dutch nurse. I had tubes to help me breathe and wires coming from almost every orifice. They suspected that I had internal bleeding and possible brain damage, because my helmet shell had smashed on impact. My hands, arms, legs and feet were swollen but, amazingly, I had not broken a single bone. My head was throbbing like in a cartoon, though.

'You want something for zhe pain?' asked the nurse. I blinked twice for yes. At this point bear in mind that my arse was brand new. I hadn't even touched it, apart from a couple of bad wipes when my finger slipped through the paper. So imagine my horror when I saw her pull on her rubber gloves, squeeze some lubricant on her finger and ram a pill the size of a horse tablet right up there. I had the worst headache imaginable, possible paralysis and hands the size of a Kenny Everett character, so the last thing I needed was for my arse to be violated. Was this what Mick Doohan had to go through to win five world titles? The answer was 'yes', and much worse.

When Dad, David and Graham were allowed to visit I told them about the suppository. 'We are going to have to tell them I'm OK so that I can go home, because I'm not having another one of them,' I pleaded, before the ginger nurse came in the room again.

'Excuse me, miss,' said Graham. 'Chris was just saying that his headache has come on strong again and would it be possible for him to have another of those nice pain relievers?' Dad and Pickworth were wetting themselves. The hospital did release me a couple of days later but warned that I still had bad concussion and that I should be kept under supervision. They would not let me fly so I stretched out on the motorhome sofa while Les drove home, and Hardwick sent a text to remind me that another $8,000 seat unit had been ordered.

Unfortunately the next round, at Donington of all places, was just a week later. I turned up on the Thursday, the Day of Champions, and received a great reception from the fans. They did not know how rough I still felt but they all knew what a hard time I was having, and there are no better or more loyal supporters in the world at times like this. I was able to provide quite a few sets of scuffed leathers for the auction, which also went down well. The team and organizers knew that I had no broken bones but wanted me to undergo a medical or two before deciding whether I could ride. I actually failed the Thursday examination despite my best Stalker flannel, so I had to see the doctors again on Friday morning and pulled a rabbit out of the hat to pass this time. But I was an idiot to even consider riding. Although the doctors found nothing wrong after poking things in my ears, shining lights in my eyes and tapping my knees, I was in no fit state to get on the bike. It showed during qualifying and the race, when I finished fifteenth and scored one poxy point instead of challenging for the top ten at my home round.

At least there was now a three-week gap until the next round in Germany, so I would have time to fully recover. I was in Tesco buying my provisions for the trip to Germany on the Monday before the race when David called.

'I think they are considering putting another rider on your bike,' he said.

22

Stalker on the Rebound

There was no way I was going to drive all the way to Germany just to be told I was getting the flick, especially when I had not even been paid. The money that the organizers had made available for a British rider was supposed to arrive back with me, but in a roundabout kind of way. And some link in the chain had obviously broken. After slamming the trolley into a display of Pringles and storming out of the supermarket, I calmed down a bit and rang David back.

'I need to know what their plans are. Have they made a definite decision?' I asked. David said he would do some more digging and rang back to say that Leon had been offered the step up to my bike. Ron Haslam had been pushing the suggestion all season, apparently. I guess it's a dad's prerogative to look after his son's best interests. Ironically, this was probably the one round Leon was looking forward to on his V-twin, because the Sachsenring is the twistiest circuit on the Grand Prix calendar. He rode the V4 for the rest of the season but crashed the monster more than I had and did not finish any higher. I felt for him.

But my crashes had been the final nail in the coffin. The team had to be seen to be taking action by HRC, although I later found out that they had already run out of money and were therefore no longer receiving new parts from Japan. Maybe that explained some of the technical problems. I was massively pissed off. I did not remember there being any performance-related clause in my contract. And what had happened to the two-year bedding-in period? I had been made a scapegoat and started to regret not taking Paul Denning's offer. But if that had worked out Paul might not be where he is today. So I guess some good comes out of everything.

For the first time since my fourth birthday I was not bothered about riding motorbikes for a few weeks. I needed some time to recover from my injuries but also from the blow, and I did not want to fall into the trap of accepting different one-off rides every week. The sack was not a nice feeling but I couldn't just mope around and feel sorry for myself. Les, who had left at the same time, found work with Shakey in the British championship but also did some engine tuning in an industrial unit in Ollerton that we had rented and kitted out as a workshop. He then went on to oversee the mechanical side of the Ducati Monster Challenge, the equivalent of today's Virgin Mobile Cup, the following year. I kept myself busy with a few shop open days and some television studio work, and the break had the desired effect. I started to miss being on a bike and eventually did some tests for *MCN* and a test for Kawasaki at Rockingham with Michael Rutter.

I also had my hands full with a new girl on the scene. I had known Lisa for seven years, so it was not something that was easy just to forget, and we managed to start seeing each other on a friendly basis again. I guess I had realized that what goes around comes around. It was not a chapter of my life that I was particularly proud of, but I suppose it was just part of life's rich pattern and it was good that we could both be adult about what had gone on. Sarah Tunnicliffe, however, was like a breath of fresh air and was exactly what I needed at that time. She was very pretty, had long blonde hair and was 5 ft 11 in tall, so I barely came up to her belly button. Sarah was a model and budding young actress and was involved in the first lesbian kiss on *Hollyoaks*. I had met her when she did grid work at a few races, and then bumped into her again during some of my recent PR engagements. It would be unfair to say that she was useless, but she was used to people doing everything for her. She could not drive, for instance, and thought she had cooked Christmas dinner when she made cheese on toast. But she was daft as a brush, really good fun and had a great family, who were probably glad that someone else was looking after her for a while. Me and her dad used to joke that she was like having a classic Ferrari – looked stunning but needed constant attention.

Despite this distraction I needed to refocus on my racing future. So I travelled to the Assen round of World Superbikes, where a lot of decisions are made for the following year, and did not see any harm in taking Sarah along with me. The paddock is a very lonely place when you have no motorhome, garage, hospitality or race truck to hang out in, especially in the rain. I felt like a *Big Issue* seller. It didn't help that I was there cap in hand rather than with my head held high. I thought it was important that I spoke to the team bosses in person, rather than through David, because I wanted them to see that I was the same happy-go-lucky lad that I was before my recent misfortunes. Every little detail can help. It's good for them to see that you don't dollop butter onto your bread, or that you drink water rather than beer with your meal. And I swear that Sarah was a factor in Harald Eckl, the Kawasaki boss, calling me back a couple of weeks later for a meeting at a German airport. He probably thought that it would do no harm to have her hanging round the garage.

Anyway, he produced a contract there and then and said the job was mine if I wanted it, and before I knew it I was on a plane to Japan for the final round of the All Japan series, their equivalent of the British championship, a development arena for new factory machinery. Eric Bostrom, second in the American championship at the time and their eventual Supersport winner that year, was also competing and was pencilled in for some World Superbike rides the following year. My team-mate was to be Hitoyasu Izutsu, a really friendly guy, although he did not speak too much English and I wasn't about to learn Japanese. Having missed the second half of the second it was a bit of a shock to be on the start-line of such a hotly contested race so suddenly, but I was seventh, ahead of Bostrom, with Izutsu winning.

Not only was it a great chance to learn the Sugo circuit ahead of the 2002 season, I was also able to meet a few other members of the team, including my crew chief, an American called Theo Lockwood. He was not a typical brash American but his wife was out of the 'we have one waaaay bigger at home' mould. Harald was sometimes a bit left-field in implementing ideas he used in his own racing days, such as jogging round the paddock in our leathers to warm up before a session. He lived in a German town called Vohenstrauss, near the Czech border, famous for … Harald Eckl's house, which stood out in its Kawasaki green paint scheme.

Their Supersport line-up was Andrew Pitt, the reigning world champion, and James Ellison, the reigning European Superstock champion. Pitty was quite reserved and level-headed, probably due to his accountancy background, but loads of fun away from the track. And having James around was one of the highlights of that year for me. He was a fantastic little rider, although he was perhaps more focused that year on his new girlfriend. But, as an enthusiastic and chirpy young lad, he was always keen to see and do as much as possible wherever we travelled and I am glad that he encouraged me to tag along.

Harald was a smart cookie and realized that, with so many changes in personnel, team bonding was essential. So at the first Kawasaki test at Kyalami, near Johannesburg in South Africa, he arranged a trip to the Kruger National Park for a horseback safari. Just what I wanted – more horses! I had only been on one once before and ended up with kidney ache trying to get into the rising trot rhythm. Here my horse, Gunsmoke, looked a shitter but was actually quite cool, although he threw me over the top a couple of times because I was gripping the reins too tight whenever he jerked down to eat some grass. There was no danger that James's horse was going to do that with a name like Tinkerbell! Apparently the wild animals don't recognize that humans are riding the horses, so we were able to go underneath the neck of a giraffe and right up close to some baby rhinos, the cutest things I had ever seen. I wanted to take one home.

From South Africa we went to an official test at Phillip Island. I immediately fell in love with the place and couldn't get my breath when I jogged with Pitty down the start-finish straight for the first time, looking straight into the ocean. Izutsu wasn't much of a trainer;

he preferred to join the rest of the Japanese contingent for a fag in the back of Haga's trailer, which needed a chimney to let out all the smoke. We were warned about two things. First were the birds; and not the female occupants of the island's one and only pub, the Isle of White – or Pile of Shite, as it is more widely known. These massive geese could land in the middle of the track during a session and have been known to dislocate a rider's shoulder. Then there were the insects. The flies had come straight from an African drought – the type that nestle in the corner of your eye or crawl up your nostril. And the various bugs and mosquitoes had a field day on my ankles, arms and neck.

Harald had been very honest with his expectations for the season. 'Kawasaki will not be in World Superbikes next year because their 1000cc bike will not be ready in time for the new rule changes. So this bike is at the end of its development and will be a bit outclassed in a few ways, but should do OK at some circuits. We don't know how Izutsu will cope with the new circuits, so you have nothing to lose. If you make gradual progress through the season there are sure to be opportunities for you next year,' he said. I didn't set the world alight in those tests because I was acclimatizing to a superbike again and regaining my confidence. But I was not far off Izutsu's pace at Phillip Island and he had already been there a few times. But it was a bit alarming to see the likes of Colin Edwards blast past you on the straight on his Honda SP-2. Our top speed was not too bad but we didn't have a lot of drive. However, our bike was nimble and agile, with lots of grip, so I was in a positive frame of mind when I returned home to put the final touches to my preparations. Surely there could not be any more pre-season calamities? Think again!

With a couple of weeks to go before the first race in Valencia I was in the thick of my training programme and went motocrossing up The Desert with Graham Overton, James Ellison and my pal Mark Davies. He was riding in the British Supersport championship at the time, but when I met him in 1999 he rode a 125 Honda at the same level. He called himself Mad Dog, although we have shortened this to Dog because he never has any money with him and is always on the scrounge, just like your dog. The practice sessions for the 125 class were often scheduled before superbike sessions, so as I arrived at the garage I would see his lovely girlfriend, Vicky, hanging over pit-wall with his board, wearing her little hotpants. I took quite a shine to her and we eventually got talking. Mark came over and joined in. 'You should let him have a go on you, Vick, if he promises to buy me some tyres,' he said. I liked him instantly.

Suzuki occasionally allowed Dog to bring his bike to our test sessions in 2000 and I followed him around for a couple of laps at Snetterton. He was so fast around the corners and was a fantastic little rider on the 125s, but struggled to make the step up to bigger bikes, where deeper wallets often dictate your success. I pulled along-side and tapped the back of my bike, indicating that I would give him a tow. He pulled into my slipstream and I constantly looked behind to see that he was still being dragged along. When he popped up from behind the screen at his normal braking point he was going 20 m.p.h. faster than usual. He missed the corner and went hurtling across the gravel, so I didn't give him any more tows.

Back at The Desert we were approaching a fast, narrow, tree-lined path. It had been 'whooped out' – made into a series of ridges by bikes skimming over the top of these bumps. Dog was having an off day and was struggling to keep up. 'For fuck's sake, pull your finger out, Dog,' I shouted across at him and he set off flat out down the path. The dips in the bumps were filled with puddles and Dog rode through one, hitting a stick that was hidden at an angle below the surface of the water. It deflected his bike straight off the path and into the trees. I was a fair distance behind and could only see smoke and steam. When I reached him Dog was lying next to a bent tree trunk with his leg pointing the wrong way. He was pale, dazed and winded, and as I covered him with my body warmer and rested his head in my lap he asked if there was any blood. We could not lie. The bone had broken the skin but had gone back inside, so there wasn't too much.

Graham rode off to an area with a phone signal to call for an ambulance and the two fattest ambulancemen in England eventually arrived on the scene, looking like they needed resuscitation more than Dog. James had to go and fetch the blankets and stretcher for them, by which time they had called for the air ambulance.

'See, it's not all bad, buddy,' I said, feeling a bit guilty that I had urged him to ride faster. 'At least you are going to get to go in a helicopter.'

'Like I'm fucking bothered,' he wheezed.

In the meantime Graham had been riding his bike backwards and forwards through a hedge to make an entrance into the trees from the field where the air ambulance would land. When they took him away I started to collect the bits of my bike, because Dog had typically borrowed one from me. It was in three separate pieces and the engine had come clean out of the frame, so the three of us had to haul this back to the van and run back to collect our bikes. It was an hour before I could go to the hospital, still in my muddy crossing gear, to see how he was. He had put his leg out to try and save himself, snapping his tib and fib before braking seven ribs, some at the front and some at the back, on impact with the tree. He had also punctured one lung and was due for an extended stay in the King's Mill Hospital in Mansfield.

I went to see him every morning and afternoon and arranged to stay over at Graham's house after going to watch Roy 'Chubby' Brown in Mansfield one evening following a visit to the hospital. I showered the next morning and got soap in my eyes for the first time since being a kid. I washed it out and then immediately got more in. 'That's weird,' I thought. I dressed and brushed my teeth, and dribbled toothpaste down my only clean shirt. It was obviously going to be one of those days. Graham said I should have a bit of breakfast because I looked a bit off, but I was in a rush to go back to see Dog, who easily got lower than lino when he was in hospital. So I just accepted a quick coffee, and spilled it all down my top. 'What's wrong with me this morning?' I thought. When I walked into Dog's room he asked: 'What's the matter with your mouth?'

'Nothing. I think I just slept really funny at Graham's. My head must have been stuck to the pillow or something,' I said. A doctor came in and told me my mouth was lopsided and that I should see someone about it. I felt fine, though, and didn't think any more of it, so I went into Nottingham to buy a few things ready for heading off to Valencia for the first race of the season the following week. I bought a sandwich and some water at Boots and promptly spilled the water down my shirt and dropped the sandwich out of my mouth. 'What the fuck is going on?' I thought.

I returned to the hospital and the same doctor said that it had worsened since the morning. I hoped that a good night's sleep would put me right but didn't sleep a wink for some reason and in the morning my mouth was even more lopsided and my eye really weepy. 'This isn't right,' I thought, and asked to see a doctor when I went back to the hospital. Their initial suspicion was that I'd suffered a stroke, so I was rushed into a bed on the level below Dog, and wired up to all sorts of machines to measure brain activity and heart murmurs. The left-hand side of my face was now paralysed. I could feel it, but not move it. My bottom lip was fully drooped at the side; I couldn't blink, which is why I had been unable to sleep; and I had no frown lines on one side of my forehead. I was also a little bit forgetful. By now I was shitting myself. I had never been overly handsome, but I didn't fancy the idea of having a full-on disfigurement for the rest of my life. I was also supposed to be racing a motorbike next week.

There were no signs of a stroke so they allowed me home the next day and I went to buy some tape for my eyelid so that I could sleep, because the plaster provided had ripped my eyelashes out. I returned the next morning to see an Indian doctor, who had once seen some thing similar and promised to do some more research overnight. His hunch had been right. I had Bell's Palsy.

'The difference between the face and the rest of the body is that the rest of the body has only one nerve controlling movement and feel, whereas the face has two separate nerves, one for each function. Bell's Palsy is caused when the facial nerves get cross-wired in a ganglion, which is like a telephone exchange for nerves, in the socket behind your ear. You could easily have had no feeling but normal movement,' the doctor explained. He then went through a list of possible causes. Had I had any abnormal facial movements? I had laughed a bit more than normal at Chubby Brown. Had I slept in a draught? I raced motorcycles for a living – my face was always in a draught. Was I stressed? One of my best mates had recently been air-lifted to hospital after I told him to ride his bike faster. Had I suffered head trauma recently? Yes, but many months ago at Assen. Did I have herpes? Not that I knew of! Did I have any insect bites? Yes, and not just normal mossies. The bites from Australia had been huge and were not going away – and there was one about an inch away from the ganglion. The doctors thought they had got their man.

Everyone understood how upset I was. Lisa popped in to see me when she heard and Sarah was desperate to come over, too, although I didn't want her to see me looking like John Merrick. When I did finally pluck up enough courage to see her she was just what I needed, always taking the piss but in a caring sort of way. When we were driving anywhere she could only see the paralysed side of my face and would lean right round the front to see if I had reacted to any of her comments. It used to spin me out.

I also had to summon up the courage to tell Harald. It was difficult to explain over the phone and I could tell that he was already wondering who else might be available for the ride. He told me that he would wait until the Monday before the race before making a final decision. But there was no way that I was not going to be riding at Valencia, so the race was on to reduce the discomfort.

This was made more difficult because I couldn't take the steroids the hospital was providing to reduce the swelling around the ganglion, as they would have been picked up in a drugs test at the race. Training was also put on hold because of sweat running into my eye, and tiredness made the condition worse. Eating was also difficult. I had to fill my mouth and then hold it shut while I chewed, and often found bits of chicken in the left-hand side of my mouth days later. But I knew that the main problem was not being able to blink. The eye quickly dried and felt like sandpaper, so I could only imagine what it would be like during a race with wind whistling through the helmet. I turned to my old motocrossing mate, Mark Robinson, for help.

Robbo stayed late at his optician's shop in Nottingham along with his contact lenses specialist, Lorna. We tried a few lenses but I instinctively knew it was not going to work. Then Lorna suggested some special eye drop gel she had heard of. They went out for a drink that night to discuss the gel, got together and are now married with kids. So, again, this particular cloud had a silver lining.

I delayed my arrival at the circuit on the Thursday before the race for as long as possible. Everyone could see there was something wrong, but I looked physically fit and able to race, and I played down the blinking problem. Most people had a double take when they saw me for the first time. I bumped into Neil Hodgson, still on the HM Plant Ducati, and he said, 'What the fuck's happened to you, you poor bastard?' You would not have wished this on anyone, even your old sparring partner. Although everyone was concerned and supportive, I couldn't help feeling very self-conscious. And it didn't help when, while chatting to Foggy, his wife, Michaela, came up and said, 'You look just like Chris Walker.' Her face dropped further than the side of my mouth when she realized her mistake.

At the riders' pre-season briefing there was the usual discussion about new rulings and I was sat next to Mark Heckles, a Scouser riding for Rumi Honda. Some of the riders were standing up to say their piece and I whispered a possible solution to one of the debates to Heckles. 'That's a bloody good idea, chief. Stand up and tell them,' he said. 'You can fuck off,' I replied. 'I'm not standing up in front of anyone looking like Quasimodo.' It was the start of another great friendship and Mark spent most of that summer travelling to races in my motorhome.

Unfortunately the gel did not work. In the heat of Valencia it became runny and the wind through my visor blew it all over the eye. I then tried eye-drops, but I could taste them on the back of my throat, which didn't seem right, and they made me feel sick. But, despite my cod eye, I went gradually faster all weekend and finished a creditable seventh in the second race.

The next few rounds were all long-hauls and in very hot climates, so I went armed with a range of possible solutions to the problem of not being able to blink, many sent in from race fans or fellow suffer-ers. It soon became clear just how common the condition was.

Having taped my eye shut for the twenty-four-hour flight to Phillip Island, once there I decided to try Vaseline over my eyebrows to help channel the sweat away. That, too, melted fairly quickly and ran into both eyes. I was also careful to use lots of insect repellent this time.

At Kyalami my plan was to soak up the sweat with a sweat band, and also to tape up my visor so that the draught didn't dry the eye. After three laps the sweat band started to work its way down my forehead and dropped over my eyes just as I tipped into the fast left-hand turn two. But I couldn't lift my visor to push it clear because it was taped down. I was blind at 100 m.p.h. in third gear and ran straight on into the gravel, but managed to keep the bike upright and had to coast back to the pits with my head tipped right back as though I was peeping underneath a blindfold. Then someone suggested swimming goggles. I thought that, if I was going to look a fucker anywhere, Japan was the place for it. They would probably assume I had devised some revolutionary system with data being transmitted onto the goggle lens, like something out of *Terminator*. But it was like looking out of a goldfish bowl, and when I opened the visor for a better view my face was instantly splattered with bugs, just like the *Me, Myself and Irene* scene. Not surprisingly my results over these rounds were fairly average, although I was often inside the top ten.

Back home I tried facial massages and, despite the needles, even acupuncture, because I still could not risk taking the steroids. My mouth slowly improved, although this meant that I now looked permanently shocked, with my cod eye wide open. So I wore the blackest visor possible because after the initial ten minutes of sympathy you become a freak show. And I don't think people ever really knew how I much I was struggling. I have never been one to feign illness, except when I wanted a day off school and would empty a can of oxtail soup down the bog and tell Mum that I had been sick. So I always tried to play it down because there was no way I wanted to be replaced halfway through the season – again. It was only really the tremendous support from friends, family and fans that I was receiving which kept me going.

The highlight of a frustrating and difficult season was definitely the British round at Silverstone. It was the wettest I had ever known, and this suited me. Not only would I not sweat as much, we would also go slower and the eye would not dry as quickly. This was the first World Superbike round at the circuit, too, so I knew the track a little better than some. I was challenging for fourth in the first race when I lost the front at the first corner and, although I remounted, could only finish fourteenth. In the second race I was again on the pace and managed to catch and pass Shakey and Hodgson to finish the top British rider in fourth place. I had not had much to smile about all year and, with Heckles having finished in sixth place in race one and Dog visiting for the weekend still on his crutches, there was every reason to let our hair down before the next round at Lausitz, where my rear BBS wheel disintegrated on the start line. The hub ripped the spokes clean out of the rim and luckily I was not collected by those behind me. It was put down to my aggressive way of starting, but that theory didn't really hold water when the same thing happened during the first race at Assen. Apart from another couple of good finishes at Brands, the other high point was my first trip to Laguna Seca – with Heckles in tow.

He got there a couple of days before me and was staying in a motorhome in the paddock until he saw the size of my hotel room. On the way to and from the circuit we became hooked on a local radio station, which was running a competition for the last tickets to see a sell-out rock concert in San Diego. The three naked male contestants had to climb in a two-man sleeping bag, were covered in Crisco cooking oil and shown non-stop porn. The winner of Fag in a Bag, or Nude with a Dude, as they called their game, was the last one to get an erection. If they looked too comfortable the men were told to change positions. You could picture them slithering around like eels while desperately trying to picture their mum naked. The presenter had been an extra in the Annabel Chong porn film, *The World's Biggest Gang Bang*. He told us listeners about the 'fluffers'; girls employed to keep the seventy men waiting in line alongside him ready for action. 'When my time came she looked like an iced doughnut,' was his classic line.

I loved Laguna and its famous Corkscrew section. I remember that master of understatement Foggy once describing it as 'just a chicane on an 'ill', but it's a bit more special than that. Some riders learn certain circuits better than others, but this one had a bit more character than the average European track that you come across for the first time. I struggled to master it straight away and was a bit overshadowed by Eric Bostrom during qualifying, although he crashed during morning warm-up and sat out the races. I was eleventh and tenth, but this was in the days when a rider kept his appearance and prize money, rather than it being paid to the teams. And in the States it was paid in cash. I was handed around $1,500 and Heckles another $700, so we were armed with dollars and dangerous. Our flight home was not for another two days so there was only one thing for it: road trip to Hollywood. We drove down Highway 1, the Pacific Coast Highway and, while it was spectacular, it went on for hours so we headed straight for Muscle Beach to kick back when we arrived. It lived up to its name: full of muscle-bound blokes and women with pecs instead of boobs, which is not right. Then we headed up to Beverley Hills and found a big hotel, with the biggest suite, right on Hollywood Boulevard. Our intention was to cruise a few bars, and the first one we came to was a massive place, done out like a Wild West ranch. In the middle of the bar was a Bucking Bronco machine that bucked girls wearing next to nothing, so invariably their boobs or Jack and Dannies would pop out from under their costumes. In the corner to our left was a pit for coleslaw wrestling. We just looked at each other and didn't need to say a word – we were living the dream. Needless to say we didn't make it out of that bar and woke up with around $300 left between us and only a hangover to show for it. After making a token effort to see the big Hollywood sign, it was a long and painful trip home.

Just as Harald had predicted, my consistency and determination had been enough to impress the other teams and Colin Wright took me to one side at Oschersleben. Neil Hodgson had been poached by the factory Ducati squad, so Colin was looking for a rider. 'Before you do anything about next year, make sure you facking talk to me,' he said, and we later agreed to meet up on the morning after the final race at Imola, one of the most memorable in Superbike history when Colin Edwards clinched the title from long-time leader, Troy Bayliss.

The series owners, the Flammini brothers, always throw a grand end-of-season prizegiving dinner, showing highlights of the season's action on a few big screens, and this was being held on the second-floor grandstand roof area in a big marquee. Heckles, in true Liverpudlian style, had managed to swipe a few extra bottles of wine, so our table was getting pretty lively. Big Jamie Gamble, the biggest of the Big Lads, dared Heckles: 'I'll give you a grand if you get one of those plasmas, Nobby.' At the end of the night Heckles had disappeared for more than an hour and I started to worry, so went to look for him. He was halfway back to the motorhome, knackered and bleeding from a wound on his leg. He had taken one of the kitchen knives with the intention of slicing his way back into the marquee and grabbing a plasma screen. It probably weighed three times his body weight, so the plan was not too ingenious. Anyway, he was met by a burly security guard at the top of the stairs, who said, 'Watta da fuck d'ya thinka ya doinga?' Undeterred, Mark went back to ground level, put the knife between his teeth, and tried to scale the grandstand from a couple of different angles. Having repeatedly dropped the knife he slipped it into his trouser pocket – and straight into his leg.

On the way back to the motorhome we went past the Aprilia hospitality, which was locked up for the night. But they had left two big manicured bushes outside, so we decided to give the new world champion, Colin Edwards, a treat by creating a tropical patio paradise outside his motorhome. The bushes weighed a tonne and we had to drag them half a mile through the longest paddock on the calendar to the motorhome area. We then placed them either side of his motorhome door, adding a few tables and chairs and a big umbrella for good measure. Colin's wife, Alyssia, opened the door in the morning and screeched: 'Colin, Colin! What on earth has been going on out here?' Nobody claimed the bushes so we loaded them in my motorhome and took them home, named them Colin and Edward, and they still have pride of place in my garden.

I was a bit worse for wear on the Monday morning and actually a bit nervous about seeing Colin Wright. I remembered my last negotiations with him for the Kawasaki job, when I dared to point out that the contract did not include a bonus for winning the championship. 'Facking championship bonus?' he said. 'Your facking bonus is a job for next year, you little cant.' This time it took next to no time to thrash out a deal. I was peaking. I would be on a year-old factory Ducati, be working with Colin and Stewart Johnstone again, had met and liked HM Plant's John Jones and GSE owner Darryl Healey, and I would have James Toseland, who had already started to show his potential, as my team-mate in an all-British assault on the title. At long last I could enjoy an uninterrupted winter of preparation. Come on, you know the score by now, right?

23

Punctured Stalker

The final act of the 2002 summer was a return to the Supermotard International Race in a Belgian town called Mettet. It's a huge event with a great atmosphere, where road racers and motocrossers take on supermoto riders on a track – half dirt and half road – through the town centre. The cream of the motocross world like Stefan Everts turned out, as well as supermoto experts like Christian Iddon and Warren Steele. I had been called up the previous year as a late replacement on a CCM for Foggy, who broke his leg badly while preparing for the race. I didn't do too badly, finishing around fifth, and was desperate for another go. This year I had to source my own bike and called in a few favours, including asking Stewie Johnstone to tune the engine of a Honda CRF450, lent to me by mechanic and magazine test rider Doc Wobbley. At the last minute I was asked whether James Toseland would like to take one of the few remaining rides. James had been a schoolboy trials champion and was pretty handy on dirt bikes, and he jumped at the chance, although I knew that the XR650 he was due to ride would be powerful but difficult to handle around this circuit.

I have never seen anyone crash as much as James did in the first twenty minutes of qualifying, including one amazing stunt when he crashed sideways into a tyre wall and landed sitting on top of the tyres as though it had all been planned. However, as ever with JT, he

272

soon had it mastered. My bike was a weapon, and although I was fourth in the first big race I was a bit miffed because my exhaust had cracked and I had lost power, allowing Stefan Everts to beat me to third. I blagged another exhaust for the second race and was dicing for third with the reigning British Supermoto champion at the time, Warren Steele. I had just overtaken him when the guy in front of me, riding a Husqvarna, clipped the tyres forming a chicane round the back of the circuit. Some tyres bounced into the track and my foot hit them as I went through – snapping my leg in two. I stayed on the bike and slowly rode back to the pits with my foot pointing back-wards, parked the bike up and leant against the wall. It was like *déjà vu* from my motocross at Abergavenny. My big break in World Superbikes had turned into a big break of my tib and fib and ankle.

'What's the matter, Nobby?' asked Graham, who had travelled out in the van with me and Sarah. I just looked down at my leg.

'Get the ambulance, will you? The job's fucked,' I said. At the hospital I thought it best for everyone to set off for home because it looked like I would have to stay in a while. Graham had a business to run, as had Dad, who had driven out on the day of the race and saw the accident, and there was nowhere for Sarah to stay. I asked Dad to ring Colin Wright and tell him that I would call as soon as I knew the extent of the damage. I wasn't relishing that call.

I woke up to the news that I needed an operation and that I would be in hospital there for a week. This was Belgium's revenge for all the shit tanks we had emptied in their motorway service stations. They explained where they were going to insert the plates and fix the foot, but all that I was concerned about was whether I would be able to move my ankle freely afterwards. However weak my leg come the start of testing I knew that I'd be OK to ride as long as I could change gears easily enough. The language barrier proved too great because when I came round from the anaesthetic, feeling like I had been hit by a steamroller, I realized straight away that my ankle had been immobi-lized. I was spewing and was straight on the phone home. Dad pointed out the obvious – that I shouldn't have been racing there in the first place. Bit harsh! Maybe I'd get a bit more sympathy from Sarah.

'Don't come crying to me, Christopher,' she shouted down the phone. 'Graham told me on the way home how you have been calling Lisa all this time.' Graham, whose company sponsored my mobile phone, had dropped me in the shit, like mates do from time to time. But all I had done was have the occasional chat and haircut from Lisa, the girl I was with for seven years.

Great! My dad is angry with me, my girlfriend is spewing, my mate has shat on me, I can't move my bastard ankle and I am stuck in the middle of fucking Belgium. The doctors would not let me leave until the swelling had died down, the wound had healed and they had placed a full cast on my leg. As soon as the plaster dried I discharged myself, hobbled with my kitbag, stolen X-rays and crutches into a taxi to the airport, flew home and took another taxi to the train station in England, changed trains twice and limped home at about 2 a.m.

The specialist at the private Park Hospital performed another operation almost straight away to remove all the Belgian metalwork and place two plates on either side of each fracture, attached by screws that could stay in permanently. The ankle screws were also repositioned so that I would have full movement when they eventually came out. Everything was timed so that any unnecessary metal would be removed the week before the first test at Valencia. In the meantime I was given a bit of a talking to from Colin, stressing how important the year was for both me and the team.

'Park that fackin' motocross bike up for the year. You don't need to train on that. We will keep you busy and fit enough with testing,' he said. 'And don't go influencing JT again. We didn't even know he was going to Belgium, so he's had a right fackin' bollocking.' Colin was right, as usual. I had been stupid to even think about doing the Mettet race. Having said that, though, you can't wrap yourself up in cotton wool and there hadn't been so much as a broken finger among the 300 riders the previous year.

After that final operation I couldn't support my weight at the test, so I had to move around on crutches and be lifted onto the bike by my mechanic, Dave Parkes. Even so, I left Valencia having gone faster than JT and stepped up my rehabilitation in the weeks leading up to the first race. I started swimming again, despite my cod eye, and threw myself into my cycling. Nobody could question just how determined I was to be as fit as possible for the first race, also at Valencia.

The bike and the team made it so much easier for me there. I was on Ruben Xaus's bike from the previous year and it was almost brand new, probably because all the parts were in fact new after he'd crashed so often. Everything seemed to be slower on a twin-cylinder compared to the busy four-cylinders that I was used to, although the Ducati was certainly not short of power and speed. Hodgson took both wins ahead of his team-mate Xaus, and I managed to stay ahead of James in the first race, although we swapped positions in race two and came away joint third in the championship. This would have been a reasonable excuse for a few beers, if an excuse were ever needed in Valencia because everyone always headed for the Irish bar in the city, O'Neill's.

The Big Lads were out in force: the ringleader Big Jamie and his mate Roger Thomason, known as Nelson because, like Nelson Mandela, he was only allowed out once every three years; Hoggy and George Clooney; and Gary Turner, a used-car salesman more commonly known as Bullshit. Dad was also with the Big Lads, although this turned out to be his last trip abroad. He was put in charge of the weekend's cash, and if anyone wanted any money for anything they had to check with John whether it was a good deal. I'm not exactly sure what went on, where they went or what they did with him, but he was scarred for life. I had driven the little team-liveried Smart car, which I attached to the back of the motorhome on a trailer, into the city centre with Heckles, who was at Valencia looking for a ride for the rest of the year. He had become a great pal, sharing many a motorhome adventure the previous season. I picked him and his huge kitbag up at South Mimms services at the start of the summer and never got rid of him! He now lives with his wife, a leading brand manager for the Guinness Group, in New York, so I don't get to see much of him any more. JT and a few of the other riders were also out, as were all the TV commentators like Whitham, Jack Burnicle, Steve Parrish and Suzi Perry.

The Guinness started to flow and it was a great atmosphere when in walked one of the North African street sellers with a rucksack full of goods including some wooden animal carvings that were actually quite good. Heckles sifted through the fake CDs, using all his Liverpudlian heritage while buying two and stuffing six others down his trousers and up his jumper. Bullshit was also keen to buy a present for his wife at the time, who was a big old girl.

'I think I'll get a giraffe for the wife,' he said.

'Sounds like a fair swap to me, Nobby,' said Jamie.

'At least it's got a neck,' said Hoggy.

'You're all bastards,' laughed Bullshit, and bought a pair of bongo drums instead. Later in the night Jamie handed Heckles a few euros and said, 'Get me a pair of bongos, Nobby. And make sure they're bigger than Bullshit's.'

At the airport the next morning Jamie and Bullshit couldn't work out why the pads of their fingertips were swollen and bleeding. It might have had something to do with them bongoing 'Show me the way to Amarillo, Gonna wipe my knob on your pillow' for a couple of hours, non-stop. Binman Andy, a binman called Andy, was another casualty, having spent the night talking to the big white telephone. We had become friends after his wife, Carolyn, had been one of my early Pillion in a Million victims – but managed to stay on.

Me and Heckles were not feeling much better. But while the Big Lads could get a taxi to the airport and a two-hour flight home we faced a 2,000 km drive back through Spain and France and a rush to get Heckles back in time for his birthday party on the Tuesday. So we were up quite early, placed the trophy on the dash and the Dunlop cap on the trophy and set off in my 39 ft Damon Escaper. I had never bothered to take the test for the correct licence for a vehicle of that size, and didn't have the correct insurance either. What we did have, though, was a tray full of Crackerwheats with Philadelphia Light and tomato sliced on top, plus a stash of Red Bull and Nurofen. Five hours later, about an hour from the French border, we heard the loudest bang. I thought something had hit us. The motorhome started to vibrate, and in the mirror I saw the wheel arch fly off and land in the middle of the road. It was a good distance before I could bring 14 tonnes of motorhome and trailer to a stop on the hard shoulder, and set off sprinting back up the road to try and salvage the wheel arch. I got to within 50 metres and it was still in one piece, but then the next lorry along smashed it to smithereens. Bastard! There was no spare wheel because they are too big to change without specialist equipment, so the plan was to coast along to the next major town on the three remaining rear tyres. There we finally found a tyre stockist on an industrial park, but after much pointing and scratching of heads we got the message that they didn't stock the correct size of tyre.

Not to worry, it was still only mid-afternoon and we were only an hour from France, home of Michelin. Surely someone would stock them there? We limped into the first town over the border, but after much pointing and scratching of heads we discovered that this size of tyre could only be ordered direct from the States. I could not believe that we could not buy one in the whole of France, where they actually made the bloody things, so I rang Hoggy to see if he could use his transport business connections to find out, while we tackled the remaining 800 miles up through France at 40 m.p.h. It was now dark and I was bored and hungry because Heckles had treated himself to one of his famous 'power naps' in the reclining front seat. I tried to increase the speed step by step, but the vibration worsened as the speed increased until at 80 m.p.h. I seemed to have accelerated through the problem. It was all starting to look a bit rosier.

Bang! The motorhome was suddenly sideways as I fought with the steering wheel to try and correct the screeching, steaming, sparks-flying slide. Heckles shat himself awake and screamed, 'Brakes would be good, brakes would be good, chief!' The remaining tyre of the nearside pair, which had been taking the whole load since the original puncture, had also blown and only the weight of the trailer kept us upright. I hadn't done too badly in reaching the hard shoulder, considering I hadn't been to the School of Motorhome Skids. But it was now 11 p.m. and the only constructive idea Heckles could come up with was to start cooking a pizza. Out of the blue a recovery vehicle pulled up in front of us, lights flashing. It was obvious he didn't speak a word of English and we were fed up with pointing and scratching our heads.

'Avez-vous des frères ou des sœurs?' I asked. OK, it would not be too useful to know whether he had any brothers or sisters, but it was one of the few sentences I remembered from school.

'Je m'appelle Mark,' added Heckles, pissing himself laughing. That was the only French he knew, but I had a few more sentences up my sleeve.

'J'ai un grand bat,' I tried. I didn't have a big cock, but my sister had a French exchange student over to stay when we were young and I thought it might be a useful phrase to learn. Heckles was now rolling around the floor and even the recovery man was smiling.

'Avez-vous des chiens ou des chats?' No, he didn't have any dogs or cats, or any vinegar, which I had also found useful when ordering chips in France. But that had pretty much exhausted my French vocabulary and we were no nearer Calais. He eventually climbed into the motorhome, trailing oil all over my Axminster carpet, and told us to listen to the radio, which he tuned into the necessary emergency frequency. Sure enough, an hour and a pepperoni pizza later a guy turned up in a big van. He didn't have any brothers, sisters, dogs, cats or vinegar, but he did have a compressor and took one of the tyres off the pair of wheels on the other side and fitted it onto the blown side. It was enough to enable us to follow him to his compound where we could spend the night while he looked for the correct tyres, which we knew didn't exist in Europe.

'Oh, by the way, happy birthday, Nobby,' I said to Mark.

'I just want to be home,' he whined. We had lost our sense of humour by now.

The new day brought fresh hope and motivation, until the guy returned with the news that there were no tyres in France of that size. No surprise there. But he had a plan. If he took the tyres off the front and put them on the two empty wheels on the back, then he could find two tyres of a different size for the front. Perfect – until the tyres arrived, he fitted them and showed me the bill: 2,000 euros for two tyres, a tow and the fitting. I pulled out my wallet, handed him the money, left his office and dropped my jeans and boxers.

'What are you doing?' asked Heckles.

'I've had my pants pulled down by old François there so I might as well keep them down,' I said.

We made it to Calais just in time for the overnight ferry and back home more than a day later than expected. Heckles had missed his birthday party and I decided to join the RAC.

There was a full month to recover from that trip home, and for my leg to get stronger, before the next round at Phillip Island. I was actually able to jog around the circuit with JT and was quite chuffed when he was out of breath at the end of a couple of laps, because he is a keen jogger and super fit. We suffered problems with the tyres delaminating in both races and I came home in seventh in the opener, when James was black flagged when his fairing came unclipped. He managed to steal fifth place from me by just seven thousandths of a second in race two but I was now in third in the championship on my own, heading for Sugo the following month.

My leg was now feeling strong and I was able to beat James 10–0 at squash at the hotel in nearby Sendai. We had to play that many games because he wouldn't stop until he won one or flaked out. I had never had lessons, just whacked the ball as hard as I could and then hurtled after it if it was returned. I knew I was back to a good level of fitness and was excited about racing at such a fun track. The weekend didn't turn out to be a whole lot of fun, though.

I struggled with the front at first and maybe had it too soft for the hard-braking areas. Stewie made a tweak on the first morning and it felt immediately better. But then I tipped the bike into the first left-hander and high-sided. The bike landed on the same leg that was broken in Mettet and the foot-rest dug into the top of my foot, which was dragged along with the bike, scraping all the skin off the top. I had broken three metatarsals, or guiders as I called them, and you could see the bone through a big hole. Colin went with me to the medical centre and when they took the boot off he said, 'Fackin' hell, you're facked.' When they started to scrub away the dirt from the wounds and cut away the frayed giblets he had to leave the room. Then they injected the wound with some fluid before covering it with a pad and bandage. I borrowed a bigger boot from another rider and the guys moved a few bits so that changing gear would be more comfortable for me. It hurt through the chicanes but I finished the wet afternoon session first on the timesheets and managed to qualify sixth on the Saturday.

I'm still not sure exactly what happened at the start of the first race, but as I tipped into the sharp first right-hander and started to accelerate Corser had missed the corner completely for some reason and crashed into the side of me. Let's make that two broken feet then, shall we? I hobbled out of the gravel, where Corser, Clementi and Chili were also lying from the same incident. The team tried to persuade me not to race in the afternoon. But I was still in a handy position in the championship and I wasn't about to just to sit it out with an updated total of five broken metatarsals. After the second lap of the race, however, I didn't have much option. I was challenging for sixth place when I lost the front at the end of the back straight. I looked like the lizard from the television advert, which hops from one foot to the other on the hot desert sand, as I scurried off the track before crawling to a safe position.

All I needed then was a twenty-four-hour *Planes, Trains and Automobiles* trip back to England. But James's manager, Roger Burnett, was really helpful, organized a flight that night and, along with JT, carried my bags as I hobbled on my heels all the way back to Narita Airport. The medics at the circuit had luckily provided me with a sleeping pill for the flight that would stop a rhinoceros at 100 paces and I was thankful to be able to sort through my abundance of collated crutches when I reached home. The doctors wanted to give me a skin graft, but I didn't have time for that with Monza just two weeks away. I was also told to keep it out in the open, so that the scab would form, until the district nurse decided otherwise and ripped the 5 mm deep scab off without any anaesthetic. That, however, was not half as bad as having to wear sandals for the first time in my life. At least I didn't have to wear the black socks too, as all Germans seem to do. The hardest thing to take, though, having reached a good fitness level before Japan, was putting my training on hold again. I could not swim with the open wound, and could not cycle or jog, so I just had to do weights and started to look like a Paralympian.

I struggled through the fast chicanes at Monza, especially Ascari, but the wound was nearly healed by Oschersleben, and I was much better prepared, both mentally and physically. I was on the pace all weekend and Superpole was declared wet, which always suited me more than the normal one lap that you get in the dry. I preferred to get dialled in and build up my pace before putting all my trust in a qualifier, rather than stand around for up to three quarters of an hour before going straight out for one fast lap on qualifying rubber. However, at the 180 degree turn in the first split I gave it a big handful of gas, earlier than when on a normal tyre – and obviously fractionally too early. The tyre gripped and gripped and gripped and – let go. And then I was picking straw bale out of my teeth.

Maybe that shook my confidence for the first race, when I was a fraction of a second off fourth place behind Regis Laconi. I wanted to make a few set-up changes between races but Colin said, 'You've been in the top three all weekend. Never mind any changes, just ride the thing like we know you can and you will be sound.' It was exactly the kind of pep talk I needed.

My motorhome was parked overlooking the first turn and Hoggy and Jamie had watched the first race from the roof, casting a huge shadow over that part of the track. I'd warned them that if I crashed there in the second race because the track temperature had dropped at that spot I would not be happy. Coming round on the final lap I could see them waving their Stalker shirts and giving me the thumbs up. I had held off early challenges from Chili and Xaus to come home third in a what turned out to be a great race for HM Plant, because JT won his first race. With Hodgson second it was the first ever all-British podium. Even better for JT, he was able to collect on a promise made by HM Plant owner, John Jones, a couple of years earlier. They had been watching Elton John perform on TV in hospitality and James, an exceptionally talented piano player, commented that he would love a go on one of the Steinway grand pianos. John said, 'If you win a race when you are still riding for me I will buy you one.' He was true to his word, and a £70,000 piano was delivered within weeks. I tried to hint to John that I would love a ride in one of the Mercedes SL500s that was featured in an advert shown in hospitality after the races, but he was perhaps recalculating his bonus packages by then!

It was hard to find something that James was not talented at. Earlier in the season he was forced to sit out a test at Almeria after damaging his right hand in a crash at Valencia. But he still came out for a beer after the test and I challenged him to a game of darts in the bar where we were eating, knowing he could not use his natural throwing hand. He still beat me with his left. So it was nice to discover an Achilles' heel during the PR build-up to the first British race of the season at Silverstone.

Jane Rose, who had handled the Old Spice PR, had arranged for the BBC to film me and James fly with the Red Arrows at RAF Scampton in Lincolnshire. I love speed, whether in cars, on bikes, on trains or in planes, but had no idea just how special it would be. The pilots were so down to earth, not your typical Wing Commander sorts, and seemed just as excited about meeting us. Having just about passed the height restriction test I pulled on my G-Force suit, which inflated around the legs at a certain speed, stopping the blood rushing down when pulling Big Gs, which cause you to faint. We were also told to eat some food, as an empty stomach moved around inside the body and caused nausea, so I stuffed about fifteen slices of toast down in the canteen. We were both given hand-held video cameras and filmed each other flicking Vs when the planes flew side-by-side. The sensation of speed when we burst from the clouds over Skegness beach and flew 50 ft above the water was incredible. Then they did somersaults and barrel rolls and flew upside down, and my pilot handed me the controls for a loop-the-loop before landing. The TV cameras rushed over when I climbed out of the cockpit of Red 9 and James pulled off his mask to reveal all the carrots that he had chucked up. I felt sorry for him but was quietly chuffed to add puking in a fighter plane to squash on the very short list of JT weaknesses.

After an average Silverstone I was much more ready for Laguna second time around. The race had been hyped up as Matt Mladin, smoking everyone in the AMA, versus Neil Hodgson, runaway leader in World Superbikes. Mladin finished fourth ahead of me in the first race, which Neil won, and didn't even take part in the second, claiming to be concentrating on his domestic championship. Neil and JT tangled early in race two, leaving me in second place behind Ruben Xaus and ahead of Aaron Yates. He crashed but Hodgson had recovered to take second spot with five laps remaining while I held on to clinch the final place on the podium. During the post-race interviews Ruben was asked what he put his performance down to. 'I rode with the Spanish hard-on,' he said. I was a Xaus fan before that anyway, but I certainly was now. I couldn't help admiring his all-action, occasionally win-it-or-bin-it, style. Plus he was one of the few Spanish riders not to have called me 'cabron'!

Brands provided a chance to make amends for my previous lacklustre round in front of the home crowd at Silverstone and the weekend started well when, in a wet Superpole, I qualified second on the grid behind John Reynolds, my best qualifying position in World Superbikes. Shakey Byrne, who was leading the British championship by miles, won this race by miles too. I was dicing with Hodgson for second place throughout the race, despite struggling with the front tyre pushing towards the end, and finished just one tenth of a second behind to complete the first ever all-British podium in England. We considered changing the front tyre for race two, but stuck with the same compound and – surprise, surprise – I lost the front going into Clearways. The bike somersaulted into the fence and the wheels were still spinning when the first kid arrived to ask for my autograph – then my gloves, then my boots, then my leathers. I had to sit and watch the rest of the race nearly naked. Again it was an all-Brit rostrum with Shakey completing the double and JR finishing ahead of JT.

I went to Assen sixth in the championship and 13 points behind Gregorio Lavilla in fifth, which was not bad at all considering my injuries in the first half of the season. Fifth place was important for me because this time I had been able to pin Colin down on perform-ance-related bonuses at the end of the season. The deal was that my ride would be secured for 2004 if I finished in the top five. Hodgson's second place was enough to secure his title but Lavilla failed to finish the first race and my 11 points for fifth place meant I was now just two points behind. Colin called me into the trailer between races and I assumed it was to discuss the deal for 2004.

It was actually to tell me that the team would not be competing next year.

24

Extreme Stalker

To say that I was smashed was an understatement. I had felt so at home with the team. Colin Wright was the best in the business, John Jones was the most relaxed sponsor possible and Darryl Healey, the GSE team owner, whilst always ensuring that every detail was perfect, was also a pleasure to deal with. James Toseland was hotly tipped for the factory Ducati ride, so even if I had finished out of the top five at the end of the year they were unlikely to change both riders. For once I expected to have some continuity during the winter and was gearing up for a genuine title challenge. Telling me the news just before a race was not the best motivational tool, but it had been leaked to a journalist and Colin wanted me to hear it from the team rather than any other source. With rumours of a possible one-make tyre rule, the manufacturers were up in arms and Ducati were unable to guarantee the best bikes. So, rather than drop their standards, Darryl had decided to sit the year out. All this was running through my mind during the second Assen race and my eighth place left me 10 points behind Lavilla with two rounds remaining.

But hang on a minute. Didn't my contract say that I was guaranteed a ride if I finished in the top five? I certainly wanted to be in a position to ask that question. My cause was not helped, however, when Lavilla out-braked both me and himself going into the top chicane during the first race at the penultimate round in Imola. I was punted off onto the Astroturf and lost the front, while he stayed on to finish fourth. I was now fighting a losing battle for fifth place going into the final round of the season at Magny-Cours. Equally important for the team, though, was that JT was only 17 points behind French rider Laconi in the battle for third place. I was desperate to do everything possible to help him out, but having seen the reaction that Hodgson received when he helped Bayliss I was not about to help manufacture any results. In fact, I didn't help James's cause when I passed him into third place with five laps remaining, and held Lavilla off for my fifth podium of the year. But James had finished ahead of Laconi, who strangely never does too well at his home circuit, despite all the frantic waving to the fans on his out-laps, in-laps, and probably trips to the toilet, too.

'Don't worry, I'm sure you'll still get that third place,' I told JT before the final race of the year. After a few laps we were locked in a tremendous dice for third place. James was faster than me in a few spots and I was quicker through other sections. Then, halfway through the race, we saw Laconi in the gravel, going mental as only Régis Laconi can do because his mechanics had not tightened his back wheel properly. James had third place in the championship in the bag but I was riding for pride, and when Neil Hodgson went missing from second place with five laps to go our battle was suddenly for second place. I had it all planned and knew where I was going to challenge James on the final lap, but made a mistake beforehand and had to settle for third. While race winner Ruben Xaus messed up his celebratory doughnut and crashed, me and James did a more successful but equally spectacular double burn-out at the last chicane. I have signed so many of those pictures. Ducati must have been impressed with our performances throughout the year, too, because Minichamps produced two model replicas of our bikes, and mine still has pride of place on my shelf.

As soon as the smoke had cleared from the burn-out I was keen to cement a ride for the following year. And Foggy eased any fears that I might have had at the end-of-season party in France. Before I had even heard that I would be losing my job the manager of Carl's Foggy

Petronas Racing team, Nigel Bosworth, had approached me at Assen. I obviously had a lot of respect for him from my early racing days and I had seen what a professional outfit he ran for Carl.

'Don't overlook us when you are thinking about next year,' he said. 'We have a lot of developments coming through and we should be up there.' Despite this brief chat, at Imola I decided to find out what my options were in the rest of the paddock and spoke to Kawasaki Bertocchi and Alstare Suzuki and a couple of other teams. But the championship was in a bit of turmoil because of the imminent control tyre rule and many manufacturers were stepping aside for a year to see how it all panned out. So I sat down with Bozzy and Carl in Italy and listened to their plans for new engine builders to improve the reliability of their Petronas triple and to increase the horsepower. The new tyre rule was expected to work in their favour, as the championship would be more of a level playing field. I was conscious that their 900cc bike would be up against a field of 1000cc bikes, as the rules now allowed restricted four-cylinders at this capacity. But I had raced 750cc machines against the 999cc Ducatis and knew that power wasn't everything. There are more corners than straights during a championship campaign and, while I knew the bike would struggle at the faster tracks, it handled well by all accounts and, given the right conditions, there was a chance of some good results. It would also keep me in World Superbikes and in a good position for one of the choice rides when the manufacturers came back in 2005, as they were sure to do. There was also a chance that, if the Petronas FP1 continued to improve, I might want to stay with that team. The pros far outweighed the cons.

Nothing was agreed at Imola but Carl made it clear during the party in France that the ride was mine if I wanted it. He had his arm round me the whole night and was introducing me to the team as though I had already signed. Back home we started to discuss terms and I held out for an extra £15,000 on their original offer because, contrary to popular opinion, Foggy's team weren't in a position to pay silly money for riders come 2004.

'That James Haydon cost us a fucking fortune this year in crash damage. There's only so much in the pot, Chris. If you insist on that

£15,000 it will have to come out of my wage,' he said. I liked him even more for pulling that one! Everything was soon agreed and I travelled to their workshop in Burton-on-Trent to sign the contract and do some publicity photos for *MCN*. The place blew me away. It was obvious this team was not going to run out of money halfway through the season. It was also good to know some of the team already. My crew chief was going to be Barry Stanley, whom I knew from my Cadbury Boost days, and Bozzy had assembled a lot of familiar faces in his team. But, before putting pen to paper, Carl called me into his office with the team's chief executive, Murray Treece, a dead ringer for Buzz Lightyear.

'We want to make you aware of something before you sign,' said Foggy. 'We are letting Bozzy go. There's no need to go into the reasons. We are not sure who is going to replace him yet, or even if there will be anyone in that role. Hope this doesn't change anything.' It was water off a duck's back by now. I knew that nothing ever went smoothly. But it was still a bit of a pisser, and I felt for Bozzy because he had been so enthusiastic when he sold the project to me. It was, however, too late in the day to do anything about it as I was already wearing the team shirt and the lights had been set up for the photoshoot!

And it wasn't long before I had my first taste of action on the bike – first test, worst test! I was actually quite excited about riding the bike at Valencia; it was beautiful to look at and the image of the team was also fantastic. There was no reason why we couldn't build on the progress that Troy had made towards the end of the previous season. But after just one lap on the thing I couldn't believe how shit it was. When I shut the throttle off for the first time the back end came round and JT came past on the factory Ducati shaking his head. 'This is going to be a long season,' I thought. My favourite race bike had always been the Suzuki 750, but my best bike had been the previous year's Ducati. So to jump straight from that onto this beast was a shock to the system – literally. I stayed out for ten laps then came into the garage with half my fillings missing and my feet still zinging. The chatter from the front and rear was unbelievable. At first it was put down to the new Pirelli tyres and we searched for a compromise set-up. It was not until the following season that the cause was finally discovered. The seat unit and tailpiece were an integral part of the chassis, and the faster the bike went, the more it vibrated.

Carl was looking a bit sheepish during the test at Valencia, but at the end of the three days he was more than happy how close I was to the lap times of Corser, who had already had a season on the bike. Troy had been one of the first riders to welcome me into the paddock when I was a wild card and I quickly discovered that his motorhome was the place to be for the post-race parties. After one race at Donington he shouted: 'You boys want some two-stroke smoke?' He then yanked the cord of his mini-moto and filled his $300,000 motorhome with smoke so thick that I couldn't see my hand in front of my face. In his heyday, I might not have been too happy leaving my girlfriend with him. He had a reputation for suffering from desert disease – wandering palms. But now he was with his future wife, Sam, and had a kid on the way, so was not so much of a party animal any more. But Troy is still an awesome rider and a great bloke.

As the season developed, though, every weekend was like being in the film *Apollo 13*. Whenever one problem was solved another one came to light. And then, on those rare weekends when everything was going smoothly, before the second race you would feel a squeeze on your leg on the start-line from Carl.

'Good luck in this one. I won't be around for the finish. I'm going to shoot off to beat the traffic,' he would say. It didn't exactly spur you on.

If I was starting to wonder what I had let myself in for after that first ride on the Petronas, it was nothing compared to the shock to the system I received a couple of weeks later at a PR event for my helmet sponsor, Shark. I had been with them for a couple of years now, ironically because their distributors, Phoenix, were conscious of a gap in the British market after Foggy retired and wanted me to switch from another of their brands, Arai. One of the clauses with Shark was that I would take part in their annual adventure race through the Pyrenees, called Shark X-trem. And extreme it certainly was.

Foggy had also been roped into taking part by Shark and was to be teamed up with Régis Laconi. I was partnered by Paul Malin, who had been second in the World Motocross championship before having to retire with a broken back. Others had promised to take part but pulled out when they heard a few more details. Our adventure didn't start too well when we were stopped in our diesel Ford Transit van, lent to me by Jamie because it was in Petronas green, by the French police for speeding. The copper didn't have any brothers, sisters, dogs, cats or vinegar, or a sense of humour, and confiscated our passports until we came back with some euros for the fine. We were stopped again on the way back to pay the fine for not stopping at a junction leading back onto the motorway. This gendarme started rattling his handcuffs as we tried to explain that his mate down the road, who was actually in view, already had our documents. This trip was going to be extreme all right, extremely bloody expensive.

On arriving in the Pyrenees we discovered we didn't have any of the necessary equipment, such as a wet suit for a 5 km kayak out to sea before the 10 k run, road-registered endurance bikes or our own insurance. What we did have, though, was a driver to follow us round from stage to stage in the van: Neil Bramwell, Foggy's manager and the team's marketing guy. 'Am I insured?' he worriedly asked when I handed him the keys.

'Is he for real?' I asked Carl. 'You don't know him,' Carl laughed. The first checkpoint for the endurance stage was an hour away and Neil pulled into the car park with the side of the van hanging off, having backed into some poor unsuspecting Pyrenean villager's prized Peugeot. I had ripped the radiator off my bike on a rock ten minutes into that section, so immediately set about blocking off a hose with some wheel nuts off the van, so that the bike would run off only one radiator. Malin thought this was ingenious and I was quietly quite pleased with myself. Foggy had already retired by this point, having dabbed his knee down and conveniently discovered 'gangrene' in the 'wound' within five seconds. We battled on until the night stage, stopping continually to pee in the one remaining radiator, which was by now also leaking. We even begged a local farmer for a raw egg to crack inside the radiator so that, when cooked, the egg

would provide a temporary seal. Yes, it did work, believe it or not –
for an hour or so anyway.

For the night stage pairs went out at two-minute intervals and
the leaders, the French legend Jean-Michel Bayle and his partner,
set off forty minutes before us and returned one minute after we
left. Me and Paul limped home three and a half hours later. My bike
didn't have lights as standard so we had fitted some shitters on,
which got brighter the more I revved the engine but were no better
than a candle when it was just ticking over. I basically could not see
a bloody thing and hit a rock bigger than a house, throwing me over
the bars and head-first off a precipice into a raging river. When Paul
appeared all he could see was a shiny pair of white Tech 8 Alpinestars boots sticking out of the river. He pulled me out, then we
pulled the bike out of the river, only to discover my lights had
fused. I had to crawl along behind Paul, using his lights to ride by
for the rest of the stage, all the way back to the bivouac tent and just
in time for the last helpings of – rabbit stew! And we were one of
the last back so had no option but to place our sleeping bags
directly underneath the village clock, which chimed at fifteen-
minute intervals throughout the night. Still, sleep or no sleep, we
were not too worried about the next day because, although we
refused to quit, there was surely no way my Yamaha YZ250 could
last another ten minutes.

Wrong! After building a temporary raft to get the bikes across
another torrent of a river, the Terminator, as we had nicknamed my
bike because it could not be killed, made it through to the mountain
bike section. After scaling a castle wall to finish the race we received
the biggest cheer of the day because everyone had heard of our traumas. Our reward? Enough cash to cover our fines and pay for the van
and bike repairs, perhaps? A nice memento or trophy? Maybe a case
of French beer or wine? No, none of the above. Our prize for surviv-
ing the most gruelling two days of our lives was … a leg of Parma
ham. A fucking leg of Parma ham! And it stank so much that we
chucked it out the window of the van after half an hour of the trip
back home!

And it was a new home I was going back to. I had rattled around the big rooms in the farmhouse in Bilsthorpe, which wasn't much fun and not very homely. So I bought an old barn in Kirklington in the summer of 2002. It needed a lot of work so Jamie said that I could move into the converted barn that was part of his house, the Corn Barn, while the work was being done. It suited him because he was just about to take his family away for the summer and I was effectively house-sitting for a few weeks. With a broken leg and two broken feet, those few weeks dragged on into a few months. Now, a year and a half later, all the work was long completed on my own barn and, although I loved it there, I had run out of excuses to stay. I had been in no rush to move because Jamie, his wife Lisa and their three boys George, Harry and Tom had made me feel part of the family. And there was a real community feel in the village of Epperstone, where Bullshit, Hoggy and Roger were also regulars in the local pub, the Cross Keys, renamed Dipper's Nightclub because the landlord, Alan, had dyed his hair and was also notorious for staying open after hours.

Jamie always liked to keep an eye on what I was up to, and the Corn Barn soon became known as the Porn Barn. Sarah had been a frequent visitor during that summer, and there were no curtains. So, if Jamie ever spotted us going upstairs, out would come his sliding ladders and he would appear at the upstairs window, hoping for a flash of Sarah's arse.

'All right, Nobby?' he said, steaming up the window and wiping it with his sleeve. 'These windows are getting dirty again.' Sarah was high-maintenance, especially if she ever came to the racing, where she would be bored after ten minutes. So we drifted apart over that summer and I found myself in the unusual position of being young, free and single. A few years earlier I had been actually put forward for an Eligible Bachelor competition run by *Company* magazine and reached the last fifty in the country, who were all invited to London for photoshoots. Readers were asked to vote for their favourite and the results were to be announced at a grand ceremony in London. There were firemen, soldiers, models, actors, tycoons and aristocracy – and me. I was the only entrant under 6 feet tall and I felt a proper wand strolling down the catwalk with a number stuck to my suit, just like in the Miss World competition. I finished eighteenth, which was no disgrace, although I'm not sure Lisa was too chuffed with the result because we were back together at that time.

Now that I was truly eligible, it didn't seem like a whole lot of fun. Jamie had invited me round for Christmas dinner, but it didn't seem right having moved out only that week. Mum and Dad were away in Devon down at Grandma's, so a couple of years after eating two Christmas dinners I was facing a Christmas Day without any. What goes around comes around, I guess. I decided to make the effort and bought a turkey and all the trimmings, but couldn't be arsed to cook it for myself. So I opened the biggest bottle of Mateus Rosé and ate endless slices of toast with Brussels pâté, before falling asleep to *Chitty Chitty Bang Bang*.

The Christmas lull in festivities was also useful from a fitness point of view, because there was a test at Phillip Island just after the New Year. I was faster than Troy on the first day and, again, not too far behind at the end of the test. There was perhaps light at the end of the tunnel. To be that close to a former world champion, and in his own backyard, showed that we had already made progress, and I was a lot more upbeat. Back home the boys had realized that I had been a bit down over Christmas and arranged a big night out in nearby Newark, when I saved a girl with the biggest mop of curly dark hair I had ever seen from having to put up with Dog's banter. And – bosh – Kathryn was on the scene, although I thought it was wise not to take a girlfriend who was new to racing to the first round of the season at Valencia, because it was sure to be a difficult start.

If a normal race weekend was like being on *Apollo 13*, then qualifying at Valencia was like being on the space shuttle *Challenger*. But we both made it into Superpole, which was a bit of a worry beforehand. Then it rained on race day morning and the conditions played right into the hands of the Petronas and the Stalker. Tyre choice was a lottery but the track was starting to dry, although it was still too wet for slicks. We opted for intermediates on the front and rear but, whatever the choice, it was going to be a race of attrition. I think Troy sniffed an opportunity to make up for his previous year's hardships and got a bit giddy early on, trying to win the race on the first lap and crashing out. Others were also dropping like flies, while the riders on wet weather tyres had cleared off. But as the track dried their tyres were useless and the riders on intermediates came through. JT, Chili and Steve Martin, all on Ducatis, filled the top three places, while I had a big cushion in fourth. That was good enough for me, as the Petronas had never finished higher than fifth.

As I crossed the line with two laps to go I could smell oil and our team were waving their arms around wildly on pit-wall. Bastard! It was no surprise, considering all the problems of the weekend, but I was still smashed. I backed off, had a look around, but couldn't see any problem. Then I saw Steve Martin at the side of the track punching his bike's tank. It had been his oil. I was in third place. As I came round for the final lap the team was this time urging me to slow down and I don't think I have ever done a slower lap to bring the bike home for its first-ever podium, one of only two during the whole project. With the line in sight I tried to pull a wheelie but there wasn't enough power. And then came the first of two special memories. As I approached the chequered flag Carl leapt over pit-wall and onto the side of the track with his arms in the air. I had not seen him so emotional since winning his last world title. It was one of my best feelings in racing.

The second lasting memory came when I pulled into *parc ferme* to see James congratulating Chili on second place. He then looked round to see who had finished third. When he saw me he did a proper full-on double-take. 'What the fuck are you doing here?' he asked.

'I came third!'

'What? On that pile of shit? Come on!' he laughed. I didn't disgrace myself with seventh place in the second race, either. But I had already achieved one goal for the season: to capitalize on certain conditions and circumstances to secure the occasional eye-catching result. This was exactly the boost the whole team needed and I was excited about the trip to O'Neill's before the second race had even finished. Carl had caught the first plane home but the Big Lads were out in force and the Petronas boys liked a pint. They needed it after the work they put in over the weekend; I have never known mechanics able to change an engine so quickly. As the night kicked off Bullshit came in for more and more stick again, having turned up in a pink Pringle jumper, with the famous white lion logo.

'What are you doing wearing that gay Peugeot jumper, Nobby?' laughed Jamie.

'Trust me, Nobby. It's not Peugeot, it's Pringle. Cost me a hundred notes. At least I don't shop at Millets,' Bullshit replied. Bad move. Jamie grabbed the sweater and yanked at it. Two minutes later Jack Burnicle was wearing one arm of the ex-Pringle sweater, JT was wearing a makeshift pink tank top and Bullshit was left with the other arm and a bit of thread around his neck. It was the perfect end to a great weekend.

Valencia had also been my first taste of the Foggy Petronas PR machinery. I had realized that I would have to do a lot of PR duties during the year, as the team was unlikely to be able to keep the sponsors happy with results. But I was not prepared for the onslaught from their PR girl, Fiona Cole. I was handed a schedule at the start of the weekend telling me where I had to be and when and why and what I was supposed to wearing and what type of aftershave I should be using. I was warned there was another event on the horizon after the Valencia race and prepared myself for a shop opening or maybe a magazine photoshoot. I was not prepared for a ten-day trip around Borneo. The sponsors, Petronas, were owned by the Malaysian government, and every year before the F1 race at Sepang they staged a PR offensive around the country, demonstrating their various motorsport achievements and interests in an effort to put something back into the community. So me, Carl and Troy joined their Sauber Petronas drivers, Felipe Massa and Giancarlo Fisichella, in Kuala Lumpur before heading off for the Malaysian part of Borneo.

Every day there was a different challenge organized with local school kids, and I lucked out on the first day, in a place called Kota Kinabalu, one of the most beautiful places I have ever seen. The aim was to build and race a car powered by an elastic band and my group contained the school kid destined to design the first real flux capacitor. One–nil to Stalker, and Foggy was spewing. It was actually great to spend some time socializing with him and we probably behaved like two naughty school kids throughout the trip. Next stop was another city in Borneo, Kuching, where the main street demonstration was to be held. The kids again spoke English better than anyone from Mansfield and this time Foggy made sure he was in the group containing the obvious Tefal boy, and they won the race for cars built from a Coke bottle and powered by compressed air. Carl even tried to turn the street demonstration into a race, probably because he was riding the race bike and we were on their road bikes.

That day made Suzuka feel like a polar expedition. And just when I thought it could not get any hotter I had to ride the FP1 road bike. How the seat unit did not melt I will never know, and it is the closest I have ever come to passing out from the heat. But the crowd of around 100,000 Kuchingians cramming the streets loved it, and I actually had a fantastic few days in Malaysia.

We were already more than halfway towards Australia so it made sense to travel straight there for the next round rather than go home first. So I spent a few days in Sydney with Neil and my mechanics, Barry and Zim. This was another place that blew me away. The city was so spectacular and, not being one for holidays, it was nice to chill out doing all the touristy things like climbing the Harbour Bridge and taking the ferry to Manley Beach. There is just such a vibrant feel about Sydney and it has fantastic restaurants and nightlife too. Australia is definitely somewhere I want to see a lot more of one day. The drive to Melbourne, however, was not quite as spectacular. Neil persuaded us to take the Great Ocean Road rather than fly there. Unfortunately the Great Ocean Road is from Melbourne to Adelaide so we drove for 1,000 km on the most boring road on this planet although, to be fair, we could see the sea for the first five minutes.

The results at Phillip Island were pretty average, although I did manage to challenge for top ten spots at all the next few rounds. A new specification of engine was introduced for round five at Oschersleben where, ironically, I had my first DNF when I had to pull in because the engine was cutting out, causing one rider to run in the back of my bike. It proved to be the start of the most testing part of the season.

25

Burning Stalker

Riders accept injury as an occupational hazard, but I don't know many who would accept having their pubic hair burnt off as part and parcel of the job! But that's what happened to me on my first lap of the Silverstone round. Even though it was on my out-lap I was doing 100 m.p.h. approaching Bridge when I started to feel uncomfortable. I looked down to see flames rising from either side of the tank, engulfing my legs. The Petronas was known to belch fire from the exhaust now and again, but this was ridiculous. I had only ever seen bikes or cars on fire in films, and they always exploded. 'She's gonna blow, she's gonna blow,' I thought, as I ran onto the grass and scrubbed off some speed before jumping off at 70 m.p.h. I rolled around in the grass to make sure that all the flames were out and then bashed my bits, which felt the hottest through the Kevlar section of my leathers, to make sure. Back in the garage I emptied the bits of singed pubes from my boxers; the rest were burnt to a crisp and snapped off later. And only half have ever grown back!

The bike was a write-off but the team built a new one from spares by Saturday morning. On my out-lap, still with bed in my eyes, I reached one corner further on from the previous day's inferno, Brooklands, touched the gas and had a huge high-side. I landed on my side and was in agony. The bike was in bits and the guys had to travel back to Burton to fetch the bike that Foggy used for PR events as a back-up for race day. At the medical centre I was told that three ribs were broken but, while the doctors did various tests and gave me injections, I could see on the monitor that I was slipping out of Superpole with only minutes remaining. Neil was with me and I asked him to get me back to the garage as quickly as possible. Just one problem: he could barely ride a scooter, so I had to give him a lift back to the garage as he held on tight to my fractured ribs. I managed to do two flying laps and squeezed into Superpole by two hundredths of a second, earning a big slap on the back from Carl – right on those ribs again! The weekend didn't get much better with a low-side crash in the first race and twelfth in the second, when the bike was cutting out again.

Fortunately there was a full month before the trip to Laguna, somewhere I really enjoyed racing – except on the Petronas. But you still have to maintain the same focus, whether you are challenging for a championship or struggling on a prototype bike. You have to prepare exactly the same and travel there thinking that you have a chance. It's not great, though, when you come away and the highlight of the weekend is walking the track with Chris Vermeulen. He hadn't raced there before so I told him, 'I know how to go fast here, even if I can't do it myself!' I pointed out to him things like not being on the gas too early at the first corner, because the next two were more important for a good lap time. He must have absorbed everything like a sponge because the little sod went and won both races on the Sunday and has since been on the podium there in MotoGP. He's a really likeable, upbeat character, too. But I left America lower than a badger's set, having failed to make Superpole for the only time ever in my career and didn't finish either race, through gearbox and clutch problems. All I needed was a nice week-long Petronas PR trip to China!

Normally I never eat or drink on plane journeys. Even bags of crisps expand at 35,000 ft and I think that's what happens to my stomach, because I can't stop farting if I eat anything. Me and Neil had decided to have a couple of beers on the twelve-hour flight to Shanghai to get over the depression of Laguna, and then the air hostesses kept filling our glasses with wine, before we moved on to Jack Daniels. And then the farts kicked in. I admit mine smelt ungodly, like something had crawled up there and died, but Neil needed a barbed-wire pull-through. At first the little Chinese girl sat next to us thought it was funny; then she turned green, covered her face with a hankie and finally turned to face away from us. We were now bored and started caning the credit cards, ringing people on the sky phone but forgetting it was the middle of the night back home. Then we thought it would be fun to throw jelly-beans at the other business-class passengers, who were busy creating spreadsheets on their computers. After four hours one of the old boiler air hostesses informed us that they had been told not to serve us any more alcohol, at which point we both promptly passed out and didn't come round until the wheels touched down in Shanghai. There were jelly-beans everywhere and we were obviously not the most popular passengers on the plane, as everyone filed through our cabin holding their noses.

If Borneo had been hot, Shanghai was like stepping into a volcano. The heat was breaking all local records and even the Chinese were dying of heat exhaustion. We were there to perform more demonstration laps with the F1 team, at a special round of the German Touring Car championship held on a street circuit in the city and sponsored by Petronas. I say we, but it actually all came down to CW. Carl was supposed to join us but had suffered an alleged jet-skiing injury, which had obviously turned instantly gangrenous. Then Troy spent the day of the demonstration in his hospital bed on a drip. He had either eaten some wubbewy chicken, or it might have been the ice used in the hotel bar at 4 a.m. in the morning! Our laps were supposed to take place between the two DTM races, but when the first started the downdraught of the cars setting off down the straight of the specially created street circuit lifted up a manhole cover, which flew through the windscreen of a car and nearly killed the driver. They spent the next six hours welding down all the manhole covers on the circuit, while we melted. When it was finally time to ride, the bike would not run properly because the fuel was evaporating, our mechanics' computer had locked because of all the sweat dripped onto it and I barely had enough strength to get into my leathers. Please take me home!

The next round at Brands Hatch did provide some home comforts. Finishing fourth there, especially after the trials of the previous couple of months, felt like winning the world championship. Carl knew that it was as good as we could possibly have hoped for and made me an attractive offer to stay for the following year, even suggesting that I recreate the dream team with Les. But, as much as I had enjoyed my times with Carl, Troy and the rest of the Foggy boys, I was a racer and wanted to be near the front. I knew that the void between the top bikes and the Petronas was only going to increase, so I started to investigate what else was on offer.

At Assen I sat down with Guido Pagani, the owner of the San Marino-based PSG-1 team that was currently running Chili's Ducati but switching to the new Kawasaki ZX10 for 2005. Most people thought Guido was a gun manufacturer but he was actually just a collector and the PSG-1 was the name of his favourite gun. He was a real father-figure, who didn't promise the earth and didn't flash his cash around. Guido had already offered one ride to Mauro Sanchini, a chilled Italian who was good friends with Valentino Rossi. But he also wanted a consistent front-runner alongside Sanchini. Their offer was nowhere near Carl's, but I had enjoyed success and a good relationship in the past with the tight-knit Kawasaki organization in the UK. Again there was the prospect of more than one year, and the chance to develop a new bike also appealed. I came away with a good feeling about it and didn't take long to make up my mind.

Kathryn had been to most of the races and was good company, but I had my reservations about any long-term future because she didn't have too much get-up-and-go. She would still be in bed when I got back from morning warm-up and just didn't seem to be very motivated about anything. It has to be said, though, that anyone who puts up with me for any length of time deserves a medal because I do show signs of a common trait among sportsmen and bike racers in particular, Obsessive Compulsive Disorder. I despise mess and untidiness and know that I am a massive pain in the arse. But I am also easily pleased, and was more than pleased with a new arrival on the domestic scene – Nobby.

I'd never really had a dog of my own before and, being away from home a lot, I wanted a placid big dog rather than a smaller one that I would have to walk five times a day. Mum and Dad were between dogs and promised to look after him while I was racing or training. I had no idea which breed to choose, so I bought a book on dogs and the Bernese Mountain Dogs were by far the cutest. Next stop was a dog show in nearby Newark, where I met a breeder who lived not too far away in Lincoln. That was the easy part. The difficulty was trying to persuade her of my suitability to be an owner. As a self-employed motorbike racer with the life expectancy of a daddy-long-legs it was worse than obtaining finance from the bank.

Once I had passed their vetting procedures I went to have the pick of the litter and even stayed in on New Year's Eve so that I would make a good impression – on the dog. The other puppies were leaping about all over the place and trying to catch my attention, but Nobby was the biggest and the coolest. When I picked him up he just stared down his little snout as if to say 'Bovvered!' There was no contest, although I actually wanted to take them all and very nearly had two. The breeder's kennel names for her dogs were inspired by film stars, for example Fern Park Cruise or Fern Park Stallone. She has since started to follow the racing and now names her dogs after famous racers, like Fern Park Chili or Fern Park Walker.

Nobby made it home without being sick, which impressed me no end. I was less impressed when, immediately inside the house, he spray-coated the plate-glass double doors with a perfect arc of diarrhoea that also landed in my favourite trainers. My OCD was kicking in and I was ready to drive him straight back to get a refund. But he was a quick learner and I rewarded him with a dog-friendly chocolate button each time he went outside to pee. It was at this point that I realized he was smarter than me. Rather than store it up and have one big pee, he quickly caught on that three individual trips would bring three chocolate buttons. So, although he ate his own body weight in chocolate buttons in the first two weeks, he was quickly house-trained and my furry son is now a huge part of the Walker family.

For the first couple of months of the year I felt like a character in *Prisoner Cell Block H*, but that was not just Nobby's fault. I had been sponsored with a Subaru Impreza WRX STi WR1 – a special edition to celebrate the World Rally title win of Petter Solberg – by a local dealership, Beechdale Motors, owned by a great bloke called Les Waterfall. As always, when you are driving a car like this, everyone wants to race you, and on the way back from testing a number of bikes for *MCN* I was telling Hoggy on the phone that I was going to buy a Ducati 749 when a cock in a bright red Ford Mondeo appeared right up my arse. So I put my foot down and soon reached 150 m.p.h. The bright red Mondeo was nowhere to be seen, but in its place was a navy blue Mondeo with flashing lights. They had clocked me at 137 m.p.h. and suspected that I was on the phone and not wearing a seat belt. Dad could not make my January court appearance and, although it was again a lady magistrate, I didn't manage to escape a ban this time. I did still swim the Channel, though, with a sixty-day ban and £1,000 fine, when I could have been looking at bread and water. The clerk of the court asked if I wanted to use the back entrance to avoid all the press. 'Press? I'm a speedo not a paedo,' I said, but nevertheless returned home to find my name all over the national newspapers and Teletext.

Once again, this cloud had a silver lining. When I wanted to go anywhere it had to be on my push-bike now. The Foggy team had been sponsored by Kona, who provided me with a trick cycle, sprayed up in the team colours and personalized with my name. The more cycling I did, the more my training became focused around it. I still went to the gym, or for the odd run, mountain-bike ride or swim, but cycling provided another step up in my training levels. The Walker family has always had the potential to carry weight; you only have to look at my sister, who is like a ginger Vicar of Dibley. My granddad carries a bit of extra baggage, Dad still jogs to keep his love handles away, and pictures from my Cadbury's Boost days show that I had, at the very least, chubby cheeks. And, while I did enjoy the occasional party as part of my work-hard play-hard ethic, training always took precedence and I never wanted to be able to say that I might have done better if I had been fitter, injuries excepted of course. Two friends in particular were very keen cyclists: Mad Dog had represented the England junior team, and Fish still raced, sometimes in red Lycra shorts, which is not right when you have an arse that big. So they persuaded me to join the local Saturday morning ride-out, for some reason called the Parrots. This was a group of between twenty and fifty cyclists, some young and fast, some old and steady, some experienced and some new to the sport. At the start of my ban my tongue was hanging on the handlebars and I was back with the granddads when we reached the midway café stop. It wasn't supposed to be a race to get there, but that's how it turned out, otherwise you were at the back of a long queue for coffee and toast at the café. A month into the ban and my leg strength had caught up and my arse could stand three hours in the saddle. I was soon up with fast lads, some of whom, like Dave Miller and Doris, have been professionals. My body fat dropped, my fitness was up and, for once injury free, I was in great shape for the start of the season and testing.

I couldn't believe how fast my motorbike was when I rode it for the first time at Valencia, and it was still effectively a road bike at that time. 'I can't wait until this thing can go round corners,' I thought. Guido was keen to cement a long-term arrangement with Kawasaki, so was spending a lot of the budget on the best bits for the chassis, as well as a top data-logging company in Pectel and French engine tuners Akira. So that was maybe why my wages didn't always come through on time! But I was gelling well with the team, and especially two of the English-speaking mechanics, Paolo, the data-logging guy, and Lorenzo, known as Lolo. My crew chief was Massimo, another great guy, and Sanchini kept a watchful eye over me, making sure the chefs understood how to cook my steak.

Joining an Italian-speaking team had been a little daunting at first, although it perhaps helped that I wasn't able to understand all the politics that always goes on, or that I would be in the dark if the team had forgotten my new dashboard or were being chased for money. But I soon felt part of their big family atmosphere and spent more time in hospitality than ever before. They enjoyed their long leisurely evening meals and were happy to sip espresso and work late, although when there was work to be done they were like a whirlwind of headless chickens and I nicknamed one of my mechanics Tornado. I guess some of that mealtime ethic has rubbed off at home, because we always make a big thing of the evening meal or Sunday dinner.

After more optimistic tests at Almeria and Valencia again, we went to Qatar for the final official test with spirits high. This was my first visit to the Middle East and it was an eye-opener. On our first drive out to the circuit me and JT went past a camel and its family cruising along at the side of their equivalent of the M1. Then, back in Doha, we saw men walking hand in hand down the street, a sign of friendship and not arse banditry over there. In a country where it's forbidden to see anything but a woman's eyes, the boys took great delight in going to the massive shopping malls and Bluetoothing porn from their phones to anyone within range, and then watching their shocked reaction. But then you should have seen the look on their faces when the clips they received back featured camels instead of women. The place was actually loads of fun for somewhere where most pleasures are supposed to be frowned on.

We made further progress during that three-day test at Losail, a circuit built in the middle of nowhere in the desert – the real desert, not the one near Mansfield. I finished seventh fastest and I was happy with our settings for the race the following weekend. That was before we were told that our bike was under the legal weight limit. All the settings proved useless on the first day of qualifying and we struggled to find somewhere to position the 7 kg of lead that had to be strapped to the bike. We tried to place small bits here and there, or all in the belly pan, or where the starter motor used to be. We finally settled on under the seat but we had lost a lot of ground on the rest of the field and were also having a few problems with front-end chatter. Things went from bad to worse on race day when the rear tyre span on its rim in the first race, causing terrible vibration. Then, after that fourteenth place in race one, Karl Muggeridge turboed me out of the second race at the hairpin.

Perhaps Guido also forgot to factor travel costs into the budget, because we travelled on Cheap Shoes Airlines to Australia for the following week's race. Most teams changed planes once in Dubai; we changed five times and arrived a day later than everyone else. So maybe I can now use jetlag as an excuse for what happened in the second race. Having struggled with stability down the straight in strong winds during qualifying and race one, the second race was stopped after a few laps when it started to rain. I had made up four places and was now starting from the head of the third row for the restarted race on wet tyres. I made another Stalker start and carved my way through the field, finally taking the lead on track from Kagayama going into Honda hairpin. OK, I was seven seconds behind Corser on aggregate, but in my mind I was leading a World Superbike race for the first time – for 300 yards before I tossed it down the road in fine fashion. I wasn't to know that four other riders had gone down at the same point, the right-hander after Siberia, where the cars bottom out and leave aluminium off their sumps on the top of the bumps, making it exceptionally slippy in the wet. But I had tried to win the race in three corners, in full-on novice style. Even so, the team left Australia peaking that we were at least capable of challenging at the front, because it had been a while since Kawasaki had been up there on the television coverage. And we all knew that I was capable of results at Valencia.

I was on the money there right from the first session and just missed out on a front-row start, although I didn't have the best of starts and got caught up in the traffic early on. I was able to climb up to fourth behind Kagayama, but knew that I could mix it with the leaders. I had a mega start for race two and passed Andrew Pitt into third place for a dice with Chris Vermeulen for half the race. I was faster in a couple of corners but his bike ate mine on the straight, and although I was never able to put a wheel in front of his the team was going wild. With two laps to go I almost lost the front going into turn two and realized the tyre was going off a little. 'Don't throw another rostrum away. Ride within the limits of the tyre,' I thought, and secured a comfortable third. The boss of Kawasaki Racing was over from Japan and the team was ecstatic. From the podium I could see Guido, who had barely recovered from my fourth place in the first race, with tears streaming down his face. Even the prospect of another Big Lads bonanza in O'Neill's couldn't tear me away from the team that night, especially after the chefs cooked me a special number 9 shaped cake.

In each of the next five races I finished one place behind Frankie Chili, who invariably passed me in the closing stages, which upset the team no end as he had left them because he didn't feel the Kawasaki would be competitive. But I was back on it at Brno, where we had tested, and where we had a new spec engine and a few new parts. These allowed me to kick the front out and realign the geometry, because the back end had been jacked up to help me turn. I was fastest in the first qualifying session and the time was not bettered on the Saturday, which meant I would be last out for Superpole. And it was a good job, too!

I wanted to use a qualifying tyre right at the end of the afternoon free practice and just before using one for Superpole. The session ended seconds after I came round for my final flying lap but just as I was entering the Stadium section Max Neukirchner, on his slow-down lap, turned into my path. I clipped his bike and we both went spinning into the gravel. It was the only time I have ever fully let go on a race track.

'You fucking twat,' I yelled, grabbed his helmet and was just about to punch him when a marshal dragged me away. 'Superpole starts in fucking fifteen minutes and you have wrecked my fucking bike.' Then it dawned on me that I didn't really have any time for a scrap. My bike was in pieces and the spare bike didn't have any of the improvements. The handlebar had snapped off on the side of the throttle so the bike wouldn't start but a marshal on a dirt bike, who had worse clutch control than Simon Buckmaster with his one leg, offered to tow me back to the pits. I held onto the rack at the back of his bike with my right arm and steered with my left, dragging a 165 kg bike and my 63 kg up the steepest hill on the calendar, on the hottest day of the year. My mechanics had forty-five minutes to put the bike back together: new handlebar, new foot-rests, new exhaust can, much of it held on by cable ties. The whirlwind blew in the garage and, although it didn't look pretty, the bike felt perfect as I pulled out for my Superpole warm-up lap. My arm, however, did not. Not only had it received a bash from the crash, my forearm had pumped solid during the tow back. After two corners of my Superpole lap my fingers cramped on the brake and I couldn't release them. I had to slide my hand down the handlebar to release the brakes and was barely able to use the brakes for the rest of the lap, but still managed to qualify sixth on the grid. It was a great first race; I caught and passed Vermeulen to go second before JT came through and I was left to dice with Laconi for third place for the final third of the race. But I had cooked my tyres early on and Laconi pulled away, although I was then thankful to hold off Chili in the closing stages; I couldn't face losing to him for the seventh consecutive race.

And I couldn't face leaving that long drive back from the Czech Republic until the next day so I set off back, aiming to make Holland before I stopped for a break. The torrential rain didn't help our progress through Germany but I was still able to cruise at 90 m.p.h. in the fast lane because, after all, there are no speed limits on the autobahn – except for when you are driving a 39 ft motorhome with a trailer, apparently. I was pulled over at a secluded rest area; just trees, a few benches and a filthy toilet. The two Gestapo officers wanted my insurance documents; I didn't have the correct insurance. They wanted my paper licence; I wasn't about to give them that because I knew I wasn't properly licensed. They wanted my log book; I never carried it because it wasn't actually registered or taxed. So they had to be content with my card licence and passport, and they seemed to swallow my story that burglars had taken all the other documents. They then insisted that I couldn't go anywhere until I found someone with the correct licence to drive the motorhome. I explained that the team was not far behind, with two qualified truck drivers. One of the Italian truckies would help out. Again they swallowed this and, while they took pictures of the motorhome chassis plate for evidence, I swiped my passport and licence back from where they had been left on the seat. Having demanded the 370 euros fine – and a signed cap, the cheeky bastards – they seemed happy enough that I was going to wait for the team to rescue me. An hour's kip later and the coast was clear, so I made a dash for the Dutch border and, within another hour, was home free.

I narrowly missed out on the podium again at Brands, finishing behind Vermeulen in both races in fifth and fourth places. With four rounds remaining, and after such a terrible start to the season, I was now only 31 points behind the reigning world champion, James Toseland, who was in sixth place in the championship and on the factory Ducati. There was still a good chance that I could achieve my highest finish in the championship.

But things tended to happen to me at Assen …

26

Smitten Stalker

I'd been locked up, concussed and had my arse tampered with in Assen; now it was time for Suzuki's revenge. Wild cards had become a bit of a rarity after the one-tyre rule, as not many teams were able to use Pirellis on a one-off basis. But Rizla, who sponsored the Crescent Suzuki team in the British championship, wanted exposure in Holland, for obvious reasons. So they arranged for the best-known Dutch rider, Jurgen van der Goorbergh, to compete there. He had a big crash in the first session and spent little time on track over the first two days, although he did finally manage to qualify, but down on the sixth row. I was a bit disappointed to be down on the fourth row and it did prove to be costly.

On the third corner of the first lap van der Goorbergh came in way too hot, trying to pass half the field in one go, and smacked straight into the back of my arm. The collision punted me off into the gravel, and I was spewing. Did he think he was going to win the race? I ran towards him and lifted my arm to gesticulate. Ouch! I think Whitham said in the TV commentary: 'Tha's not gonna hit anyone with that arm, lad.' Van der Goorbergh stayed on, wobbled through the gravel, escaping my wrath and finishing the race in twentieth place. Meanwhile, at the medical centre, I was told that my arm was broken above the elbow and at the joint itself. There was no way I could start the next race, and the next round was the following week in Germany. I would have to miss that too. Yet again I was going to be denied my rightful place in the championship through injury. But I was also again determined that the paddock vultures would not steal my ride for the rest of the season.

I managed to drive the motorhome back with one arm and headed straight for Ipswich to see the Laserman. I actually stayed there for a week, leaving the motorhome in the car park of a DIY store, and right next to a bingo hall. Every night I tried to sleep to the sound of 'Get your dibbers and your dobbers and your dabbers!' It drove me round the bend but the sessions in the hyperbaric oxygen tank were working and I promised Guido that I would be fit for Imola. Fonsi Nieto, who had come from 250 GPs but struggled on the Caracchi Ducati and lost his ride at Assen, had already been on the bike and on the rostrum at a round of the Italian championship. More importantly, he was bringing a bit of much-needed cash to the budget from his personal sponsors. So Guido promised that if I could prove my fitness at Imola the team would build a third bike for Nieto for the final two rounds.

I was able to do press-ups before leaving for Italy and Guido had never felt a handshake like it when I greeted him there. In truth my arm was still weak but the damp conditions played into my hands for the first race and the second was cancelled due to torrential rain. That provided a bit more time for Guido to sit me down and ask if I wanted to race for them again next year. He explained that Sanchini would be released and that Nieto had also been offered a ride. The money that Nieto brought would help with the budget and also allow them to catch up with my payments. Kawasaki would also be more involved in the funding, because we had been helping to develop their new bike, the ZX10R. We had actually been out to their test track in Japan, Autopolis, a couple of times during the summer to test the pre-production model and I was excited about being so closely involved with the factory and their development programme.

Another bonus was that I instantly liked Fonsi. He was married to a Spanish supermodel called Ariadne Artiles and they were effectively the Posh and Becks equivalents of Spain. Becks had even been to his wedding, which was covered in *Ola!*, or whatever they call the Spanish version of *Hello!* He lived in a mansion in Ibiza and had all the trick cars and yachts. Me and Heckles thought we had been living the dream in Hollywood, but Fonsi actually did live it and there would always be celebrities around his motorhome, like footballer Patrick Kluivert and golfer Sergio Garcia.

Fonsi's arrival was good news from another point of view, too, because I had heard rumours that Régis Laconi might be my team-mate. This was a little worrying because Laconi was despised as a team-mate by JT who, however aggressive he is on track, has not got a nasty bone in his body off it. Laconi just always seemed to be a bit over-enthusiastic with not just verbal diarrhoea, but French verbal diarrhoea.

I finished the season with a fifth at Magny-Cours and the team seemed really happy with my seventh place in the championship, especially considering that I had effectively missed two rounds with my broken elbow. So I was starting the winter all upbeat about the following season, until I received a call to say that the team would be running three riders. This meant a total of six bikes and eighteen mechanics in the team. Hang on a second! We had been skint all year. It didn't add up. I was reassured that there were incentives to keep the only French rider in the championship and that there was no need to worry about being paid. I'm not a materialistic person, but I did need to earn a living.

And this was not the only money issue around then. Not long into seeing Kathryn I discovered that she was married when we first met. I had assumed it was just a boyfriend she was splitting from and was happy to help with the legal bills surrounding the sale of their house until she was in a position to pay me back.

Shortly before the end of this season she received a call to say that her ex-husband, who had made a new life with someone else, had died in a car accident. But he had forgotten to take her off his insurance, so she was due a large settlement. The family of her ex was furious that she was considering accepting the money and I instantly thought that it was not right for her to take it. I saw a different side to her – and one that I wasn't sure I wanted anything to do with. When we split up that side of her showed again when she chased me for £17,000, supposedly the amount she would have made if she had bought property with the money she received from selling her half of the house. There was no way I was going to hand that over without a fight and I was glad to see the back of her in the end.

As luck would have it, the NEC Show was just around the corner. I knew from experience that meeting girls there could be a recipe for disaster. But onwards and upwards! Kawasaki were not known for pushing the boat out on promotional girls, but this year their choice seemed a lot better. And I took a shine to one in particular – a tall blonde with an athletic figure. 'She's a minter,' I thought and during one of my interviews on the stand, with Martin Lambert, Kawasaki's marketing guy, I was lucky enough to stand alongside her.

'I find all this stuff really embarrassing,' I whispered.

'You shouldn't be embarrassed. From what I've seen you're really good at it,' she said. We got talking and I immediately knew that she was a bit different, upbeat and genuine, and obviously not just out for what she could get, like a lot of the girls were. I discovered her name was Rachel Freer, that she went to boarding school at the age of 11 to study dance and then went on to the Royal Ballet School. She did some modelling and promo work between dancing contracts. I watched her over the next couple of days and I was smitten. But, for some reason, I couldn't pluck up enough courage to ask for her phone number. Time was running out because I wouldn't be around for the final weekend, as I was off testing the new bike again in Japan. It was now or never.

'It would be really nice if I could take you for a drink once the show is over,' I said.

'That would be lovely,' she said. 'I'm glad you asked. I was wondering whether to give you my number but I didn't want to be too forward.' Two things had worked in my favour. Firstly, she had overheard a conversation I had with Martin, who was asking me when I was going to settle down and have kids. 'I'd love to have kids one day, but only when I click with the right girl. I will know when it's right,' I told him. Secondly, I had asked Rachel if we could meet *after* the show. She was used to lads, who were trying to do as much damage as possible during their two weeks at the show, constantly hitting on her and was impressed that I wanted to do things properly.

As soon as I reached the hotel in Japan I tried ringing from my hotel room phone, but couldn't figure it out. Then I went to buy a phonecard and that wouldn't work. So I finally went to the shop to stock up on loose yen before calling. Her phone just rang out. Had she given me a Radio One Flirt-Divert number, the number the radio station gives out for people to use when they want to give someone the slip, and then play the recorded messages received on air? I rang again thirty minutes later.

'I knew it was you. It's the last day of the show and I was on the stand with my phone on vibrate in my boot. I was getting some funny looks!' she explained. We just about managed to arrange to meet in Cambridge, where she lived, when I returned to England. Then my sackful of yen ran out.

It turned out to be the perfect date. We met and went to a restaurant called Vaults and didn't stop chatting for hours. Then, at the first point when there was that inevitable awkward silence, a guy came over, shook my hand and asked for my autograph. 'That wasn't bad timing, Nobby,' I thought. All those hours of standing in the garage for pit-lane walkabout with broken ribs and burnt pubes had finally paid off, although I was a bit embarrassed. Towards the end of the dinner I leant over and gave her a gentle kiss on the cheek, thanked her for booking the restaurant and we headed off to a couple of bars before I returned to my hotel. More brownie points for booking myself a hotel, because she obviously now knew that I wasn't there for one thing only.

We arranged to meet the next morning, and that didn't go quite as smoothly – it's not easy trying to park a Hummer in Cambridge and it was even trickier negotiating the low archway into the car park of the pub. But not as tricky as leaving through the exit archway, which was even lower. I eventually had to ask passers-by to sit in the back seat to compress the suspension. I then let the tyres down and managed to squeeze underneath. The Hummer had to go – but not before I had taken Nobby to see Rachel at the Dirt Bike Show at Coventry, where she was doing more work for Kawasaki.

She had been desperate to meet Nobby but I didn't tell her that he was in the car, parked just outside. Rachel was doing some dancing at the show but had made me promise not to watch and I didn't even have a sneaky peek. But she couldn't understand why I wanted her to go outside into the freezing cold, dressed in only a skimpy little outfit and a big overcoat. When I opened the boot it was love at first sight. I swear there were little hearts floating up from both of them, and I have never seen Nobby so excited. 'Nobby's found a mum,' I thought to myself, 'and I've found myself a proper bird at last.' That's Stalker-speak for I was falling in love!

It was all change on the home front, too. A major bypass had been built 50 yards from my barn conversion and it felt as though lorries were hurtling through the lounge at 5 a.m. It wasn't the safest place for Nobby, either, although he rarely strayed any further than the bottom of the stairs. As ever I was on a cycle ride when I stumbled upon my current house. I turned down a dead-end lane expecting to find the River Trent at the bottom. Instead there was an old gamekeeper's cottage that used to be part of the old village manor. The surrounding buildings had been turned into about fifteen beautiful homes. The cottage was over 200 years old and had lots of little rooms, an orangery and an annexe for a gym. It was much more homely and perfect if my bachelor days were coming to an end. I eventually sold the barn and moved in the week before Christmas. I spent Christmas Day in Cambridge with Rachel, her mum, Jan, and her brother, Stephen, a photography student. Rachel had lost her dad, Charles, a doctor at the Cambridge Hospital, who helped pioneer the MRI scanner, eleven years earlier to cancer. Having been away at boarding school she had missed out on a lot of time with him. Rachel travelled back up to Nottingham with me on Boxing Day – and never really left!

The guys in the team had heard that I had a new girlfriend and were desperate to see her at the first round of the new season in

Qatar. When I saw their faces I could tell they were thinking: 'Mama mia! Stalker's gone massive!' And Rachel instantly fitted into the team. Without being asked she always made sure my drinks bottle was filled and was the first person ever to wipe my visor halfway through a session. After my first real winter of continuity, when nothing had gone wrong, I was genuinely excited about my chances at the first round. So it was somewhat inevitable that I scored no points – my worst start in years! I was forced to stop in the first race with a fuel starvation problem and then Giovanni Bussei crashed into me in the second, breaking my rear calliper. Things didn't improve much at the second round in Australia, with two tenth places. The 2006 bike was not as agile as the previous year's specification. Our lap times were faster, but that was probably down to an improvement in the Pirelli tyres and also because the team was no longer new to the bike. Developments in the chassis, engine and traction control were coming all the time, but they did not seem to be helping us on track. The only consolation was that the other two riders, Nieto and Laconi, were struggling more than I was.

And by Valencia I was starting to struggle with Laconi. It was now clear that he wasn't a great fan of me and Fonsi, and I found some of his habits a bit odd. Before each session he would stand in a corner, talk to himself out loud and beat himself on the chest, roaring like Tarzan. Then, halfway through the first race, as I went to pass him going into the final corner, he pushed me onto a damp part of the track and I lost the front end. I remounted and finished twenty-third instead of my usual third there. And the Big Lads had brought their party frocks in preparation for the podium celebrations. I didn't say anything to Laconi but I did think: 'What comes around goes around.'

When Monza came around the team told me and Fonsi that one new spec engine was available and that Laconi would be using it. But, hang on a minute, I was supposed to be the number one rider. I was spewing. Their reasoning was that the reliability was questionable, and also that he would be able to provide better feedback to the French engine developers. There was no point kicking up a fuss, and in any case after the first day he had been the fastest of the three of us on the old spec engines. It just made me even more determined to beat him. There was no chance of that, though, when the teeth sheared off the back sprocket in the first race. That confused the traction control, which constantly thought the rear wheel was spinning and caused the bike to judder down the first two-thirds of each straight. In the second race I was slipstreaming with Fonsi when we saw Laconi's bike parked up at the side. At 200 m.p.h. we looked across at each other and I don't know whether he could see that I was smiling, but I could certainly see that he was.

Silverstone saw a turnaround in my fortunes and I qualified third during a wet superpole, in which you are allowed to pass start-finish twelve times in fifty minutes. My fastest lap was my last but I had miscalculated and was about to go round once more when I spotted a marshal waving his hands frantically for me to turn down pit-lane instead of going through the chicane. He knew that my best time would have been erased if I had carried on. Tommy Hill claimed pole in his first World Superbike race and nearly made the same mistake, but he crashed on his final lap. He is a rider I really rate – totally focused in all the right ways. From the front row I had the chance to make a Stalker start count and I was first into the first corner against all the guys with launch control. Not bad for someone who still just used his back brake and clutch, just as I had in my motocross days. I managed to hold onto the lead at the end of that lap and the grandstand erupted, reminiscent of the time I knocked Hodgson off. But I melted my tyres trying to stay with the faster bikes in those early laps and slipped back to sixth, with a similar story in race two.

The team were excited going to Misano, and not just because it was their home round. We had tested there earlier in the summer and I really struggled for the first two and a half days, before a tweaked offset turned my fortunes around and I left fourth fastest. We used the same setting for the race, along with an improved rear linkage from Japan, and were immediately on the pace again. But I was a little impatient in the first race and lost the front trying to pass Haga because the leaders were pulling away. I had Haga in my sights again during race two in one of my best ever race-long battles. We swapped positions for half the race, but with a couple of laps remaining I missed a gear and lost the momentum to challenge for the final podium place. Still, the team were peaking again at the extended TV coverage, because any dice with Haga is bound to be spectacular.

Another great thing about having Rachel around was the incentive to start seeing something of the places where we raced. I didn't know how many more years I would have in the world championship and I didn't want to miss out on seeing parts of the world that racing has given me a chance to visit. With the team based in San Marino, that nearby Misano round provided a perfect chance to spend some time with what was now our extended family and also to visit the principality. I can't believe how many riders have never been to San Marino. It's a stunning town set on the top of a massive rocky outcrop, with tiny medieval streets. I just wish that someone had told me that there was a cable car to the top because turning a 39 ft motorhome and trailer round was even more difficult than parking a Hummer in Cambridge.

Before the next round, at Brno, was a test at Lausitzring, and this time Rachel wasn't able to come because she had to look after Nobby. So I took Rat Boy, Stuart Easton, who was riding in the World Supersport championship, Craig Jones, who was riding for Petronas, and his mechanic, Chris Anderson, known as Spanner, to Colditz. Rat Boy, not a nickname I was involved with, must spend a lot more time watching Discovery Channel than he lets on and was pretty clued up. But I had to pretend that there were motorbikes involved for Jonesy to even consider coming along, so we pretended it was the set for *The Great Escape*, where Steve McQueen jumped the fence. The fact that the prisoners of war had used an Oxo cube tin to dig through solid rock went straight over his head. 'Where are all the prisoners?' was his first question. I think he was actually expecting to see them in their loincloths, digging a tunnel. But the place blew me away and it put my chain jumping its sprocket at Monza into perspective. I spent a lot of time with Jonesy that year, and really rate him. I tried to help him out whenever I could, not always with racing tips, but with gems like how to avoid the German authorities when you have a head-on collision without a motorhome licence.

After more consistent results at Brno and Brands there was a long gap before the next race at Assen, and Rachel and I decided to make up for the time we had been away by treating Nobby to a trip down to Devon. Rachel actually spoils him rotten. If we are having steak for tea, Nobby has his own bit of steak. If we are having spag bol, she cooks spag bol for three. Big dogs normally slaver a lot but there is really only one food that makes him drool: cheese. In fact he turns into a waterfall for any dairy products, so we call him Dairy Dog. Cheese on toast sends him over the edge and he starts to howl like a werewolf. The big drawback with his size and his big thick coat is that he is always too hot, and our house is always nice and warm. He's a big softy at heart and loves affection, so when we go to bed at night we always hear soft footsteps creeping up the stairs behind us. While we are brushing our teeth he seizes his opportunity to lie on the bed, ready for his goodnight cuddle, which means we usually have to climb under the duvet either side of him, often with my arse hanging out under the covers until he overheats after ten minutes and creeps back downstairs. Sure enough, at around 7 a.m. every morning we will hear those same steps on the stairs and then you are suddenly aware of being closely scrutinized while he rests his head on the mattress and sighs until he has been acknowledged. Nobby also now has his own spot on the sofa where I should be!

But Nobby wasn't the only precious goods on this trip. There was also an engagement ring. I wanted it to be a special surprise so had taken the risk of choosing it on my own. For nights on end I would wait until she went to sleep then feel her fingers to try and gauge the correct size. I also made the mistake of telling Roger of my intentions, so every half hour on the hour for three days he was texting me things like 'Have you done it yet, chief?' or 'Is today the big day?' The big day had been planned with military precision. We were going to take a picnic on the steam train from our hotel in Brixham to my grannie's in Kingswear. From there we could walk along the coastal path to a spot I remembered from being a kid – Brownstone Battery. Gun emplacements were built into the cliffs, and one was in a sheltered and secluded spot. Rachel didn't know I had packed champagne and strawberries and cream, but Nobby did know that I had packed cheese sandwiches and started to get over-excited as we laid the rug down. Then I brought out the big box containing the ring. Rachel thought it was a watch, and was privately peaking about that.

We were already sitting on the rug so there was no need to go down on one knee when I opened the box. 'Will you marry me?' I asked.

'Who, me? Are you sure?' she said.

'Well, I didn't mean Nobby and there's no one else around. Of course I'm sure, you silly thing,' I laughed. She leapt to her feet, climbed on a ledge and shouted out to sea at the top of her voice: 'We're getting married!'

It was the sweetest thing I had ever seen.

27

Stalker the Winner

'Do you know your zhpeed?' asked the Dutch cop, who had pulled us over ten minutes before we reached the circuit on the Wednesday before the race. This was Assen, of course, so I had been prepared to come down to earth with a bump after our engagement. The trip had started off eventfully enough. I normally left it to the last minute to board the ferries across the Channel but misjudged it on this occasion and the Norfolkline boat was just pulling out of dock when we pulled up. Luckily Norfolkline were one of my personal sponsors and one of their directors, Wayne Bullen, had become a personal friend. He rang to check that I had made it on time.

'Don't worry. Give me five minutes,' he said. Five minutes later he rang again. 'It's coming back for you,' he said. Sure enough, we could see the ferry heading back to Dover and we were not exactly popular with the other passengers when the boat finally set off again with our motorhome safely on board. 'You must be pretty bloody important if you can stop a cross-Channel ferry. Are you fucking royalty or something?' one person grumbled.

'No, I race motorbikes actually,' I replied sheepishly.

Maybe the same thing would work with the Dutch cop. 'Ah, you race zhe motorbikes, eh? We have problems every year with you guyzh. I let you off zhis once if you promise to win the race for me zhis weekend,' he said. Right-oh, chief, anything you say!

This was the first time we were on the new, shorter layout of the circuit, and I really liked it. But, after two days of dry qualifying, it bucketed down on race day and morning warm-up became the compulsory wet-weather practice session. Then Steve Martin, without knowing, did a full lap on his Petronas with oil spewing out and it took ages to clear the track of oil. The session finally finished at 11.15, just forty-five minutes before the start of race, and I was second fastest. I knew our bike and traction control worked well in the wet and it was looking promising, until my engine started to cut out on my in-lap because there was water in the electrics. 'Here we go,' I thought. 'The Stalker curse strikes again!'

I was desperate not to use my spare bike but the guys only had thirty minutes to solve the problem before pit-lane closed. We missed the cut-off point by seconds and I would have to start from the back of the grid. As I left the garage to join the warm-up lap, Guido said, 'Just remember it's a long race, so stay calm.' Then Rachel gave me a hug and said, 'If anyone can do it, you can do it.' 'Does anyone realize I'm starting from the back row here?' I thought, as I pulled away down pit-lane.

I made a good start and had cut my way through the field by turn one when someone tried to go up the inside, got it wrong, and crashed into the side of my bike, pushing me into the gravel. I still don't know who it was. My little legs paddled away and I managed to stay upright and rejoin the race in last place, without another bike in sight. 'They were not wrong. This is going to be a fucking long race now,' I thought. But everyone else was struggling and by the end of the fourth lap I was back in a point-scoring position. After eight laps the heavens opened again and I could see a bunch of four or five riders ahead. I passed them all in one lap and that probably kept me out of trouble, because those sticking to the racing line, where there were puddles on the apex of the corners, were falling left, right and centre. When I looked at my pit-board for the first time I was P6 with twelve laps remaining. Then Bayliss crashed, then Josh Brookes, and then, despite having a lead of about twenty seconds, Haga went down. I was third behind Pitt and Michel Fabrizio with ten laps to go. 'I could pinch another rostrum here,' I thought.

I caught and passed Fabrizio into second place, but he proved hard to shake off. Then the new leader, Andrew Pitt, was suddenly in my sights. I could tell immediately that I had more grip than him around half the track. The rain slackened and the lap times improved. By lap 15 I was right up his arse, and at the left-hander before the final chicane I lined him up and pulled off a clean out-braking manoeuvre. The grandstand went wild. The team went mental on the pit wall. And I shat myself. I was leading a World Superbike race. There were still eight laps to go. The last time I led a race, I binned it after 300 yards. Would Pitty have enough to get back at me? Had Bayliss remounted for the third time? Was anyone else closing in? Had I jumped the start? Had I overtaken on a yellow flag? Concentrate, for fuck's sake! Just concentrate!

Those last few laps lasted an eternity. But at the start of the final lap I had a four-second lead. I couldn't afford to back off straight away so kept up my pace for half the lap and then took the rest of it so, so gingerly. The crowd were on their feet as I came through the final chicane and the tears started to form inside my helmet. Rachel had been right. She had told me I could do it. I've only gone and done it. I've won the fucking race.

I was in pieces and couldn't even think about elaborate celebrations. I just waved at the crowd during the slow-down lap and pulled into parc ferme, where I was only ever used to parking at the number three spot. This time I was in the centre, at number one. I climbed off the bike and launched myself into the arms of the team. But I needed to find Rachel. I finally spotted her in the corner of parc ferme, crying and shaking. I picked her up and squeezed the life out of her.

Holding that trophy above my head was like the climax of the search for the Holy Grail and I couldn't wait to ring Mum and Dad, who had been working and missed the race. Dad had two favourite sayings: 'You would fuck a new cunt up, you would!' which he used when I had done something wrong, and 'Shit hot that, youth,' which he used on this occasion. Mum just warned me not to get carried away and to be careful in the next race. It was good advice because on the sighting lap I discovered the tyre was out of round. So we changed it on the grid and I couldn't believe how much grip the new tyre had for the first couple of laps. After three laps I was sideways into every corner. I struggled home in fourteenth and said, 'Just check that bastard tyre, will you?' As I suspected they had fitted a qualifier in by mistake. If that hadn't brought me down off cloud nine, there was worse to come.

An Italian journalist came up to me after the races and asked, 'How do you feel about losing your ride after just winning your first World Superbike race?'

'Eh?'

'There is a story in the Italian press that PSG-1 will only be running two riders next year and it looks as though you will be the one to go,' he explained. OK, Nieto brought money and there were incentives to keep Laconi, but this couldn't be true. I had helped develop the bike in Japan, never moaned when their payments were late, was ahead of the other two in the championship and had just won them their first race. But the rider is always the last to know in these situations, and it dawned on me that nothing had been discussed for next year yet. And I couldn't help thinking that Laconi had already wheedled his way in with his Italian-speak. I went to find Guido's right-hand man, Ricardo Drisaldi.

'What's all this about me being axed for next year?' I asked.

'I am sorry. I do not understand the question,' he said with a shrug. 'That's funny,' I thought. 'You have been able to understand every word I have said all year.' I could not believe that my fortunes had turned around so quickly. I was in bits, but although it was obvious their minds were made up I was determined not to let it put a dampener on my big day. Rachel had to leave for the airport straight after the second race to be at an audition the following morning for a big winter show in Norfolk, the Thursford Christmas Spectacular. She was really nervous but I assured her that if I could win a World Superbike race then she would walk the audition. So after a couple of beers I found myself back in my motorhome, alone with my Corona podium trophy in one hand and the winner's trophy in the other. I was in bed by 9.30 p.m. but just as happy as I would have been if

I had partied until the small hours. There aren't many trophies on display at home, but those two have pride of place, where they glint in the morning sunshine.

My win had simply made the team's decision more awkward, yet not a word of explanation was given to me during the final two rounds. I tried the main man from Kawasaki Italy, Mr Yoshitaka Tamura, but he said it was a team decision, although they would consider me for a Supersport ride. But I was a superbike racer. I wasn't ready to switch to 600s just yet. Guido never did find the heart to tell me officially and Ricardo didn't have the spine. After the final race, when I beat Kagayama home in eighth after a race-long dice, my mechanics said how sorry they were to lose me and, with a tear in his eye, Guido simply thanked me for doing a great job. So that was that – it looked like the dream of competing at world level was over for the time being.

When I had realized what was going on I started to speak with other teams in the World Superbike paddock, but their bikes would not be as competitive. OK, the Kawasaki was not the best bike out there, but it was still a good little bike. I wanted to be with a team that had a chance of challenging for rostrums and race wins. And it was looking like my best chance of finding such a team was back in British Superbikes. I had always said that I wanted to go back there one day and try and win the title. And I knew that a couple of good, professional teams were not totally happy with their mounts. Rizla Suzuki, for instance, had been through more riders in the previous three years than the *MCN* Babe Squad.

I realized that I had not been high on Suzuki's shopping list ever since that horrible split in 2000. But I had managed to patch things up a bit with Paul Denning since then. I bumped into him at the start of the year, when Dorna allowed us to share the Kawasaki MotoGP team's facilities at a test at Sepang. When I went to catch up with Chris Vermeulen, Paul and I had a laugh about what had happened and I admitted yet again what a twat I had been. I left there with a renewed feeling of what a good bloke Paul was and it was nice to know that it had all been put behind us. So before our final round at Magny-Cours I sent Paul that first ever email, albeit spelling Rizla with two 'z's. He replied that Simon Buckmaster was being appointed as team manager and the final decision would rest with him. That wasn't what I wanted to hear, given that we had not exactly gelled when we last worked together with Kawasaki in British Superbikes.

By Magny-Cours, Rizla had already announced that one rider would be Cal Crutchlow, the new British Supersport champion. He travelled out to France with Fish, part of a three-week celebration of his title. Jonesy and Rat Boy were ready to party at the end of their seasons and the Big Lads were also out in force. So, after such an emotional farewell to my Italian family, we were all just starting to power-drink when I received a call from Paul Denning.

'Chris, the team is going to enter the Race of the Year at Mallory. Cal is going to ride one bike and we want you on the other one. We test there on Friday,' he said. I went over to Rachel and whispered, 'It looks like I've got a job interview.' We put the cork back in the wine bottle and sneaked off for an early night so that I would be fresh to ride again in a few days' time.

There was just one condition. Before the test Paul asked me to go and sit down with Buckmaster and patch up our differences. He had already told *MCN* that, for personal reasons, Chris Walker would never ride for a team that he was running. And I don't suppose it helped that he had kept my job open as I dilly-dallied at the end of 1999, eventually costing him the chance to sign one of the top riders. So I drove up to his home in Louth and we were soon reminiscing about our year at Kawasaki. I was keen to point out that coming home to race in Britain was very important to me and not just a PR stunt. I was open that I had reservations about the chances of me winning the British title in my first year back but I was keen to be with a team, and with competitive machinery, that would give me that chance. And Rizla had assembled a great team over the years. My bro, Les Pearson, would be my chief mechanic, and the other guys earmarked for my crew, Mark Hanna, Dale Meech and Chris Anderson, were all very experienced.

Simon explained that he remembered me as a disruptive member of the team, unwilling to share info with the other rider. I wasn't actually aware that Steve Hislop, with his experience, had needed any help from me. And, when all is said and done, I was a racer whose job was to go out and win races, although I was never aware that I had deliberately withheld any data or had even created that impression. Simon then went on to explain that the team were looking for someone to help bring Cal Crutchlow on.

'Cal is on the brink of either being a really good lad or turning out to be a cock,' he said. 'I don't want someone around who is going to help him be the latter.' I thought that was a bit harsh on us both.

It was time to fight my corner, because Simon wasn't aware of the work that I had been doing behind the scenes with the Vivaldi team in 2005. Halfway through the season I'd received a call from the team boss, Richard Wilson, asking if I would come to the British rounds whenever there was no clash with my schedule, and help out their young riders, Richard's son, Ben Wilson, Tristan Palmer, Ollie Bridewell and Aaron Zanotti, who were riding Kawasaki ZX10s, as I was. I really enjoyed passing on whatever knowledge I could and developed a great rapport with them all, and Ben in particular became a good friend. Although no longer in an official capacity I carried this on whenever I could the following year, and still walk the track this year with Ben before race day. I had also been trying to help Jonesy whenever I could in World Superbikes, tapping my seat unit as I went by so that he could follow me and learn the right lines at circuits that were new to him. And I'd actually already become friends with Cal, who came to some of my boxercise sessions and on some cycle rides with me and Fish.

When I left Buckmaster's we were both pleased to have cleared the air and to be setting out on a professional footing. I was actually quite nervous about Mallory. It was as much pressure as I had put myself under in years. If I won the race everyone would say that I was expected to win, having come from World Superbikes. If I hurled it down the road, doubts would be raised. If my lap times were crap, there would be no ride. But it was not going to be easy – riding a new bike, on a circuit I had not been at for years, and on a new generation of Dunlop tyres.

I was desperate to impress at the test and, in particular, not to let Paul Denning down. I knew that he had stuck his neck out with Suzuki in both the UK and Japan to smooth things over after my acrimonious departure in 2000. The Mallory race was effectively make or break for the job. Fortunately I won by seven seconds, although Cal would have been much closer had he not crashed in qualifying, forcing him to use his spare bike. Johnny Rea, who would have been the favourite to win, also failed to make the race after a crash during practice. The result was not the most important thing, however. We had been using the old circuit, without the new chicane half-way round Gerard's. And I had been under the lap record from the previous year on that circuit. They could not really have asked for any more than that and Simon told me he would let me know during the week.

It was a long week. I knew that Michael Rutter, who has strong personal sponsors, had said that he would ride for free. Neil Hodgson was also in the frame but was holding out for a World Superbike ride. And their current rider, Shakey Byrne, had not been officially told that he would not be retained. But the call finally came. 'The ride's yours if you want it,' said Simon. Of course I wanted it. My only other talks had been with the MSS team, who were running the ZX10 the following year, but we had not reached the negotiation stage and so I accepted Suzuki's offer there and then.

So my job was sorted, and Rachel had also been accepted for the Thursford Christmas Spectacular. The downside of this was that she would be stuck in the middle of nowhere in Norfolk, which is itself in the middle of nowhere, for the three months running up to Christmas. I missed her like crazy. Whenever I could find a gap in the Suzuki PR duties I drove down to Norfolk with Nobby to stay in the tiny cottage she was renting and finally was able to see her dance live for the first time – with next to nothing on. 'Any danger of a dressing gown to cover up my fiancée?' Rachel had taken me to see the show the previous year and I was blown away by the scale of it. This year they had pre-sold around 130,000 tickets. So when Mum and Dad came to watch I think they were expecting a glorified nativity play. Dad never shows much emotion but when he walked into the venue, which is a steam museum for the rest of the year, I could see in his little face that he was thinking 'This is a bit of all right.' Then, when the dancing girls came on, that changed to, 'Christmas wasn't like this when I was a lad!' Having dragged Rachel all round the world to watch me racing all year, it was really nice to take so much pride in what she was doing.

We were both keen to marry the following summer, but choosing a date had been a nightmare. We tried to fit it in around the British Superbikes, World Superbikes and MotoGP calendars, and, having chosen Jamie as best man, around his holidays. Jamie is the sort of bloke who is always stitching everyone else up, but is rarely on the receiving end. So this was the perfect way of getting back at him. He started his best man speech by saying, 'Being best man is like being asked to sleep with the Queen; it's a great honour but nobody really wants to do it.' I was also keen to arrange the date as soon as possible so that I could concentrate on my training.

Suzuki took this very seriously and sent all their riders to a company called Pro Performance, based in Surrey. Before Christmas I went with Cal for our initial tests, such as VO2 max for lung power, lactate threshold for stamina, resistance tests of muscle strength, and also mental conditioning exercises. We returned in the New Year for the results and to receive the specific programmes they had devised. I had always taken my fitness seriously. Essentially the main job of a racer is to stay in peak condition for the race weekends. I was fascinated by this scientific approach and pleased to learn that I was in excellent shape, essentially fitter than Cal, although he was a bit stronger. My four-month programme, on top of my usual crossing and cycling, was designed to build my strength in key areas, while maintaining my aerobic fitness.

Winter testing could not have come at a better time. Just after Christmas I had picked up a BMW M6 and took Rachel for her first ride in it the very next day. 'This is the bollocks,' I said. 'I'm going 170 m.p.h. and there are two still two gears left. Look, it even projects the speed onto the windscreen.' But it wasn't only Rachel who saw the speed I was doing – so did the cop car behind. They clocked me at an average speed of 111 m.p.h. and, with John, my lucky charm, not at the court hearing again, I was banned for twenty-eight days with a £500 fine. Luckily this started the week before winter testing and finished the week after, so I was only off the road for a couple of weeks. But I didn't risk keeping the car and owned it for less than the number of days I was off the road with the ban.

All the signs from those first few tests in Spain were good. I was third fastest at the Dunlop test at Guadix, with Johnny Rea already stamping his authority and Shakey flying. So all I needed was for Buckmaster to start shouting his mouth off in the press about how I was going to smoke Shakey this year. Throughout my career I had never ever mouthed off about how I would do this or do that. It's just not my style. I never even thought those kind of things, let alone said them publicly. And the expectations on me were big enough already, I didn't need my own team boss adding to the pressure. In the following week's *MCN* Shakey's boss, Paul Bird, retaliated by saying that Simon was all fur coat and no knickers – which I liked! It all started to spiral out of control while me and Shakey were just horrified bystanders in their little publicity game. Buckmaster was eventually reined in by Suzuki, because he was about to announce that he had put money on me finishing ahead of Shakey, having laid the bet off at various bookies. It was getting beyond a joke.

I also finished third fastest at the next test at Albacete, the last before heading back to Britain. I knew that there was still work to do, however. We did not have a complete traction control package and were still undecided about set-up on certain constructions of tyre. There was also some doubt over which rear linkage to use. But, all in all, I could head to Brands Hatch with high hopes.

I had always said that I would one day return to the British Superbike championship, to try and win the title that eluded me for so many years. And when that day arrived – the first race of the season at Brands Hatch – it left me feeling humble, appreciated and overwhelmed.

Of course I was nervous going back to the British scene after six years away on the world stage. There was huge expectation and, riding for a team like Rizla Suzuki, lots of pressure on my shoulders. This was where I cut my teeth in superbike racing and it held a lot of memories. And although the team colours and names had changed, it was still essentially the same and I bumped into lots of old pals around the paddock over the weekend.

There was, however, one thing that completely blew me away – the reception from the supporters. The queues during pit-lane walkabout were phenomenal. I looked out from the garage on a sea of light blue wigs and Stalker T-shirts, which were apparently sold out after a couple of hours on the Friday morning. Maybe they had only brought half a dozen with them! It all gave me a real feel-good factor going into the races.

I knew it would be a lot to ask for me to come back and start smoking the likes of Kiyo, Johnny Rea, Leon Haslam and Greg Lavilla from the word go. Returning to the majority of the circuits for the first time in six years and instantly finding all the right lines with pinpoint precision at the speeds generated on a superbike was always going to be a big ask. I knew that I would need a period to re-acclimatize.

But Brands is one of the circuits I have been to every year since leaving British Superbikes in 2000, after that heart-breaking titanic battle with Neil Hodgson. So I was hopeful about my chances. Everyone was caught out to some extent on the tyre front by the unusually high temperatures, although it was pleasing to get away to a typical Stalker start before the tyre started to delaminate as both races went on. But it was like the good old days: sideways into every corner and as loose as ever. I was in second place for half of the second race, when the pace car came out, and could hear the roar of the crowd every time I came round into the grandstand areas. My spine was tingling on every lap.

I genuinely don't know why I receive so much support. It's not as though I'm a Foggy who has gone out and won titles for them. I do know that I have always had a lot of time for everyone who comes to watch us race. After all, it's those people who make the racing world go round. It's an honour when somebody asks for my signature, and that has always been the same, whether it was my first or my thousandth autograph hunter.

Maybe it's something to do with my style on the bike, as everyone can see that I try my heart out on every lap of every race. I have had that attitude right from my motocrossing days and up through the road-racing ranks to Grand Prix and World Superbike levels.

Apart from all the emotion of my return to British Superbikes at Brands Hatch, I was also given the results of the recent tests that I had undergone at the end of my fitness programme. I don't think Cal ever went back for his results! My body fat was down 2 per cent, my resting heart rate was now in the 40s rather than the 50s and my VO2 max and lactate thresholds had increased. I still wasn't the strongest rider they had ever seen but I was now officially the fittest.

It was even more reason for optimism for the rest of the year – until the next round at Thruxton. At Brands I had managed to overcome any set-up gremlins by gritting my teeth and biting the screen. Here, the harder I tried the slower I went. There was no doubt that the bike was one of the most powerful and fast out there, but it was a bit unruly and quite difficult to get the power down to the ground. I struggled in the first race, following Cal home in ninth and then, after a better start, my bike blew up in the early stages of race two. Over the course of a season something goes wrong for every rider, so I just put that one down to experience, although it did provide me with the shock of my life. As I parked the bike up at the side of the track I looked up to see none other than Jean the stalker, with her camera right in my face. So I ran across to the other side of the track, only to bump straight into Deaf Geoff. We can only speculate what had happened to Two-Litre Rita during the time I had been racing abroad – maybe someone had whisked her off her feet. Maybe Jean had also mellowed over the years, or maybe she had turned her attentions elsewhere. But if anyone had wanted to stalk me this year, they would not have had a problem. My new European-style Burstner motorhome, provided by an old motocrossing mate, Richard Wood, who owns the RDH dealership near Mansfield, came complete with stickers of my logo that were bigger than me.

Fortunately the next round was at Silverstone, another track I knew from World Superbikes. And although I was only something like a hundredth of a second off qualifying on the front row, I was still struggling a bit with my set-up. Then, before morning warm-up, Les came up with a stroke of genius. It was reinventing the wheel, changing the head angle, offset and swinging arm pivot point, but –

bosh – it worked. Straight away in the races I was able to run consistently half a second a lap faster and I was away with the leaders. Kiyo and Johnny Rea pulled away and at one point it looked as though I would have a comfortable third. But then Leon Camier started to close in. With four laps to go my pit board said +1.5, then +1.0, then +0.5 and then the dreaded +0. I knew someone was right behind me on the final lap and going into the Brooklands complex for the final time I glanced up at the big screen to see that it was Camier. It was better than having mirrors. At the final right-hander before the chicane I braked more than normal and, as I glanced at the screen again, I could see Camier sit his bike upright. In motocrossing it's called a brake check and I'm not convinced it's either sporting or legal! But it secured my place on the podium and it was great to be spraying that champagne again before a good solid fourth place in a shortened race two.

After two decidedly average rounds at Oulton Park and Snetterton, I was desperate to be challenging at the front again. These were tracks I had enjoyed in the past, but now with an extra 50 bhp it was like I had never have been there before. And this was the start of the monsoon season. It rained all the way to Ireland and didn't stop until after morning warm-up so, at a completely new circuit to me, I did not have a setting for the two dry races, after which it immediately started to rain again. There were more than just dark clouds hanging over this meeting, however.

Throughout the weekend I had been hearing stories that Neil Hodgson was due to test my bike and that I was going to lose my ride. Of course, there was a wall of silence from the team until the usual post-race debrief, when Buckmaster passed it off as though it was the most natural thing in the world. I was seething but just kept my mouth shut, shook my head and left the meeting.

Apparently the original idea was to let Yukio Kagayama ride the bike to provide a second opinion on our obvious set-up problems. It's never ideal when a team turns to another rider for help, but at least Kagayama was riding a GSXR1000 and had been on one since the bike's introduction, so I could see some logic in that. But there was not a scrap of sense in bringing in Hodgson for those two days at Cadwell. He was out of work and touting himself around for the following season, so he was never going to be completely honest about any deficiencies in the bike. And if he was fast on it there was every chance that he would be offered the job there and then, because this team did have previous for giving riders the flick. As it turned out Neil was two seconds slower than Johnny Rea on the same track on the same day and it only took me and Cal fifty laps to better a time he had set over 120 laps there.

From someone with very few man-management skills to begin with, this stunt reached new lows. Neil and I are pals now and have often tried to make plans to go motocrossing together, but was Buckmaster trying to motivate me by picking the guy who nicked my championship in 2000? This seemed like he was driving a huge wedge into his team. I had done everything in my power to put myself in the best position to come back to Britain to try and win the title over the next two or three years. So this was just taking the piss. It made me exceptionally angry and still does.

MCN had obviously heard the rumours so were knocking on my motorhome door and ringing every hour. But what could I say? I certainly couldn't tell the truth. So I thought it would be best to stay silent and honour my next PR commitment, a Rizla Suzuki track day at Knockhill. The only consolation was that on the actual days of Hodgson's test I would have the distraction of being on my first stag do, the one for my more athletic friends.

Here's the line-up: Mad Dog, Fish, Cal, Jonesy, Ben Wilson, Tommy Hill and Magpie, who needs to be introduced. Magpie is more loyal than a Patterdale Rescue Terrier and is an integral part of the Stalker clan. But I didn't know his real name was Stuart Hall until I was sorting his usher's suit for the wedding. Everyone knows him as Magpie because he likes shiny things. For instance, his crosser is more tricky than Stefan Everts', although he rides it like Steffi Graf! He makes socks for a living, which isn't ideal when you are trying to pull birds, so he goes to great lengths to get laid, including making fake business cards. One had a picture I took of him wearing a retro

Davida stars and stripes helmet, alongside a picture of Evel Knievel. It read: 'Wrecks Cramer: Part-time sock knitter, full-time Danger Seeker'. I met Magpie through the local motocross shop where another mate, Steve Cottam, worked. Cott, or Wee Man, had been a great motocross mate from an early age and we still ride together most weeks. Unlike Magpie he has trouble avoiding sex – from his amorous wife, Max. After motocrossing we always have to stop off at the pub on the way home for a pint of Guinness and some peanuts to build his energy up.

There were two other participants on the first stag, although they didn't do the 100-mile off-road ride from the village of Milngavie to the foot of Ben Nevis. Rat Boy turned up for the final beers in Fort William and Dean Gregory volunteered to drive the minibus. Deano is an animal. This first came to light when, at a recent winter party, he invented the new sport of naked quad-biking in the snow. Then, the following morning, he was frying bacon on my Aga and dropping fag ash into the pan while his piss tank (belly) rested on the oven. Not pretty!

By the end of my lane, 0.24 miles long, everyone was into their first can of Guinness, except Tommy Hill, whose resolve weakened at Newark, two miles down the road. When the ride started Tommy set off like a bat out of hell, complete with a police siren microphone to startle any unsuspecting ramblers. But he calmed down (ran out of steam) after his big crash. Fish was the other liability. He is in my phone as Bingo Wings, although the phone's voice alert recognizes him as Wings Bingo. This is because, while the rest of his body is chiselled, the backs of his arms flap around, especially when his bike has no front or rear suspension. With plenty of weight over the back end, every time Bingo hit a pebble his rear tyre punctured – a total of five times out of a group total of five. It was an awesome few days over rough terrain and with spectacular scenery.

Back in Scotland for the round at Knockhill, I could hardly bring myself to talk to Buckmaster. Hodgson had since announced that he had a ride in America lined up anyway, so his ride on my bike made even less sense than before. The atmosphere was so awkward, especially for Les and the rest of the team. But at least the races went well. It was the start of a spate of wet races – a key feature of the season. Dunlop would always be my tyre of choice and we had the pick of the bunch from Phil Plater and the boys in the dry. Even so, there were certainly some tracks where the riders on Michelin had an advantage. But the combination of the HM Plant Honda and Michelin wet-weather tyres was unstoppable. Johnny Rea was phenomenal round there and, on wets, was under the Superstock dry lap record. You only have to look at the picture in this book, with one boot around my ear while the other is scraping on the track, to see how I struggled, despite coming fifth and sixth.

In the gap between races there was just about time to squeeze in my second stag do, for my less athletic friends. It was originally going to be Fit Lads and Fat Lads, but that would have been unfair to a couple of the participants on the second trip, including David Pickworth and my dad. This was a slightly more sedate affair than the first: a trip to Sandown Races – on Ladies' Day, of course. (I was still allowed to look at the menu, as long as I dined at home.) By coincidence, Suzi Perry, the BBC MotoGP presenter, was hosting the day and I was dragged into presenting the prize for the Best Dressed Lady. It wasn't easy being interviewed in the Parade Ring after six pints of Guinness by 3 p.m. A few of us came good on the last race, thanks to a tip from Barry the Gardener. Luckily this included Cott, who would have been forced to pay Maxine in kind if he had lost any money.

A few of the Big Lads faded as the day wore on, ending in a night-club in Kingston, where David had arranged VIP treatment through his Mad Croc energy drinks company. I'm not sure that my dad real-ized he had drunk his own bodyweight in Mad Croc and vodka, but he was certainly buzzing until at around 3.30 a.m. he began to fade – at least until the wet T-shirt competition started. Being a couple of inches shorter than me, he couldn't see a thing, so me and Mad Dog boosted him onto our shoulders and let him watch from on high. What we didn't realize from down below was that the bloke who was wetting the girls was also hosing Dad down, and he was dripping wet when we helped him down. It was another fantastic day, but now I had to refocus on the racing.

We had made progress on a wet-weather setting and I was more dialled into the circuit when we returned to Oulton for the second time. I was battling with Haslam and Shakey for much of the race and finally finished third by a whisker for my second podium of the season. But maybe I was pushing that little bit too hard when I ran into the gravel and fell over in race two. I frantically waved the marshals so that I could restart and climb back up to eighth.

I was quite optimistic going to Mallory Park, too, having tested there earlier in the year. While my results were decent, the whole weekend was marred by the death of Ollie Bridewell during qualifying on Friday and I couldn't wait for it to end. I had watched Ollie for a number of years, particularly when helping the Vivaldi team in 2005, I'd read his column in *Motorcycle Racer* and there was never a dull moment with him around. He was the most unlikely-looking racer, with big milk-bottle glasses, a mass of ginger curly hair and long lanky legs, but he was very well-educated and polite. He was a pleasure to be around, and a talented rider. I am not good with words on these occasions so, after the minute's silence on the start-line on race day, I simply gave his bike a little pat and a wink, and wandered off. It was hard for everyone to think about racing on that day, but I am sure it is what Ollie and his family would have wanted.

After a flying start I was battling for the lead for a while and came home in fourth. I was also up there in race two before the pace car came out and I slipped back a few paces with front brake problems. The race was stopped three laps early and it suddenly dawned on me: 'Fuck me, I'm getting married next week!'

28

Lucky Stalker

Earlier in the year the team tried to arrange a test around my wedding date. I didn't want to be testing the week before, as we had so much to arrange. And I didn't want to be testing too soon after because, not being a beer monster, I guessed I would feel a little fragile for a couple of days after the carnage of the big day. So I agreed to start the test on the Saturday after the wedding, allowing us four days at Hotel Posillipo, situated at the top of a mountain near to the PSG team's base in Italy. It is nothing flash, although it's somewhere that Valentino Rossi and his chums hang out, but has fantastic views over the Adriatic coast. It was exactly what we needed to wind down after such a hectic time and we just chilled out, allowing the waiter to choose wine from their encyclopaedia of a wine list and watching the sun set under the electric canopy on the terrace. It was a perfect spot for newlyweds and we could have stayed there for fourteen days, never mind the four we had available. As it turned out, on our return to England, we discovered that we could in fact have stayed there for fourteen days. The team had cancelled the test months ago but failed to tell me.

There was no point throwing my toys out of the pram. I already had a good inclination that I wasn't part of their plans for the following season. Rumours were strong that a Japanese rider called Atsushi Watanabe would be coming over and the team was already talking about renewing Cal's deal. Yet I was still enjoying riding the bike and was looking forward to the final few races, although the omens for the next round, at Croft, were not too good.

I had raced there just once before, at a one-off meeting that was a bit like the Mallory Race of the Year, when I won one race and John Reynolds the other. So I was anxious to get to know the lay-out again at a two-day test that the team had arranged earlier in the summer. At the end of the back straight there is a great right hander, followed by a fast kink left and then a fast kink right. On the first morning I was just starting to build up speed, when the front folded going into the left-hand kink. But instead of me just sliding off and the bike doing its own thing, it pushed itself back upright onto its wheels and took me along with it, balancing on the petrol tank rodeo-style, without a hand on the bars or a foot on the pegs. And it was like this that we set off into the corn field at 120mph. All I could see was a blur of straw, and the occasional startled fieldmouse, before the grass brought us to a sudden stop. I passed out for a few seconds but when I came round, as I lay curled up in a ball assessing the damage, I could tell my neck was really sore and my eyesight was not right. It was obvious that my brain had taken a bit of a battering inside my skull when the sudden stop lashed my head forward. Apart from that there was not a scratch on me and I could hear a faint shout: 'Chris! Chris! Where are you?'

There had been no usual scraping sound of bike on Tarmac and so the marshals didn't see me disappear into the field. Luckily Shakey witnessed everything and was able to provide an approximate grid reference for the search party.

'I've found the bike, but not Chris,' I heard someone cry.

'Fucking hell,' I thought, 'he sounds a long way off.' When the first guy arrived on the scene he checked to see if there were any obvious broken bones, that I was breathing okay and then asked if I could squeeze his hand. My grip must have been really weak because he then asked: 'Do you have a pain in the neck?'

'Only Buckmaster,' I whispered back.

Needless to say, after the bang on the head, I wasn't allowed to finish the test and things didn't go much better at the race meeting. I was eighth in the first race and confident I could improve second time out but Tommy Hill high-sided in front of me on the opening lap and I had to take to the grass. Although I fought my way back into the top ten I collided with Karl Harris at the slow hairpin and had to start all over again, eventually coming tenth.

So I was pleased to be heading from there to Cadwell Park, a meeting I had always looked forward to. It's held over the August Bank Holiday and has an atmosphere like Assen in World Superbikes, where everyone camps overnight and makes the most of the weekend. But, thanks to the decision to use Neil Hodgson for the test earlier in the year, I hadn't been to the narrow, undulating and twisting track for seven years. And now I had 50bhp more and they had thrown in a couple of tight chicanes for good measure. So, by the end of race two, I was doing the sort of lap times I should have been doing on the Saturday morning and I had two mediocre results. It was still mega fun to ride, though, especially the notorious Mountain section. This had been resurfaced since I had last been to Cadwell, making the Mountain easier to jump – and easier to get wrong, especially on the most unstable bike I had ever ridden over there. I later saw a picture of Johnny Rea jumping it with one hand off the bike, showboating to the crowd. I also had one hand off a few times but it wasn't to please the crowd, because I nearly ended up in them. I lost count of the number of times me and Cal landed with our feet dangling off the sides and there were a number of crashes over the weekend, none worse than that of Leon Camier. I don't know Leon too well but I like what I have seen and I really rate him highly. Now I like the odd horror movie and don't mind a bit of gore. But I didn't really fancy seeing his legs flapping around in that famous crash, which the rest of the world was soon watching on YouTube. I guess that when you have legs that are twice as long as mine, something has to give when you land a jump that badly. Maybe, now I know that he has recovered and that I won't be going back there for a while, I might have a quick look.

After Cadwell there were only two bites left at the cherry for me to try to persuade Suzuki to keep me on. It would have been a crying shame to leave after just one year having done all the hard work in a development year for their new bike, as had happened so many times in the past, because I knew it would have been better the following year. The fact that Buckmaster was unlikely to be around, because there were already rumours of a new team manager being appointed, would have been a bonus. I hadn't joined the team expecting to win the championship, but I had expected to be more competitive. I am always the first to put my hands up when I have not done a good job. But the year's results were down to a combination of me, the bike and the team. Sure, there were times when I didn't get my head around the bike until way too late in the weekend, and you don't stand a chance from the third row of the grid when you are up against the riders and machinery that we were facing. That's not to say the same hunger wasn't there every time the lights went from red to green. I just don't think anyone at Suzuki had expected the changes on this 2007 bike to be significant enough to turn it into what was effectively a new and very finicky bike. That said, when me and good old Les did get it sorted as we managed to do at the next round at Donington, it could be a fantastic machine to ride.

The last time I had raced at Donington was in the 500cc GP in 2001 and, having tested there earlier in the year when I saw the fantastic new facilities for the first time, I was desperate to put up a good performance in the races. Also, as I only live just over 30 minutes away from the track, there was always a good turnout of family and friends. I was on the pace all weekend and missed out on pole position to Leon Haslam by less than a tenth of a second, my first front row of the season. I led the first race for a few laps until the same type of front tyre that we had used throughout the first two days suddenly turned to blancmange. I dropped back down to sixth and then, strangely, it was fine again for the final few laps. Maybe I just copped for a dodgy one. Having changed the front for the second race I was a whisker off a rostrum place. Okay, I was challenging for the honours and nearer where I wanted to be on a regular basis, but I was gagging for a podium and therefore a bit disappointed after the race.

My efforts had obviously been appreciated, however, because I even earned a 'good job' from Buckmaster. Ever since we both realized we were going to be replaced he'd been much more pleasant, even acknowledging that riders were part of a race team. He actually does a good job at the administration side but he is just not much of a people person and it's a shame we couldn't have been on better terms throughout the year, as I am sure he would have got more out of me if I'd felt that everyone had been pulling in the same direction.

Rob Mac also patted me on the back after the race, pointing out that it was easy to tie yourself up in knots on such a technical circuit. It was good to hear from him because Virgin Mobile Yamaha was one of the teams I wanted to talk to about a potential ride for the following year. At the time, though, Rob's team were using Pirelli tyres, against the best Dunlop and Michelin rubber, and were unlikely to be in a position to win races. So I also spoke to Neil Tuxworth at Honda, but he didn't seem too interested, and Colin Wright had plans to take the Airwaves Ducati team to World Superbikes, and they already had two obvious choices in Leon Haslam and Greg Lavilla if that was going to happen. So I was left with the likes of Hydrex Honda and MSS Kawasaki. While these were good teams, with good bikes, they were up against teams with better bikes and better funding. I had taken backward steps before in the World Championship in the hope of moving forward eventually, but at this stage in my career I didn't have enough time to make any more strategic moves. And, off the back of a fairly average season, these options in the British championship didn't appear to be obvious steps in the right direction. There was only one thing for it. 'Pack the bags, Rachel. We're off to Magny-Cours.'

The final round of the World Superbike is always a busy market place for riders and teams and I was flattered by the interest in me. People seemed to have noticed my decent results but ignored the average ones, and the win at Assen was still fresh in their minds. I spoke to a couple of Italian teams that were switching from 250cc GPs to World Superbikes, and I was chased by the new Triumph Supersport teams. I also approached Yamaha Germany but the most serious talks were with the Kawasaki Supersport team, Gil Motorsport. I was actually offered a ride with them at the end of 2006 because Kawasaki didn't want to lose me, especially after the Assen win. But at the time my heart was still in superbike racing and a return to the British championship seemed a positive move.

However much I had enjoyed seeing all the familiar faces back in Britain, though, it was not a world championship. After the first round of the season, we had made it back home from Brands just before our local Indian takeaway, the Muchak, closed at 10 o'clock. So that then became a Sunday night ritual on race weekends: three poppadums (one each for me, Rachel and, of course, Nobby, who has since been put on a crash diet which does not include Indian food, dairy products or fillet steak), chicken tikka jalfrezi, pilau rice, a side order of saag aloo and a garlic naan. The only time it looked like we would not be back in time, after Knockhill, we rang them at 9.45 to ask them to stay open, which they were happy to do. While it was nice to be back at home on the sofa each Sunday, we both missed the whole world championship atmosphere and, believe it or not, the travelling to some extent.

Kawasaki was offering me the chance to compete in a world championship again, albeit on a smaller 600cc Supersport machine, which I had always jokingly referred to as shopping bikes. In Kawasaki's green and black colours I guess that it might look like I was riding for Asda! I also knew that the Gil Motorsport team was a good little squad, and had won the Australian race that year with Fabien Foret, who had moved to Yamaha Germany after finishing third in the championship. The results were not the most consistent, though. While they were up near the front for some races, they were also two-thirds of the way down the field at others. But Kawasaki always carefully chose the teams they supported technically and financially, so this gave me some peace of mind.

I didn't accept their offer there and then, because I had one last chance to turn a few heads at the final race of the British season at the Brands Hatch Indy circuit. And I was at Magny-Cours for another important reason – to see James Toseland lift his second World

Superbike title. Being the team-mate of another rider always seems to be kill or cure: either you form a lasting bond or you never see them again. With JT it was definitely the former. Our paths don't cross as much now but I'd like to think we will always be close friends, and I was desperate to see him clinch the title. He knew I was at Magny-Cours but I am no lucky charm, so I didn't go out of my way to wish him luck before race day. In fact, I think most riders run the other way if they see me coming before a race, in case my curse rubs off on them. We watched the final race on the garage monitors and kept moving from garage to garage in case he was doing any better on another monitor. James kept us on pins until the final lap but I was so proud when he stood on the podium with his trophy, not only because he is a friend but also because Britain could celebrate another true world champion. I felt like an older brother when I caught his eye and our little nod and wink said it all.

It's a long time since Britain motorbike racing fans have had a rider they can really get behind. There is a lot of exciting talent around, such as Tom Sykes, Johnny Rea, Jonesy, Leon Camier, Leon Haslam and Tommy Hill, but they are all a long way behind JT right now. I think that what he achieved in 2007 elevated him to the next level of public awareness and it was great to see him ride onto the stage at the BBC Sports Personality of the Year awards and play his piano. I remember seeing Foggy interviewed on that show after his fourth title. The interview lasted a nanosecond and you could almost hear the producers saying: 'Get rid of him quickly, he's a rough-arsed biker.' It takes something like James's performance for people to realize that bike racers are human beings with other interests and talents. But whatever you think about James's racing skills, you can't help but admire the way he conducts himself. He is dedicated and a gentleman, but he is also a lot of fun to be around. That doesn't always come across in interviews, maybe because of the way he has been groomed for PR. But he certainly knows how to let his hair down and has done a fair bit of partying in his time. He just does all that in private, because the likes of Anthony Gobert, who do it in public, are the first to be knocked when it all goes pear-shaped. I wish

JT all the luck in the world in his MotoGP career and believe that, if he can just dig in when the chips are down for the first season and then pick up good results at the circuits he knows, he can make the kind of transition that Chris Vermeulen made from World Super-bikes to MotoGP, be a consistent top five rider for years to come and then, fingers crossed, a champion again.

Consistency hadn't been the theme of my British championship season but I went to Brands Hatch with high hopes of a grand finale. Rizla Suzuki, with the prospect of a non-English speaking Japanese rider for the following year, were keen to squeeze every last ounce of PR out of me, too, so there was a heavy schedule of autograph sign-ings, dinners and garage tours. I had PR coming out of my arse, a fitting end to a season in which I did more PR days than days on the bike. I knew the bike was in good shape after Donington and I loved the Indy circuit, having won the last time I raced there in 2000. So when I finally switched from my PR hat to my helmet, I was ready to dig deep for two good days of qualifying. So, almost inevitably, I threw the bike down the road on the Saturday morning.

It was one of my biggest 'What happened there?' crashes. I acceler-ated out of Druids in a tall second gear, probably at around 120mph. Then I shut the throttle off and was just about to touch the brake going into Graham Hill Bend when I was suddenly going backwards after a corner entry high-side. I was flicked over the top and I landed flat on the base of my back and hips before the bike caught me as it cart-wheeled into the grass. The head-stock had snapped, the forks were bent and the engine was hanging out. It was a write-off and I didn't feel too much better. I was stretchered to the medical centre and, although I wasn't a wheelchair case, I had no strength to move my legs and couldn't stand up. This was all I needed. Kawasaki, having offered me the World Supersport ride, were sure to be watch-ing my performance with interest this weekend, along with all the other teams that remained interested. My head hadn't been banged so I would be allowed to go out in the crucial afternoon qualifying session, as long as I could get on the bike. All I needed to do was post a time so that I made the grid for the races, when I might be feeling a bit better. But there was already a big blood clot on my kidney and bleeding into my hip joint. My mechanics had to tip the bike right over and lift me onto it just to get me out of pit-lane. Going into the dip after Paddock Hill Bend felt like someone was giving me a kidney punch, but I somehow still managed to better my time from the first day and qualified 11th on the grid.

I was still second hand in the morning but gritted my teeth to finish seventh in the first race. I was sure I could have been up at the sharp end had I been fit but it was the best that could have been expected in the circumstances. Although I managed to catch and pass Tom Sykes in the second race to come sixth, with the leaders always in sight, it was all a bit of an anti-climax. It's amazing, however, what half a dozen bottles of Grolsch, force-fed to me by various members of the team, can do to numb the pain of a bruised kidney and arse. Fish and Mad Dog had travelled down for race day, not knowing that I only had one working leg. Not wanting to be a party pooper I struggled over to the Indian restaurant just outside the circuit with them and returned to the paddock for a few more end-of-season drinks with a few of the teams. The carnage commenced when Rachel went to bed. I had started to feel a bit ropey by then and was hobbling towards the motorhomes area when me and Dog stumbled across a couple of old mountain bikes, leant up against a truck.

'Dog, just grab those bikes. It'll be a lot easier for me to ride around than walk,' I urged.

'No, no, no. We can't do that. We don't even know who they belong to,' said Dog.

'Just do it, will you? I'm in agony here.'

He reluctantly wheeled them over and Stalker was suddenly mobile, with second wind. The first motorhome we came to was that of Scott Smart, who had a few mates round in his jacuzzi at the back. At the time it seemed like a good idea to throw the bikes into the pool, although I probably wouldn't have done it if I'd realized that James Haydon was in there with the others. Looking back, it might not have been all that clever, especially if a front sprocket had landed in someone's forehead. Naturally enough, the bikes came flying back at us from the pool and the front wheel of 'mine' was now badly bent. I was just picking it up when the real owner appeared around the corner. Dog had seen him coming and had done one, like you do.

'I'll be taking that now, Chris,' the bloke said, obviously regretting his schoolboy error of leaving anything unguarded in a race paddock at the end of the season.

'Yeah, here you are mate. I was just about to bring it back because there's something wrong with the front wheel,' I innocently replied.

Normally the last round of the season would have been as good a time as any to suffer a serious injury. Not this year! The following Sunday was the 25th anniversary of the Weston Beach Race and the TV commentator, Jack Burnicle, had persuaded me to take part, on the condition that I could have the number 9. Events like that are no fun without your mates so Mad Dog had also entered, Magpie and Cott were coming along to support and the hotels were booked. But my injuries worsened over the next couple of days and by Tuesday I had a big purple love handle which looked like someone had stuck my liver on the outside of my hip. I couldn't sit, stand or lie down to make myself comfortable. And to make matters worse my head was a shed over my ride for the following year. Hydrex Honda and Virgin Mobile Yamaha were still interested for a British Superbike ride, as were the two Triumph World Supersport teams and, of course, Gil Motorsport. Suddenly, from having little on the table, I was in demand. I just needed a couple of days free from pain and hassle before making up my mind to take the Kawasaki ride in World Supersport. I still wanted to be in a position to win a major title, for my own pride and satisfaction and also to reward all the people who have helped me along the way. Nothing could replace all the amazing memories that I had been fortunate enough to have accumulated, on and off track, but a title would be the icing on the cake. And this seemed the best chance of achieving success.

The next big decision was whether to go ahead and compete in the Beach Race. My name was in the programme, my mates were looking forward to it and I'm not one to let anyone down. My waist was so swollen and sore that I couldn't get into my own clothes and had to wander round the house looking like Albert Steptoe in my dad's favourite George jeans and his Y-fronts. (My mum assured me these were new but I wasn't convinced.) But it was only Wednesday and I had four more recovery days before the race.

This was a big year at Weston, the 25th anniversary of the race, with a massive 1,380 starters and around 15 previous winners in the field. Something like 70,000 spectators turned up over the weekend and the atmosphere was even more special than usual. I could tell that the scrutineers were worried on Friday whether I was fit to start but I assured them I would be okay after taking a couple of Nurofen. On the morning of the race we were up early to set up our pits on the beach. I would only know how painful it was going to be when I was half-way down the start straight with 1,400 other riders. Correction! I found out as soon as I tried to get into my motocross gear. I must have struggled for half an hour in the back of Dog's van, trying to pull my crossing pants over my external liver. There was no way I could wear my body belt or hip pads and I was in agony when I attempted to sit on a bike. My Weston dream looked over until Dog found an old and bigger pair which at least allowed me to bend at the hip. Rachel and Dog's girlfriend Vicky were in position with their air horns and big rubber hands so that we could spot them and I took my place in the start area set aside for the invited riders. When the flare went off to signal the start I was swept up in one of the most amazing spectacles and noises in sport – hundreds of bikes all aiming for one tight corner at the bottom of a mile-long stretch of beach – and was relieved to get over the first dune before the mayhem started behind me.

It goes without saying that I fell off three or four times but my leg actually started to feel better once it was loosened up. With around 20 minutes remaining I stopped at our pits for the final tank of petrol and told Rachel: 'If I go missing don't worry. The bike is starting to overheat and misfire. I don't think it's going to finish the race.' Sure enough, after riding for two hours and forty minutes, as I got to the end of the long straight the bastard thing backfired and expired. But a finish was in sight if I could only cross the line and there was no way I was going to give up, so I started to push the bike home on my one good leg. A couple of mates from my early motocross days spotted me struggling and climbed under the fence to help me heave the bike across the finishing line. I was losing places with every second but I was determined to see that chequered flag. But, when I did eventually collapse across the line, the red flag was also out. A marshal told me that a spectator bridge across the track had collapsed and the race had been stopped 20 minutes earlier – the 20 minutes it had taken me to push the bike to the finish. So the standings at the end of the previous lap would count and not only had I finished, I'd finished 23rd and not 223rd.

'Fuck me! Result,' I thought. 'Stalker's just had a bit of luck!'

Acknowledgements

To Rachel, for putting up with me on book days.

To mum, for feeding us on book days.

And to Neil Bramwell, my co-author, for sending me over the edge on book days.